Mastering
Marketing management

G000135577

Palgrave Master Series

Accounting
Accounting Skills
Advanced English Language
Advanced English Literature
Advanced Pure Mathematics
Arabic
Basic Management
Biology
British Politics
Business Communication
Business Environment
C Programming
C++ Programming
Chemistry
COBOL Programming
Communication
Computing
Counselling Skills
Counselling Theory
Customer Relations
Database Design
Delphi Programming
Desktop Publishing
Economic and Social History
Economics
Electrical Engineering
Electronic and Electrical
  Calculations
Electronics
Employee Development
English Grammar
English Language
English Literature
Fashion Buying and Merchandising
  Management
Fashion Styling
French

Geography
German
Global Information Systems
Human Resource Management
Information Technology
Internet
Italian
Java
Management Skills
Marketing Management
Mathematics
Microsoft Office
Microsoft Windows, Novell
  NetWare and UNIX
Modern British History
Modern European History
Modern United States History
Modern World History
Networks
Organisational Behaviour
Pascal and Delphi Programming
Philosophy
Physics
Practical Criticism
Psychology
Shakespeare
Social Welfare
Sociology
Spanish
Strategic Management
Statistics
Systems Analysis and Design
Theology
Twentieth Century Russian
  History
Visual Basic
World Religions

www.palgravemasterseries.com

Palgrave Master Series
Series Standing Order ISBN 0–333–69343–4
(*outside North America only*)

You can receive future titles in this series as they are published by placing a standing order. Please contact your bookseller or, in case of difficulty, write to us at the address below with your name and address, the title of the series and the ISBN quoted above.

Customer Services Department, Macmillan Distribution Ltd.
Houndmills, Basingstoke, Hampshire RG21 6XS, England

Mastering
Marketing management

Roger Cartwright, MA

Business Series Editor
Richard Pettinger

palgrave

in association with
St Antony's, Oxford

First published 2002 by
PALGRAVE
Houndmills, Basingstoke, Hampshire RG21 6XS and
175 Fifth Avenue, New York, N.Y. 10010
Companies and representatives throughout the world

PALGRAVE is the new global academic imprint of
St. Martin's Press LLC Scholarly and Reference Division and
Palgrave Publishers Ltd (formerly Macmillan Press Ltd).

ISBN 0–333–94897–1

This book is printed on paper suitable for recycling and
made from fully managed and sustained forest sources.

Cataloguing-in-publication data

A catalogue record for this book is available from the
British Library.

A catalogue record for this book is available from the
Library of Congress.

10   9   8   7   6   5   4   3   2   1
11   10   09   08   07   06   05   04   03   02

Printed and bound in Great Britain by
Creative Print and Design (Wales), Ebbw Vale

■ ⍓ Contents

◼ ⌄ Preface

This is a book about marketing management and thus is also about the management function *per se*.

In the early 1990s, when the Management Charter Initiative (MCI) introduced the first set of management standards in the UK, it took the important step of emphasising the holistic nature of management and the need for specialists in marketing, personnel, finance etc. to understand generic management concepts. This holistic nature has also been stressed by professional bodies such as the Institute of Marketing and the Institute of Personnel and Development (IPD). Both these bodies include generic management as a key component in their professional qualification programmes.

As this book will show, marketing is a concern and responsibility not just of marketing specialists but of all those employed in an organisation and especially those in a managerial role. Whilst there may be a dedicated marketing or advertising department, the image of the organisation and its relationship with its customers transcends departmental boundaries and indeed hierarchies. As an example, a receptionist's attitude to customers and suppliers is just as important as that of the Chief Executive and may be as influential in gaining (or losing) business.

Marketing is fundamentally concerned with the relationship between the products/services delivered by an organisation and the needs/wants for those products/services by customers. As such, marketing includes developing a knowledge and profile of and maintaining a positive relationship with the customer. Marketing is much more than shiny advertisements and catchy phrases, at its heart is a long-term supplier–customer relationship.

In order to demonstrate the multi-faceted nature of marketing management, examples are taken from real organisations. The author is grateful for the assistance provided by Icelandair, the national airline of Iceland, which offers an alternative route from the UK to North America. Icelandair was chosen as a major case study because of the interesting nature of its operation and because it has been able to satisfy some particular needs of its potential customer base. Whilst much information was provided by Icelandair and other organisations, any comments etc. remain purely the views of the author.

The book is laid out in a series of sections. At the end of Chapters 2 to 14 will be found suggested Recommended reading and a set of questions. It is hoped that these will be useful both to tutors for assignment purposes and for the general reader as a series of points to consider.

The world of business is changing rapidly. Many previous books related to marketing have contained a section on 'International Marketing' as distinct from the operations of more local organisations. The author has taken the view that this distinction is no longer valid. Globalisation and the development of e-commerce using the Internet have made international borders much less relevant in marketing terms.

This does not mean that organisations can ignore cultural differences and norms in their marketing efforts but then again these should be recognised even within a national context. There are UK organisations that approach marketing in Scotland in a slightly different manner to the approach in England. The rules for marketing do not change substantially across borders, only the approach and the language.

Thus the decision has been taken not to separate out international marketing, as it is believed that this reflects the trend towards globalisation so prevalent today as seen in supra-governmental groupings such as the European Union (EU) and NAFTA (North American Free Trade Association).

The operations of Icelandair, the national airline of Iceland, are referred to throughout this book both in the text and at the end of many of the chapters. Where a chapter ends with airline-related case material the aircraft symbol shown below will be displayed:

The Icelandair web site can be found at:

www.icelandair.co.uk

Who is this book for?

It is unusual to find any management development programme that does not require participants to study and understand marketing and the marketplace. Programmes for those in work from supervisors upwards usually require a fairly detailed examination of marketing management. This book will provide useful and comprehensive materials for those undertaking NEBS Management, CMS and DMS programmes in addition to those engaged upon N/SVQ programmes in management and customer service at all levels.

The book also provides material for those undertaking professional qualifications with a marketing element and qualifications purely in marketing.

Students engaged upon business studies related HNC/HND and degree programmes will find that there is much useful material contained in this book.

Finally the book has been written to be of use to general business readers who wish to know more about the role of marketing within their organisations.

For additional support to this book, please see our website at
www.palgrave.com/studyskills/masterseries/cartwright

■ ✓ Acknowledgements

The author and publishers wish to thank the following for permission to use copyright material:

CACI Ltd for 'CACI ACORN profile of Great Britain' (1993).

Every effort has been made to trace the copyright holders but if any have been inadvertently overlooked the publishers will be pleased to make the necessary arrangement at the first opportunity.

The author would like to acknowledge the assistance of the headquarters staff of Icelandair in the provision of case study material. He would also like to thank his wife June and BB & BB, Suzannah Burywood his editor at Palgrave and Richard Pettinger the series editor for their support and assistance.

Part One

Introduction

☑ **1** What is marketing?

Definitions – Customer driven and product led – Conscious and unconscious marketing – The organisation seen from the customer's point of view – Definitions of organisations – Typologies of organisations – SMART and C-SMART criteria – Customer chain – Motivation – The value chain – Internal and external customers – Facets of marketing – Marketing as a management activity – The marketing mix, 4/7Ps and 4Cs – Products and benefits – Products and services – Introduction to cases

Wilmhurst (1984) quotes the definition of marketing used by the professional body for marketing, the Institute of Marketing. According to the Institute, marketing is '. . . the management process responsible for identifying, anticipating and satisfying customer requirements profitably'.

This definition encompasses all that marketing is really about, i.e. finding out what the customer wants both now and in the future and being in a position to service both current and future requirements. The need to keep in contact with the customer and to seek feedback might be a useful addition to the Institute of Marketing definition. This addition is made to emphasise the point that satisfaction, in order to be of benefit to the organisation, should lead to repeat business or at least a recommendation to other potential customers.

Marketing is often thought of, simplistically, as something to do with advertising. Advertising is an important part of marketing but far from being the only facet. Consider a customer who wishes to purchase a motor car. Every newspaper and magazine will contain glossy, well–produced advertisements for such products but what is actually being sold? Is it a vehicle *per se* or a benefit – the ability to have one's personal transportation? More than likely the customer is actually acquiring the latter. There may well be factors such as convenience and image to consider but what is actually being bought is a benefit.

The customer will have a certain amount of money available with which to purchase the vehicle, money that is either cash or credit facilities, and the manufacturer will want to sell at a price that ensures that costs are met and a profit made but one that is not so high as to put off the customer by engendering a feeling of overcharging. The manufacturer can only do this if he knows exactly what the customer needs, wants and is prepared to pay. It is also important for the manufacturers and suppliers of products and services to recognise and comprehend the competitors within a particular marketplace. Price-setting etc. has to occur within a frame of reference that takes account of the actions of competitors.

For many years, up to and including the beginnings of the second half of the 20th century, less regard was paid to what the customer actually required and more to what the organisation wanted to produce/deliver. Strange as it may seem today, many organisations stayed in business by being what has become termed as **product led**. The organisation developed the product that it wanted to sell and then offered it to the marketplace. Marketplaces were perhaps more local in nature with less global competition, but even into the second half of the 20th century this was not an unusual manner of introducing a new product. In the field of transportation Ford introduced the technologically advanced Edsel (named after Henry Ford's son) in the late 1940s. A wonderful product, except that the customers didn't like it! Even later, Sinclair introduced the infamous C5 electric micro-vehicle, again technologically advanced but with little appeal to customers. In aviation the Vickers VC10 and the Convair Coronado CV 880/990 series of jet airliners were introduced without much customer analysis and both failed to make the massive sales of the Boeing 707 and Douglas DC8s of the time. Even Boeing has been criticised for not really talking to its customers to find out their requirements, until the company realised that it would lose business by offering another version of the 767 and opted instead to work with its customers to develop the 777 (Sabbach, 1995). Product led has never been a satisfactory outcome for the customer but it did give suppliers the luxury of supplying what was easiest for them. As the customer base has become much more sophisticated and global in nature, even the recent expansion of mobile telephone sales has seen manufacturers offering what they believe customers might want, e.g. WAP technology, rather than what they have stated that they need. In the UK the take-up of prepaid mobiles was appreciably higher than WAP-equipped models, perhaps indicating that this was what customers, especially parents who could control prepayments for their children, actually required.

The current perceived wisdom is that organisations should be much more **customer driven**, i.e. find out what the customer actually wants and then develop and deliver it. Finding out about customer requirements is as much a facet of marketing as is advertising.

Conscious and unconscious marketing

In biology and medicine the autonomic nervous system is that part that operates automatically, whereas the somatic nerves control limbs etc. over which individuals have, in normal circumstances, a measure of control. That the control is never absolute is demonstrated by the reflex test where the doctor taps the knee and the leg jerks, and it is only incredible will power that can override this reaction.

This book introduces two related types of marketing – conscious marketing (somatic) and unconscious marketing (autonomic). Many organisations believe that all of their marketing is carried out consciously by the marketing department. However, much of what the customer learns of the organisation may be from other staff, talks with fellow customers and suppliers, and the evidence of their eyes and ears when on the organisation's premises or using the products/

services. These messages are of vital importance to effective marketing and form the basis of Organisational Body Language. Organisations which discount the autonomic marketing functions do so at their peril because the messages that an organisation sends out without thinking are, like human body language, often stronger than the conscious messages. Telling customers that they are valued but actually ignoring their needs will produce considerable resentment. The experience nearly always wins out over the advertised message when there is a conflict between them.

The organisation seen from the customer's point of view

Marketing is perhaps best described as a two-way communication process between an organisation and its customers. Even such an apparently simple statement is actually rather complex. To fully understand the concept it is necessary to consider what is meant by the terms 'organisation' and 'customer'.

Organisations

Chris Argyris (1960) has defined organisations in the following terms:

> 'Organisations are intricate human strategies designed to achieve certain objectives.'

For many organisations, the objectives may appear to be relatively straightforward. Icelandair's (the national airline of Iceland whose operations are introduced at the end of this chapter) objectives are basically to provide an efficient, safe transportation system at a profit; a local authority's objectives will centre on providing a defined set of services to those who live within its area. These services, education, social services, libraries etc. will have certain performance standards set for them and there will be financial limitations. The objectives come first; the organisation is the human response to achieving them. Sections, departments, branches etc. are part of the system that has been designed to deliver the stated objectives.

A second definition by Pugh in 1971 suggests that:

> 'Organisations are systems of inter-dependent human beings.'

Note that this definition stresses the vital role of the human resource in achieving organisational objectives.

There are a number of recognisable sectors in which organisations operate according to their objectives. These sectors can be seen throughout the world:

1. *Private sector organisations.* These organisations have the maximisation of profits as their prime objective. They can be divided into three types:
   (a) manufacturing, for example, ICI, Ford and Airbus Industrie;
   (b) supply, for example, Shell.

(c) service, for example, shops, banks, private schools, professional sports teams and transportation organisations such as British Airways, Great North Eastern Trains, Stagecoach and Icelandair.

Many private sector organisations may fit into more than one of the above categories, for example Shell is concerned not only with the supply of oil and petrol but also with retailing the product to the consumer, and thus is both a supply and a service organisation.

2. *Public sector organisations*, such as local authorities, government departments, the Health Service, Colleges and Universities.

3. *Voluntary sector organisations*, such as charities, Church organisations and amateur sports clubs.

Prior to the 1970s, the different sectors employed differing styles of management but the recent trend has been a convergence to a more 'business' orientated management style, making the differentiation between sectors more difficult to define. Examples of this can be seen in the development of local management schemes in the Education and Health Services and the Management Information Systems employed in major charities.

There are four basic typologies of organisations, defined by ownership and prime function ('for profit' and 'not for profit' as the terms are generally understood), as shown in Figure 1.1.

In terms of size, the current position in the UK is that the for-profit/private ownership and the not-for-profit/public ownership sectors are in fact by far the largest components in terms of economic activity. The former includes the majority of all commercial activities and the latter the entire public sector including national and local government, the National Health Service, education and the armed forces. Prior to the 1980s, the for-profit/public ownership sector was also very large and contained some huge monopoly or near monopoly organisations. These included the steel, coal, gas, electricity and ship building industries, British Railways, British Airways and other nationalised concerns. Under privatisation these have been moved into the for-profit/private ownership

	Public ownership	Private ownership
For profit	Nationalised industry	Commercial organisations
Not for profit	National/local government	Voluntary sector

Figure 1.1   Typologies of organisations.

quadrant and are in many cases unrecognisable in terms of culture and means of operation from their nationalised predecessors.

Pettinger (2000) states that organisations consist of individuals, groups and relationships. Objectives, structures, systems and processes are then created to give direction and order to activities and interactions.

Objectives

Given the prominence that objectives receive in organisation definitions it is prudent to consider how objectives are set. Managers have, in the past, been taught that objectives should always be written in SMART criteria, i.e. they should be:

- **Specific** – that is, laid down in clear, concise terms.
- **Measurable** – in order to see if something has been achieved it must be capable of measurement. This will have been a success if . . . etc.
- **Agreed** – those responsible for the setting of objectives and those responsible for meeting them must agree that they are applicable to the situation and actually within the capability of the organisation and its employees.
- **Realistic** – there is little point in setting unrealistic objectives, as this only leads to failure and frustration if they are too high and complacency if they are set too low.
- **Timely**, i.e. with deadlines and time scales attached.

In a companion volume to this (*Mastering Customer Relations*) the author suggested that SMART should be amended to C-SMART with the all-important *customer driven* being the most important. He quotes the example of the failure of the Ford Edsel motor car in the late 1940s and mentioned earlier in this chapter. The vehicle was well-designed and built but nobody appeared to want to buy it. Interestingly it is now highly collectable to classic car enthusiasts.

The Ford Edsel met all of the SMART criteria: there was a *Specific* project, the outputs were *Measurable*, all of the Ford executives *Agreed* to the project, it was *Realistic* and it was built on *Time*. Unfortunately it was product led and not *customer centred*, i.e. it was the car the designers wanted to build rather than the one customers wanted to buy. If only *customer centred* had been the main objective, much investment would not have been wasted.

The next chapter of this book looks at organisations and the way they function in more detail.

Customers

A key performance criterion for most organisations is repeat business. The exceptions include health, policing and prisons where repeat customers are seldom wanted. Without customers, all endeavours of the organisation are worthless.

For those working in a retail or direct service environment, 'Who is the customer?' may appear an easy question – it is the person who is served. However, as will be shown, the true picture is more complex yet still easily understood. What will be introduced here is the concept of a customer chain, each member of which having his or her own wants and needs. For the enterprise to be a success, all of the members of the chain need to be at least satisfied and preferably delighted.

One can distinguish between satisfied and delighted customers, as mere satisfaction *is no longer enough*, it being delighted customers who provide repeat business. To comprehend this it is necessary to consider the differences between needs and wants, two concepts that are frequently confused and sometimes treated as synonymous, which they are not.

A need is something that we cannot do without; a want is the method by which we would like the need to be satisfied, in many ways a want is a need with added value, just as delight adds value to mere satisfaction. Needs and wants receive detailed coverage in Chapter 6 of this book which examines the links between marketing management and motivation.

A customer can be defined in simple terms as:

One for whom you satisfy a need

It should also be obvious that needs are very basic and it is wants that grow in importance once basic needs are satisfied.

Unfortunately many people in organisations behave as if the definition above is enough and that all that is required is to satisfy a customer's needs. This may be true if the organisation only wants to see the customer, but most organisations want to retain their customers.

Whilst there are exceptions, once an organisation has an external customer (the difference between internal and external customers will be considered later in this chapter) they normally wish to retain that customer be it an individual or another organisation.

If you are starving, a meal, any meal, will suffice to satisfy your basic physiological need for food. Once the means (usually money) exist to choose how the need is satisfied, then it is wants that are important. 'I need breakfast, I want bacon, eggs, mushrooms and fried bread!'

It used to be thought that customers had to be satisfied, but in today's competitive world satisfaction is not enough – in order to retain customers they need to be delighted. Needs can be satisfied but to delight a customer it is necessary to understand their wants.

In modern society, basic needs are satisfied using money and money has to be earned, giving rise to what may be termed a *facilitory* need, a term first introduced in a companion volume to this, *Mastering Customer Relations*.

In order to earn money, large numbers of people *need* to travel to work (they have little or no choice) and thus transportation is a facilitory need in order to fulfil basic needs. Their preference for transportation forms their wants; they may want a motor car or for environmental or cost reasons prefer to travel on public transport. Put succinctly, they do not need a motor car but they do need transportation in order to gain the money to fulfil the basic needs of food and shelter etc.

The earlier definition of a customer can be refined to:

One for whom you satisfy a need and who you delight in respect of their wants

Organisations that follow this definition are much better placed to retain customers over the long term. Their customers are also much more likely to provide favourable comments to their friends, colleagues and relations, and as such perform an autonomic marketing function (see earlier) for the organisation.

The value chain and the customer chain

The following example is taken, with permission from *Mastering Customer Relations*. It is your child's birthday and sitting proudly in his bedroom is a new computer system bought from a major retailing chain.

In this section it is intended to use the above simple, but familiar scenario to demonstrate the importance of firstly the *value* and then the *customer chain.*

A modern home computer system consists of a number of components manufactured mainly from metal and plastic. The total cost of the metal and plastic is a very small proportion of what will have been paid for the system. What happens is that each step in the manufacturing, distribution and retailing process adds value to those bits of metal and plastic. The individual value of the materials in a memory chip may be only a few pence whilst the value of the completed chip is many times that (even though prices fell steadily throughout the 1990s). In assembling those components, value was added to them. At each stage of the assembly process, the part completed system is potentially worth more than at the preceding stage. Those who are interested in the more esoteric motor cars, boats or even aircraft know that it is possible to buy a kit of parts, a part assembled kit or a completed product, each costing more than the other to reflect the value that has been added during the various assembly processes.

By the end of assembly a diverse set of metals, plastics etc. will have made into a coherent computer system which the manufacturer/assembler can then sell to a retailer at a profit.

Profit according to accountancy practice is the situation where the book value of a company is greater at the end of an accounting period than at the beginning. That book value includes the worth of buildings, machinery, stock, cash held and monies owed. Thus it is possible to be in profit but to have no cash to pay bills. For the purposes of this chapter profit can be defined as the:

added value left when all the costs have been taken into account

When the computer leaves the factory for the retailers it will have incurred direct costs relating to the materials and labour used and the indirect costs of heating, lighting, administration, marketing, packaging etc. apportioned to each unit.

Provided it is passed on at an added value price greater than these costs then a profit will have been made. It is the customers' decision as to whether they have received value for money and whether the price charged is realistic – too high a price and it ceases to be added value and is perceived as a 'rip off'.

Retailers also add value to a product. In a later section of this chapter it will be shown how convenience is an important part of the marketing mix, but in addition to convenience the retailer may offer extra services such as advice, after sales service and even (in the case of computers) training if required.

Each step in the chain 'adds value' and within each step there is a customer relationship. If you bought the computer you are clearly a customer of the retailer who is in turn a customer of the manufacturer/supplier. However, each step in the manufacturing process has a set of customer relationships. If, to carry out a job, a person in a factory needs a computer delivered to a workstation in a certain condition and by a certain time, then such a person is a customer of the previous person in the process. The person is an *internal customer* and quite clearly fits the definition of a customer given earlier, namely:

One for whom you satisfy a need and who you delight in respect of their wants

Anecdotal evidence suggests that the better the internal relationships are, so the likelihood of the external customer being delighted increases.

One company that has recognised the importance of internal customer relations is Princess Cruises, the US operation of the British P&O Cruises Company. Passengers on their cruises are asked to submit the names of those who have given them excellent service with the view to an award. Whilst this is a laudable idea, passengers only come into contact with a minority of the ship's crew and thus the company has a parallel scheme whereby those crew members who interact with the passengers on a regular basis are able to nominate colleagues behind the scenes who have provided them with excellent service. A table steward can only provide the highest standard of service to a passenger if all those working unseen in the galley have provided the steward with a high standard of service, good food, cleaned plates etc.

Thus there are two main categories of customers – **internal** and **external** – and whilst the latter are important for the final profit, the former add value and have a vital role in quality.

In the computer purchase scenario introduced earlier, you bought the computer but gave it to your child as a birthday present – who was the customer, you or your child? It was your money that paid for it but it is your child who will (hopefully) be delighted with it. You may never use it. In this case you were a *purchaser* but your child was the *end-user*. The purchaser is the customer and the consumer is the end-user. Often the same, they may nonetheless be different individuals or even organisations.

The *customer chain* can be represented as shown in Figure 1.2.

It is important to realise that the purchaser and the end-user may not be one and the same but that there is likely to be considerable feedback between them,

Person 1 ●⟶ 2 ●⟶ 3 etc. ●⟶ Purchaser ●⟶ End User

Internal Customers   *External Customers*

Figure 1.2   The customer chain.

so good customer care can double the potential for repeat business. The purchaser may come back again for something else but if the end-user is delighted with what the purchaser has provided for them and the purchaser relays a good report on the service they received, then the end-user may also become a purchaser.

We have presumed in our scenario that your child is delighted with the computer. However, if the child is dissatisfied then the retailer has probably lost a customer even if the service to you was good – you have become vicariously dissatisfied. One should not, perhaps, refer to the parent–child relationship as part of the customer chain but in the scenario examined that is precisely what it is; your child is in effect your customer, and if the child is dissatisfied then you are likely to be also.

It is easy to see the relationship between internal and external customers and purchasers and end-users in the retail and commercial segments of business but less easy to understand the customer relationships in other areas such as the public service. Who are the customers of the Prison Service, is it the prisoners or is it the taxpayers who pay for the service? Other areas of the public sector face the same dilemma and many use the term *client* for the end-user to distinguish the users of a service from those who pay for it.

Facets of marketing

Marketing is the key link between the organisation and its external customers. A simplistic view of marketing might equate it mainly with advertising as stated earlier but, as this book will show, marketing is a multi-faceted activity with implications for all the areas of organisational operation.

The chapters of this book will introduce the major elements of marketing and relate these to the management function within organisations. These major elements are:

- market knowledge, which considers the nature and operation of the markets served by the organisation and its competitors;
- market research, i.e. the acquisition of market intelligence;
- competition;
- customer needs and wants;
- products and branding;
- product life cycles;
- customer relations and behaviour, i.e. understanding the customer and his or her relationship with the organisation;
- grudge purchases, a term used for those products and services that are needs but definitely not wants – insurance is an example, obviously important but most people begrudge paying for it;

- costs and benefits relating marketing to the financial activities of the organisation;
- quality;
- advertising;
- sales;
- public relations;
- technology as applied to marketing activities;
- distribution channels.

Each of the above forms a chapter in this book, chapters which are linked by their applicability to marketing and the management function.

Marketing as a management activity

Supervision and management can be described as 'getting things done through the activities of others'. Often it will mean having direct responsibility for others but in some cases one will merely be reliant on others, having no direct control over their activities but needing their co-operation in order to ensure that tasks for which the manager is responsible are carried out.

Henri Fayol, writing in 1916, defined management in the following terms:

'To manage is to forecast and plan, to organise, to command, to co-ordinate and to control.'

By the 1950s, motivation had taken the place of command so that Brech defines management in terms of a social process consisting of planning, control, co-ordination and motivation (Brech, 1957).

An even more recent definition, that of Koontz and O'Donnell in 1976 (quoted in Cole, 1993), followed a similar line:

'The five essential managerial functions are: planning, organising, staffing, directing and leading and controlling.'

Contemporary organisations have tended to specialise in managerial functions. Examples to be found in a great many organisations include; financial management, strategic management, human resource management, quality management, operational management, supply chain management etc. Whilst such distinctions may serve to fit categories of managerial activity into the sub-structures of the organisation, they can disguise the holistic nature of management. It is, in fact, very difficult to pigeonhole types of management. It is difficult to manage the human resource without taking account of the financial implications of staff changes, training etc., and it is almost impossible to consider human resource management without thinking about the operations and activities that those people carry out and the quality standards to which they work.

Marketing is very much an holistic management activity. One of the problems that organisations face when they set up distinct functional areas is that staff in other areas may begin to perceive, wrongly, that they have little or no role in a function outwith their own area. Setting up a quality assurance department may, in practice, be counterproductive as it can detract from the fact that quality is a part of everybody's job and not the preserve of one particular part of the organisation. Wille (1992) has stressed the importance of quality pervading the organisation, and so too should marketing as the relationship with the customer is the concern of all staff and not just those in the marketing department.

This book is just as relevant for those working outwith the formal marketing function as for those with marketing in their job title.

The marketing mix – 4 and 7Ps/4Cs

Marketing, as discussed earlier, comprises a number of elements. The relationship between these facets has become known as the marketing mix, a term coined by Philip Kotler (1980). Just as a cake will not be complete or appetising without all of its recipe ingredients present in the correct quantities, so the marketing mix provides a recipe for effective marketing. Just as the recipe for a successful meal requires a careful balance of ingredients and processes, effective marketing is based on the right balance of marketing elements and processes depending on the nature of the product, service or idea being marketed. It is these ingredients that make up the major sections of this book. They are introduced below and then developed in Parts Two to Five of this text.

4Ps

Initially, marketing authorities used a marketing mix consisting of 4Ps: **Product**, **Price**, **Promotion** and **Place**. For success it was necessary to have the **product** or service the customer required, at the right **price**. **Promotion** channels needed to bring details of the product to the customer and delivery needed to be at a time and **place** to suit the customer. For many years the 4Ps provided a useful vehicle for discussing the marketing mix.

7Ps

Later writers on marketing added three further Ps to reflect the complexities of the market in the second half of the 20th century. In addition to a mix comprising **Product**, **Price**, **Promotion** and **Place** were added **People**, because it is people who are ultimately responsible for the development of the supplier–customer relationship, **Process**, i.e. the actual mechanics of the product/service acquisition and **Physical evidence** including packaging etc.

It is possible to argue that these extra 3Ps were actually included in the original four. **Physical evidence** can well form part of the **product**, especially where it is a supplementary product (see Chapter 7) and there may be a **people** and **process** aspect to all of the original 4Ps.

4Cs

A concept that is of considerable use is that of Kotler's (1980) 4Cs. By replacing **Product** with **Customer value**, **Price** with **Cost**, **Promotion** with **Communication** and **Place** with **Convenience**, a much more useful and manageable marketing mix can be developed that reflects contemporary 21st century practice. The 4Cs are summarised below and will then be considered alongside the related 4Ps in Parts Two to Five of this book.

Customer value

As stated above, this is the term that is used instead of product. It reflects the fact that it is not the product *per se* that the customer buys or uses but what he or she perceives that product to be and how he or she values it, i.e. a benefit.

Price/cost

A five-dollar bill, a twenty-pound note or a hundred-rupee note has no intrinsic value. The value is that which the person who uses it ascribes to it.

How much is your home worth? Assuming that you own your home (if you don't, then the answers relate to your landlord), there are a number of possible answers:

- how much you paid for it;
- how much it would cost to rebuild it;
- how much you could sell it for.

The last amount is the nearest to the truth; the value of any product or service is that which a customer is prepared to pay. A supplier may have the best product or service in the world, but if the price is deemed too high, then there will be few customers. Conversely, if the price is too low, questions may be asked about quality.

Price is what is charged for your product or service, and all products and services have a price attached to them. In government it may be the taxpayer who provides the resources indirectly but nothing comes free.

The price is built up by looking at all the costs that go into the provision of the product or service: those which are fixed (i.e. the organisation would have to pay them whether they made one or a hundred items, or serviced one or a hundred people); those that are variable (these include materials that are needed more of as more product is produced); overhead costs (heat, light, marketing and distribution); the desired level of profit; and what the market will bear. The difference between the organisation's costs and the price that the customer is prepared to pay represents the margin or profit.

For those working in the public sector the word 'profit' may not apply, but profit is the added value that is received over and above costs. In situations where money does not change hands, profit could be considered in more subjective terms. For example, schools do not make a profit but they should add value;

charities may see profit in terms of alleviating distress or saving lives, hospitals may be able to generate extra income to allow improved health care facilities to be installed. In balance sheet terms, a company has made a profit when it has more assets at the end of an accounting period than at the beginning. In educational terms, a school or college could have made a 'profit' if the pupils were more capable at the end of a term or a semester than at the beginning, Equating such ideas from the private sector into the public and voluntary sectors has proved difficult, but it is not impossible given some lateral thinking.

Promotion/communication

Organisations spend large sums on advertising. If they have the right product at the right price, it is pointless if nobody knows about it. Promotion, including advertising, lets people know and, often just as important, keeps the product and service in their minds. Individuals working for organisations have two roles to play:

1. They need to know the promotions that their organisation has underway so that they anticipate customers' requests and queries.

2. The way they deal with customers can be an advertisement for the organisation and its products/services *per se*.

All customers talk to their friends and colleagues and tell them about good and bad products and services. Personal recommendations are very important in purchase decisions.

The term *communication* rather than *promotion* is preferred because communication is a two-way process and allows customers to give feedback. All interactions with customers, whether face to face, on the telephone or by letter, are communications and the way they are handled can promote the product or service and give signals about the type of organisation that the customer is dealing with.

Place/convenience

Does your customer come to the organisation or does it go to the customer?

Not all transactions take place on the supplier's premises and recent years have seen a move towards making the provision of products and services convenient to the customer. New technologies including the *Internet* offer exciting prospects, especially for the delivery of services. With domestic video conferencing through Windows® on a PC, a whole range of consultancy opportunities in the health, financial advice and educational markets are being opened up.

Products and benefits

Modern selling techniques have shifted the emphasis away from the product or service and onto the benefits to the customer of acquiring that product or service.

In describing the SCRS (Sales Control and Record System), Fenton (1984) makes a point of introducing the benefits straight away – it is not just a system that the customer is purchasing, it is a means of doing business. In a similar vein, a car is not just an object but it is personal transportation, it is freedom, it may even be a method of expressing an image. Indeed image is a very important supplementary to a number of products, possession of which sends out a message regarding the customer's status.

Products and services

It was once thought that there was an intrinsic difference between products which were tangible, i.e. could be touched etc., and services which were more intangible. Whilst there are undoubted differences say between a motor car and an operation in a hospital, when considered in terms of benefits then identical rules apply. This book does not make a distinction between products and services, concerned as it is with customer value. Throughout the book there will be references to product/service, as the opinion of the author is that they are really one and the same.

This Part of the book continues with a consideration of the organisational analysis that needs to be undertaken prior to considering the marketing management and strategies to be employed, a discussion of what is a market, market research and finally the nature of competition, before considering the marketing mix in Parts Two to Five.

 ## Introduction to Icelandair case

The following provides an introduction to the major Case Study (Icelandair) that is used in this book.

Case study introduction – Icelandair

The marketing operations of Icelandair, the national airline of Iceland, form a major Case Study running throughout this book. In order for the reader to gain the maximum understanding of the importance and relevance of this case material to the text, it is necessary to consider a degree of background material.

The operations of any organisation depend on a whole host of both internal and external factors, and a consideration of these factors is required in order to understand the nature and direction of the organisation.

In order to comprehend the importance of Icelandair to the marketing concepts that will be developed in this text, it is necessary to understand certain facts about both the airline industry and the geopolitical situation of Iceland.

As the text will show, Icelandair have been growing in the Western Europe–North Eastern USA market, one of the most competitive airline markets in the world. To comprehend how a very small airline from one of the smallest European nations (and one that is at the extreme geographic periphery of the continent) has been so successful requires a study that will be somewhat technical but also, it is hoped, interesting.

Icelandair – a brief history

The roots of Icelandair can be traced back to 1937 with the formation of Flugfélag Akureyrar, renamed Flugfélag Islands (Islands is the Icelandic for Iceland) in 1940 when the headquarters were moved from Akureyei on the North Coast to the Icelandic capital, Reykjavik. It was this company that later adopted the trade name Icelandair. In 1944 another company, Loftleidir, was formed, soon changing its name to Icelandic Airlines.

The first commercial international flight to operate out of Iceland was on 11 July 1945 when a converted Catalina seaplane began a service to Larges Bay in Scotland.

Iceland and World War II

In World War I, Britain had nearly been brought to its knees by the operation of German submarines (U-boats) attacking the vital North Atlantic convoys. The introduction of the convoy system brought not only much needed food and military supplies but also troops from Canada and, from 1917 onwards, the USA. As an island nation, Britain depended on being able to secure the sea routes leading to and from the British Isles. Airpower was in its infancy and convoy protection depended upon destroyers and sloops ringing the convoy and forcing away the U-boats. Britain was in fact very late in instituting a convoy system, experts deriding the idea of putting merchant ships in convoy and believing that such a concentration would make the job of the U-boat commanders easier, not harder. It was not until as late as 1917 that convoys became the norm for vessels crossing the North Atlantic (Warner, 1975). In 1939, at the outbreak of World War II, the British were quick to reinstitute the convoy system, although again they suffered heavily at the hands of a new generation of U-boats and their commanders.

One new weapon against the U-boat was the long-range patrol aircraft. Even with the development of the snorkel device by the Germans later in the war, diesel-powered submarines still needed to surface to recharge their batteries and were thus vulnerable to air attack at this time. It is not often realised that a diesel-powered submarine is much faster on the surface than submerged, and thus U-boat commanders were often obliged to stalk convoys whilst surfaced. Unfortunately for the allies, there was a huge gap in the centre of the North Atlantic which could not be patrolled by aircraft operating from the British Isles or the USA/Canada and it was not until 1941 that small escort aircraft carriers converted from merchant ships were available. To give an illustration of the scale of the problem, 564 allied merchant vessels with a tonnage of 2,926,339 million gross registered tonnes were sunk between September 1941 and May 1942 (Watts, 1976). Not only did this represent a major loss of precious ships and cargoes but also of the lives of the merchant seamen. New ships can be built but lives cannot be regained.

At the start of World War II, Iceland was a dependency of Denmark. Germany overran Denmark (but not Iceland) in the Spring of 1940. Situated towards the North and the centre of the Atlantic, Iceland occupies a key strategic position to the North of the convoy routes.

As an ally of Denmark, Britain despatched military forces to Iceland in 1940 and set up anti-submarine operations using maritime patrol aircraft. This went someway towards bridging the North Atlantic air gap and was to be crucial when the Western Allies began to ship supplies to Russia after the German invasion of that country in 1941. The British operation was turned over to the USA in July 1941 and, as the USA was then neutral, ships sailing from the USA to Iceland could do so with a neutral escort, the British then escorting vessels from Iceland to the UK. Neutrality proved little bar to some U-boat captains and a number of US Navy escorts were actually attacked and one, the *USS Rueben James*, sunk prior to the US entry into the war in December 1941.

With the US entry into the war and the need to move the huge US armies to Europe, the continuing need for supplies from the USA to Britain and the Russian convoys, operations out of Iceland multiplied and led to the construction of an air base at Keflavik. This base became the NATO air base of Keflavik after World War II and was and remains an important part of the NATO defence operations. It also provided Icelandair with modern facilities and long runways.

The importance of Keflavik to NATO operations was demonstrated when the fictional taking of Iceland by the Warsaw Pact was used as a major part of the plot in the best selling novel, *Red Storm Rising* (Clancy, 1987).

In the late 1940s into the 1950s, Icelandair expanded its international operations into other parts of Western Europe with services to London, Luxembourg, Stockholm, Amsterdam, Copenhagen and Helsinki. In 1953 the first services to the USA were introduced with fares that were significantly lower than their competitors, albeit using slower aircraft.

Hubs and spokes

Icelandair uses Keflavik Airport and air base as what is known in the airline business as a 'hub'. Other hubs include Heathrow (British Airways), Luton (easyJet), Atlanta, Georgia (Delta Airlines) and Brussels (Sabena).

The airport is the hub and the routes flying out of it are the spokes. Passengers fly into the hub on a spoke and then transfer to another plane that takes them out along another spoke. Such an operation maximises aircraft utilisation and helps ensure that passengers remain with the same airline. Where the latter is not possible, airlines negotiate agreements with other carriers, often as part of a code sharing agreement. Icelandair's partners include British Midland (whose hub is the East Midland's Airport in the UK) and Scandinavian Airline Systems (SAS).

Situated as it is in the middle of the most trafficked international air route in the world, Europe to North America, Iceland Keflavik is a very important and useful hub and accounts for the importance of Icelandair in the North Atlantic market and the airline's inclusion in this text. As will be shown later, the position of Iceland allows Icelandair to use the same aircraft on its Iceland-US services as used on the Iceland–Western Europe ones.

Using the Autumn 2000 timetable as a guide, the operation of the Icelandair hub and spokes can be clearly seen. All times are local (Summer time) and for simplification, to illustrate the principle, only those services connecting with a flight to North America are shown. In addition there are non-connection services purely to Iceland and a large number of services from other towns in Europe, which connect to the services shown. Thus the flights from Copenhagen to Iceland are fed by flights from Aalborg, Aarhus, Brussels, Dusseldorf, Gdansk, Geneva, Gothenburg, Hamburg, Helsinki, Luxembourg, Munich, Vienna, Warsaw and Zurich. Madrid and some German/Swiss cities are a direct service during the Summer but indirect in Winter.

Travelling from Europe to North America, the timetable is shown in Figure 1.3.

Travelling from North America to Europe the timetable is shown in Figure 1.4.

Thus, each afternoon, eight flights arrive at Keflavik from Western Europe between 1500 and 1600 and then between 1750 and 1845, six flights leave for the Eastern seaboard of North America with onward connections to California etc. The same pattern is repeated each morning with a series of transatlantic flights connecting with ones to Western Europe.

Diagrammatically the hub and spokes can be represented as shown in Figure 1.5.

With the exception of Glasgow and Frankfurt, the Western European direct services are to capital cities. Frankfurt is the home of the European Central Bank and also falls in the area covered by United States Army and Airforce operations for NATO, and Keflavik is a major USAF base. Glasgow will be covered throughout this text when considering Icelandair's marketing in Scotland. Whilst Glasgow is not the capital of Scotland, it has long been known as the 'second city of the Empire' after London.

Air services across the North Atlantic

The North Atlantic route between Western Europe and both the United States and Canada has been one of the most densely travelled of all trade

INBOUND FROM EUROPE

Departure Airport	Time	Arrive Keflavik
Amsterdam	1400	1520
Copenhagen	1425	1535
Frankfurt	1400	1535
Glasgow	1400	1510
London	1300	1500
Oslo	1445	1525
Paris	1415	1545
Stockholm	1410	1520

OUTBOUND TO NORTH AMERICA

Depart Keflavik	Arrive	Destination
1650	1845	Baltimore
1645	1820	Boston
1655	1835	Halifax, Nova Scotia
1630	1750	Minneapolis
1640	1840	New York
1635	1845	Washington

Figure 1.3   Icelandair operations Europe–North America.
(Note: Eastern USA is 4 hours behind Iceland, 5 behind UK. Iceland is 1 hour ahead of the UK and 2 hours ahead of Western Europe.)

routes. Up to the introduction of regular air services, much national prestige was put into building the biggest, fastest and most luxurious of ocean liners to operate across the North Atlantic. However, once aircraft could make the crossing in safety, the days of the classic Atlantic liner were numbered.

The Atlantic was first flown by the British aviators Alcock and Brown in 1919 using a converted Vickers Vimy bomber. The first solo crossing was that of Charles Lindbergh in 1927. However, up to the late 1930s there was no commercial aircraft available that could carry passengers across the Atlantic. It was not until 1937 that the first airmail services across 'the Pond' (as the ocean is known) commenced, followed by both Pan Am and BOAC (British Overseas Aircraft Corporation) flying-boat services from the Eastern seaboard of the USA to the UK. World War II then intervened but whilst the war put an end to commercial flights across the Atlantic, it did act as a great spur to the development of larger aircraft with much greater ranges and payloads.

In 1933 Boeing launched a small monoplane airliner with only two engines – the Boeing 247. Prior to this, airliners had been of a box like construction and there was a belief that a minimum of three engines were required to cover any commercial range with safety. The Douglas Aircraft company followed suit with the DC1, which developed into the famed DC3

INBOUND FROM NORTH AMERICA

Departure Airport	Time	Arrive Keflavik
Baltimore	2045	0625
Boston	2130	0630
Halifax, Nova Scotia	2230	0545
Minneapolis	1920	0620
New York	2050	0620
Washington	2045	0625

OUTBOUND TO EUROPE

Depart Keflavik	Arrive	Destination
0745	1255	Amsterdam
0805	1305	Copenhagen
0725	1250	Frankfurt
0755	1100	Glasgow
0745	0045	London
0735	1205	Oslo
0745	1305	Paris
0740	1235	Stockholm

Figure 1.4   Icelandair operations North America–Europe.
(Note: Eastern USA is 4 hours behind Iceland, 5 behind UK. Iceland is 1 hour ahead of the UK and 2 hours ahead of Western Europe.)

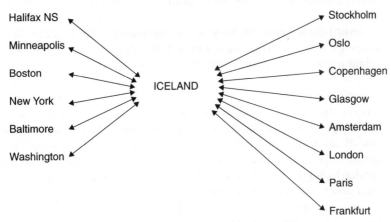

Figure 1.5   Icelandair's hub and spokes.

or Dakota that first flew in 1935. By the end of World War II, thousands of Dakotas had been built for the USAF and the RAF and many were demilitarised to form the nucleus of a growing commercial airline sector.

In the late 1940s the technology existed for propeller driven aircraft of sufficient size and range to carry a commercial payload across the Atlantic although, in the early days, refuelling was often necessary at Gander in Canada, Prestwick in Scotland or Shannon in Southern Ireland. Indeed the increase in traffic brought temporary prosperity to these airports, vital as they were for the North Atlantic traffic. The Boeing Stratocruiser, the Lockheed Constellation and the Douglas DC6 and DC7 began to bring North Atlantic air travel to a mass market. However the airlines were not in the market for economy passengers and law suits were filed against those operators who tried to offer cut price fares, the airline cartel being very strong at the time and determined to keep prices high, especially as demand far exceeded supply.

Of engines, speed and range

The propeller driven aircraft of the late 1940s and early 1950s had one problem. A propeller begins to lose efficiency the closer the speed of the airframe approaches that of the speed of sound. The speed of sound (Mach 1, named after the scientist Mach) varies according to the density of the air. An aircraft moves forward because the propulsion system moves a column of air backwards. Newton's Third Law of Motion states that for every action there is an equal and opposite reaction. Thus the reaction of the engine moving air backwards is for the engine and its airframe to move forward. Unfortunately for the propeller, it is theoretically only possible for it to move an airframe at about a maximum of 500 mph. If power is increased, the propeller tips are moving so fast as to distort the backward movement of the air column and there is no increase in forward motion.

Nevertheless, slow as they were compared with modern jets, the propeller driven aircraft were much faster than the ships on the North Atlantic route. The engines were however very complex, as piston engines tend to be, and there were not enough aircraft to provide competition for the shipping companies and prices were high. Speed, as was shown by the fares charged for Concord flights, commands a premium price.

The opening up of the mass market for North Atlantic (and indeed, the world) air travel came with the introduction of the Boeing 707 into commercial service in September 1958 and the Douglas DC8 which entered service in September 1959. The UK had been first into the jet market with the Comet, which made its first commercial flight as early as May 1952 and its first commercial crossing of the North Atlantic in October 1958 in an enlarged form thus beating Boeing by days. The Comet, however, despite being the first commercial jet airliner, suffered from fatigue problems and a lack of payload and was not a commercial success.

Whereas the maximum speed of a Lockheed Super Constellation (perhaps the ultimate in commercial piston engined designs) was around 300 knots (nautical miles per hour), that of the Boeing 707 approached 500 knots at 35,000 feet (where the air is thinner) thus cutting considerable time off the North Atlantic crossing. It was this ability to cross the

Atlantic in half a day that spelt the end of the North Atlantic shipping industry.

The thinner the air is, the faster an aircraft can fly. Thin air occurs at high altitude but at such heights passengers cannot breathe. Thus the development of pressurised aircraft ran alongside the development of propulsion systems.

By the late 1960s a new type of jet engine (the fan jet) that was highly efficient and which could lift greater and greater payloads had been developed, and this let to the introduction of a series of wide-bodied (i.e. with twin aisles in the passenger cabin) airliners, the Boeing 747 (Jumbo) being the first followed by the DC10, the Lockheed Tristar and the Airbus A300/310 series. These aircraft could carry hundreds of passengers across the Atlantic and with their introduction fares became much more affordable for the tourist as well as for the business user. These engines were also much more reliable, an important consideration in the Icelandair story.

Twin city pairs

The most cost-effective routes for airlines to operate are those known as twin city pairs, where the two destinations generate enough traffic to fill up an aircraft to past the breakeven point. London–Paris, London–New York and Los Angeles–Chicago are good examples. Such routes can justify large aircraft being deployed on them. For less densely trafficked routes, especially those which feed the hubs mentioned earlier, smaller aircraft have been developed. As the major players in the airframe market both Boeing (which now includes McDonnell Douglas) and Airbus in Europe have a family of aircraft ranging from short-haul to long-haul products. All but the largest of these are twin engined.

Twin-engined aircraft are cheaper to purchase and to run but, owing to a rule known as ETOPS (Extended Twin-engine Operations), they may be restricted on over-water routes.

ETOPS

Even the largest Boeing 747 or Airbus A340 does not need the full power from four fan-jets whilst cruising, indeed one or two engines will keep it in the air. However, should an engine fail on a four-engine plane, there are three more; on a twin-engined plane there is only spare in the event of a failure. The Federal Aviation Authority in the USA developed a 60-minute ETOPS rule for twin-engined aircraft. The plane must only fly on routes where there is a suitable airport on which to land within 60 minutes of an engine failure. This restricts the ability of twin-engined aircraft on the North Atlantic routes. However, as Sabbach (1995) has shown, modern engines can run for as many as 20,000 hours without removal for major maintenance and thus the chances of a second engine failure are very slight indeed.

If an aircraft has to be within 60 minutes of a diversionary airstrip it is impossible for a twin-engined model to fly across even the North Atlantic from Europe to North America. However, if a 180-minute ETOPS certification is approved, i.e. one where the aircraft must be three hours from an airport, then the world and the ocean routes are opened up to twin-engined aircraft so certified. Indeed, there is only a small area in the middle of the Pacific Ocean, and Antarctica, that are forbidden to such aircraft. The profitable North Atlantic routes are thus opened up to aircraft that cost less to buy and less to operate than three- or four-engined models.

The three-engined medium-range Boeing 727 launched in the 1960s was one of the world's most successful passenger jets, having operating costs, range and payload that met airline requirements almost exactly. Its replacement in the 1980s was the twin-engined Boeing 757, a single-aisle, narrow-bodied plane much in demand for the operators of charter flights linked to package holidays. Equipped with identical instruments to those used in the wide-bodied Boeing 767 (introduced in 1982), pilots can be certified on the 757 and 767 simultaneously. The Boeing 757 is the main airliner operated by Icelandair for which it carries 183 to 189 passengers (22 of whom are in business class).

The Boeing 757 and 767 received ETOPS 180-hour rating after 2 years of commercial service had demonstrated the incredible reliability of the engines. It was this reliability that led Boeing to seek certification for the wide-bodied Boeing 777 immediately upon its debut into commercial service in 1995, which involved extensive pre-introduction testing, a process described in detail by Sabbach (1995). Operating just one major type of aircraft on both sides of the hub (Iceland–North America and Iceland–European mainland) gives Icelandair considerable economies in maintenance etc. The UK 'no-frills' airline easyJet, which has been the subject of television documentaries, uses the same approach, operating just one type of aircraft as a cost-control measure.

Thus Icelandair has the use of Keflavik with its huge runways situated across the major air route between Europe and North America and operates a fleet of Boeing 757 aircraft that are rated for extended flights across ocean areas.

Icelandair first came to the attention of the author when flying home to Scotland from Vancouver in Canada. The transatlantic flight flew almost directly over the author's house and then on to London where there was the need to change terminals and catch a flight to Glasgow, adding considerably to the journey times. There are a few direct flights from Glasgow to the eastern seaboard of North America, mainly to New York and Toronto, but they tend to be more expensive than flying a twin city pair of London to New York or Toronto. Flying from Scotland via London involves setting off in almost the opposite direction from that desired. Although maps show New York etc. to be west of the British Isles, because the earth is a globe the most direct route is a great circle that involves a north-west track out over Iceland, then west to Greenland and finally south-west over Canada and the maritime states of the USA.

Owing to a phenomenon known as the jetstream, a high-altitude wind that blows west to east over the Atlantic, airliners normally cover the North America to Europe leg faster than the Europe–North America one. The average time taken between Glasgow and New York via London is about 12.5 hours, allowing for the change of terminals in London. Via Iceland, the time is just over 9.5 hours.

What will be demonstrated throughout this text is the manner in which Icelandair have marketed the geographic position of their hub etc. in order to appeal to the European and especially the Scottish market for transatlantic air travel.

Flugfélag Islands and Loftleidir merged in 1973, and in 1979 the brand name Icelandair was adopted as the international tradename. Keflavik was developed as the major hub from 1989, with the smaller airport at Reykjavik handling domestic traffic. This coincided with an easing of cold war tensions, thus releasing some of Keflavik's runway capacity.

Icelandair also owns extensive hotel and tourism operations in Iceland itself and is the largest private company in the country, employing over 2000 staff.

The company introduced a new livery, uniform designs and logos in 1999 as part of a process to stay ahead in a highly competitive market.

The market

Icelandair are, in fact operating in a number of separate but linked markets, namely:

- the transatlantic market;
- the market to and from Iceland;
- the Iceland vacation market.

As such, those in charge of marketing management need to balance the needs of these various markets and see how they can have a synergical effect upon each other. For instance, transatlantic travellers who take a two-day break in Iceland are utilising two different markets. The skills and knowledge required to run a transatlantic airline are different from those needed to support part of the vacation industry, and the organisation needs to be and is aware of this.

Iceland has been steadily expanding its share of the lucrative but highly competitive European Cities Short Break market. Reykjavik and its environs are well placed to offer a very different experience from that of many other cities, and Iceland and Icelandair have been marketing this uniqueness.

Throughout this book, Icelandair operations will be used to support the concepts covered to provide a practical example of how marketing concepts are applied in a commercial and competitive environment.

Icelandair's Scottish market

Icelandair's Glasgow–North America operation, as an example of how the airline operates, accounted for 34% of the airline's UK sales in 1998. In revenue, 87% of these sales were in economy (known as coach in the USA) with 13% being business-class, hence Icelandair's wish to boost business-class sales. As premier tickets, these generate much more revenue per passenger mile than economy tickets.

The breakdown of North American destinations from Glasgow using Icelandair in 1998 was:

Boston	28%
New York	26%
Florida/Orlando	25%
Baltimore/Washington DC	10%
Halifax, Nova Scotia	6%
Minneapolis	4%

Given the importance of Florida as an outbound UK tourist destination, it is no surprise that it is the third highest. New York is served by Continental Airlines from Glasgow, but Icelandair are the quickest to Boston from Scotland thus giving the airline a prime market position.

According to Icelandair, the issues that the Scotland–North America operation face are:

Low brand awareness

Despite advertising, many potential customers are not aware that Icelandair offers a convenient service to North America. This is being addressed via newspaper advertising and special promotions, and advertising on the sides of buses etc. in an attempt to create awareness over a wide cross-section of the population.

Low share of business-class sales

This issue is being addressed by targeting potential corporate groups using a dedicated sales team.

Overdependence on consolidators

The operation of consolidators is best seen in the pages of the weekend newspapers. They consolidate ticket sales by buying from the airlines at a discount and then offering tickets directly to customers. Overdependence on consolidators means that every ticket is being sold at a large discount and thus the airline is not gaining maximum revenue.

Alliances

As will be covered in Chapter 5, 64% of airline business is conducted through members of one of the major airline alliances. The major alliances are:

Oneworld: British Airways, American Airlines, Canadian Airlines, Cathay Pacific and Qantas.
Star Alliance: Air Canada, Lufthansa, SAS, British Midland, Thai Airways, United Airlines and Varig of Brazil. Icelandair has major links to this alliance.
KLM/Northwest: KLM, Northwest, Continental and Alitalia.
Atlantic Excellence: Delta, Swissair, Sabena, TAP (Portugal) and Austrian Airlines.

Overall, Icelandair has 0.71% of the global market, making it a fairly small player in global terms but one whose market share on the North Atlantic will need to be taken into account by the larger players. The company has grown faster than most European Airlines over the past few years (13% on average, according to Icelandair's figures) and has a very young fleet of aircraft.

In addition to the threats posed by the established airlines, the latter part of the 20th century saw the growth of a low-cost airline sector prompted by government deregulation of airline operations in the developed world. Operating as 'no-frills' airlines, operators such as easyJet in the UK rapidly built up a route network and began to challenge established players. easyJet have been profiled by Swarbrooke and Horner (1999) and there is no doubt that established operators need to take these newcomers into their calculations when planning future developments and setting prices.

Summary

This chapter has introduced the major facets of marketing, stressing the holistic nature of marketing as an organisational management function. Up to quite recent times, many organisations operated on a product-led basis, developing products and services with little regard to the actual needs of customers. The contemporary approach is one that is customer driven, based on researching the needs and wants of the customer base and then satisfying the needs and wants in a manner that is cost effective for the organisation. Not all organisations operate for profit but even those in the public sector need to market their products and services and adopt a more customer-driven approach to all aspects of their operations, including the setting of objectives.

Marketing may be somatic or autonomic. Whilst the former may well be a function of a dedicated marketing department, the latter involves all the staff of the organisation and may also include actions by current customers who can provide both positive and negative marketing by their comments to those they are in contact with.

The marketing mix of the 4/7Ps and 4Cs provides a useful starting point for an examination of marketing management.

Useful website

www.icelandair.com   Icelandair website

■ ⓥ **2** Understanding the organisation

The importance of the external environment – Sectors of business and organisations – Mission and objectives – Internal and external analyses and the links between them – BACK analysis – Culture – PEST/PESTLE/SPECTACLES analysis – SWOT analysis

The importance of the external environment

No organisation exists in a vacuum. Whatever the typology and function of an organisation it has to co-exist with other organisations in a complex, increasingly global external environment. In many cases it is actions taken by those outside the organisation that are a major influence on organisational decisions, and for this reason it is important that decision makers have as clear a picture as possible as to what is happening in the external environment and can then relate such data to the internal environment of the organisation. Whilst organisational decision makers may wish to believe that they are the masters/mistresses of their organisation's destinies, in reality that destiny is shaped by governments, customers, suppliers and other stakeholders, including competitors.

Sectors of business and organisations

Traditionally the world of business used to be divided into two main sectors – private and public – as discussed in the previous chapter, with a third, the so-called voluntary sector (charities etc.) gaining in prominence in the second half of the 20th century. As was shown earlier, these are really descriptions of the typologies of organisations and actually describe ownership. Sector is a description of the type of core activity that the organisation is engaged on. Whilst the list can be never-ending, the main business sectors may be described as:

- government, including armed forces;
- financial service (banks, insurance etc.);
- information services;
- manufacturing;
- building;
- transportation (airlines, bus companies, taxis, railways, shipping);
- hospitality;

- tourism;
- care (hospitals, nursing homes etc.);
- entertainment;
- education;
- services (including plumbers, electricians etc.).

Each sector can have further subsectors as illustrated in the brackets. For example, the transportation sector includes railways, shipping, airlines, road transport etc. It is not always clear without a careful study as to exactly which sector or sectors an organisation belongs to, especially as large conglomerates may operate in a variety of sectors. An airline such as Icelandair, whilst predominantly in the transportation-by-air sector, may also be involved in tourism operations.

Vision, mission and objectives

All organisations have been set up to do something, whether it is to run a country, provide a holiday, manufacture a motor car or sell groceries. Whilst the ultimate objective of a for-profit organisation may be just that – profit, in order to achieve that objective the organisation needs to deliver a product or service to its customers. Modern organisations usually produce a statement of their mission that encapsulates what business they are in and where they see themselves positioned within the particular market or markets that they serve. Unfortunately many mission statements, originally intended to motivate staff and to inspire customers have become, in the words of Clutterbuck *et al.* (1993), 'woolly platitudes' that do reflect actual performance.

Vision

Everybody it seems who has ever commented on entrepreneurship and successful organisations mentions vision. Without vision it is impossible to be an entrepreneur. Bill Gates of Microsoft has it, as has Sir Richard Branson. Those who have written about them all comment on the way they have almost clung to their vision. Even their detractors, such as Tom Bower (2000), who has been highly critical of Branson, appears to concede that the man has both a specific vision and vision in general. This is also a clear message from Manes and Andrews' (1994) study of Microsoft's Bill Gates.

Vision could be described as a dream with direction. Visionaries not only dream about something, they almost experience it in real time. A dream is experienced; a vision is lived in.

William Heinecke (1990) considers that entrepreneurs should set goals but go easy on vision. Setting goals is very important but without vision the daring steps are never taken.

Vision, whilst it is often centred on the individual holding the vision, also has to be such as to appeal to the customer. One of the most difficult tasks that the formulator of a vision has to accomplish is to communicate that vision to others in such a way as to fire enthusiasm.

Vision does need to be focussed on something tangible. There is no use in having the vision that you want to be the most successful person in the world, this is far too broad. As Heinecke also points out quite rightly when discussing vision, Bill Gates did not set out to be fabulously wealthy, his vision was the best software program in the world. That vision was focussed and could be worked towards in a systematic sort of manner.

Internal and external analyses

In order to understand the functioning of any organisation it is necessary to analyse the internal and external operating environments within which the organisation works. This is especially true of marketing, as marketing is fundamentally concerned with the relationship between the organisation and its customers. Customers form a very important component of the external environment.

The links between internal and external analyses

It is important that both the internal and the external environments of an organisation are considered in a systematic, analytical manner as part of any organisational planning process.

Three fundamental analyses are considered in this chapter. Firstly a BACK (Baggage, Aspirations, Culture and Knowledge) analysis, then an analysis of external factors, PESTLE/SPECTACLES, and finally a SWOT (Strengths, Weaknesses, Opportunities and Threats) analysis in which the internal strengths and weaknesses of the organisation are matched to the opportunities and threats that may affect the organisation and which come from the external environment. The analysis of the product/service portfolio offered by the organisation forms the core of Chapter 8.

Just as every organisation is unique in terms of its history, culture, product/service mix, staff etc., so it follows that the results of any analysis will be unique for the organisation in question. In effect, these analyses produce an organisational fingerprint.

BACK analysis

This is an analysis devised initially to support personal development programmes but then used by a number of organisations with considerable success as an aid to understanding organisational behaviour. The analysis was further refined in a companion book to this volume, *Mastering Customer Relations* (Cartwright, 2000) from which this section is adapted with permission. The analysis is designed to provide an overall picture of an organisation. The acronym stands for: **Baggage**, **Aspirations**, **Culture** and **Knowledge**.

Baggage

Imagine a person on holiday with suitcases, hand baggage and souvenirs trying to exit a hotel through a set of revolving doors. In order to make progress they are going to have to put down one or more pieces of baggage. So it is with both organisational and personal life. 'Baggage' is collected as the organisation or individual moves through life. Life also presents a series of revolving doors which being fixed in time means that, unlike the holidaymaker above, baggage once set down may not always be retrieved. Often it is the case that some baggage must be relinquished in order to make progress. The problem with baggage is that both individuals and organisations become very attached to it even when it no longer serves a practical purpose. How many lofts, garages and garden sheds are filled with those things that people cannot bear to throw away, just in case it might be useful! In organisation terms, baggage can include procedures that were once relevant but are no longer needed.

Procedures, policies, rules and even products themselves all need to be looked at when considering baggage. Much baggage is necessary but organisations should review on a regular basis if they are still doing things that at best are of no practical use and at worse actually impede the relationship with the customer or supplier. Surplus baggage always consumes organisational energy and should be dropped as soon as possible. The best way to ascertain the baggage that an organisation carries with it is to talk to members of staff not only about what they do but why they do it. If they don't know the answer to the second question, then this may indicate a piece of baggage that should be dropped.

Organisations need to be careful about dropping any baggage that may identify them positively to their customer base. British Airways provoked an outcry in the late 1990s when the company decided to change the traditional tailfin logo for a set of non-country specific designs in an attempt to express the global nature of the operation. Unfortunately many in the UK did not agree with this decision and a reversal of policy ensued.

Aspirations

If baggage is about where the organisation has been, then aspirations are about where it wants to go. In conducting a BACK analysis it is useful to ask staff at various levels within the organisation as to what they see as the main aspirations. Sensible management ensures that all those in the organisation have an understanding of where the organisation is heading. In that way there can be maximum, informed input into the planning process. Mission statements and statements relating to organisational objectives may also provide valuable clues that truly reflect aspirations and are not just a set of sound bite platitudes.

Aspirations can only be realised if they are unhindered by baggage, fit into the culture of the organisation (to be covered under the next heading) and if the organisation possesses the necessary knowledge. This shows the interlocking nature of the four components of the BACK analysis. As mentioned above, it is important that an organisation and all who work for it have an idea of its aspirations and that they are realistic. It is only if one knows where one wants to go that proper plans can be made and implemented. Unrealistic organisational aspirations, like unrealistic personal ones, may lead to frustration because they are incapable of fulfilment.

Culture

Organisational culture is an internal factor. Culture, when referring to organisations, is a function of 'the way we do things around here'. As in definitions of national cultures, it is made up of a set of underlying values, assumptions and beliefs.

It is possible to write whole books about organisational culture, as has indeed been done. Charles Handy (1976; 1978) has produced a simple-to-understand but highly effective descriptive method for illustrating organisational cultures. Handy has identified four types of organisational cultures, each with its own distinctive behaviours.

Role culture

The *role* culture that Handy visualised as a Greek temple, a highly stable structure, represents the typical bureaucratic organisation.

Such organisations often have a plethora of rules and regulations with departmental boundaries clearly defined. They are often slow to change, seeing in stability their means of survival. The role culture places great emphasis on stating what a person's job title is rather than what the person actually does. There tend to be barriers to inter-departmental communication across the pillars of the temple. Communication tends to be up and down individual pillars. Such a structure is typical of many large organisations and has often been identified with the traditional public sector/governmental organisations. In recent times many organisations have been trying to move away from the inflexibility that such a structure produces. Handy ascribes the god Apollo to this type of culture, as Apollo was the Greek god of order and rules.

Club/power

The god Zeus is ascribed by Handy to the spider's web of the *club/power* culture. Power rests in the centre, often with a single individual with a strong personality. It is not unusual for that person to be the founder of the organisation. Power flows outwards from the centre. This is a culture that suits the entrepreneur who can keep an eye on operations. Club cultures can respond very quickly but only in the direction personally favoured by those at the centre. The UK based Virgin Group with Richard Branson in the centre became a byword for entrepreneurship in the

1990s with operations that included an airline, rail operations, music, personal finance and publishing – all interests of Sir Richard.

Task culture

In the 1980s and 1990s many larger organisations began to adopt a *task* culture (represented by Handy as a net or matrix) approach as they moved away from the role culture discussed earlier. The task culture has been ascribed by Handy to Athena, the goddess of craftsmen. Power in a task culture lies in expertise and creativity. Whilst in a role culture, promotion and advancement are regulated by rules relating to position in the hierarchy and time served, for those in a task culture advancement is purely on ability. Task cultures actively break down departmental barriers and thus are much more flexible organisations to deal with.

Existential culture

This type of culture is represented in Handy's work by the god Dionysus, the god of wine and song. Handy (1978) points out that the role, power/club and task cultures all have one thing in common: the individual employee is there to serve the organisation (it might be argued that this does not apply to the individual or to the small group at the centre of a power/club culture). In the *existential* culture, the organisation exists to serve the needs of those in it. A partnership of doctors, architects, lawyers etc. are examples of an existential culture. Such organisations suit professionals who may well appoint a manager to oversee the day-to-day running of the organisation, but the professionals themselves operate on the basis that they are all equal.

There are very interesting inter-reactions that can occur when two different organisational cultures interact in either a competitor situation or a customer–supplier relationship. Similar situations can occur when different national cultures work together. In the 1980s and 1990s the rivalry between British Airways and Virgin Atlantic led to a series of court actions initiated by the latter (Gregory, 1994). In terms of organisational culture, what was actually happening was that a role culture (as BA was at the time) was competing with a power/club culture (Virgin Atlantic), with interesting results.

It is not difficult to imagine the frustration those in a role culture might experience if they become the customers of an existential supplier; the former's rules may well be alien to the latter. One can look at the possibilities of a whole range of combinations.

There is a useful concept from George Bernard Shaw and used by Handy in 1989: Shaw remarked that all progress depends on unreasonable people. Reasonable people adapt themselves to the world whilst those who are unreasonable persist in trying to adapt the world to themselves. A successful organisation will attempt to adapt itself and thus its culture to the customers, and not force customers to adapt to its methods and procedures. The two ends of this continuum are known as product led and customer driven, as described in the previous chapter.

National cultures

When Fons Trompenaars published *Riding the Waves of Culture* in 1993, he produced one of the most influential business texts of the late 20th century. In 2000, R. D. Lewis published *When Cultures Collide*. Both texts are recommended reading to anybody looking at marketing and organisations in the global economy.

As the world, especially the world of business, becomes smaller through improved communications, so, paradoxically, does the importance of understanding cultural diversity become more important. Cultural change is generational and responds at a much slower rate than technological change. Thus, whilst communications between different cultural groups are much quicker and much easier, the differences between those groups still remain. Only perhaps in the field of popular culture is there rapid global convergence.

It stands to reason, therefore, that as organisations undertake their operations on an increasingly global basis, the need for cultural understanding becomes greater and greater, especially within the management of the marketing function in order to ensure that the message received by a different culture is the one that the organisation actually wishes to send. The importance of the correct reading of national culture is an important component of advertising, as is covered in Chapter 12.

Trompenaars set out to explore the cultural diversity aspects of business and one can only recommend his work to the reader in the highest terms.

Trompenaars considered cultural diversity in terms of a series of differing attitudes held by various national groups. It should be noted that such attitudes are always just a tendency – not all Britons will react in one way to a particular set of circumstances, all Americans in another and all Japanese in yet another, but his research did show a series of national tendencies. The attitudes Trompenaars believed were most critical were:

- attitude to time;
- universal v. particular;
- individualism v. collectivism;
- emotional v. neutral;
- specific v. diffuse;
- achievement v. ascription;
- attitudes to nature.

To these can also be added:

- attitudes to age;
- attitudes to gender.

None of these concepts is absolute, national tendencies lie on a continuum between two factors. In the following section the factors are described and, where appropriate, the cultures lying at each end and in the middle are given. Trompenaars spent many hours researching this, often by asking multiple choice questions requiring a response to a certain set of circumstances; for example, how much right does a friend have to expect you to lie for them in a certain set of circumstances? The responses were interesting as in some cultures it is expected that friends will support each other come what may (a particular response), whilst in others if a friend breaks the rules then those rules should apply whatever the circumstances (a universal response).

Attitude to time

It might be thought that time is a universal concept as an hour is an hour whether it is in London, New York or Shanghai. In looking at the cultural effect of time, however, it is not the absolute nature of time that is important but the attitudes towards it.

Eastern cultures often have a reverence for ancestors and historical precedent. The USA, according to the research, was less interested in the past and much more in the future. Even the importance of time is an issue. In many Western cultures, punctuality is, as many of us had to write as lines at school 'a very desirable virtue'. In other cultures, punctuality is perhaps of less importance. This can immediately lead to a cultural clash. Different cultures have different norms within their value systems.

Those working across cultures need to adapt their ideas to those they are working with, and to understand and adopt the prevailing attitudes to time in the culture within which they wish to do business. There will be times, of course, when it is necessary for delivery dates etc. to be met and here a sympathetic method of insisting is required, with the reasons being clearly stated and not just a blanket insistence made.

Universal v. particular

In some cultures a set of rules or laws is universally applied (or so perceived wisdom tells us, despite the fact that there is sometimes one law for the rich and one law for the poor, as the old adage goes). In others, rules and norms may be applied contingent upon the circumstances. Trompenaars points out that relationships such as friendship may confer special rights and obligations in a particular oriented culture which are less welcome in a universal one. In a universal culture your friend has much less right to expect you to cover up for them than in a culture where particularism is the accepted norm. In general, the USA and Japan were very high on universalism when tested, whereas the former Yugoslavia and certain Far Eastern countries (excluding Japan) tended towards the particularism end of the continuum, although it must be stressed that the overall tendency was that there should be universal rules followed by everybody. The UK tended towards the universalism end but to a lesser degree than did the USA.

In dealing with a culture at the particularism end of the spectrum, organisations need to know exactly which rules are being applied and to whom.

As Trompenaars points out in his excellent tips for doing business with different cultures, in a universalist culture there will be one way of doing things whilst in the particularist there may be a number of alternatives.

Individualism v. collectivism

Basically, do people regard themselves as a member of the group first and an individual second or vice versa? Perhaps not surprisingly, the USA is an individualism-oriented culture whereas the Japanese came out, together with countries such as Nepal, East Germany under the communist regime and other Far Eastern groupings, as tending towards a more collectivist approach. This should not be surprising given the political and social creeds of many Eastern areas and of communism. The UK was fairly individualist, but again less so than the USA.

In conducting business, it is important to realise that it may be the group as opposed to a key individual that needs to be satisfied in a collectivist-oriented culture, and that the building of collective relationships will be of great importance.

Emotional v. neutral

To what degree is it culturally acceptable to show feelings, especially in business relationships? In the UK and Japan it may be frowned on, less so in Italy and France. Latin cultures tend to accept displays of emotion more readily than those designated as Anglo-Saxon. Emotion is a good psychological safety valve and maybe this, plus the use of olive oil instead of fat for cooking, may go part of the way to explain the apparent lower incidence of heart disease in Latin areas. Whereas a display of emotion and even temper may be acceptable in Italy, it will certainly be less likely to produce effective results in the USA.

Specific v. diffuse

In many cultures there is expected to be a personal relationship between those involved, whereas in others the relationship is more organisation to organisation. In some cultures, work and home are closely related; in others, people are not expected to bring domestic issues into their workplace. This invites the question of how one is supposed to leave a problem at home? – it is the belief that the two should not mix and not the actual reality that is important here. Trompenaars quotes China as a very diffuse culture, using the example of how many respondents would refuse to help their boss paint his house. In China, 72% would help whereas in the much more specific culture of the UK only 8% would agree to give up their own time in this way (the US figure was 11%). Similarly in China, 89% of employees believed that the organisation had a responsibility to help house its employees compared to 55% of Japanese, but only 18% of those in the UK and 15% of USA respondents. There has been a change here in the UK, since during the late 19th and early 20th centuries, organisations often provided housing for staff. The relationship between suppliers and customers is very important to marketing management and may need to be considered differently if dealing with a specific rather than a diffuse culture.

An organisation in a specific culture may appear to those also adopting that culture to be much more focussed on its objectives, whereas in a diffuse culture time may be spent talking about non-organisational related issues. Neither is right or wrong, as both suit their cultures. It is again a matter of knowing, understanding and reacting in a culturally acceptable manner.

Achievement v. ascription

An achievement-oriented culture ascribes status dependent on what people have done, whereas ascription is about position, connections and even birth. The USA is the most achievement-oriented culture studied. In the USA it is believed that with hard work and education anybody can rise to the top, as the careers of many early emigrants and their immediate descendants showed. As Trompenaars points out, achievement societies ask what somebody has studied, whereas ascription ones may be more concerned with where the studies occurred. To that extent even the USA with its Ivy League of Universities (Harvard, Yale etc.) is not a wholly achievement culture and nor is the UK. India, where the author of this book worked for some time, was characterised to him by the degree of detail about his education (including the names of colleges and universities attended) that seminar audiences required before any work was undertaken. Titles and qualifications are much more important in ascription-oriented cultures and great offence can be caused by omitting them or quoting them incorrectly.

Trompenaars listed attitudes to age and gender in this category but for the purposes of this book they are being treated as separate factors.

Attitudes to nature

To what extend does a culture believe that it is right and proper for mankind to try to control nature? The developments in genetic engineering in the USA and the UK suggest that these cultures believe that this is acceptable. Trompenaars claimed a score of 35% in the UK and 38% in the USA who believed that it is worth trying to control nature, compared with only 10% in Japan. His highest score was Brazil with 53%, but perhaps this will decrease as Brazilians realise the importance of the rain forest and the global effects of too few trees.

Environmental issues are now very important and people are beginning to realise that one cannot trifle with nature as global warming etc. have shown.

There is also a related issue as to how much people feel they are the masters or mistresses of their own destiny. In the Western world, people believe this far more than those in communist regimes did. Controlling one's own destiny and controlling nature are closely linked, as is the concept of individualism v. collectivism. Fate, so important in many Eastern cultures, plays a much lesser role in the cultural psychology of the West.

Attitudes to age and gender

Different cultures have very different attitudes to these issues. Age is revered in many Eastern cultures, whereas it may be difficult for an over 40 to find employment in the West. This is despite results from a UK Do-It-Yourself chain which found that employing over 50s brought immense benefits in productivity, timekeeping, punctuality etc.

Similarly the position of women differs from one culture to another. Sending a young man or woman to negotiate on behalf of the organisation may be good practice in certain cultures but frowned on in others, especially if they are ones that denigrate the position of women or revere age. Sensitivity is required with these issues.

Organisations that discriminate against people on the grounds of age, gender or even race do themselves a grave disservice, as well as breaking the law of many developed jurisdictions. Sex and race discrimination are illegal in the UK and to these are added age in the USA. They also lose customers!

Knowledge

It is common sense that certain things cannot be accomplished without prior knowledge and experience. If an organisation wishes to pursue a particular strategy or set of goals it needs people with the relevant knowledge. This is one area where consultancy has grown, as it allows the organisation to obtain the knowledge and skills when needed without long-term payroll costs.

Organisations that value the knowledge held by their people and which have the development of people as a clear part of their overall strategy can be termed 'Learning Organisations'. An organisation that develops its staff also acquires organisational knowledge, which permeates through the organisation. As part of the BACK analysis it is important to consider those aspects of organisational knowledge that can form entries in the SWOT analysis that follows later in this chapter.

External analysis

As was stated earlier, no organisation operates within a vacuum. Organisational decisions and planning are contingent upon external factors. There may well be a market for a particular product/service but the successful development to meet that market may depend on a range of external factors including government approval, legal requirements, social attitudes, the costs of borrowing etc.

For many years the key external factors were referred to as PEST, standing for **Political**, **Economic**, **Social** and **Technological**. To these were later added **Legal** and **Environmental** factors, making the acronym PESTLE.

Cartwright (2001) in *Mastering the Business Environment* expanded this analysis to SPECTACLES, standing for **Social**, **Political**, **Economic**, **Customers**, **Technological**, **Aesthetic**, **Cultural**, **Legal**, **Environmental** and **Sectoral** factors. These are the key external factors that influence the direction that the organisation can take.

Components of a SPECTACLES analysis

As covered in the preceding section, the SPECTACLES analysis has grown out of the traditional PEST/PESTLE analyses. The additional components have become necessary to cope with an increasingly more complex business and social environment. The following sections are designed to act as an introduction to those components and to show the interrelationships between them.

Not only do each of the components of the analysis impact upon the organisation, they also impact upon each other.

Social analysis

Sociology is the study of the organisation and functioning of human societies. Margaret Thatcher, the UK Prime Minister from 1979 until 1990, is reputed to have remarked that 'there is no such thing as society there are only individuals and their families'. Part of the Thatcher philosophy was to stress the rights and responsibilities of the individual and that in many respects we are all responsible for our own destiny. However, in the main we all live and work in close proximity to other human beings whom we rely on for certain services and products. It is these relationships that form society.

The social analysis component of SPECTACLES is concerned with examining the changes in the societies with which the organisation interfaces and what trends within those societies are likely to have implications for the organisation. Included within this part of the analysis is a consideration of the phenomenon known as consumerism, a concept that will also be used as part of the customer analysis and the role of the media in communicating with society and influencing societal views and changes. The recent trends in the priority accorded to green/environmental issues are considered so important as to merit a separate analysis of their own, although it must be noted that it is society itself that has raised these issues as a priority and thus whilst the growth of green issues is also a rightful part of the social analysis, the addressing of those issues forms part of the environmental analysis.

The social analysis also includes a consideration of the demographic changes (size, age etc. of populations) that may impact upon an organisation. For instance, there has been a considerable change in the market for mobile telephones. Once a business tool, more and more are now used by the youth sector of the market. In 2001 it was estimated that well over half of the young people (including children) in the UK had their own mobile telephone. This trend has been accelerated by the introduction of child/parent friendly purchasing arrangements, such as pre-paying for calls. This allows parents to top up their child's telephone account and decreases the risk of unexpectedly large bills.

Political

Politics is the art and science of government. The citizens of any country are normally subject to a complex series of governmental layers. In Scotland the lowest level of government may be a Community Council, followed by a District

Council, the Scottish Parliament and the UK Parliament at Westminster. As the UK is a member of the European Union, Scots as UK citizens are also governed to an extent by the European Parliament.

Each layer of government has its own responsibilities and normally some form of revenue raising power. As the various layers may well be controlled by parties with differing political ideologies, this can make any analysis by an organisation quite complex.

Governments produce legislation and legal issues also form a separate part of the analysis. The political analysis is concerned with those external policy developments that affect the organisation. As even the smallest organisations begin to trade globally, then it is not enough to consider indigenous political policies but also to have due regard for policies in the national regions of customers and suppliers.

Economic

All organisations depend on sources of finance. Economics is always the source of much debate and the subject of countless books. The analysis of the economic environment considers the sources of finance for organisations and then the effects of regional, national and international economies, including exchange rates, interest rates and inflation.

Money does make the world go around but it must be stressed that there are considerable interrelationships between political and economic factors. Governments have a vested interest in managing their economies and some may be much more interventionist in the economic field than others.

Cultural

Much human and therefore organisational behaviour can be traced back to culture. As has already been discussed, there are distinct types of organisational culture each of which needs to interact with organisations displaying different cultures. An understanding of the culture of suppliers, customers and competitors forms an important part of the analysis of the environment.

There are also national cultures and as the world of business becomes increasingly global in nature, so organisations need to take much more cognisance of the cultures they will encounter. Good products can fail because those supplying them have not carried out a sufficiently in-depth analysis of the culture of the target market.

Technological

It almost seems as if last year's technological miracle is this year's major best-seller. Technology has been moving at an almost exponential pace.

The development of the use of computers, from purely scientific through business and then domestic markets, forms part of the analysis, as does the implications of the Internet and e-commerce, developments that affect nearly every organisation world-wide.

Aesthetic

Modern technology allows organisations to produce even the most mundane products and services at very high levels. High quality is now becoming an essential. In such an environment those involved externally with an organisation, especially customers and potential customers, become more and more influenced by the intangibles that surround product and service delivery.

The aesthetic analysis considers the way in which those in the external environment respond to organisational image and design – design of products, packaging design and even building design. In a link to culture, it is a fact that many organisations from the Far East would not consider the design of a new building without the assistance of a Feng Shui consultant, so important is this aspect of culture.

Organisations need to analyse the message they put out to the external environment through the Organisational Body Language they display.

Customers

Every organisation, no matter what its type or products/services, has customers. Indeed, customers are the most important stakeholders of any organisation. No customers eventually equals no organisation.

Organisations need to analyse the needs of current and, most importantly, potential customers. What are the needs and wants of customers and how can they be met in a cost-effective way?

The customer base for many organisations is growing not only in geographic and number terms but also in sophistication.

Legal

All organisations need to be aware of and take account of the law in those areas where they operate. Each national jurisdiction has its own set of laws and whilst many of them may be based on the same principles, there will be national and even local differences as seen between the States making up the United States of America.

Whilst a detailed analysis of legal aspects in the external environment is rightly a subject for specialist lawyers, it is important that all those involved in carrying out an analysis of the external environment are aware of current legal practices and proposed legislative changes that may impact upon the organisation.

Environmental

One of the major movements of the late 20th century was that of environmentalism. No longer can organisations ignore the environmental implications of their actions and the effects these may have on waste disposal, pollution, biodiversity etc.

An environmental analysis is rightly accorded its own section in considerations of the factors affecting an organisation. Indeed an environmental impact analysis may well be a condition of planning permission or funding for new projects.

Sectoral

The final component of the SPECTACLES analysis concerns other organisations operating in similar markets. This includes collaborators and competitors. The actions of both of these can have a dramatic effect on an organisation.

Analysis of the competition (and collaborators) includes looking at their strengths and weaknesses plus analysing the competitive forces that are operating within the marketplace.

Links

The ten components of the SPECTACLES analysis plus the organisation itself provides for no fewer than 55 possible interactions (the number of pathways that join 11 points together).

To give an example of the complexity of the relationships between the analytical components of SPECTACLES, consider the hypothetical case of a UK supermarket that decided in 1999 to offer a range of genetically modified (GM) foods.

In 1999 there was a massive debate about the safety of such foods ongoing in the UK. Such a decision would require an analysis not just of the *technological* possibilities but also an analysis of the *social, legal, environmental* and *customer* aspects at a minimum. It would not be enough to look at the opportunities that the technology had provided, but also at the threats that the other components might present.

That simple example shows how important the interrelationships are and also the criticality of ensuring that all are represented in an analysis of the external operating environment.

SPECTACLES analysis for Icelandair

The following, based on a SPECTACLES analysis (an expansion of the traditional PEST/PESTLE models), uses the Icelandair case study introduced at the beginning of this book to show the type of factors that an organisation (in this case an airline) needs to consider. This information will later be referred to in the SWOT analysis section that follows.

Each of the components of the SPECTACLES analysis is considered briefly in turn.

Social

- Vacation patterns, especially for short breaks
- Longer holidays
- Air travel more the norm and less an exception

Political

- Privatisation of State-run airlines
- Political agreements on routes and fare structures
- Opening up of Eastern Europe

Economic

- Fuel prices
- Interest rates
- Increases in disposable income
- Spending patterns, especially on vacations

Cultural

- Scandinavia's and Iceland's reputation for cleanliness and efficiency
- Cultural vacations
- Use of the English language
- Links between Scotland and Scandinavia/Iceland

Technological

- ETOPS (see Chapter 1)
- Hub and spoke operations (see case study)

Aesthetic

- Liveries
- Organisational Body Language

Customers

- Business passengers
- Vacation passenger patterns
- Increased customer expectations
- Problems with deep vein thrombosis (DVT) on long flights are alleviated by changeover in Iceland – this is an issue that began to grow in prominence in 2000

Legal

- Governmental agreements
- ETOPS (see Chapter 1)

Environmental

- Iceland as a natural wonder etc.

Sectoral

- Low-cost airline competition
- Competition from major carriers
- Partnerships
- Ability to link with holidays in Iceland

The above are very simplistic but show some of the factors that an airline such as Icelandair need to consider when planning its future business. Organisations within other sectors of business will have different factors directly related to the sector in question, although it should be noted that interest rates and fuel prices may well be common to the vast majority of organisations although they may be affected in different ways. Organisations within the same sector are likely to produce very similar SPECTACLES analyses, as what affects one player is likely to affect others. These factors form an important part of the threats and opportunities section of the SWOT analysis to be covered next.

SWOT

A SWOT (Strengths, Weaknesses, Opportunities and Threats) analysis is a common component of organisational planning.

A SWOT analysis is a two-part analysis: the first part looks at the strengths and weaknesses of the organisation and is thus an *internal* analysis; and the second part considers the threats and opportunities facing the organisation from the external environment which are derived from the *external* analyses that form the subject of the previous section.

The *strengths* of an organisation are those things it does particularly well, especially when viewed against the operations of its competitors, whereas its *weaknesses* are areas in which it is less strong than the competition.

Opportunities are those external factors where the organisation can use its *strengths* to outclass the competition, and *threats* are those factors from the external environment from which the organisation may suffer because of its *weaknesses*.

The aim should always be for strategies that build on *strengths*, minimise *weaknesses*, exploit *opportunities* and defend against *threats*.

A SWOT analysis is usually displayed as a quadrant, as shown in Figure 2.1.

Items may appear in more than one quadrant. The large size of an organisation may be seen as a strength when it comes to economies of scale but as a weakness

STRENGTHS INTERNAL	WEAKNESSES INTERNAL
OPPORTUNITIES EXTERNAL	THREATS EXTERNAL

Figure 2.1   SWOT analysis.

in respect of communications. It is perfectly legitimate to place it in both quadrants.

To achieve maximum effect, a SWOT analysis should be carried out at a minimum on an annual basis. It is best done as a group activity involving people from across the organisations and at differing positions within the hierarchy. Different views may thus be represented. In large organisations it is not unusual for individual departments, sections etc. to complete their own SWOT analysis on their part of the operation. When this is done, what one part of the organisation may see as a strength may be regarded as a weakness by another; again this is perfectly legitimate if it aids discussion. To give an example, a large transport concern carried out such an exercise with groups of its employees. Those in engineering saw the highly competitive nature of the then Chief Executive as a weakness as it affected their professional relationship with engineers who worked for other, competing organisations and who were sometimes less willing to provide information to help solve problems. (The balance between helping as a fellow professional and not helping because you are a competitor is one that can bedevil professional relationships.) The staff in the customer services department however saw the CEO's approach as a major strength as they relished the cut and thrust of competition. Different views of the same issue can produce different perceptions.

It must be stressed that there is no point in undertaking an analysis of *strengths* and *weaknesses*, i.e. an internal analysis, without then going on to link that analysis to one of the external *opportunities* and *threats*.

SWOT analysis for Icelandair

The author is grateful to Icelandair for providing details of the SWOT analysis that it carried out on its Scotland–Iceland–USA market (Figure 2.2) and also for the general Iceland market (Figure 2.3).

STRENGTHS	WEAKNESSES
• Schedule, shortest elapsed time Scotland to Boston, Baltimore/ Washington, Minneapolis and Halifax, Nova Scotia	• Marketing of off-line cities • Publishing of prices • Business class product weaker than competition • Long turnaround time at Glasgow, leading to delays
OPPORTUNITIES	THREATS
• Corporate sales • Improved frequent flyer programme • Iceland stop-overs • Reduction in DVT • Partnerships	• Overcapacity in the transatlantic market • Strength of Continental Airlines in the USA and who also operate services to Glasgow • Increased competition • Other airlines' alliances/partnerships

Figure 2.2   SWOT for the Scotland–Iceland–North America market. [*Adapted from material by courtesy of Icelandair.*]

STRENGTHS	WEAKNESSES
• Good media coverage for Iceland • Frequency of UK–Iceland flights both from London and Glasgow • Good relationship with tour operators	• Lack of Tourist Board support • Having to use own sales staff, limited resources and cope with a growing demand • Small advertising budget
OPPORTUNITIES	THREATS
• Cultural status of Reykjavik • Off-season programmes • Incentives • Internet as a distribution channel • Links with Ireland	• Negative development of nature tourism in the high season • City break market for other European cities • Low-cost/'no frills' airlines driving down fares • Lack of hotel rooms in Iceland to meet anticipated demand • Competition with other airlines considering Iceland as a potential market • High Icelandic prices

Figure 2.3   SWOT for the general Iceland market. [*Adapted from material by courtesy of Icelandair.*]

Many of these issues will be referred to throughout the text. The task of Icelandair managers is to build on their *strengths*, minimise their *weaknesses*, exploit the *opportunities* and defend against the *threats*.

Summary

Organisations do not operate in a vacuum. All organisations interact with other organisations and individuals. Organisational planning needs to take into consideration the analyses of both the internal and external environments. An internal BACK analysis and an external PEST/PESTLE/SPECTACLES analysis can be used to produce a SWOT analysis that links the internal strengths and weaknesses of the organisation to the external threats and opportunities that the organisation should exploit (in respect of the opportunities) and guard against (in respect of the threats).

QUESTIONS

1 Why is it important for organisations to carry out an external analysis when engaged upon organisational planning? Illustrate your answer using components of the SPECTACLES analysis.

2 'Aspirations are useless without a knowledge of the baggage and culture of an organisation and also require the requisite organisational knowledge'. Discuss this statement with reference to at least one organisation with which you are familiar.

3 Conduct a SWOT analysis for an organisation with which you are familiar, explaining how you derived the factors which make up the various components.

Recommended reading

For further consideration of organisational cultures you are advised to read *Gods of Management* by Charles Handy (1978), and for national cultures *Riding the Waves of Culture* by Fons Trompenaars (1993) and *When Cultures Collide* by Richard D. Lewis (2000). A full consideration of the SPECTACLES analysis is the subject *Mastering the Business Environment* by Roger Cartwright (2001). Analysis in general for marketing subjects is covered well in *Strategic Market Management* by David Aaker (1984), especially chapter 2.

Useful website

www.virgin.com   Virgin website

■ ⌄ 3 Understanding the market

What are markets? – Segmentation – Profit – Segment typologies – Geographic – Virtual – Demographic – Social groups – Societal changes – Psychographics – Segmentation continuum – Differentiation – Internal customers and markets

The word 'market' can be used to describe something as local as a set of stalls laid out in a public space, as still seen in a number of market towns throughout the world to this day, through to the international transactions required to purchase oil or aircraft.

In simplistic terms, a market is the forum for an exchange between parties. Whilst 21st century shopping malls throughout the world may seem to have little in common with the medieval markets depicted in films and books or the thriving markets of many African or Asian countries, they are in fact just a modern version of the same mechanism for exchange.

By bringing a seller and a buyer together, a market facilitates the exchange process. In the vast majority of cases the exchange is one of goods and/or services for money, although it may involve barter, i.e. the seller exchanges his goods/services as required by the buyer for goods/services that the buyer holds and that the seller requires. Such barter is not unusual in trade between governments, especially where oil or weapons are concerned.

In the days when travelling was difficult, it made sense for people to carry out as many transactions as possible at the same time and in the same place. Medieval towns vied with each other for the right to hold a market and as such a right was often within the patronage of the local ruler, considerable political machinations could occur. Even in 21st century Britain there are weekly markets held that can trace their origins back to the granting of a Royal Charter many centuries ago.

Markets were in effect the early equivalent of the modern concept of a one-stop shopping mall where all the facilities from retail outlets, banking, eating places and toilets are grouped together in one convenient location. As people may have travelled considerable distances either as buyers, sellers or both, ancillary operations connected to accommodation, food, entertainment and financial activities became linked to the market itself.

The Trafford Centre outside Manchester, opened at the very end of the 20th century, shows the link between modern developments and the medieval market. Not only is there a wide range of retail outlets but the Centre also has restaurants, banks and even nightclubs. Like the medieval market, these huge modern developments draw from a wide catchment area. The author well remembers the old-fashioned market at Stockport, just a few miles from Trafford, in the 1950s, and the differences with the Trafford Centre are more in terms of modernity and comfort than the operational concept.

In contemporary terms, a market is usually described by means of a particular product or service. Hence one of Icelandair's prime markets is that of business travellers from Scotland to the USA and Canada and vice versa. That particular market is made up of two major components, a who and a where. The who is the business market and the where is self-explanatory. Another linked market is the leisure one to and from Scotland to North America whilst a third is the leisure market for vacations in Iceland. These concepts are known as market segmentation and are covered in more detail later in this chapter. There are thus at least three major markets that Icelandair are aiming products at – each market having its own characteristics.

In Chapter 1, marketing was defined (according to the professional body for marketing, the Institute of Marketing) as: '... the management process responsible for identifying, anticipating and satisfying customer requirements profitably' (Wilmhurst, 1984).

For any one product or service, there may well be a number of quite disparate markets and customer bases as shown by the Icelandair example quoted above. Needs and wants form the major part of Chapter 6 but it will be obvious that the precise needs of a business traveller from Glasgow to New York may well be different from those of a Scottish family undertaking a short break in Iceland. Successful organisations are able to offer products that can satisfy a range of needs and wants. Airlines can rarely provide a separate aircraft for each particular customer group (Concord was the exception, being all first class). They therefore divide up the cabins on their aircraft to cater for the different customer groups. The business traveller may well book into business class whilst the family are in economy. In effect they will partake of the same core product (the flight) but with levels of service and space that suit their particular needs and pockets.

Market segmentation

Morden (1991) defines market segmentation as 'the analysis of a particular total demand in terms of its constituent parts, so that sets of buyers can be determined'. As an example, let us consider the market for motor cars in a particular country. The need of customers is actually for personal transportation; the defined want will be a motor car as there may be other means of satisfying the need for personal transportation. This was an area of policy that was exercising the mind of the UK government in the late 1990s and early 2000s as it wished to reduce the number of motor vehicles (especially private cars) on Britain's roads for environmental reasons, but needed to replace the private car with an acceptable mode of transport that was as efficient, as flexible and as personal.

Within the total market there will be a variety of segments. For instance, there will be those who wish for a family car, those whose ideal is a sports car, those who wish for a basic vehicle, and those who can afford and want a luxury model.

There will also be companies who wish to purchase a fleet of vehicles for the business use of members of their staff. Organisations that need staff to travel around as an integral part of their duties may well provide a vehicle to facilitate this. In many cases the vehicle will also be available for the individual member of staff to use domestically. The Inland Revenue will also assess the necessity of the journeys made and whether the vehicle is really vital or just a 'perk' – if the latter, then a considerable amount of tax may need to be paid.

For the individual, the burden of insurance and maintenance is taken from them and laid on the employer. For vehicle manufactures, the benefits of large fleet sales can be considerable although the more vehicles an organisation purchases, the greater the discount it will expect. The fleet market in the UK is a very important segment, as organisations tend to change vehicles more frequently than individuals do.

Each of these groups form a segment of the total market and it may well not be possible for a single supplier to meet the requirements of each segment. Later it will be demonstrated how a company can service a variety of segments through the careful branding of a family of products.

Whilst there are organisations that cater to wide market segments, others concentrate on specific segments. For many years Boeing were not considered as a serious contender in the civilian airframe market, the majority of its business being with the United States military (Eddy *et al.*, 1976). As both Eddy *et al.* and Irving (1993) have demonstrated, Boeing made great efforts from the 1940s onward to appeal to the commercial airline segment, with the result that it was one of the two major airframe manufacturers (Airbus Industrie being the other) in the world at the start of the 21st century.

The more segments of a market an organisation can service, the less dependent it becomes on the success or failure of any particular segment although there is the danger that in trying to serve everybody, nobody actually receives the standard they require.

Morden (1991) distinguishes between consumer goods markets and industrial goods markets, the former being more influenced by demographics and lifestyles. In effect, Morden is saying that some products and services are marketed at individuals whereas industrial goods tend to be aimed at organisations. Very often the goods and services supplied to the industrial segment are used as part of the value chain covered below and thus facilitate goods for the domestic market.

Segment typologies

The segments relating to any particular market can be expressed in terms of three typologies:

- geographic;
- demographic;
- geodemographic.

The positioning of any product or service will be in terms of all three typologies.

Geographic markets

Prior to the introduction of Internet trading (e-commerce), most organisations operated in defined geographic markets. Whilst the Internet has allowed many more organisations to trade world-wide, as discussed later, the vast majority of organisations still operated in discrete geographic regions.

Geographically, markets can be defined as:

- local;
- regional;
- national;
- international;
- virtual.

However this is somewhat simplistic, as it is necessary to distinguish between the product and the means of getting that product to the customer. For instance, a chocolate bar may be national or international in its appeal but because of the means by which it is sold, the actual point of sale may serve a purely local market. A great many products and many services are actually national/international whilst the point of sale may be purely local. In the car industry, most sales are through a local dealer. The actual car may be only part of the product with the after sales service etc. being an important factor in the decision to purchase. The purchaser will in effect be acquiring an international product but with the service etc. being fairly local. Because of the high cost of vehicles in the UK when compared with other parts of the European Union (EU), a growing number of UK motorists began buying directly from other parts of Europe in the 1990s. Despite (illegal) attempts by manufacturers to discourage this trend, it grew to the extent that specialist organisations to facilitate such purchases were formed with a fair degree of success.

Local

Organisations operating locally are perhaps among the most familiar. They include the vast majority of small owner-managed organisations. Their operations are designed to serve a local market. Being part of the locality they can often react and adapt to changing local conditions more rapidly than can organisations operating in a wider region. However, because of their smaller size, they are often unable to compete with larger organisations on price and range of products/services. The average corner shop in the UK has found it very difficult to compete with the large national supermarket chains. Initially such shops were able to compete by opening earlier and shutting later, but some supermarkets now operate on a 24-hour basis. In more rural areas they have the advantage of being closer to their customers but they are still unable to match the economies of scale offered by the supermarkets, with their ability to buy in huge bulk quantities. A number of corner shops have banded together in a confederation (Spar is an example) and are then able to buy in bulk and gain the advantages of economies of scale.

There is no doubt that as shopping malls and out-of-town supermarkets etc. grew in the developed world throughout the latter years of the 20th Century, it was the smaller retailers who felt the pinch and the increasing number of closures of such retailers in UK towns was evidence of this.

Other organisations, such as local builders, plumbers, electricians etc., have managed to hold on to their business as it easier for them to provide an immediate service (if you need a plumber, you need one now) than larger national organisations.

One other method for the local organisation to gain the benefits of size which accrue to regional/national/international organisations is to become part of a franchise. Perhaps the best known of these is the McDonald's® chain of fast move restaurants which offers almost identical menus and service standards over much of the world, the vast majority of the operations being franchises.

As fashions change and the product life cycle (see Chapter 8) for many consumer goods becomes shorter, it can be much more difficult for local organisations, especially in the retail sector, to carry the necessary stocks. Where they have an advantage, and this applies especially in the service sector, is the ability to develop a long-term relationship with the customer. Customers may well use a local supplier who is a little more expensive than a regional or national one if they receive a more personalised service.

Regional

In geopolitical terms, a region can be described as an area with clearly defined boundaries. Such boundaries do not have to be political or geographic, they can be cultural, e.g. the Basque Region which straddles parts of the Franco–Spanish border.

The UK is often divided up into a series of regions: London and the Home Counties, South East, South West (and the West Country), Midlands, North West, North East, Northern Ireland, Wales and Scotland. Scotland, Wales and Northern Ireland, together with the Isle of Man, the Scilly Isles and the Channel Islands, also have their own devolved government (that of the Isle of Man being one of the world's oldest parliaments), together with (Wales excepted) their own versions of the standard Sterling currency.

The United States is often divided up into regions for marketing purposes, i.e. the North East Corridor, the Pacific Northwest, the West Coast, the Deep South etc.

Regions can often exhibit quite different cultural norms, as anybody who has lived in both London and, say, the North West of the UK or has moved from California to New York will appreciate.

In the UK there are a number of organisations that operate on a purely regional basis. There are, for instance, a number of organisations that operate almost exclusively in Scotland. Scotland, together with Wales, was a separate country until the advent of James I of England (but the VI of Scotland) in the 17th century, and the formal Act of Union was not passed until 1707. In certain market sectors, e.g. foodstuffs, there are products that sell almost exclusively in Scotland. Reviewing the top ten brand names in the UK in 1999, the most popular brand in Scotland (Irn Bru – a soft drink) did not appear at all in the general UK list. Marketers need therefore to keep a careful eye on regional trends. Whilst many products now exist in a global market, there will always be those that are purely regional in demand and the supply of such products may present a useful niche to a regional marketplace.

National

A trend of the late 20th century carried on into the 21st has been for the development of products and services that have a more than purely national appeal. Motor car manufacturers such as Ford, Chrysler, BMW etc. have been developing models that appeal to more than one nationality. Indeed the Japanese may be considered to have started this trend when, as part of the rebirth of the Japanese economy after the World War II, they developed motor vehicle products for the European market rather than for specific countries. In Western Europe, where there are countries with very similar road networks and infrastructures, it is not difficult to design a model that can appeal to different nationalities, with only superficial details being changed, often just the brand or model name (see Chapter 7). The UK and Irish market is somewhat more problematic, given that both countries drive on the left rather than the right, but modern manufacturing techniques make light of that problem. Interestingly, it is not a problem for the Japanese who also drive on the left.

The vast majority of organisations operate within their own national borders; hence brand names that are familiar to the people from one country may be unknown to those from others. As will be shown in the next section, there are however some products and names that have become truly international.

The advantages to remaining within a single national segment are those of language, currency and law – factors which tend to be consistent within national entities, albeit with some deviation. For example, laws differ between US states and between Scotland and England, and certain regions may speak a different language although there is nearly always a common tongue. In Europe the advent of the Euro may well make currency transactions easier although at the time of writing not all EU members had joined the Eurozone, the UK appearing very unenthusiastic. The issues of selling similar products in different countries will be discussed in Chapter 7 under branding.

Products such as literature, many TV programmes, some motion pictures and comedy often do not work when placed in another culture, and these may well remain national in character.

International

Ford, Sony, McDonalds, Shell etc. are household names across much of the globe. These organisations do have a national home – the USA for Ford and McDonalds, Japan for Sony, the Netherlands for Shell (the company is actually Royal Dutch Shell) – but in fact operate on a global basis with headquarters, manufacturing, distribution etc. in either individual countries or pan-national regions. Products and services may be developed for particular national groups or the same product may be sold everywhere with only slight changes to reflect particular usage etc. For instance, North America works almost universally on 110 volts for the electric supply compared to 220/240 volts in Europe. If you are manufacturing electrical goods, certain different components will be needed, depending on the voltage in the area of sale. It is noticeable that consumer electrics designed for travel, such as electric razors and laptop computers, often come equipped as dual voltage appliances.

Somebody from the UK studying the goods on sale in a New York department store might conclude that the market is becoming more and more global, and they would be right, notwithstanding the fact that some goods and services do not travel as well as others. Just because something has been successful in one market does not guarantee similar success in others, however similar. Whilst some US convenience foods and drinks (two soft drinks ending in the word Cola spring to mind) have been highly successful globally, other such items have failed to penetrate global, especially the lucrative European, markets.

Virtual

The latter years of the 20th Century saw a dramatic growth of the so-called dot com organisations linked to the Internet. Whilst it was initially thought that there might be vast sums of money to be made trading internationally over the net, in reality there were some outstanding financial failures but some successes, especially in book retailing and home banking. Christopher Price (2000) has looked at a group of Internet pioneers and concluded that although the losses up to 2000 were considerable, the eventual long-term gains will make the virtual market an inevitable success, especially for those such as Davis at Lycos, Yang at Yahoo! and Schrock at AltaVista who are supplying search engines etc. to facilitate Internet use. On a smaller scale, many purely local retailers and manufacturers were able to reach a much larger market by taking on-line orders and providing product/service information through their web pages. The Chairman of IBM was certainly wrong (spectacularly so) when he said in 1943 that there would be a world market for only five computers (quoted in Aldrich, 1999). It is to be expected that there will be a growth in this type of marketing, especially as customers become more confident in the security of credit card transactions and delivery mechanisms.

Working on-line frees an organisation from any local/regional/national constraints and allows it to be truly international, but perhaps at the loss of the personal touch.

The virtual or digital marketplace is now a fact of life, although it will take some time for consumers to change their buying habits. UK anecdotal evidence in January 2001 suggested that there was still a reluctance of UK consumers to buy over the Internet, security being quoted as the largest barrier. Aldrich (1999) makes the point that whilst the Internet and the digital marketplace may provide further empowerment for consumers by widening their choices, this by no means ensures that the consumer knows what he or she wants. Increased choice can lead to increased frustration.

Although from the late 1990s onwards the Internet has produced some successes, Amazon in the book-selling field being a prime example, the dot com revolution also led to some spectacular failures with companies disappearing almost as quickly as they arrived. What the digital/virtual marketplace has produced is a shift in the balance of power from supplier to consumer because of the choice available to the latter (Aldrich, 1999). One has only to consider the IT skills of the average child in the developed world to see that these will lead to a marketplace filled with much more sophisticated consumers, who will present new challenges to manufacturers and suppliers and who will be able to seek satisfaction and delight across a much wider market.

Demographic markets

Any society consists of different groups of members. Approximately 50% of any general society will be male, 50% female. These will further be split up by age. For example, in the UK in 1997 out of a population of 59 million, 61.4% were between the ages of 16 and 65, i.e. of working age, 7.2% were over 75 and 20.5% were below the age of 16. These are figures which are changing all the time.

Certain products and services are designed for different genders and different age groups. As will be seen later, the groups using a product may change. Perfumes and jewellery for men have been a growing market in recent years and grey currencies, i.e. disposable income spending for those over 65, have also been increasing, creating new market segments. Carnival Cruises, an organisation to be examined later in this chapter, has one of its products (Holland America Cruises) designed to appeal to the older holidaymaker much more than the Carnival brand itself, which is targeted at a younger age range.

Age is a very important factor. Studies over many years have shown that patterns of spending, saving, home ownership, types of car owned, holidays etc. vary throughout a person's lifetime. Phipps and Simmons (1995) refer to a family life cycle that is analogous to the organisational and product life cycles used in this text. Whilst such a life cycle may well vary between individuals, for many it is in their 20s and 30s that they spend and borrow (often for a property), whilst in later years they may well spend and dis-save, i.e. dispose of their savings. It is in our middle years that we tend to save so that there will be sufficient disposable income in old age.

The family life cycle and its implications for consumer behaviour are discussed in detail in Wilmhurst (1984), where it is shown how the young bachelor or spinster living at home has few long-term financial commitments and use their disposable income (after contributing to the household) on mainly fashion, entertainment and vacation products. Such individuals are often living with parents or in rented accommodation. The young married couple with a child will have very different spending patterns as will a solitary survivor who is retired. The former will be spending money on their child and also perhaps saving for the child's future educational needs. The latter may be 'de-saving', i.e. spending previously saved income on care in old age, holidays etc.

The family life cycle can be related to the aspirations that people have for themselves and their families at varying stages of life, and it is aspirations that often drive the patterns of acquisition of goods and services.

Societal groups are also differentiated in terms of not only income but in the way in which income is used. No society is homogeneous. From earliest times

Grade	Category	Occupation of the nominal head of the household
A	Upper and Upper middle class	Senior professional/higher managerial
B	Middle class	Junior professional/managerial/senior administrative
C1	Lower middle class	Supervisory/middle administration
C2	Skilled working class	Skilled manual
D	Working class	Semi or unskilled manual
E	Subsistence	Low-paid workers, unwaged or living on basic pension

Figure 3.1 UK social groups (simplified).

there have been attempts to place people into set categories. Early methods included dividing British society into the Monarchy, the Aristocracy, the Clergy and the Commoners. Such a system would be very difficult to use today, as well as being irrelevant to 21st century social organisation.

The UK currently uses a system based primarily on occupational area (which has a loose connection with income). The UK system (other countries use similar methods) is based upon six categories with a grade and category based upon the occupation of the nominal head of the household (Figure 3.1).

The use of categories such as lower working class has been attacked as being politically incorrect and patronising, but the gradings do provide a basis for segmenting society.

There may have been a time when one could see a clear correlation between progression up the social grades (if that were possible, and for much of history such progression has been actively discouraged) and income. However, today it is perfectly possible for somebody in category C2 to earn as much if not more than somebody in B, hence it is more important to examine how income is disposed of rather than income *per se*. Rates of saving or spending on educating children provide a better example of the relationship between money and values than do pure income figures.

The surveys one is often asked to contribute to on the street or when returning from a package holiday seek, in addition to gaining information about experience of a product or service, to determine the type of person using that product or service. Thus there are usually questions relating to occupation, household income, house ownership and newspapers read. The latter is very important information to an organisation as it can help determine advertising strategy. Certain groups of people tend to read certain types of newspapers. If you are involved in marketing an executive-price motor car in the UK, then advertising in a tabloid newspaper may bring less favourable results than advertising in one of the respected broadsheets. Similarly cut-price holidays to the Costa del Sol may be more effectively advertised in the tabloids. In Lynne and Jay's brilliant satire, *Yes Prime Minister* (1989) there is an explanation of exactly who reads each particular UK newspaper, an analysis that whilst humorous is probably not far from the truth!

Different groups of people have different interests, perhaps even different aspirations, and a knowledge of this can assist organisations in ensuring that the products and services they develop meet the demands of those parts of society they wish to form their customer base.

Providers of many products and services target these at particular groups of society. Even certain cars may be targeted at particular groups. BMW and Mercedes in the UK are mainly aimed at categories A and B. Ford target categories B and C1 with many of their products. Rover's target market is also B but at the slightly higher end. These social classifications have very elastic boundaries, and organisations are not in fact targeting an income group but a lifestyle. It is interesting that those rating cruise ships have recently moved from describing products in terms of cost to a categorisation that includes life style.

Changes in society

For much of human history the society people lived in was ascribed to them by their birth. Even in the early 20th century there were still people living in the UK who had never travelled more than a few miles from their place of birth.

It is true to say that up to the start of the 19th century, the lives of the vast majority of people were bounded by the family, the village or town (and the latter were small by today's standards) where they lived, the tribe to which they belonged etc. Communities were much smaller than those seen in today's vast cities and urban areas. These changes are ongoing and thus not only are life styles changing but so are the habitats that we live in. This can be important for those managing marketing, as a concentrated urban market may be much easier to service compared with a scattered rural one. The growth in mail order which has been translated on to the Internet began as a means of satisfying the expanding rural communities of North America where distance made a visit to the major shopping centres very difficult.

Psychograpics

Linked to demography is the concept of psychographics which deals with the more qualitative factors of attitude, motives and values, all of which are important when considering life style.

Crimp (1990) produced five typologies of motorist but they are just as applicable to other forms of goods/services acquisition. The key point is that each of the five types will behave very differently as a consumer and they cannot all be treated the same. Her five types of motorist were:

The uninvolved: Drives because they have to and are heavily reliant upon garages and dealers.

The enthusiast: Loves cars and is a good target for accessories etc. Likely to carry out much routine servicing themselves.

The professional: Often has a vehicle provided by their employer. Unlikely to carry out repairs etc. themselves. Unlikely to buy many car related products.

The tinkerer: Likes to carry out their own servicing etc. either because this gives them pleasure or from economic necessity. Tends to be male and own a collection of tools etc. The car may be the hobby but it is ownership for use, unlike the collector below.

The collector: These people collect cars as others (perhaps less wealthy) collect stamps. Tend to be very knowledgeable. At the extreme, they may go in for extensive renovation.

Such an analysis can be applied to a large range of goods and services.

Geodemography

As Phipps and Simmons (1995) have pointed out, both the geographic and the demographic typologies can be combined to produce a hybrid that is of considerable use in marketing. Even casual observation will suggest that in many areas there is a considerable degree of life-style convergence of the inhabitants. Look around any British housing estate and one is likely to see similar cars on the driveway and similar entertainment systems etc. inside. Indeed, the commonality may extend to entertainment outside the home and to holiday preferences.

As each UK area has its own postcode (ZIP – Zone Improvement Plan codes in the USA), it is possible to make certain generalisations about life styles within a particular post code area. Such techniques are used extensively within the insurance industry when assessing the risks attached to household and motor vehicle insurance. In some cases this has led to addresses within certain postcode areas being virtually uninsurable as those areas have a reputation for high crime rates. A statistical analysis of car crime by postcode areas will show that cars parked regularly in certain areas are far more likely to be broken into or stolen than those in other areas. Thus different premiums can be applied depending on the postcode of the insurer's home. Such techniques are not foolproof. At the margins of any postcode area there may be places with a totally different life style, and vehicle insurers may not ask where the insured works and thus where the vehicle may spend the working day.

Areas also change in character. Many of the run-down inner city areas of the UK are being redeveloped and a process of 'gentrification' is occurring. The area around the docks in the twin cities of Manchester and Salford was very run-down at one time but since the closure of the Manchester Ship Canal has been undergoing a transformation with a large number of quite expensive residential properties being built or converted from existing commercial buildings. This can completely alter the character of an area and thus the general life style of its inhabitants.

ACORN (A Classification Of Residential Neighbourhoods), developed by Weber in the 1970s, is one such postcode classification providing a means of classifying the various UK postcodes according to 54 neighbourhood types arranged in 17 Acorn Groups. The ACORN profile is shown in Figure 3.2. There are a number of other such profiles, some using financial information etc.

CACI ACORN PROFILE OF GREAT BRITAIN

The ACORN© consumer targeting classification was developed by CACI Information Services. The table below shows the ACORN classification's 6 Categories, 17 Groups and 54 Types (plus 1 'unclassified' in each case), and their share of the GB population in 1991. The ACORN classification is derived from the Government's 1991 Census of Great Britain.

ACORN Types		% of 1991 population		ACORN Groups	
	ACORN Category A: THRIVING	**19.8**			
1.1	Wealthy suburbs, large detached houses	2.6	15.1	Wealthy achievers, suburban areas	1
1.2	Villages with wealthy commuters	3.2			
1.3	Mature affluent home-owning areas	2.7			
1.4	Affluent suburbs, older families	3.7			
1.5	Mature, well-off suburbs	3.0			
2.6	Agricultural villages, home-based workers	1.6	2.3	Affluent greys, rural communities	2
2.7	Holiday retreats, older people, home-based workers	0.7			
3.8	Home-owning areas, well-off older residents	1.4	2.3	Prosperous pensioners, retirement areas	3
3.9	Private flats, elderly people	0.9			
	ACORN Category B: EXPANDING	**11.6**			
4.10	Affluent working families with mortgages	2.1	3.7	Affluent executives, family areas	4
4.11	Affluent working couples with mortgages, new homes	1.3			
4.12	Transient workforces, living at their place of work	0.3			
5.13	Home-owning family areas	2.6	7.8	Well-off workers, family areas	5
5.14	Home-owning family areas, older children	3.0			
5.15	Families with mortgages, younger children	2.2			
	ACORN Category C: RISING	**7.5**			
6.16	Well-off town & city areas	1.1	2.2	Affluent urbanites, town & city areas	6
6.17	Flats and mortgages, singles & young working couples	0.8			
6.18	Furnished flats & bedsits, younger single people	0.4			
7.19	Apartments, young professional singles & couples	1.1	2.1	Prosperous professionals, metropolitan areas	7
7.20	Gentrified multi-ethnic areas	1.0			
8.21	Prosperous enclaves, highly qualified executives	0.7	3.2	Better-off executives, inner city areas	8
8.22	Academic centres, students & young professionals	0.5			
8.23	Affluent city areas, tenements & flats	0.4			
8.24	Partially gentrified multi-ethnic areas	0.7			
8.25	Converted flats & bedsits, single people	0.9			
	ACORN Category D: SETTLING	**24.1**			
9.26	Mature established home-owning areas	3.3	13.4	Comfortable middle agers, mature home-owning areas	9
9.27	Rural areas, mixed occupations	3.4			
9.28	Established home-owning areas	4.0			
9.29	Home-owning areas, council tenants, retired people	2.6			
10.30	Established home-owning areas, skilled workers	4.5	10.7	Skilled workers, home-owning areas	10
10.31	Home owners in older properties, younger workers	3.1			
10.32	Home-owning areas with skilled workers	3.1			
	ACORN Category E: ASPIRING	**13.7**			
11.33	Council areas, some new home owners	3.8	9.8	New home owners, mature communities	11
11.34	Mature home-owning areas, skilled workers	3.1			
11.35	Low rise estates, older workers, new home owners	2.9			
12.36	Home-owning multi-ethnic areas, young families	1.1	4.0	White collar workers, better-off multi-ethnic areas	12
12.37	Multi-occupied town centres, mixed occupations	1.8			
12.38	Multi-ethnic areas, white collar workers	1.1			
	ACORN Category F: STRIVING	**22.8**			
13.39	Home owners, small council flats, single pensioners	1.9	3.6	Older people, less prosperous areas	13
13.40	Council areas, older people, health problems	1.7			
14.41	Better-off council areas, new home owners	2.4	11.6	Council estate residents, better-off homes	14
14.42	Council areas, young families, some new home owners	3.0			
14.43	Council areas, young families, many lone parents	1.6			
14.44	Multi-occupied terraces, multi-ethnic areas	0.8			
14.45	Low rise council housing, less well-off families	1.8			
14.46	Council areas, residents with health problems	2.0			
15.47	Estates with high unemployment	1.1	2.7	Council estate residents, high unemployment	15
15.48	Council flats, elderly people, health problems	0.7			
15.49	Council flats, very high unemployment, singles	0.9			
16.50	Council areas, high unemployment, lone parents	1.9	2.8	Council estate residents, greatest hardship	16
16.51	Council flats, greatest hardship, many lone parents	0.9			
17.52	Multi-ethnic areas, large families, overcrowding	0.6	2.1	People in multi-ethnic, low-income areas	17
17.53	Multi-ethnic estates, severe unemployment, lone parents	1.0			
17.54	Multi-ethnic estates, high unemployment, overcrowding	0.5			
	Unclassified	**0.5**			

Figure 3.2 CACI ACORN profile of the UK. [*Reproduced with permission.*]

The use of geographic, demographic and geodemographic data related to segmentation allows those involved in the management of the marketing process to identify customer groups in a manner that is analytical rather than random.

Segmentation in practice

If one analyses the contemporary cruise holiday industry it is found that as a sector it provided some superb examples of segmentation.

In simple terms there are four main geographic markets for cruise customers. These are the markets in which the customers are domiciled, not the places that the ships visit. The four major geographic markets with approximate customer figures for 1998 according to the Maritime Evaluations Group (Ward, 1999) are:

North America	5,750,000
Asia	1,000,000
UK	635,000
Rest of Europe	818,000

The total customer base world-wide for 1998 was in excess of 8.4 million, thus making the sector a major player in the tourism industry.

Within the total cruise market there are a large number of companies but, in fact, the market is dominated by four major companies with another four snapping at their heels. In 1999, the dominant company in terms of market position was the Carnival Group with nearly 30% of the market followed by Royal Caribbean, P&O Cruises and Norwegian Cruise Lines. These top four account for over 80% of the market.

Not only are there four major geographic markets but there are also four demographic/life-style markets, namely:

- standard;
- premium;
- luxury;
- niche.

The niche market includes sailing ship and expedition cruises.

Carnival in particular, followed by P&O (a UK company), has been very successful in filling the segmentation matrix for cruising. The matrix is shown in Figure 3.3.

NORTH AMERICA				
UK				
ASIA				
EUROPE				
	STANDARD	PREMIUM	LUXURY	NICHE

Figure 3.3   The cruise industry segmentation matrix.

NORTH AMERICA	Carnival Cruises Costa Cruises	Holland America Cunard	Seabourne	Windstar
UK	Share in Airtours	Cunard		Windstar
ASIA	Plans with Hyundai postponed in 1998			
EUROPE	Costa Cruises	Cunard		
	STANDARD	PREMIUM	LUXURY	NICHE

Figure 3.4   The cruise industry segmentation matrix for Carnival Group.

By acquiring a series of companies and operations and retaining their brand names, Carnival Group (which began with one ship in 1972) has been able to dominate the market (see Figure 3.4).

By careful branding and retaining the brand names of companies it has acquired e.g. Holland America, Carnival is able to offer a product to a large range of the overall market.

P&O in the UK acquired the US based Princess Cruises as a means of entering the US market where the P&O brand was unknown, and has recently done the same to enter the German market.

The segmentation continuum

Some products and services appeal to a wide range of market segments, others are targeted much more specifically.

A product which appeals to the widest possible range of segments can be described as a broad band product, whilst one having only a narrow appeal falls into the niche category. This continuum follows the pattern of the one based on volume and margin. Most products and services are sold on a continuum that ranges from high volume–low margin to low volume–high margin. The reason for this is simple. A profit of £1000 can be made by selling 100 items with a profit of £10, i.e. high volume–low margin, or one item with a profit of £1000, i.e. low volume–high margin.

It is important for those involved in marketing to appreciate exactly which segment of the market a product or service is aimed at because, as will be shown later, different segments have differing perceptions of value and are prepared to pay different prices.

The analysis of a market is a key task of all those involved in marketing management. Individuals (and corporate buyers) may have a series of reasons that account for their demand for a particular product; these are known as attribute sets. From market research (see Chapter 4), correlations between the factors can be sought. Factors can include price and ease of purchase.

Three basic types of market can be identified, namely:

- homogeneous markets;
- diffused markets;
- concentrated markets.

Homogeneous markets

A homogeneous market is one where most of the likely customers share a common perception of the benefits of the product/service and the price they are willing to pay. Any organisation seeking to supply the market is likely to be competitive with all other suppliers. The price charged in any geo-economic area is unlikely to vary much between suppliers. Indeed such a market often involves suppliers co-operating with each other and producing generic products. Proprietary medicines, anti-freeze and supermarket own-brand essential products are examples of a homogeneous market.

Diffused markets

A diffused market, of which the brown goods market (television sets, hi-fis etc.) is a good example, contains a large number of clusters. This relates to the widely differing price bands and the often huge range of differing models available.

Concentrated markets

Concentrated markets, e.g. the family car market, usually contains a relatively small number of discrete clusters, each relating to a specific market segment. The differences between the products themselves and the prices charged are quite small and thus the market is clustered around a particular set of attributes and price levels.

The changing nature of segmentation over time

Market segmentation is not a static phenomenon. Chapter 8 will examine the product life cycle and steps that can be taken to extend the life span of a product or service.

Products and services which appeal to a particular market segment may, over time, appeal to different geographic/demographic groups. The Morris Oxford car was very popular in the 1950s and early 1960s in the UK. As newer, more sophisticated models were introduced, UK sales fell. However there was a ready market for a comfortable but unsophisticated car in the Indian market, and the Morris Oxford is now manufactured and sold in India as the Hindustan Ambassador. The Honda 50 motorcycle has seen a similar shift in geographic markets from Japan to the USA to Europe to India, and latterly to China. As one market segment declines, it may well be that another one opens up.

In demographic terms, bank accounts were once an upper and middle class phenomenon in the UK. As more and more people were paid by cheque etc., so the demographic market for bank accounts expanded. Facsimile machines were, on their introduction, purely for the commercial market, now there is a domestic market. Similarly the computer was never considered as a domestic item at its introduction. Today there are more and more people using a computer at home.

Those involved in the management of the marketing process need to keep a careful eye on the behaviour of not only current market segments but also potential new segments. Anything that extends the life of a product or service is to be welcomed, especially if a segment can be exploited with the minimum of investment, a concept that will be considered in more detail in Chapter 8.

Differentiation

Within any segment of a market there may well be a number of similar products and services competing for a finite number of customers. Competition is considered in detail in Chapter 5 but it is important to consider differentiation alongside segmentation.

Differentiation is that which distinguishes a particular product or service from a competitor. There are three basic ways a product can differentiate itself from competitors, the first of which is really a sham but still legitimate:

- appear different but be really the same;
- differentiate on price;
- differentiate on quality/service.

Appear different but be really the same

There have been times when the same (or virtually identical) motor car has appeared from two apparently rival manufacturers. The vehicles may be aimed at the same market segment. What has happened is that both manufacturers have had a gap in their product range and they have shared manufacturing capability and expertise between them. By ensuring a family of products they are able to encourage product loyalty and trading up. All that is really different is the badge but branding can be very important, especially when related to image and life style.

It may well be that the same manufacturer produces a series of similar products but differentiates each on price, as shown below.

Differentiate on price

There is very little difference between products from the VW brand and the Skoda one. Hardly surprising, as Skoda is in fact part of VW. The Skoda may have fewer supplementary products (see Chapter 7) but it is nearly always cheaper than the equivalent VW branded product – this is what the market expects, and buyer perception is that a Skoda will cost less than a VW even when the two models are nearly identical.

Because they are able to operate a single type of aircraft, Icelandair have been able to compete on price terms with much bigger airlines.

Differentiating on price always runs the risk that the organisation will be undercut by a competitor and that a price war will result, which only ends when one organisation begins to sell at a loss. Selling at a loss, in the short term, is an acceptable sales practice if it leads to building market share and the sales of more expensive, profitable items. The use of loss leaders to entice customers has long been a practice of many organisations.

The reason why similar products cost the same may be because of price fixing (illegal in many jurisdictions) but is more likely to be because competing organisations have similar costs and because there will be a price beyond which customers will not go.

Differentiate on quality/service

The third major way to differentiate is on quality or service. It is difficult to raise quality much beyond a competitor without raising the price. If organisation A can keep the price down and yet raise quality, organisation B, their competitor, will do their best to follow suit.

It may be possible to raise service levels by recruitment and training or by offering a local, more personalised service. A small organisation may be able to compete with a larger one in this way.

Internal customers and markets

The term 'the internal market' came into vogue as part of the Conservative Party policy for the public sector during the 1980s and early 1990s. In an attempt to improve efficiency in the public sector, organisations such as the National Health Service were required to deal with their constituent parts in a manner as near to replicating market forces as possible. In practice this proved difficult, especially when dealing with organisations operating in a not-for-profit environment. In such an environment the cheapest service might not always be the best, but the concept did focus attention on the importance of the internal customer.

As demonstrated in the value/customer chain covered earlier in this book, there are a series of steps to nearly every business operation, with the external customer being at the end of the process. Within the process there are a series of internal customers, and writers on customer care have stressed the importance of applying equal standards of care to both the internal and external customer. Indeed, if the internal customer does not receive good service from his or her internal supplier, the danger is that they will fail to pass on the best in quality and service to the next part of the chain.

Whilst this book mainly considers the external market, readers should bear in mind that the concepts introduced are equally applicable to internal customers and the internal market within organisations.

Icelandair, airlines and the market

The airline industry provides a useful tool for exploiting market changes. It is a market that has seen not only incredible growth but one which has shifted into varying segments with great rapidity.

From the Wright Brothers first flight in 1903 until 1930 there had been a mere 34 actual or attempted flights across the Atlantic. Seven were by airship and were all successful; of the 27 aircraft attempts, 16 had ended in failure causing 21 deaths (Stewart, 1986). By 1976, 34 million adult Americans were taking a flight at least once per year (Eddy *et al.*, 1976) and by 2001 it was difficult to find anybody in the UK who had never flown.

Interestingly, the early airlines did not expect nor welcome the idea of air travel becoming a mass market. At the end of World War II, Juan Trippe, the CEO of Pan American Airlines (Pan Am), had tried to introduce a tourist class fare at $275 on Pan Am's USA–London service. The British, supported by IATA (the International Air Transport Association), refused landing rights to flights operating such a tourist class service, forcing the airline to land in Ireland and transfer passengers. Eventually, in 1952, IATA and the governments concerned accepted the concept of the tourist class fare and began the age of mass air travel (Irving, 1993).

The jet aircraft, with a speed that allowed it to be used to carry more passengers than its predecessors, brought with it operating costs that allowed fares to be set that were attractive to a larger percentage of the population.

The introduction of medium to short haul jets from the late 1950s onwards heralded the massive increase in foreign package holidays, especially in Europe where the beaches of Spain were easily accessed from the colder climes of Britain and Northern Europe by the new jets. Families that had traditionally gone to Blackpool or other UK seaside resorts soon discovered the delights of the Costa del Sol in the first instance and then longer haul destinations such as Florida and Thailand.

Vladimir Raitz, founder of Horizon Holidays, organised the first package holiday by air in 1950 and, by 1970, 2.7 million inclusive holidays were undertaken from the UK (Laws, 1997). One of the results of this expansion was the development of a series of large resorts, especially in Spain, resorts that were often isolated from the original village communities and where a homogenised experience could be obtained by the holiday maker – in effect, Blackpool with sun and sangria!

For the first time, holiday makers from the UK came to share their experience with those from other European countries, and the residents of the resorts (plus an increasing number of ex-patriot entrepreneurs) began to modify their commercial behaviour to cater for the huge numbers of tourists. British pubs and German Bier Kellers began to open, each catering for their national groups. From the 1980s onwards, concerns began to be expressed that many of the resorts were being ruined by a combination of cheap holidays attracting a younger and younger clientele and the effects of cheap alcohol leading to unruly behaviour.

According to the UK Civil Aviation Authority, the three market leaders in the UK package holiday business, Thomson, Airtours and First Choice, took over 5.5 million holiday makers by air on package holidays in the Summer of 1994 (Civil Aviation Authority, 1994).

In 1939, few Europeans or North Americans had travelled outside their own national boundaries and even fewer had been on an aircraft.

By 1985, US citizens were spending in excess of $8,000,000,000 per annum on foreign travel and over 10 million Britons were undertaking an annual foreign package holiday (Lavery and Van Doren, 1990).

The early developments in foreign package holidays were to regions within easy flying distance of North America and Northern Europe, giving Mexico, Spain, Portugal and Greece a head start in the development in mass tourism. Longer haul tourism, especially to less developed countries, has been slower to develop although the latter half of the 1990s saw Thailand become the most popular UK long haul destination. In 1950, 66% of the international tourist market share was held by Europe, with the Americas accounting for 30%. Europe has maintained its position, still accounting for 64% in 1990, but the Americas had slipped to 20%, whilst Africa held 3.3%, with Asia and the Pacific Rim having grown from virtually zero in 1950 up to 12% (Harrison, 1992).

By 1980, the package holiday trade was well established and moving from short haul destinations to medium and even long haul packages. Prices were coming down fast compared to average earnings, and a foreign holiday was no longer a once-in-a-lifetime event but an annual experience.

Air travel has moved from being confined to a particular segment of the market, i.e. the well-to-do business or leisure traveller, to encompass a series of markets, often within the same aircraft – hence the different cabin configurations, economy (known as coach in the USA), business class, first class and a number of in-between classes. Some airlines have introduced business class style seating but economy class food that suits the needs of many business travellers who want the leg room but are not necessarily bothered about champagne and canapés. Icelandair has a two-class service and this is adequate for the length of sectors it flies, and the type of aircraft that it operates. The passenger mix is very much one of the leisure market and the business traveller seeking a cheaper and (from Scotland and Northern England) more convenient method of reaching the Eastern seaboard of North America.

As the popularity of Iceland as a short break destination grows, then the more leisure passengers will be carried. In the main, such passengers are more concerned with price than facilities and tend to travel in economy class, as they will often be on a tight budget, especially as Iceland is not likely to form their main holiday destination in any one year. Similarly the growth in short breaks in the USA for European travellers is likely to be using economy class seats. In revenue terms, business class accounts for 13% of the Glasgow–USA business for Icelandair, whilst economy class generates 87% of the revenue. In 1998, Glasgow generated £4.5 million, this being 34% of Icelandair's UK sales. Whilst the Heathrow market is the larger of the two, the Scottish market is a significant one-third of the market and one that the airline is seeking to increase.

As business class constitutes 11% of the capacity of a Boeing 757 (22 seats out of 189), and yet is much more expensive than coach, it can be seen that a business class revenue of 13% leads to considerable room for growth, and Icelandair have recognised this opportunity in their SWOT analysis.

Summary

Markets are an age-old human strategy for bringing buyers and sellers together in a convenient location. The modern marketplace is diverse and complex, being segmented both geographically and demographically and indeed on a mixture of both. In recent years, the use of the Internet has led to the development of a virtual/digital marketplace that is becoming truly global and is encouraging a much more empowered consumer base. Products and services add value to basic components and this is shown through the value chain. The external customer, whilst the purchaser of a product or service, may well not be the end user. Products and services can be differentiated from competitive products using price, quality etc. as the differentials.

QUESTIONS

1 Explain, using examples, what is meant by *market segmentation* and why it is an important concept in marketing management.

2 For a product or service with which you are familiar, illustrate the relevant value and customer chains, indicating how value is added at each stage and how each component of the customer chain relates to the one before and the one following it.

3 How can similar products be differentiated from competitors? Give at least one example of products that are indeed similar, one example of price differentiation and one of quality differentiation.

Recommended reading

You are recommended to read D. F. Aldrich (1999) *Mastering the Digital Marketplace* and Christopher Price (2000) *The Internet Entrepreneurs* for a consideration of the digital/virtual marketplace.

Useful websites

www.traffordcentre.co.uk   Trafford Centre website
www.mcdonalds.com   McDonald's corporate website
www.carnivalcorp.com   Carnival website

◪ 4 Market research

All enterprises, including commercial ones, carry an element of risk. Sabbach (1995) has spoken of the Unk-Unks (Unknown Unknowns) that were encountered during the design and building of the Boeing 777. No plan, it is often said in military circles, ever survives the first contact with the enemy.

Markets are composed of people, and not all human actions are rational and logical. However, the more information an organisation has about the market, the customers and the competition, the less likely it is to be taken by surprise. The bringing of a new product or service to the marketplace can be a costly undertaking in terms of both money and time, and the organisation will want to know as much as possible about the potential customer base in order to guarantee the highest possible measure of success. As Giles (1990) has pointed out, market research can never eliminate risk entirely but it can reduce it and give an objective indication of the probability of the success of various possibilities. This chapter examines the marketing research that organisations need to undertake in order to achieve the maximum possibility of success for their products and services.

Market research can be defined as the objective and systematic collection, recording, analysis, interpretation and reporting of information about (a) existing or potential markets, (b) marketing strategies and tactics, (c) the response to current and potential products/services and (d) the composition and dynamics of the current and potential customer base.

The importance of conducting such research is shown by the following, now famous examples of not listening to the marketplace. As mentioned earlier in this book, just after World War II, Ford designers had developed what they believed would be the best automobile they had ever produced, the Ford Edsel named after Henry Ford's son. Unfortunately they never consulted with the potential customers and whilst the vehicle might have been technologically advanced, it did not meet the needs of the customer and very few were sold. Similar charges can be perhaps levelled against the suppliers of WAP mobile telephones. Whilst the suppliers were convinced that this was technology that the market wanted, sales were very slow indeed, suggesting that not enough research had been carried out. Asking the customers what they actually want can save a lot of organisational heartache.

It is now generally accepted that systematic, formal market research as a business activity commenced in the USA in the early years of the 20th century. Giles (1990) reports that the first formal marketing research company was founded in 1911 in the USA and that from small beginnings a whole flourishing subsector of business has developed.

Information in isolation can be very dangerous. Just knowing that sales in a company are rising is meaningless without a knowledge of what is happening to the market. If a competitor's sales are rising even faster then the company is losing market share and, as market share is a key success indicator, the company is actually failing. If sales are rising faster than those for the competition, market share is being gained and this makes the company a good choice for investors as it is acquiring market share.

Market information is such an important tool in business planning that it has developed into a whole subsector of marketing, with organisations dedicated to researching the market for clients ranging from multi-national companies to smaller retailers and even political parties.

In general, the market questions that organisations need answers to are:

- What is the market size and trend, i.e. is it falling, static or rising?
- How is market share allocated between the competitors in a market?
- What demographic trends are occurring within the customer base?
- What are the main channels by which customers acquire the product or service?
- Who are the main competitors and what strategies do they employ?
- Are there likely to be any new competitors or substitute products entering the market?
- What products/services do customers prefer, and why?
- How are customers likely to receive new products/services?
- Do customers perceive any major problems with current products/services?
- How effective is the organisation's advertising – is it reaching the target population?

The above are some of the major questions that organisations use market research to answer. The wording may change depending on the sector that the organisation is in, but the questions themselves are quite basic. Not-for-profit organisations, such as local authorities and the NHS, are as concerned as retailers about the demographic trends in their customer base and to provide the services that people actually need. Market research can assist in developing such services.

The specialist nature of market research

Major organisational decisions are often made based on the results of market research, and this makes the proper application of market research techniques extremely important.

Market research staff need to be able to view the organisation and its products/services objectively. A deeply held belief about the organisation or the researcher's loyalty to a product can be disadvantageous. The market researcher needs to be able to distance himself or herself from his or her own point of view.

The skills and techniques of market research require a good working knowledge of certain mathematical concepts, statistics and especially probability being very important. Market researchers have not only to gather information in an objective manner but they must be able to interpret it and then present it to the organisation in a robust but understandable fashion.

Over the years, three separate but linked groups have become the major focus for conducting market research, as will now be detailed.

In-house market research departments

Market research specialists are often to be found on the staff of the marketing department in larger organisations. Such people have the benefit that they are well aware of the organisation's modes of operation and should have an excellent knowledge of the product or service. As internal members of staff, they will be less costly to employ than outside researchers, but issues of bias need to be guarded against. Because they work for the organisation it may be less easy for them to acquire detailed information about competitors.

As such people are nearly always attached to the marketing department, it can be very difficult for them to take anything but the party line put out by the department. This can cause conflicts of interest.

Advertising agencies

A good advertising agency works closely with its clients. As such it is often well placed to assist in the gathering of market research. Indeed, in order to develop an effective advertising campaign, the agency will have had to consider many of the questions posed earlier in this chapter.

The client organisation needs to be aware, however, that the advertising agency is itself marketing its own product and thus there can be a conflict of interest in the information provided and particularly in its interpretation.

Market research companies

These are companies whose product is market intelligence for their clients. As this is their sole relationship with the client, bias and conflict of interest are less likely to occur.

Such companies are used by many organisations. Political parties will commission them to run polls, especially in the run-up to an election. MORI has become a household name in the UK, with the results of their polling being pored over by politicians and media pundits as they try to assess not only voting intentions but also the impact of both the party's and its opponents' policies.

Market research companies are able to stand back from the organisation and provide objective information. Acting on behalf of the organisation, they are able not just to carry out polls and questionnaires but can also conduct focus groups and monitor demographic information.

Whatever type of group is used for market research, the information sought will be of two types – primary and secondary.

Sources of information

Primary research data is that which is specifically sought as part of the market research process, whilst secondary data already exists and is accessed to support the market research process. Thus the government of the UK conducts a census (primary research). The information is then collated by the Office of National Statistics and becomes secondary research data for other organisations.

Primary research

There are three basic methods of acquiring primary data – surveys, observation and experiment. The last is often used in scientific work and perhaps less so in commercial market research, but it does have an important role to play if used sensibly.

Surveys

The citizens of developed countries sometimes seem to be barraged by surveys of one type or another. We are constantly being asked questions about our preferences, life styles and future intentions.

Before considering the types of questions that a survey should contain, it is necessary to distinguish between the four major methods that are used to survey individuals. These are: face-to-face interviews, telephone interviews, postal questionnaires and discussion/panel/focus groups. Each has advantages and disadvantages, and the type chosen has to be a balance between the ease and cost of acquiring the information and the validity of the information received. The problems in choosing the size and the nature of the sample to be used are discussed later in this chapter.

Face-to-face interviews

Provided that the questions asked are suitable and robust, this method, when used by an experienced researcher, can lead to the most reliable results. Part of this is due to the influence of body language. It is very difficult for people to disguise their body language and from childhood we have become very adept at picking up body language clues. If the person says 'yes' but the body language suggests 'no', then 'no' is the real response. By interviewing somebody face to face, the researcher is able to pick up all the non-verbal and intonation clues that will lead to the recording of a reliable response.

Interviewing face to face also allows for a relationship of trust to be built up between the parties. It is important that the relationship remains professional as, if it becomes personal, there is the danger that the respondent will say what they believe the interviewer wishes to hear and not what they actually think.

The interviewer will normally have a fixed set of questions and such interviews can be carried out almost anywhere. Indeed, people who fit the required sample may often be approached in the street and asked if they can spare a few minutes of their time to assist in a survey.

Telephone interviews

As more and more of the population have access to a domestic telephone, so there has been a growth in use of this medium for market research interviews. Such interviews maximise the use of the interviewer's time as they can remain in a warm place, out of the elements and work their way through the questions over the telephone.

A distinction has to be made between the use of the telephone for genuine market research and the growth in telephone sales. Telephone sales techniques often have the interviewer claiming to be conducting a survey, whereas the aim is actually to sell a particular product or service and the survey is just an opener to attract the interest of the respondent. Anecdotal evidence suggests that much telephone selling is not backed up by any market research, with countless tales of those who have just moved into a newly built house being offered replacement kitchens, windows etc. over the telephone. Proper market research would suggest that these are the least likely people to be in the market for such products as the new house will, in all probability, be well provided with such items.

Telephone surveys carry with them a cost for the use of the telephone line and also do not permit the interview to assess the body language of the recipient. There is also the danger that a telephone call may be at an inconvenient moment and that this may alienate the respondent – making a telephone survey call during a popular soap opera is to be avoided at all costs!

Postal questionnaires

Postal questionnaires, which here can include questionnaires in magazines and newspapers, can be a useful way of reaching a large number of potential recipients within a target market.

There is no question of being able to assess body language, nor indeed is it possible to be completely accurate about the sample. Just because somebody indicates that they are a male over 50 does not mean that they necessarily are. Face-to-face and telephone questioning are more reliable in this respect.

The two main problems with this type of survey are biased returns and the level of returns.

If you set out to survey people who have had complaints on holiday and this is done via a postal survey, in all probability it will be those who have had a problem who respond. Assume that 200,000 copies of a magazine with your survey in it are sold and that 8,000 people respond. Analysing the responses, it is found that 5,000 of them indicate some form of holiday problem. Can you conclude that out of 8,000 holidays sold, 5,000 will be the subject of some form of complaint when the customer returns home? No!

Firstly, not everybody complains even when dissatisfied and, more importantly, what about the 192,000 people who did not respond. Were they all happy with their holidays, indeed how many of them went on holiday? The problems with drawing conclusions from this type of data are self-evident.

If the survey is more carefully targeted, then conclusions with a higher degree of validity may be drawn. If it is sent to current customers then there may be a higher response rate, as it is known that they are interested in the product or service in the first place. If it is in a specialist publication, perhaps dealing with a hobby, again responses may be higher. It is the response rate that is all important. Many organisations offer incentives for people to complete and return the survey, and this can often lead to better results.

Modern versions of the postal survey include those, often single-issue polls conducted on teletext pages and by Internet providers where a response to a particular question is sought. As with postal surveys, the more interested a person is with an issue, the more they are likely to respond, leading to a biased final result.

Discussion/panel/focus groups

The use of some form of panel or focus group is one of the most expensive methods of acquiring primary data and yet, if managed properly, the data produced may be the most useful.

These groups work by bringing together customers and suppliers etc. and by careful chairing of the group to allow discussion to take place. The responses are likely to be somewhat looser than in a face-to-face interview as members of the group will, in all probability, feed off each other. As the members of the group gain in confidence they are likely to provide much in-depth information about their true feelings for a product/service – information that might be difficult to acquire in any other forum. The use of focus groups has grown sharply in recent years, the concept now being used not only by retailers but also by political parties.

Focus groups are an excellent means of testing the suitability of new products and services, as the group setting is likely to generate a degree of emotion that a one-to-one situation cannot. As Phipps and Simmons (1995) have pointed out, the synergy from a focus group may lead the organisation along a new path entirely.

Other methods of collecting primary data

Other such methods are discussed below under Experimentation.

Observation

Simplistically, observation is able to tell the researcher what a respondent does, but fails to give an indication of their motivation and feelings. This makes it somewhat limited as a market research technique unless it is followed up by careful questioning. It is possible to use observation to see how easy a product is to use and whether there are any problems associated with the use of the product. It might be beneficial if the manufacturers of products which require a degree of construction by the customer were to use more observation of average customers carrying out the assembly using the manufacturer's instructions prior to placing the product on the market.

Where observation techniques are used they may be secretive, where the respondent does not know he or she is being observed. Modern CCTV equipment makes it possible to observe customers acting naturally, although there may be legal/ethical issues related to the data. Techniques may be non-participative and non-secret, where the respondent knows that they are being observed but the researcher takes no part in the process. The problem with this technique is that behaviour can change if somebody so much as believes they are being observed, and thus a result may be obtained that is different from the result that the respondent would produce if he or she was unaware of any observation. The researcher can also participate, in which case they become a part of the process. Going up to a person and asking why they have made the decision they have would fall into this category, but there is the danger that the respondent will give the answer that they believe the researcher requires.

Observation can be very useful when considering the movement of people, for instance past a display or through a shopping mall. Modern CCTV equipment makes this relatively simple. Such research in the USA showed that people move faster past banks and that shops on either side of a bank were at a slight disadvantage in this respect, as potential customers spent fractionally less time looking at their window displays.

Experimentation

Whilst direct questioning remains the main method of collecting primary data, other variations that are more experimental, such as word association, sentence completion, descriptions to a third person and thematic appreciation tests (TAT), where the respondent is asked to interpret an event, and even role playing are used to gather detail. These techniques are all very specialised and require those with a knowledge of psychology to interpret the results. As such, they can be a very expensive method of gathering data.

Experiments are normally designed to test an hypothesis and thus start from the premise that there is an hypothesis or big question that can be answered. An example would be the relationship between the type and design of packaging used and sales figures. To find out if there is such a relationship, scientific research methods are used.

Firstly, all of the possible variables are considered. The dependent variable would be the sales figures and the independent variable, i.e. the variable that the researcher can manipulate, would be the packaging design. There are also extraneous variables that are not under the control of the researcher but which may affect the results. The behaviour of the economy is a good example. If the economy is booming, then sales might increase regardless of packaging. These can be taken into account by 'discounting', i.e. by considering the general market trends and allowing for that in the figures.

It should then be possible to set up an experiment with different packaging sold in similar areas. The latter is important as the experiment must compare like with like. If a particular packaging proves more attractive than another does, then the experiment will have pointed the way to the desired action by the manufacturer. If the sales appear similar regardless of the packaging, then the experiment has still been a success as it will have shown not that packaging is unimportant but that all of the packaging used is equally attractive.

As with all scientific experiments, it is important that market research experiments contain a control group who are not subject to the experiment. Pharmaceutical research uses placebos (inert compounds that have no effect on the body) that are given to the control group, whilst the drug in question is given to the experimental group. If both groups show an improvement in symptoms, then it is likely that just being a part of the experiment may be producing the change. In management, Maslow's classic Hawthorne Studies showed that just being part of an experimental group could produce a change in work output regardless of the variables changed by the experimenter (Maslow, 1970).

Samples

It is rarely possible to question or observe the whole of a potential customer base as part of research. In an election situation, the only time when the whole of the possible population is able to be questioned is on the ballot paper itself. Even then, there will be those who do not vote and so their views and intentions (other than apathy etc.) remain unknown. Similarly in market research, it is difficult to obtain data from all customers. After sales activities may produce results from a high proportion of customers but that will be after the buying decision has been made, and what is often required is information prior to the buying decision.

Researchers therefore use a representative sample of the population to question, and then extrapolate the results.

The sample size is usually represented by the letter n. When $n = 1,500$, this means that a sample size of 1,500 was used in the study.

There are two types of sample that can be used, these being probability and non-probability samples. Probability samples, often referred to as 'random samples', are ones where the individual members of the sample are drawn in a random fashion from the total population. Non-probability samples, as the name implies, consist of individuals who are selected on a predetermined basis. The two are not mutually exclusive. If, for example, it is believed on the basis of past experience that it is mothers who generally buy clothes for children, then it might be considered sensible to sample the population of mothers if research is being conducted into purchasing decisions for children's clothes. The selection will not be a random one as they will all have being female in common and will possibly be within a certain age range. What the researcher will do is to use a stratified random sample of the population of mothers. It will be random as regards the mothers chosen, but it will be from the population of mothers only.

Random samples

How does a researcher ensure that the sample is random? There are a number of techniques that can be used. Firstly, the geography of the sample is important. If the sampling is only carried out in one location, there is the probability that the sample obtained may not be purely random. If all sampling were carried out next to a public house, there might be more of those who use public houses than would occur by chance. Similarly, if the sampling were carried out in a fashion store, then the sample is perhaps representative of those looking for new clothes. The more variation in the geography, the more likely the sample is to be random.

It is also necessary to guard against always asking questions of the same type of person. Researchers need to ensure that the sample balances the profile of the general population or the population being studied. If people are chosen purely at random then the larger the sample, the more representative of the population it is likely to be. Quota sampling, to be covered later under Non-probability samples, seeks to alleviate these problems.

Many researchers use systematic sampling where they will interview every 5th person, or 4th household or 6th driver etc. Again the larger the sample, the more likely it is to be representative of the population.

Cluster sampling

Market research is often a very expensive process, especially if a national sample is required. Cluster sampling, where the sample is conducted in a more con-centrated geographic area, can help to reduce costs. A particular town or area can be chosen from which to draw the sample, thus cutting down on travel costs. In using cluster sampling, the researcher needs to ensure that the area chosen is actually representative of the whole population and that unique factors are kept to a minimum. For instance, the use of Kingston-upon-Hull in the north-east of England for a study on transport in the UK would be problematic, as Hull has poor north–south communications (recently eased with the opening of the Humber Bridge) and much better east–west ones because of its position on the Humber Estuary (Jowett, 1993). An inland town with good all-round communications would be a better choice from which to draw a sample.

Non-probability samples

There are three major methods of non-probability sampling. The first, *judgemental sampling*, relies on the researcher's judgement in choosing whether or not to include an individual. This is fraught with danger as it provides a temptation to choose those who are likely to respond positively to the researcher's hypothesis. The second method also carries dangers. It is known as *convenience sampling* and uses a population convenient for the researcher – colleagues, friends etc. As such people may already have many things in common, they may provide biased results.

Quota sampling (mentioned earlier) provides the best form of non-probability sampling and indeed can be regarded as a means of ensuring that the sample is as random as possible. By dividing the population up into attributes such as gender, age, race etc. it is possible to ensure that examples of each are sampled. Thus the sampler may be instructed to question 10 women and then 10 men, 10 young people, 10 older people etc. In this way the sample profiles the population.

Sample size and determination

Effective market research requires a balanced sample of sufficient size to inform the decision-making process. It is important that the sample size (n) is not so small as to make the results unrepresentative. Adler (1969) makes the point that even a nation-wide survey in the UK will have a sample size of only 2,000 and that it is rare for this to rise as high as 5,000. This means that the members of the sample need to be chosen with great care if they are to represent a large population.

Whilst some surveys may wish to consider the total possible population (say of the UK), most are concerned with specific populations, such as the population that buy chocolate or drink beer, or drive motor cars etc.

In order to identify a population, it may be necessary to approach a much bigger sample than required and ask some simple questions to see if the subject is part of the target population. If the research is into gardening equipment, then perhaps asking 'do you have a garden?' may, repeat *may*, allow the researcher to discard those who answer 'no'. It may be that some negative respondents are required – perhaps it would be useful to know why they do not have a garden. Approaching a large number of previously unknown people in this manner is known as random sampling (see earlier). Where individuals can be targeted either as a result of a previous random sample or because their preferences are already known (perhaps they already form part of the customer base) is known as quota sampling (also discussed earlier). A supermarket sampling shoppers leaving the premises already knows that they are customers. To be effective in a case like this, previous qualitative analysis should have been carried out to ascertain a gender, age etc. profile. If it is known that 65 of the customers are female and that of those 40% are over 35, then the sample for the market research should replicate these proportions in order to provide a true picture of the customer base. This is in line with the ideas of quota sampling covered earlier.

The design and use of questionnaires

The vast majority of surveys, however conducted, use a questionnaire and thus ensure a commonality of questions asked.

The results from any survey need to be both valid and reliable. Validity means that the results reflect what they are meant to represent. Thus if a researcher wished to study radio listening, valid questions would consider how long the radio was on, not how many times it was switched on and off. A radio could be switched on and off six times and yet total daily listening could be 2 hours; it could be switched on only once but be listened to for 5 hours.

A reliable questionnaire will produce similar responses from similar respondents over a period of time. Questionnaires are like most research tools –

garbage in equals garbage out. The results can only be as good as the questions asked.

The main rules for questionnaire use and design are:

1. The interviewer should always explain the nature and purpose of the research.
2. Respondents should always be asked if they can be contacted again for further information if necessary, as the interviewer may well not be responsible for interpreting findings and the actual researcher may have additional questions as a result of the responses provided.
3. Keep the questionnaire as short as possible. If the respondent is asked to fill it in on their own they may become bored and if they are being interviewed, they may well have other things to do with their time.
4. Questionnaires that are based on a single topic tend to be the more reliable. The more topics that a questionnaire tries to cover, the more the respondent may become confused, and there is a danger of drawing conclusions that are not valid.
5. Use language that the respondent will understand, and avoid technical terms and jargon unless they are very well known.
6. Always ensure that there is space for a different response from those planned. 'Don't know' and 'other' can be useful to the researcher as they may provide ideas that had not been considered.
7. Care should be taken to ensure that questions are ordered in such a way as not to force a response to a later question from the response to an earlier one.

Questions

There are four basic types of questions, the first of which should be used with considerable care if market research is to be useful.

Closed questions

Closed questions are those which require an 'either/or' response. They often require a 'yes/no' response. Whilst there are times when they are required, they allow for little variation unless followed by an open question. 'Do you own a car?' is a legitimate closed question that might be very important if researching into attitudes to car ownership. It should be followed by an open 'why?'/'why not?' question.

If purely quantitative data is required, then closed questions may be ideal, and multiple-choice closed questions are often used in surveys. How would you vote if there was a general election tomorrow?, followed by a list of political parties, is an example of a legitimate multiple-choice closed question.

Open questions

Open questions are concerned with eliciting a why?, how?, when? etc. response. They can be completely open, for example, 'what is your favourite breakfast cereal?', with room for responses following; or they may be constrained, for example, name three reasons for owning a food processor'.

Open questions are, unfortunately, harder to analyse than closed questions, as the responses may be much more varied. They are more likely to represent the views of the respondent more closely.

Analysis

Whatever survey methods have been used, there need to be measures of the responses. In many cases this can be achieved at the time of questioning by using a response scale that asks the respondent to rate an aspect etc. of a product or service along a mathematical scale. For example:

How likely are you to take a foreign holiday in the next 12 months?

Very likely   *Unlikely*

1   2   3   4   5   6

Another method is to ask respondents to rate something. For example:

Using 1 for your preferred choice and 2 for your next choice, rate the following take-away food establishment types according to your preferences.

American style fast-food outlets   _____
Chinese   _____
Fish and chip shop   _____
Indian   _____
Other (specify)   _____

Such responses are relatively easy to analyse as the analytical program can be set up on the computer and just needs the numerical response to each question to be entered.

Thereafter the analysis enters the field of statistics. This book is not intended to consider statistics, as there are many suitable volumes that the researcher can refer to. Suffice to say that statistics can and are manipulated to say what the sponsoring organisation requires, and numbers can never tell the whole story.

Secondary research

Secondary research is that which uses information that is already available. It is often referred to as 'desk research'.

The Internet has become a Mecca for secondary research as governments and supra-national official bodies, e.g. the European Union, have a considerable amount of data publicly available at the click of a key. Just by entering a few key words into an Internet search engine, researchers can access a wealth of up-to-date material.

There are also technical journals, the statistics provided by professional and trade bodies, governmental statistics and the research conducted by others. Most researchers are quite happy for their research to be used once it is in the public domain, provided that credit is given for it.

The major problem with the use of previously published material relates to currency. In the fast moving commercial environment of the 21st century, data can become out of date very quickly. It is important therefore to ensure the current validity of material used in secondary research. A glance at the statistics for mobile telephone ownership in the UK between 1991 and 2001 will illustrate a sector that has seen a rapid rise in the degree of ownership from single figures to over 50% of the population (higher in younger age groups), and changes in the market segmentation (see previous chapter). Initially, mobile telephones were bought almost exclusively for business use. By 2001 there was a huge market for leisure use of the technology, especially by children.

Books and journals are dated and thus it is easy to judge currency. In this age of instant information, it is likely that the role of books in the future will not be to provide up-to-date data but to stimulate thought. There are now much more efficient methods of obtaining secondary data.

The media are also other useful sources of secondary data. Newspapers and magazines conduct their own surveys and publish the results and, provided that care is taken to ensure that it is valid and reliable data, these can be a useful research source. The information contained in newspapers is likely to be much more up to date than that in books.

Whatever the source of secondary data, care needs to be taken to ensure that there is allowance made for any bias of the author. Newspapers etc. often have particular lines of argument that they pursue and even have their own political affiliations. Authors may have pet theories etc. and may present facts skewed in such a way as to support their personal viewpoint. This is perfectly legitimate but researchers using secondary data need to ensure that they are aware of any such bias.

Some data, such as that related to fashion, dates much more quickly than other data, and the researcher needs to consider how the data was gathered and what research rules were applied.

It is also worth the researcher considering the qualifications, experience and expertise of the author of any secondary data that they are considering using. Is the person a recognised authority in the field? Writers for the popular market may be less well qualified than those writing for the specialised academic field. This is not always the case and some very well qualified writers have had considerable success in bringing their subject to a wider audience without compromising accuracy etc.

Conducting market research

Whether the research is carried out by a specialist agency, an academic institution or in-house within the organisation, there are certain steps that need to be followed. These can be defined by the acronym DICAR, standing for:

- Definition;
- Identification;
- Collection;

- Analysis;
- Reporting.

Definition of objectives

Whenever there is a decision to be made or a problem to be solved, decision-making/problem-solving models almost always begin with requiring an objective and carefully thought out definition of the issue – precisely what is it that the researcher is trying to establish. The wording of the definition of the issue is of critical importance as it sets the parameters for the research activities that follow.

It is often also necessary to define what the issue is not. Research costs a great deal in both monetary and time terms, and it is imperative that the research issue is closely designed. It is, of course, possible that the research may throw up other issues that will need their own research.

Once the research issue has been defined it should be referred back to the sponsor for approval. The sponsor is the organisation or part of the organisation that requires the answer to the particular question. The sponsor is usually also the customer as well as the end-user, as they normally foot the research costs. As such, their agreement and understanding need to be sought during the research process. It can be all too easy for a researcher to become carried away and end up researching questions that they would like the answer to but that may be of less relevance to the sponsor.

The issue may be related to the type of research required, as covered earlier in this chapter. The researcher may wish to know about current or future preferences or how a product is perceived within the marketplace. They may be interested in how consumers differentiate between competitors of the effectiveness and value-for-money of advertisements. Whatever the issue, the clearer it is defined, the more useful will be the information that is gained through market research.

Identification

Once the issue has been defined, the sample to be used must be identified. It is normal to use a confidence interval of 95% for the sample. In statistical terms, this means that the researcher is confident that there is only a 5% chance that the true population statistic will fall outside the indicated margins for error. 95% confidence intervals are a norm in statistics, basically meaning that for every 100 people interviewed, at least 95 of them will be of the population required.

Some research will require the use of a wide-ranging population. The polls conducted in the run-up to elections use a balanced sample of (in the UK) those aged from 18 upwards who are eligible to vote. Unless it is a by-election, the interviews will be conducted across a geographic and type (rural, urban, city centre etc.) range of constituencies. For the polling before a by-election, only voters in the constituency concerned will be chosen.

Some sample attributes may be obvious to the naked eye, gender and age being the most obvious. Residence, occupation etc. (hidden attributes) can only be determined by questioning, and thus it may be necessary to start the questioning process and then reject the respondent if their hidden attributes do not fit those required for the research.

If the research is being overtaken over a period of time, it may be necessary to adjust the sample as time goes on to eliminate any imbalance in previous samples. Researchers also need to take account of temporal differences. The population of consumers in a particular shopping mall may be different on weekdays than weekends, and this should be reflected in the sample. Supermarkets are aware that different sections of their customer base shop at different times. Those in work are more likely to visit the supermarket in the mornings, evenings and at weekends, whilst those not in work may well choose the middle of the day.

Collection

The logistics for the collection of data may be quite complex. It may be necessary to transport researchers to particular locations. They need to be equipped with the relevant questionnaires, pens, clipboards etc. If telephone surveys are being used, the telephone numbers of respondents need to be gathered and care needs to be taken, especially in the evening to avoid a call during popular television programmes. Ruin a respondent's viewing of their favourite soap opera (so named because the first of the genre were sponsored by US washing powder manufacturers – see Chapter 12) and this can provide a negative image of the organisation/product/service that the researcher represents.

Identity cards need to be issued. It is very important that the respondent feels secure with the researcher. The latter should explain what they are doing and why, and should always offer proof of identity and authorisation.

Training for those conducting the field research is also important. Large-scale projects usually entail employing staff to conduct interviews and these people need to be trained in interview techniques and to understand the nature of the research so as to be able to answer queries from those they are approaching.

Analysis

Once all the data is in, it needs to be analysed using standard statistical techniques. There are computer programs that will perform the necessary calculations and provide the types of probability information required. Statistics is beyond the scope of this book but there are a large number of texts that can be consulted. A useful example (Anderson *et al.*, 1990) is provided in the Recommended reading at the end of this chapter.

The aim of analysis is to convert the raw data gained as a result of the research into information that the sponsor can use to aid the decision-making process.

Reporting

The final stage of the market research process is the report from the research team to the sponsor. Referring back to the original issue, the researchers need to show the position as clearly as possible, with reasons. The use of graphs and charts is useful here as simplicity is normally of more use than complexity, provided that there is not an attempt to oversimplify. The researchers should bear in mind what the sponsor is going to use the information for and present the information in a suitable format. As with statistics there are any number of texts that will provide information on presentation skills, Bradbury (2000) being a good example.

As far as the researchers are concerned, it is their report that will influence the sponsor's view as to whether the research has been worthwhile. Whilst it may be tempting to embellish reports to say what the researcher knows the sponsor would like to hear, this is usually counterproductive as it will flaw the research and this is bound to become evident at some stage.

The information that comes out of the research process is only as good as the data that enters the system – *garbage in equals garbage out*!

Pseudo market research

Market research type activities have been used not as a marketing tool but as a selling ploy. Many people are familiar with the method of telephone selling that begins with the line: 'Good evening, I am not trying to sell you anything but I am conducting a survey into . . .', the person then proceeding to attempt to sell a new kitchen, guttering, double glazing etc. Whilst a rudimentary survey may well be carried out, its purpose is not to gain information for marketing purposes but to keep the person listening long enough for a hard sell to be attempted. This type of selling involves what may be termed 'pseudo market research' and is often attempted over the telephone.

Forecasting

An important area of co-operation between those involved with the management of the marketing function and those responsible for sales occurs in the area of forecasting.

As Wilmshurst (1984) quite correctly states, those involved in sales are often the closest in the organisation to the market. Not only can they gather important market research detail as part of their work role but they are also a useful source of forecasting information.

The ability to forecast demand for a product or service is obviously vital for any organisation. If demand is underestimated, not enough product will be available to the market and, as will be shown in the section on costs, this can drive the price up. Although this may, in the short term, be beneficial to the organisation, there is also the danger that the organisation, having stimulated demand, will then be unable to supply that demand, thus opening the market up to competitors, as happened to Sinclair Computers in the UK in the 1980s.

If demand is overestimated, then resources will have been committed to production/delivery that cannot be recouped, especially as oversupply tends to drive the market price down.

It is important, therefore, that sales forecasts are as accurate as possible although such forecasts, being set in the future, can never be completely accurate.

Forecasting also allows organisations to provide a more quantitative answer to the 'what if?' scenarios that organisations need to consider when planning future strategies and new products/services.

In addition to the views of the salesforce mentioned above, the basic methods of sales forecasting are.

Market surveys

By querying customers and potential customers about their future purchasing intentions, a picture of demand can be developed. Many commercial buyers may be cagey about revealing future strategies and, in any case, an intention does not always translate into action. For instance, both Pan American (Pan Am) and the Chinese announced their intention to buy Concorde but no actual sales were made to airlines other than British Airways and Air France (Donald, 1999).

Using intentions as a reliable forecasting tool works best in stable situations where there are a limited number of buyers and sellers. The aircraft industry fits this description, and intentions and options usually translate into sales unless the product proves less than satisfactory – the Comet being such a case. In the case of the Ford Edsel motor car, already covered in this book, the sales predictions fell far short of the forecast because, in part, intentions were not translated into sales when the vehicle was released to the public, who did not in fact like the car.

Time series analysis

Time series analysis uses past patterns and behaviour to attempt to predict future levels of activity. This technique depends very much on the interpretation of trends rather than the results of 'moment in time' results. The example of sales figures given in Figure 4.1 shows how important trends can be. Although at point y the sales have actually dropped from the previous level, the trend is still upward. Careful analysis of trends will show the rate of growth or decline (or indeed, stagnation), and this can then be used to determine the figures for potential supply.

Time series analysis is also useful for the prediction and analysis of cyclical or seasonal trends. Airlines such as Icelandair are only too well aware of the seasonal nature of travel. Many operators manage this through seasonal pricing. It is

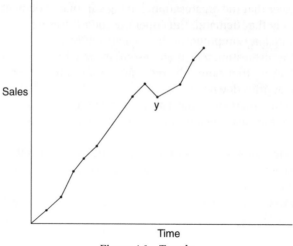

Figure 4.1 Trends.

usually more expensive to travel during the holiday season or at Christmas when demand is at its highest and therefore supply is more problematic.

Those undertaking such an analysis will also need to take account of the PESTLE/SPECTACLES factors covered in Chapter 2 to ensure that as many as possible of the external factors are accounted for, and their effect noted and allowed for in future predictions if they are likely to reoccur.

Market factor analysis

Wilmhurst (1984) defines a market factor as an element in the market that can be quantitatively measured and that has a direct relationship to the demand for a particular product/service. As the relationship is a direct one, a change in a market factor should lead to a consequent change in demand. By analysing such changes in the market, sales projections can be made.

The further into the future the organisation looks, the less accurate the predictions are likely to be.

MDSS/MkIS

Modern marketing is able to benefit from the advances in computer technology that makes large amounts of information and data easier to analyse. Kotler (1980) has defined a Marketing Information System (MkIS) as the people, equipment and processes required to gather, sort, analyse, evaluate and distribute both timely and accurate market information to the key decision makers. Information technology can aid the whole of this process using both data processing and e-mail.

A Marketing Decision Support System (MDSS) is used to support but not supplant management decisions in relation to marketing activities. Such systems can be applied to price, promotion and location, and provide an interaction between the intuition of people and the analytic ability of machines.

Summary

Market research was developed in the USA in the early years of the 20th century and is now an important part of the business sector providing information on consumers etc. to aid decision-making. All organisations need to answer questions about their products and services, and the needs and wants of their customers. Increasingly the research into the marketplace is a specialised function utilising the talents of either specialised agencies or dedicated in-house teams. Primary information is that collected in the field by the examination of properly selected samples, whilst secondary information is derived from previously researched material etc. The Internet has become a valuable source of secondary information. The information that comes out of the research process is only as good as the data that enters the system – *garbage in equals garbage out*! The market research process can be defined in terms of DICAR: Definition – Identification – Collection – Analysis – Reporting. Pseudo market research occurs when market research is used as a cover for covert selling. Part of the market research effort is usually devoted to forecasting sales etc. so that production/delivery schedules can be set.

QUESTIONS

1 'In the modern global marketplace it is important to have as much information as possible about customers and competitors'. Discuss this statement with reference to an organisation you are familiar with.
2 Why is it important to use a properly balanced sample? What problems can occur if the sample is not chosen with considerable care?
3 Design a questionnaire for investigating the popularity of a chosen product. Who would you wish to have included in the sample to be questioned?
4 Why is forecasting so important? Using a product or service with which you are familiar, indicate some of the major market and external factors that need to be taken into account when forecasting sales/demand.

Recommended reading

A comprehensive text for data analysis is D. Anderson, D. Sweeney and T. Williams (1990) in *Statistics for Business and Economics*. Useful guidance for presentation skills can be found in A. Bradbury (2000), *Successful Presentation Skills*. A good description of market research techniques is given in A. R. Morden (1991), *Elements of Marketing*.

Useful websites

www.gallop.co.uk   Gallop Polls website
www.harrispollonline.com Harris Polls website
www.icmresearch.co.uk   ICM Research website
www.mori.com   Mori Polls website
www.nop.co.uk   National Opinion Polls website

Some useful statistical web pages can be found at:

www.europa.eu.int/en/comm/eurostat/facts/wwwroot/en/index.htm
               (European Union statistics)
www.statistics.gov.uk   (UK Government Office of National Statistics)
www.open.gov.uk   (UK public sector information)
www.odci.gov/cia/publications/factbook/index.html
               (*World Factbook* – CIA USA)

■ Ƴ **5** Competition

*The nature of competition – Monopolies – Duopolies – Oligopolies – Freeopolies –
Cartels – Competitive forces – Competition between existing suppliers – New
entrants – Organisational growth – Re-forming – Substitutes – Re-entry –
Bargaining power – Competitor analysis – Customer accumulator – Competition
legislation – Parallel importing*

The nature of competition

With very few exceptions, all organisations face a degree of competition. There
are still a small number of monopolies, i.e. organisations that have no
competitors within their chosen marketplace, but they are few and far between.
One of the legacies of the long period of Conservative government in the UK
(1979–97) was the breaking up of a number of public monopolies through a
programme of privatisation. Many of these monopolies had been private sector
organisations operating within the type of competitive environment described
in this chapter before they were nationalised. The reason for nationalisation of
the railways, the national air carrier, steel making, coal mining, energy production and shipbuilding, the majority of which were nationalised by Labour
administrations, was quoted as the national economic interest. Certain other
sectors, most notably the Post Office, had always been in the public sector. Whilst
the concept of private utilities providing gas and electricity etc. might have
seemed revolutionary in the 1980s when the majority of privatisations were
implemented, it was no more than a return to the early years of these industries
when they had been very much in the private sector. Size can and does bring
greater efficiencies and this is one of the reasons often quoted by politicians for
the combining of smaller organisations, although there must be the suspicion
that ideology plays as much a part as economics in such decisions.

The story of Britain's railways is a good illustration of the policies of merger,
nationalisation and privatisation. As early as the 1840s, mergers were beginning
to occur among the many smaller railway companies that had sprung up in the
previous decade. Where there were no outright mergers, there were complex
operating agreements designed to facilitate long-distance journeys, examples
being that between the London and North Western Railway (itself an
amalgamation of a number of smaller concerns, including the Grand Junction
and the Manchester and Birmingham), the Caledonian and the Highland to
provide, respectively, a London to Carlisle, a Carlisle to Perth and a Perth to

Inverness service with only the engine changing throughout the journey, the carriages travelling through from London to Inverness. At the end of World War I there were more than 150 standard gauge railway companies in England, Wales and Scotland. Some had huge extensive networks, like the Great Western Railway (GWR), whilst others were very small, an example being the Isle of Wight Central Railway. Britain's Railways had done a sterling job during World War I. The Grand Fleet stationed in Scapa Flow in the Orkney Islands required huge numbers of coal trains to be run from the coalfields of the UK to the North of Scotland, and these trains ran day in, day out without fail. However the government believed that there was too much competition and too much duplication of routes, and that a rationalisation would aid the necessary reinvestment. There is a logic to the concept that reinvestment will be easier for a smaller number of large organisations as opposed to a very large number of smaller ones. Thus the 'grouping' of 1922 occurred in which the vast majority of the railways in the UK were formed into four major companies: the Great Western Railway (GWR), the Southern Railway (SR), the London and North Eastern Railway (LNER) and the London, Midland and Scottish Railway (LMS). These companies were in existence until 1948 when the post-war Labour government, faced with massive rebuilding costs for the war-damaged UK rail system, decided to nationalise the rail operations and form a single nationalised entity – British Railways. Whether nationalisation was a success or not is perhaps a political decision but the Conservative administration of the 1990s decided to privatise the system by forming a company (Railtrack) to own the track, stations etc. and then to lease geographic operations to a series of franchise holders for fixed time periods. Save that the franchise holders only operate the trains and do not own the track, the wheel has come full circle. In fact it has returned to a business state earlier than the railways because, as Rolt (1955) has pointed out, the first railways were supposed to operate on the same basis as canals, the basis being that it was unfair for the owner of the canal (or track) to operate their own boats (or trains). These actions in the UK have been followed in many parts of the world, so that there are far fewer State-run monopolies at the beginning of the 21st century than there were in the 1980s.

It used to be thought that any consideration of competition only applied to the private/commercial sector. Today, all organisations need to consider their competitors when looking at the market. As mentioned above, in the UK alone, since 1979, airlines, electricity, water, gas and telephone utilities, shipbuilding, steel and even banks have been returned to the private sector, and more and more competition has been introduced.

India, the ex-Eastern bloc countries, and many other countries, especially in Western Europe, are looking at placing more and more commerce and industry further away from governmental control, mirroring the situation that has always been prevalent in the USA. That is not to say that the US government has not been interested in ensuring fairness. US anti-monopoly legislation has always been very robust and the actions of the US authorities in attacking the vast combines that developed in the transportation sector are well documented.

Charities, as part of business world, need to compete with each other for donations, and other types of organisations for disposable income. The whole voluntary sector has become more and more commercially oriented as competition has increased. The growth of charity shops on many British high streets has led to calls for controls and commercial rents/rates etc. from retailers who perceive that these shops may have become a real competitive threat, especially as many have moved into selling new items in addition to pre-owned clothes, books etc.

As soon as there is competition, there is a need for knowledge of the market. As Cartwright and Green (1997) put it in one of their 'Golden Rules for Customer Satisfaction', in a free market economy the customer always has a choice. Even in a monopoly there is possibly the choice to use the product or service or not to use it, i.e. in any commercial situation there is always a modicum of choice.

There are fewer and fewer monopolies in the 21st century world. A monopoly can be defined as an organisation that has no competitors. Yet, as markets become more global, it is increasingly difficult for governments to force consumers to use a monopoly.

Other terms that are used in this area of marketing are:

Duopoly: the possession of the delivery of a product or service by only two suppliers.

Oligopoly: the possession of the delivery of a product or service by a limited number of suppliers.

To give practical examples, the railway service in an area may be a monopoly if there is only one operator (as covered earlier when considering the nationalised rail service in the UK prior to the late 1990s). If there are two operators it is a duopoly, such as the situation after 2000 between London and Scotland where Virgin Rail operated down the West Coast and Great North Eastern down the East. If there are more than two but not a large number, it is an oligopoly; the air service between London and Scotland is an oligopoly with British Airways, British Midland, easyJet, Go, Ryan Air and a number of even smaller operators offering a Scotland to London service after 2000. If coaches and private cars are considered, there is a fairly large choice for consumers wishing to travel between say Edinburgh and London. There is no longer a sea service between Scotland and the South of England but there was a limited service on cargo passenger boats until fairly recently. Monopolies thrive in *command* economies, where the decisions about who can supply what are decided centrally, usually by the government. This is not always a bad thing; too much competition can be unhealthy, as it may mean that no supplier has enough business to flourish. Amtrak, the national passenger rail service in the USA, is an example of a monopoly; they provide all of the long-distance passenger rail transport in the USA. Amtrak is an interesting (and for the USA, unusual) example of a monopoly, as the organisation was formed in 1971 to prevent the total collapse of a service that had a large number of suppliers, most of whom were in dire financial circumstances. It was the failure of the merged New York Central, Pennsylvania and New Haven concerns that prompted the move (McGuirk, 1999) as, without government intervention, long-distance passenger rail transport, decimated as it had been by the competition from airlines, was doomed. There was (and is) however still a market for long distance trains in the USA and new rolling stock has allowed Amtrak to capture over 30% of the lucrative North Eastern Corridor (Boston–New York–Washington DC) business.

Demand economies, where the market, through customers, decides on the number of suppliers, are more likely to produce non-monopoly situations and have become the norm in the Western democracies. Monopolies thrived in communist regimes but as these fell from the late 1980s onwards, monopolies became rarer even in those countries which retained considerable central control of the economy.

The car ferry market between Dover and Calais was primarily a duopoly with two big operators – Stena Sealink and P&O European Ferries. The introduction of *Le Shuttle* and *Eurostar* trains through the Channel Tunnel added substantial extra competition and led the UK government to approve a merger between the ferry companies, as this would not lead to a monopoly situation. Prior to the advent of the Channel Tunnel such a merger would not have received approval. There will always be times when the market is only large enough for one player, and in cases like this governments often have rules to ensure that customers do not suffer. Whilst Dover–Calais might have been a route that could support more than one operator prior to the building of the Channel Tunnel, the ferry service between Aberdeen and Orkney/Shetland cannot sustain more than one operator and thus the Scottish Executive, the UK government and the European Union take considerable interest in the level of fares and service.

As early as the 1930s, the US government had acted to break up the large combines that were beginning to dominate the fledgling US aviation industry. The Boeing, United Airlines, Pratt and Witney (aircraft engines) and Hamilton Standard Propellers combine was ruthlessly broken up following a report from a committee headed by Senator Hugo Black of Alabama. At the time, the US government, through the allocation of postal routes, was the major customer of the airlines and the administration of F. D. Roosevelt was ideologically against such huge industrial might dictating terms to a vital national service (Irving, 1993). This was not the first time that a US administration had expressed concern about the power of huge, monopolistic tending conglomerates. The well-known US businessman J. P. Morgan had run foul of the government in the early years of the 20th century. It is little known that whilst the infamous *Titanic* was built in Britain, registered in Britain and crewed by Britons, she was in fact ultimately owned by the International Mercantile Marine Company (IMM), a Morgan creation (although registered to White Star Line, a British component of IMM). The organisation and finances were complex but the aim of Morgan appears to have been a virtual monopoly of the lucrative North Atlantic traffic. The British government were so concerned at the loss of national assets that they provided subsidies to Cunard to enable the company to remain out of Morgan's clutches and insisted, as a condition of the company, that the majority of Cunard shares remained in British hands (Davie, 1986). It was not until the late 1999 that the Cunard brand eventually fell into US hands, being acquired by the Carnival Cruise Group from Trafalgar House. The US inquiry into the loss of the *Titanic* held in New York in April 1912 provided Senator Smith, the chair and instigator of the inquiry, with a unique opportunity to investigate the shipping trusts of which he was an opponent and the operations of Morgan (Davie, 1986). The financial cat's-cradle that represented IMM led many in Britain to say that Smith had no right to investigate the sinking of a British ship in international waters but few, even in the government, were aware of the actual ownership of the *Titanic* and White Star Line. As the real ownership was in the USA, it can be argued that Smith and the Senate were well within their legal and moral rights. The British Government did not, after deliberation, object to the US inquiry although the British government run Board of Trade held its own inquiry into the tragedy.

The oligopoly situation exists where there are a few, fairly large players in the market. London–New York air flights (of which Icelandair is a player) and the major supermarket chains in the UK are easily recognised as belonging to this category. The oil industry is an often quoted example, with a few very well-known names including Shell, BP, Exxon and Mobil supplying gasoline products to large areas of the world.

Cartwright and Green (1997) introduced a new category:

Freeopoly, where there are no restrictions, save those imposed by the potential demand, on the number of possible suppliers.

In other words, in a freeopoly there is no restriction on the number of potential suppliers of a good or service; the actual number of organisations involved is determined by the number of potential customers. Monopolies, duopolies and oligopolies are constrained by the laws of most countries (anti-trust legislation in the USA and the Monopolies and Mergers Commission plus European Union rules in the UK) from fixing prices. However, common sense tells us that if the public will pay X for the product or service from one supplier, they will not pay much more than X for it from another supplier unless there is considerable added value. Thus, within any given area, the price for similar products and services will be roughly the same even if there has been no collusion between competitors to fix prices at a certain level.

As an example: a small town can only support a limited number of pharmacies; the only restriction on that number is the market. Too few and the demand will not be supplied; too many and there will not be enough business to support all the suppliers. Sooner or later the weakest will either close or merge with one of the stronger suppliers. The optimum number is determined by the market. There is as near to true competition as possible. The danger of a monopoly, duopoly or even an oligopoly is that the participants can fix the prices at an artificially high level. In a freeopoly, prices are determined by the market. Most situations tend to evolve away from a freeopoly because of the natural inclination of organisations to grow and merge with or take over previous rivals.

Monopolies, as discussed earlier, as situations where one organisation provides the sole source of supply, are legislated against in the UK, the USA and many other countries. They are only allowed, as has been pointed out, where the market can support only one supplier. The European Union has very strict rules that allow a monopoly in certain situations, but only where there is an open bidding process to supply the service. The winner may receive the contract to operate for a fixed period, after which there will be another bidding competition.

Organisation	Customers	Market Share
A	200	20%
B	200	20%
C	200	20%
D	200	20%
E	200	20%

Figure 5.1 The initial market.

Organisation	Customers	Market Share
A	180	18%
B	180	18%
C	180	18%
D	180	18%
E	180	18%
F	100	10%

Figure 5.2 The market with one new member.

Governments have realised that a lack of choice leads to dissatisfied consumers, and dissatisfied consumers can display their frustration through the ballot box. Organisations, whilst espousing the ideal of competition publicly, often try to achieve as near a monopoly situation as possible. For the supplier, a monopoly is the ideal situation as it gives them total control of the market and prices. For the customer, as much choice as possible without destroying the market is ideal. Competition usually means lower prices and higher quality. It is important that there is some form of control of competition. All organisations need a critical mass of customers to survive. Too many organisations chasing the same number of customers could lead to a situation where the market is so divided between them that no organisation actually has enough customers to survive. To illustrate this mathematically, Cartwright (2000) demonstrated a scenario based on actual experience.

Suppose that the total market for a product is 1,000 customers and that, to survive, an organisation must have a minimum of 200 customers. If there were 5 organisations, all selling at the same price and the same quality, then the chances are they would each have the required 200 customers (Figure 5.1). This is somewhat simplistic but demonstrates the principle that increased competition can eventually lead to a restriction in choice.

If a sixth organisation joins the market, then either they will fail very early on because they attract no customers or they will (more likely) attract some customers from the original five (Figure 5.2).

There is now a situation where no organisation has enough customers to be viable. What is likely to happen over time is that the market will expand as organisations create demand and that there will be mergers and take-overs. In three years' time the market may have expanded to 1,500 customers and the position of the organisations may look like that shown in Figure 5.3.

Organisation D now looks ripe for a take-over, leaving the customer with only

Organisation	Customers	Market Share
A (+ B + F)	700	47%
C (+ E)	500	33%
D	300	20%

Figure 5.3   The market after 3 years.

two choices. Competition can remove choice almost as easily as it creates it. For legislators, the aim of competition is to widen the market and create choice; for organisations, it is to remove the competition and gain as much market share as possible. Market share is an important indicator of an organisation's success, as it is one of the aspects of performance given considerable prominence by investors.

Customers seem to be best served by organisations that are either big enough to offer such economies of scale so as to be able to compete on price, or small enough to offer a personal, exclusive service. Supermarkets have developed rapidly in the UK, as have the smaller, more specialised food shops and delicatessens. It has been the middle of the size range organisations that have been squeezed, in many cases out of business.

In the main, competition increases with the number of suppliers and as there are fixed limits between what we will pay for a product or service, as has pointed out, the degree of customer satisfaction becomes an important part of gaining market share.

There will always be situations where a monopoly situation is the only viable one. As pointed out earlier, the cross-channel ferry market between the UK and France was, prior to the building of the Channel Tunnel, sufficient for more than one operator. It was in fact a market that grew steadily throughout the 20th century, especially with the introduction of car ferries and the opening up of new holiday destinations. The market for ferries between the Scottish Islands and the mainland, also covered earlier, is sufficient for only one operator. The European Union's strict regulations relating to both competition and the payment of subsidies by governments to support non-profitable services relieve the monopoly situation in cases like this by forcing competitive tendering for the service at regular intervals in order to protect customers. Subsidies are permitted only when the tendering process has shown that they will assist customers in obtaining the best deal possible.

Duopolies and oligopolies are prohibited, in theory, from operating as cartels and from fixing prices between them. US anti-trust legislation is very strict, as has been seen in the problems Microsoft encountered at the end of the 20th century. The Windows® operating stem may not have had 100% of the market share but it certainly dominated much of the world's market for computer systems. Whilst there were competitors, billions of people used Windows® and software written for the system, especially for Internet access. The US government was concerned that Microsoft should not possess a stranglehold on software development by owning both the operating system and the software titles to run on it, and suggested splitting up the company. The legal issues were unresolved at the time of writing.

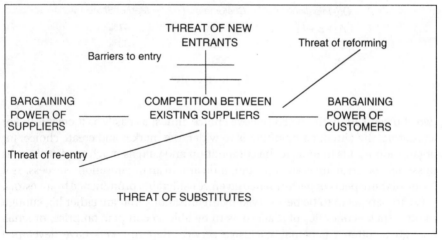

Figure 5.4 Competitive forces. [*Adapted from M. E. Porter by Cartwright and Green (1997).*]

Competitive forces

Competition is a dynamic, fluid process. Whilst organisations may say that they welcome competition, deep down they would possibly prefer to be a monopoly and thus have all the market. However, for other stakeholders especially customers and governments, it is competition that keeps quality high and prices down, provided that it is not so cut-throat as to cause too many organisations to leave the market – hence the need for a delicate balance.

Michael Porter (1980; 1985) provided an interesting model to help explain the nature of business competition. The model was expanded by Cartwright and Green (1997) with additions to explain the nature of late 20th and early 21st century business (Figure 5.4).

Competition between existing suppliers

As would be expected, the greatest competition comes between the current players in a particular market. Even where prices are very much the same, there is competition on levels of service, supplementary products and geographic provision. It is important, however, that even well-established organisations keep a careful eye on the various other options and threats that may occur, as well as considering what the established competition may do to enhance their market share.

Whilst competition between existing suppliers can appear cut-throat, they will often come together to co-operate on safety issues and to defend the market from new entrants. As more and more projects become global, then they may be beyond the capacity of a single supplier.

As mentioned earlier, cartels, i.e. the banding together of similar organisations to manipulate the market, are banned under many jurisdictions. As the world trade grew after World War II, writers such as Sampson (1984) demonstrated how the international airlines and oil companies were operating cartels so as to divide up the market between themselves and defend themselves against any new entrants. Provided that there is sufficient competition, then strategic alliances between competitors or suppliers/customers are a perfectly acceptable method of reducing costs etc. Most of the world's major airlines have partnerships with other carriers. In their annual report for 1999, Icelandair states that the major airline alliances, One-World, Star etc., account for as much as 65% of airline business. Icelandair itself has limited marking agreements with numerous airlines both in Europe and the USA. Code sharing allows passengers to travel on a multi-sector journey using the same ticket. Thus, prior to its decision to operate its own flights on the North Atlantic, British Midland could sell a ticket with a BM code from East Midland's to New York but using Icelandair for the transatlantic portion. British Airways (BA) has been a leader in developing partnerships and franchises where independent operators have their aircraft in BA livery, staff in BA uniforms and use BA codes whilst operating independently but to BA standards. The importance of strategic alliances has been considered by Lorange and Roos (1992), who conclude that they are a means to an end whereby competitive success can be made more likely by co-operation, even if it is with a competitor, and that this may be a more realistic attitude for organisations to take in an increasingly global marketplace.

Many of the large projects that have been so prevalent in the years since World War II – Concorde, the Channel Tunnel and the International Space Station – are beyond the resources of any one organisation. Companies such as Boeing, which closely guarded its proprietary information, have been forced to share expertise. As Sabbach (1995) has shown, the Boeing 777 has required Boeing to work with a host of subcontractors across the world in order to produce a competitive product. These subcontractors bear part of the financial risk and the spreading of such risk is a trade-off to the loss of the proprietary information (organisational knowledge – see the BACK analysis covered in Chapter 2). The organisations that formed the post-war European aircraft industry could not compete with the US dominance led by Boeing and Douglas (later McDonnell Douglas, and now part of Boeing) and many of them came together to form the highly successful (and competitive) Airbus Industrie that has revitalised the European aircraft industry and has challenged the US hegemony. Car manufacturers have also formed strategic alliances to share manufacturing plants etc. The balance between competition and co-operation is a delicate one and not all such alliances survive in the long term, as witnessed by the Honda–Rover alliance in the UK. Very often such alliances are for a single project or for a short period of time, as the circumstances that led to the alliance change. A full consideration of strategic alliances can be found in *Strategic Alliances* by Peter Lorange and Johan Roos (1992).

New entrants

The provision of some products and services has very high barriers to entry indeed and this may make new entrants very few and far between. You need considerable cash resources to set up a transatlantic airline as Sir Richard Branson did with Virgin and, even if those barriers can be overcome, the organisation still has to establish credibility in the market and may face intense pressure from existing suppliers. The problems Virgin believed it faced have been analysed by Martyn Gregory in his book *Dirty Tricks – British Airways' Secret War against Virgin Atlantic* (1994). Whether it is concluded that Virgin was a recipient of dirty tricks or whether BA were legitimately defending their markets is irrelevant in the context of this book, what is important is the fact that new entrants have considerable hurdles to overcome, especially if they present an out and out challenge to established providers. easyJet, the 'no frills' airline in the UK operated by Stelios Haji-Ioannou and based on the US Value Jet operation, has been profiled by Swarbrooke and Horner (1999) and shows how, with enough cash, even a relatively difficult market to enter can be penetrated if the product and service are sufficiently attractive to the customer base.

If the organisation is large and rich enough, it can enter a new market by buying an existing player (see Re-forming later in this section). Whilst this strategy may seem attractive, the buying organisation may not have the expertise, culture and knowledge to operate successfully in that particular market environment. Peters and Waterman, in their book *In Search of Excellence* (1982), talk about successful companies 'sticking to the knitting', i.e. staying close to what they do well. In the 1920s, automobile makers like Ford believed that it would be relatively easy for them to enter the aircraft making business. It wasn't. Ford only made one well-known aircraft product, the Ford Trimotor, and then left the market to those who understood it. The skills required for plane making were in fact very different from those needed for the automobile industry, despite superficial similarities. On the other hand, Disney have proved quite adept at moving into new markets where these are complementary to their main market; in addition to the theme parks, they operate hotels, retail outlets both within and outside the USA, and even a cruise line.

It used to be perceived wisdom that some areas of business/service were immune to new entrants, e.g. governmental activities including local authority services, but experience with privatisation and market testing in the UK has shown that even those services previously supplied by national and local government can be entered by the private sector, e.g. refuse/garbage collection, school meals and social service provision. In many cases the government has changed its role from being a provider to that of a facilitator, i.e. the role is now to ensure that a service is delivered to the prescribed standard rather than actually delivering the service in its entirety.

Aaker (1984) has a series of strategies for entry into a new market. These include:

Internal strategies that use existing resources and talent

Whilst this can mean that extra resources are not needed and may indeed provide a stimulating challenge for staff, it can take a long time and there is little guarantee that the resources will suit the new market or that staff will have sufficient skills without major retraining.

Acquisitions

This is a common method for entering a market and allows the customer base of the acquired operation to be retained, but may well be costly and require the divestment of those part of the acquired organisation that do not fit into future developments. Acquisitions also bring staff with the required expertise into the organisation although retaining them may be problematic, as such changes can be very unnerving for the employees of an acquired organisation.

Licensing/franchises

As mentioned earlier, British Airways have been a major player in the franchising of airline products. By franchising off BA, the franchisee airline is able to benefit from the economies of scale in training, supplies etc. of a much bigger player. Organisations can license or franchise from an existing player in order to gain a foothold into a new market although if they are not already conversant with that market, any franchisor may be reluctant to allow its name to be used.

Organisational growth

Organisations grow, whichever of the above means are used to acquire a position in new markets, by a process known as *integration*. There are four types of integration:

- inorganic;
- unrelated;
- horizontal;
- vertical.

Inorganic integration

This term, first introduced in this book, refers to the process whereby the only change to the organisation's activities is purely size. The organisation continues doing exactly the same but more of it. It is actually fairly rare as most organisations grow by branching out. A supermarket chain that grows only by opening more and more supermarkets selling the same products and services is growing inorganically.

Unrelated integration

There are a number of global companies whose actual business is to own other, often unrelated, companies purely for the financial benefit of the parent company. Such companies do not follow a strategy of buying other companies because there is a relationship with their product or service but purely for their contribution to the parent company's bottom line. As such, acquisitions may be totally unrelated and are often stripped of their assets and then resold.

Horizontal integration

Carnival Cruises, by acquiring other cruise operations (Cunard, Holland America etc.) operating across a variety of the industry's sectors, has practised horizontal integration. What its acquisitions have in common is that they are all cruise operations. Kingfisher's ownership of Currys, Dixons and PC World in the UK shows a similar form of horizontal integration. Such integration allows the organisation to concentrate on a similar core activity, albeit within different markets.

Vertical integration

Vertical integration occurs when the organisation begins to acquire various components of the supply chain. The UK holiday group Thomson, has a travel agency, a package holiday arm, an airline (Britannia) and cruise operations. Airtours and First Choice, two of its main rivals, have also acquired components of the supply chain. This allows them to offer a seamless web of service to their customers, but organisations integrating vertically need to be aware that the various segments may require different skills and knowledge.

Vertical integration in manufacturing has come under threat in recent years as brand owners have outsourced more and more of manufacturing to contractors. This has been particularly prevalent in the clothing industry, with some major names owning none of their own manufacturing and just supplying the branded image to items made by contractors. A full review of this practice is contained in *No Logo* by Naomi Klein (2000). In effect, the organisation and the brand are what are being sold and not the product, paradoxical as this may sound. Many of the contractors operate in low wage economies and Klein also considers the economic and political consequences of this trend.

Re-forming

The acquisition of market share by purchase can be termed *re-forming*. In essence, the purchasing company buys an existing player and then re-forms it to fit in with its own operations. This is clearly a threat to existing players in the market as the purchaser usually brings a degree of financial 'clout' to the operation and can become a major player very quickly, as P&O did in the US cruise market following its acquisition of Princess Cruises and Sitmar Cruises in 1974 and 1988 respectively. Re-forming has been the major growth mechanism for the Carnival Cruise group, as discussed earlier in this book. The group has effectively bought market share, to become the market leader in that particular subsector of the tourist industry.

Re-forming can also occur when a competitor moves out of the market but sells on its expertise and plant to another company, who can then take the competitor's place in the competitive situation without the major barriers to entry that would normally occur. In the early 1990s, DAF, the Dutch truckmaker, who, in 1987, had taken over the truck-making section of the recently privatised British Leyland, sold the UK operation via a management buyout. The UK company was thus able to become a player in its own right very quickly, as the plant was already in operation.

Substitutes

After World War I, there was intense competition between the various US railroads operating transcontinental services, whilst at the same time shipping companies introduced new and more luxurious tonnage on the lucrative North Atlantic routes between Northern Europe and the Mediterranean and the Eastern seaboard of the USA. The UK, the USA, the Netherlands, France, the Scandinavian countries and Italy introduced considerable new tonnage and competition between the established players, many of them household names, such as Cunard, United States Lines, French Line etc. was intense. Yet when Boeing introduced the 707 jet airliner into commercial service with Pan Am in 1958, the transatlantic shipping industry was decimated very quickly. Not only could these aircraft cross the Atlantic in a fraction of the time that ships could, but they established new standards of safety and comfort. They could also cross the USA much faster than a train. Journeys that used to take days were now reduced to hours. Whilst the British built Comet, introduced in 1952, was the world's first commercial jet aircraft, the 707 was the first successful model, carrying over 150 passengers compared with the Comet's initial 44 (later stretched to 94) in the Comet 4B.

Cunard and the other shipping companies were no longer in the shipping business and the US railroads were no longer in the railroad business; they were in the business of mass transportation over a long distance, and the new jet airliners could do the job much faster. A classic example of substitution. The shipping companies looked for new markets within the cruising market but ships designed for the 'liner' trade were not really suitable for the vacation market, and many of the companies collapsed and their vessels were laid up. The railroads could not compete at all and eventually, in 1971, all long-distance passenger trains in the USA came under the Amtrak banner (see earlier) and the route network was cut severely.

However, both in Europe and the USA, railways operating high-speed trains are now challenging the airlines on shorter routes. The flight from London (Heathrow) to Paris (Charles de Gaulle) takes a mere 35 minutes, but the airports are a long way from the city centres and there is also the time taken to check in to be allowed for. Eurostar trains using the Channel Tunnel complete the journey in 3 hours, city centre to city centre. In a similar vein, by using newer equipment Amtrak have gained 33% of the market share between Washington DC and New York by offering a city centre to city centre service in just over 3 hours.

Re-entry

Organisations that were in the market and have left it but still possess expertise and a 'memory' held by customers may pose a threat of re-entry. The organisational knowledge (see BACK analysis) is still in place even if it is not being used. As demand ebbs and flows, British Airways re-enters markets that it has left, as they become more attractive or politically more stable. As the political situation in the Middle East has fluctuated so a number of holiday companies have entered, left and re-entered that particular area as a market for their customers. Beirut was once a tourism jewel, then it was a devastated city. By 2000 it was reappearing as a cruise destination. Brands may be reintroduced after a period of time; Rover Cars as a brand disappeared when a number of UK car manufacturers were nationalised under the British Motor Corporation (BMC) banner, only to reappear when British Leyland, as BMC became, was privatised. Customers still remembered, however, the Rover brand.

Re-entry is more likely where there are fewer problems about buying expensive plant or where the organisation can use its cash resources to buy out one of the remaining suppliers or, as in the case of an airline, it already possesses all the necessary hardware.

Bargaining power

Depending on the monopoly–freeopoly situation, suppliers and customers have varying degrees of bargaining power.

In general, a supplier wants to supply the minimum acceptable quality at the highest possible price, whilst the customer wants the highest possible quality at the lowest possible price. There will be a point where, however attractive the product/service is, there is a price beyond which a customer will not go. It is also often the case that there is a lower limit that the customer will not drop below, for fear that there is a catch. The behaviour of customers towards value will be considered in Chapter 10. If somebody is offered something that they perceive as being worth £300 for £50, they may well suspect a catch or even that the product may be stolen!

If the supplier has a monopoly, it can demand a higher price from the customer up to the point where the ultimate choice – to do without – is made. In a free market economy there is a point of quality below which a customer will not drop, regardless of the price. Indeed, because customers often (wrongly in many instances) equate price with quality, as mentioned earlier, too low a price may send the wrong messages.

The more suppliers of goods and services to a customer there are for a given product or service, the more the customer, be it an individual or an organisation, can force the price down and the quality up. The more competitors an organisation has, the more likely it is that its prices will need to come down, whilst its quality needs to be as high as possible.

In recent years, organisations have sought ever closer relationships with their suppliers, offering them training, making them a full part of the manufacturing/ service process and including them as strategic partners (see earlier). This has advantages for both sides in that the supplier has a greater degree of guarantee of work, but conversely the supplier becomes tied to the fortunes of the contracting organisation.

Competitor analysis

Aaker (1984) makes the very valid point that whatever analysis an organisation carries out on itself, it needs also to carry out a similar analysis on its competitors. An organisation will wish to know the position of a competitor in relation to:

- performance;
- objectives;
- strategies;
- culture;
- strengths and weakness.

(Strengths and weaknesses form part of the SWOT analysis introduced in Chapter 2.)

By carrying out such an analysis, the organisation can begin to determine either its own or its competitors' best and worst features and can thus plan accordingly.

Given that lost customers do not just disappear but often go to a competitor, a single lost customer may mean a net difference of two, as shown by the customer accumulator (see below). Market share is one of the aspects of an organisation's performance given considerable weight by investors. This is obviously only a factor with private, for-profit organisations, but it is an important one as the effect of a drop in market share on investor confidence can be quite dramatic.

The effect of a loss of customers to a rival is not an arithmetic progression but follows what may be described as the 'customer accumulator' (Cartwright, 2000), in the following way. Imagine a situation where there are two shops in a town and each has 100 customers initially. For the purpose of this exercise it is assumed that the total customer base will remain at 200. Let us examine the effect of shop B gaining 1, 2, 10, 25 and 50 customers off shop A (Figure 5.5).

Shop A has lost half its customers but is now three times smaller and thus perhaps three times less attractive to investors than shop B. If we assume for the exercise that each customer generates £10 of profit, the situation is as shown in Figure 5.6.

Not only is shop B now three times bigger in terms of market share, but it is three times more profitable, and the comparison of profitability is a key ratio in deciding the relative strength and success of organisations.

Shop A customers	Shop A market share	Shop B customers	Shop B market share	Numerical difference B – A	Relative size of B compared to A
100	50%	100	50%	0	equal
99	49.5%	101	50.5%	2	1.02
98	49%	102	51%	4	1.04
90	44%	110	56%	20	1.2
75	37.5%	125	62.5%	50	1.6
50	25%	150	75%	100	3

Figure 5.5 The customer accumulator.

Shop A customers	Shop A profit	Shop B customers	Shop B profit
100	£1000	100	£1000
99	£990	101	£1010
98	£980	102	£1020
90	£900	110	£1100
75	£750	125	£1250
50	£500	150	£1500

Figure 5.6   The effect of the customer accumulator on profit.

Thus, losing customers to competitors not only weakens the overall position of the organisation but it also strengthens that of the competition at very little cost to the competitor. One of the most important lessons any organisation needs to learn is that a lost customer may not be lost to the sector. Such customers often do not disappear, they simply switch supplier.

Competition legislation

As mentioned earlier, monopolies do not always serve the interest of the consumer. Since the Industrial Revolution it has been recognised that monopolies may pose a threat to trade. Anti-trust legislation in the USA was used as early as 1933 to force the breakup of the Boeing Corporation, which then included Boeing Aircraft, United Airlines, Hamilton Propellers and Pratt and Whitney Engines on the grounds that such a concentration was anti-competitive. In the UK, the Director General of Fair trading (DGFT) has the power to order an investigation by the Competition Commission (the renamed Monopolies and Mergers Commission) into any organisation that controls over 25% of a particular marketplace. In 1980 the Competition Act was passed, which allows for investigations into anti-competitive practices even when monopolies or near monopolies are not involved.

In July 1999, British Airways (BA) was fined £4 million by the European Commission for making what were deemed unfair bonus payments to travel agents. The ruling stated that BA had abused its dominant position in the marketplace contrary to Article 86 of the Treaty of Rome. This was yet another twist to the long saga of BA's bitter rivalry with Richard Branson's Virgin Atlantic, as covered in *Dirty Tricks* by Martyn Gregory (1994) and showed the willingness of the European Union authorities to use legal processes where it was deemed that anti-competitive activities were taking place.

Parallel importing

In the 1990s, organisations became concerned about the phenomenon of parallel importing. This was an issue that affected, among others, the pharmaceutical and the music industries as a result of the lowering of trade barriers, especially within the European Union.

Many of the concerned manufacturers had been accused of price fixing in the UK by supermarkets and discount retailers who had been unable to obtain supplies directly to sell at a discount. The manufacturers, it was claimed, wished to keep prices at a higher level in the UK than elsewhere.

The prices of many products fluctuate according to supply and demand and may be relatively lower in one country than another; the price of CDs in the USA compared to the UK is a good example.

The supermarkets and discount retailers dealt with the problem by buying supplies from abroad at local wholesale prices, re-importing them into the UK and selling at a discount. This is known as parallel importing.

In 2001 the UK supermarket giant, Tesco, and the US jean's manufacturer, Levi Strauss, became embroiled in a legal argument when the latter tried to stop Tesco selling its product at discounted prices. Tesco were importing the jeans using parallel import methods, much to the chagrin of the manufacturer whose regular retailers were charging a much higher price.

Manufacturers claim that the specifications may be different and that this accounts for the differences in price – a claim that is currently under investigation by the Competition Commission.

 ## Competition within the airline industry

The airline industry is both highly competitive and highly regulated, although governments began to deregulate airline operations to a con-siderable degree from the 1970s onward when the US passed the Airline Deregulation Act.

As early as 1944, as it became clear that World War II was drawing to a close, the Chicago Convention drew up what became known as the Five Freedoms of the Air, to which two more were added later. These freedoms regulated the relationships between an airline's home country and those that it served. The freedoms consist of:

Freedom 1 The right to overfly the territory of another country, thus an Icelandair flight from Keflavik to Boston is allowed to overfly Canada.

Iceland ◄——— Canada ——► USA

Freedom 2 The right to stop in another country to refuel or for technical reasons.

Iceland ◄——— Canada ——► USA
(fuel)

Freedoms 1 and 2 are known as technical rights.

Freedom 3 The right to fly to another country from the home country and to land passengers.

Iceland ————————► USA

Freedom 4   The right to pick up passengers in another country and land them in the home country.

Iceland ◄————— USA

Freedoms 3 and 4 are often subject to bilateral agreements whereby an airline from country *X* is granted a route to country *Y* provided that one of country *Y*'s airlines is allowed to fly from *Y* to *X*.

Freedom 5 is the right to land and pick up passengers in intermediate countries en route, e.g. the Turkish Airlines route from Istanbul to London via Paris.

Istanbul ⇄ Paris ⇄ London

Freedoms 3, 4 and 5 are known as traffic rights.

Two subsequent freedoms have since been added:

Freedom 6   The right to pick up passengers in one country and fly them to another country via the home country. As operated by Icelandair:

Glasgow ⇄ Iceland ⇄ USA

Freedom 7   The right for an airline to operate in countries other than the home countries on routes that do not involve a flight to the home country.

Tokyo ⇄ Seoul
US airline

Cabotage

A so-called 8th Freedom is that of *cabotage*, an ancient term from the days of sailing vessels. Cabotage is the right to operate solely within the territory of another sovereign state. Air France had cabotage rights to operate internal air services in Morocco for many years as a result of the colonial connection (Hanlon, 1996).

Cabotage is only granted rarely, as it can put home carriers at a disadvantage. Even in the year 2000, Cruise ships that visited Hawaii having left a US West Coast port, such as Los Angeles, had to return to either Mexico or Canada; to return to a US port would have contravened US cabotage law which states that only US flagged vessels (of which there are very few passenger examples) may sail on a voyage that begins and ends in a US port.

Cabotage is, in effect, government protection for its own carriers.

In order to operate a route, an airline must approach the governments concerned for permission. The existing competitors in the particular market may lobby against the granting of a licence. Deregulation, as is being practised in both the USA and Europe, means that licences are granted much more freely, being based on technical and safety considerations rather than commercial ones. Deregulation also includes fares, on which governments used to have considerable say. Deregulation has brought about a number of low cost airlines, some of which have been ephemeral, but others such as easyJet in the UK have grown to operate a considerable route network.

The North Atlantic, dividing as it does the deregulated North American and European airways is, paradoxically, still highly regulated, with licences being very valuable.

In addition to government regulation of routes, airlines are also limited by the number of landing slots they can obtain at an airport. There are a finite number of aircraft movements that can occur in any one day, and just having permission to fly from New York to London does not mean that there will be convenient slots available at London Heathrow. There might, of course, be space at London Gatwick but airlines prefer to fly to a city's major airport wherever possible. Traffic loads increase considerably if Heathrow is used instead of Gatwick – passengers are sometimes perverse!

The North Atlantic Airways are highly competitive. Between the UK and North America, scheduled services are operated by the carriers shown in Figure 5.7.

In addition, there are airlines such as Air India that have freedom rights to pick up and land in London en route from their home base plus the charter operations out to Florida etc. This makes the North Atlantic highly competitive. To show how competitive the North Atlantic is, in April 2001 the following prices were obtained from a booking agency on the Internet and refer to an outward flight on 4 May 2001, returning on 12 May 2001, for one passenger. It was possible to fly from Glasgow to Boston in the USA with Icelandair for £209 plus tax. A major UK carrier was quoting £373 plus tax, and a US carrier £320 plus tax.

At the same time, the quoted price for an internal Glasgow to the Shetland Islands flight was £254, i.e. more than that for the Icelandair flight to the USA. There is more competition on the North Atlantic and thus prices are more competitive.

Airline	Nationality	Notes
British Airways	UK	Routes to USA and Canada
British Midland	UK	Commenced US operation 2001
Virgin	UK	Routes to USA
American	USA	Routes to USA
United	USA	Routes to USA
Continental	USA	London and Glasgow to USA
Northwest	USA	Routes to USA
Delta	USA	Routes to USA
Icelandair	Iceland	London and Glasgow via Iceland to USA and Canada
Air Canada	Canada	Routes to Canada
Canadian	Canada	Routes to Canada
Canada 3000	Canada	Routes to Canada

Figure 5.7 Scheduled airlines, UK–North America.

Were the passenger to require business class, Icelandair were very competitive, charging a minimum of £1,060 compared with £3,243 and £2,430 for the British and US carriers respectively. Icelandair admit that its business class is inferior to that of many competitors and that this as an area where it can make major improvements.

It must be stressed that these are prices quoted off the Supranet website and that shopping around might produce a considerable difference, as would different travel dates etc. However, the example illustrates, firstly the relative cheapness of North Atlantic flights compared to domestic ones, secondly the ability of Icelandair to offer a competitive service, and thirdly the premium paid for business class.

The importance of these premium passengers is seen from the example below of an Icelandair 757 fully loaded at the prices quoted above:

		% of capacity	% of revenue
Economy class revenue:	£ 209 × 178 = £37,202	89	55
Business class revenue:	£1,060 × 22 = £23,320	11	45

Thus whilst business class is only 11% of the aircraft capacity, it can generate 45% of the revenue – hence the importance of business class passengers.

Airlines compete very fiercely in all aspects bar one, and that is safety. Safety information is routinely passed between competitors.

The current trend, as covered earlier in the chapter, is for there to be increasing co-operation between air carriers through the growth of strategic alliances.

Summary

Competition, whilst often considered to be part of the private sector, exists in fact throughout the business world. The public and voluntary sectors are just as prone to competitive forces as are the private sector organisations. Monopolies are highly regulated in the contemporary business world but still have their place. More common are duopolies and oligopolies. The balance between a cartel and a strategic alliance may be delicate, and the latter also involves the sharing of proprietary information as the price to be paid for sharing financial risk. Michael Porter's work on competitive forces (as adapted by Cartwright and Green, 1997) provides a useful means of describing the means by which markets are entered (and left), organisations compete with each other, and customers and suppliers demonstrate their bargaining muscle.

Not only must organisations analyse their own operations, they need also to analyse those of competitors to establish the position of their respective places within the market.

The customer accumulator demonstrates the effects of losing customers to competitors and the implications this has for respective market shares.

Competition and anti-competitive practices are regulated by governments and by the EU for member states.

QUESTIONS

1 Explain the competitive forces acting on a market. Why might it be easier to enter some markets than others?
2 'Monopolies are not always a bad thing for the consumer'. Discuss this statement using examples showing where a monopoly might or might not be appropriate.
3 Explain the importance of the customer accumulator in considering competition and customer behaviour.

Recommended reading

The work of Michael Porter cannot be too highly recommended. His *Competitive Advantage* (1980), *Competitive Strategy* (1985) and *On Competition* (1996) will provide useful additional information. Also see *Strategic Alliances* by Lorange and Roos (1992).

Useful website

www.poprincesscruis.com   P&O/Princess website

▪ ⅴ   **Part Two**

Product/customer value

Part One of the marketing mix is concerned with the nature of the product or service itself and the value placed upon it by the customer.

Part Two of marketing management is concerned with the motivation of customers, i.e. their needs and wants, the nature of the product itself and also such intangibles as service, the life cycle of the product or service, and the behaviour of the customer.

If an organisation is to be successful, it is self-evident that it must provide the products and services that its customer base (and potential customer base) needs, wants and considers to be beneficial and of value.

ᵛ 6 Needs and wants

Needs and wants – Motivation – Maslow's hierarchy – Lower, middle, higher level needs – Primary, secondary, tertiary needs – Facilitory needs – Herzberg's motivators and hygiene factors – Customers, definitions of – Lifestyle and motivation – Counterfeits and fakes – Vroom's theory of motivation – Value expectation – AIDA – Evaluation – Grudge purchases

In Chapter 1 the marketing mix was introduced and Part Two of this book (Chapters 6–9) covers the product/customer value component of the marketing mix.

To commence the study it is first necessary to consider the differences between needs and wants – two concepts that are frequently confused and sometimes treated as synonymous which they are not; in fact, there is a very fundamental difference between them that is crucial to the effective marketing of a product or service.

A *need* is something that we cannot do without; a *want* is the method by which we would like the need to be satisfied. In many ways a want can be described as a need with added value. As humans, we cannot do without an intake of so many calories per day supplemented by vitamins, roughage etc. Our want is the type of food we decide to eat when we have a choice. The need for calories has nothing to do with taste – it is a basic requirement for chemicals and energy. For somebody living in a remote area, communications may be a need; the latest mobile telephone technology, however, is a want if a basic two-way radio could fulfil the necessary communications' need.

Abraham Maslow (1970) is one of the most important writers in the field of motivation. He suggested that needs were hierarchical in nature and that a need can only be truly satisfied when the lower level ones have been dealt with to the satisfaction of the individual.

Maslow proposed that human beings have five levels of needs, as shown in Figure 6.1.

Maslow's concept was that humans (and other animals) would put physiological needs, food, water etc., before safety, which come before belonging etc. Esteem needs are only met when the needs up to and including belonging have been satisfied, and self-actualisation only becomes a motivator when all other needs have been fulfilled. The Maslow model has some inconsistencies; it fails to explain how an artist or poet can starve in an attic whilst working on their masterpiece – the model postulates that such self-actualisation should not take precedent over physiological needs. Food should take precedence over creativity

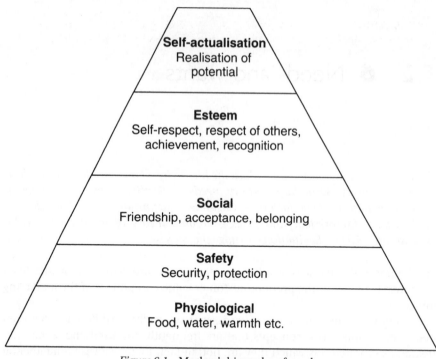

Figure 6.1 Maslow's hierarchy of needs.

but all too often, in humans, it does not and thus leads to the image of the writer starving in a garret. Maslow's concept does, however, explain the risks that animals will take to obtain food and water even in the face of apparent danger. A human equivalent is that of sailors who have been shipwrecked and have taken to the lifeboats, drinking seawater that they are well aware can be fatal – basically because the need for water (physiological) overrides that for safety.

Maslow's hierarchy is useful in that it allows us to distinguish between levels of needs. In respect of human beings, physiological and safety factors can be described as *lower level* or *basic* needs, belonging as a *middle level* need, and esteem and self-actualisation as *higher level* needs. It may well be that these are unique to humans. The role of any supplier of goods or services is *at a minimum* to satisfy the respective need. Unless the basic need is satisfied, then it is very unlikely that there will be any possibility of repeat business.

Thus a baker, in selling bread in a village outlet, is satisfying the lowest or most basic need – a staple food. Whilst bread may seem a mundane, everyday product, it receives many mentions in religious texts testifying to its importance as not only a food but a symbol of basic human needs, and bread has achieved political significance when its price has risen and rioting has broken out! The function of bread as a food is the *primary* need that the baker fulfils.

There is also a need to be able to purchase the bread in safety and convenience, which can be described as a *secondary* need, and a baker (and any other retailer) should ensure that their shop is attractive and that the purchaser feels safe,

MOTIVATORS, presence of which leads to satisfaction	HYGIENE FACTORS, absence of which leads to dissatisfaction
Achievement Recognition Work issues Responsibility Advancement Growth	Policy and administration Supervision Relationships Work environment Salary Personal life Status Security

Figure 6.2 Summary of Herzberg's findings.

secure and comfortable in it. Later in this book there will be a consideration of the effects of quality, price, convenience etc., but for the moment take some time to consider whether a purchaser will be more motivated to buy bread that is more expensive at a place that is perceived as being safer or more convenient (in this context it would be fair to consider that having to undertake a vehicle journey might entail more risks to one's safety than walking around the corner), than one where the bread is much cheaper.

Given that man is a social animal, there might also be a *tertiary* need of some recognition of belonging (see the consideration of Maslow's work earlier in this chapter). Physiologists are beginning to recognise that there is a social as well as a commercial aspect to shopping. 'Shopping therapy' may have started as a gag from comedians but it is possible that there is a serious side to the concept. Despite the growth in on-line shopping, it appears that many people enjoy the social interactions that occur when out visiting the shops and that such interactions may form part of the motivation in undertaking a shopping trip.

Herzberg (1962), writing in the context of work, concluded that there were factors which led to satisfaction and thus motivated people, he termed these *motivators*, and those which did not motivate but led to dissatisfaction and thus demotivation, which he named *hygiene factors*. His results are summarised in Figure 6.2.

His research showed that recognition and achievement are important motivators and, whilst Herzberg was primarily concerned with motivation at work, there are important lessons for those concerned with marketing. Achievement and recognition can be considered both from the point of view of the customer who may receive satisfaction from the achievement of an excellent product or service – after all, it is their buying decision that has acquired the product/service and they can take satisfaction in their good choice! It is a rare customer who does not relish recognition. Even the simple use of the customer's name during a transaction can lead to considerable satisfaction. The person delivering the product or service to the customer should be more motivated when a satisfactory transaction is concluded than when there is dissatisfaction. It is an axiom in the field of customer relations that recognition of good service nearly always reinforces that service.

Among certain customer groups, especially at the younger end of the age range, the recognition that members gain from others in their peer group may well be related to the fashions they wear and even the artefacts that they use. Peer pressure can be a very strong motivator. Peer pressure is often seen as a bad influence and in the case of drugs, alcohol etc. it most certainly is. Hence there is an ethical issue for marketers to be aware of. The success of many of the Christmas toys sold each year may well be due to the peer pressure to acquire them, linked as it is to the recognition that the owner receives. The need that is being satisfied in this example is not that for play (an important need in young animals throughout the world of nature) but of recognition through owning a particular artefact.

The effects of fashion on the product life cycle will be discussed in Chapter 8, suffice to say that fashion can change a want into a need by its effect on an individual's standing and recognition within his or her peer group.

Based on the above, a customer can be defined in simple terms as:

One for whom a need is satisfied

It should also be obvious from what has gone before that needs are very basic, and it is wants that grow in importance once basic needs are satisfied.

Unfortunately, many people believe that the definition above is enough and that all that is required is to satisfy a customer's needs. If an organisation only wants to see the customer once, this may be true; but most organisations want to retain their customers, repeat business being a very important indicator of success.

If a person is starving, a meal, any meal, will suffice to satisfy their basic physiological need for food – a low-level primary need. Once the means (usually money) exist to choose how the need is satisfied, then it is wants that are important: 'I need breakfast, I want bacon and eggs, toast and coffee!'

It used to be thought that customers had to be satisfied in order for a transaction to be successful but in today's competitive world satisfaction is not enough – in order to retain customers they need to be delighted. Needs can be satisfied but to delight a customer it is necessary to understand their wants. It is delighting customers that makes them much more likely to return with their repeat business, and for them to recommend the organisation and its products/services to friends, relations and colleagues.

In modern society basic needs are satisfied using money, and money has to be eared, giving rise to what may be termed a *facilitory* need.

In order to earn money, large numbers of people *need* to travel to work (they have little or no choice) and thus transportation is a facilitory need in order to fulfil basic needs. One of the major changes in UK society over the past 200 years has been in the effects of improved transportation links that have enabled workers to live further and further from their employment. In 1800, people lived right next to where they worked. By 1900, tramways and suburban railways had allowed the better off at least to live some distance from work. By 2000, it was not that unusual to meet people who commuted from York to London. Transportation is thus a very important need in the lives of most people. An individual's preferences for transportation modes forms their wants; they may want a motor car or, for environmental or cost reason, prefer to travel on public transport. Put succinctly, they do not need a motor car but they do need transportation in order to gain the money to fulfil the basic needs of food and shelter etc.

Given all of the above, a customer can be more accurately described as:

──────

One for whom a need is satisfied and who the organisation delights in respect of their wants

In the developed world, many, indeed perhaps a majority, of the population will pay scant attention to needs but will concentrate on their wants. It is only when disaster strikes that we become aware of the difference and needs become very clear indeed.

Lifestyle and motivation

Lifestyle is a very important method of describing the position of an individual within a particular society and is of great importance to those involved in the marketing process. Attached to a particular lifestyle are the artefacts and behaviour that distinguish that lifestyle from another. Whilst it may be perceived that some lifestyles are better than others, experience suggests that quality of life produced by certain lifestyles may be much more satisfying in the long-term than a lifestyle that may produce wealth etc. but contains little quality in other respects.

For most people there is the lifestyle that they actually have and the lifestyle that they aspire to. In much of the world the difference between the two is in the artefacts etc. possessed and thus can be measured in terms of wealth. There is a perception that greater wealth will lead to a better lifestyle. In some cases this is true but, as many of the winners of lotteries around the world have found, increased wealth does not always bring true happiness.

A great deal of advertising is based on the projection of a type of lifestyle attached to a product or service, and operates by creating firstly a want in the recipient for that lifestyle and then a belief that the want can be met by acquiring the product or service. It speaks volumes for the gullibility of many that they continue to be taken in by these advertising ploys (a theme to be continued in Chapter 12). More and more there is a perception that possessions define who we are. Note the use of the word 'perception', as we are dealing with beliefs and feelings and not facts in this instance. Perhaps there becomes a point in life or wealth when it is no longer necessary to 'show off' but many people seem to take a long time to reach that stage, if in fact they ever do. Observation and experience suggest that very few people, having bought the latest model car, put it straight into their garage – it often spends some time on the driveway where the neighbours can see it!

Many of the products and services that people acquire have a lifestyle component in addition to their tangible value. A particular car may be chosen over similar models because of the image attached to it. The need for young people to have a particular brand for their clothes etc. is also connected to lifestyle and the need to belong to a particular peer group.

One of the more disturbing retail phenomena of recent years has been the growing number of counterfeit items on sale. In the UK, counterfeit items such as clothes, perfumes, software (especially games), CDs and watches can be found openly in markets throughout the country. Trading Standards Officers and, of course, the manufacturers of the genuine products are rightly concerned at this growth. In effect it raises the price of genuine articles for the law-abiding majority and can cause a distrust of the genuine products if the fakes are of low quality, as they often are. Nevertheless, there is growing evidence that many of those who buy a fake are well aware that it is not the genuine article. Apparently it is not necessary to own the genuine product, only for others to think that you have done, as demonstrated below. In the context of this book it is a fact that it is the name or brand attached to the product that is often the reason for buying the fake. In December 2000, a UK television company interviewed buyers of certain counterfeit items. What was surprising was that the majority of these people knew that they were paying for low-quality fakes but they wanted the name as it said things about their apparent lifestyle! This is an issue that is picked up again in Chapter 7. The author has often considered that one of the saddest things that could happen to the buyer of a counterfeit watch is being mugged for it in the street!

Vroom's expectancy theory of motivation

One of the major theories of motivation is that proposed by Vroom (1964) and commonly known as *expectancy theory*. Vroom's concept was that the perceptions that effort will lead to effective performance, that effective performance will lead to rewards and that such awards are available, produce a motivational effort on the part of an individual, this effort leads to performance, and the performance to some form of reward. Achieving the award starts a feedback loop in that it reinforces the original perceptions. From Vroom's ideas it is possible to develop the concept of value expectation, covered below.

Value expectation

Based on the ideas of Vroom (see above), the concept of value expectation, first introduced by Cartwright (2000) in *Mastering Customer Relations*, uses the model shown in Figure 6.3.

The model is based upon four basic perceptions held by the customer. The first is a widely held one that has some, but not a complete basis in experience, namely that there is a direct relationship between price and quality, an issue to be explored in Chapter 11. In many cases the higher the price, the more likelihood there is of higher quality. There are, however, many exceptions and indeed this is what often leads to customer dissatisfaction.

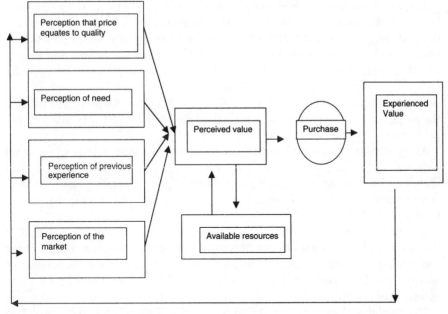

Figure 6.3 Value expectation.

The second perception is based around the strength of the customer's need (or want) as discussed earlier for the particular product or service. Highly felt need will tend to enhance the 'value' of the product in the customer's mind.

Thirdly, there are the perceptions gained from previous experiences. If they have been bad, then there may be an expectation of dissatisfaction. An excellent previous product or service from the same supplier will lead to an expectation of quality. This is important to the discussion of consistency in Chapter 11. What has happened in the past is of considerable importance when considering motivation, as it is the only objective thing that an individual has to gauge what will happen in the present and thus, by definition, becomes a predictor of future events. If the present differs from the past, then future predictions will also become changed.

Lastly, there is the perception of the customer in regard to the market. How well does the customer know the alternative products, services, suppliers etc.? Some customers will have a wide knowledge of the market that they can bring to bear on their deliberations, others may be completely new to the market and have only the perceptions of others to assist them. The experience of the friends and colleagues of a customer are very important. The problem with a dissatisfied customer is not only that he or she never returns, but that they also tell their friends, relations and colleagues. It has been suggested that for every ten customers who say something positive about a product, service or organisations, there are twenty five who will put forward negative points. Put simply, customers are far more ready to tell people about disasters than triumphs!

These four perceptions feed into an overall perception of value. If the customer has a good idea of the true relationship between price and value, i.e. they understand that prices are based on costs (see Chapter 10), and if they have a high level of need, good previous experiences and know the market and what is on offer, then there will be the likelihood of a high perceived value. The opposite could also apply; bad previous experiences, ambivalent need, and lack of understanding of both the market and prices can lead to a low perceived value. If the perceived value is equal to or greater than the available resource to match the price, then a buying decision is likely.

After experience of the product or service, the customer is able to make an objective judgement of the actual value to them of their purchase. This can then feed back to inform revised perceptions of price v. quality. There are new experiences, a measure of need fulfilment and enhanced knowledge of the marketplace.

The model provides a theoretical underpinning of the concept of a 'free trial'. If the customer is able to experience the product before making an actual purchase then their perception of value will be much more objective, and if the product or service is in fact value for money (VFM), then the customer will be far more willing to part with cash.

The model also emphasises the importance of individual perceptions. Two people experiencing the same product or service at the same time may have very different perceptions of the value. This is one of the great problems of customer relations – each customer is an individual as emphasised by the Disney Corporation in its training.

A partial answer to the problem lies in ensuring that an organisation listens to and understands where its customers are coming from and what their expectations, needs and wants actually are.

AIDA

AIDA is an important concept in marketing, standing for: **Attention**, **Interest**, **Desire** and **Action**. These are the four key processes that a potential customer goes through. As will be pointed out below, without some form of feedback the process cannot be deemed complete, and thus this book will talk about the AIDA loop to represent the fact that after action comes evaluation, and this feeds the continuation of the process.

Advertising and its impact on organisations and customers are discussed in Chapter 12 but, suffice to say, one of the main reasons for advertising is to draw the attention of a potential customer to a product or service, and then to convince that customer to take action to acquire the product/service. The AIDA loop is the process that the customer goes through from attention to action.

Attention

We are bombarded by organisations wishing to gain our attention. At the back of the brain is a network of cells known as the reticulatory activating system, and these cells act as a form of gatekeeper to the information we receive from the outside world. You may be aware of the so-called 'cocktail party effect'. You are standing in a room, crowded with jabbering people. You can hardly hear yourself speak. At the other end of the room somebody says your name to a colleague. Despite the noise, your ears prick up because you have heard your name mentioned. Our name is one of the most distinguishing things about us and, despite filtering out much of the noise as irrelevant, our brain will normally let such highly personalised pieces of information through. The cells act so as to pass through information that may be important to us but to restrict extraneous information so that our brain does not suffer from information overload.

Other examples of this phenomenon in action occur when you buy a new red Ford car and on driving it home discover that the road is full of red Fords, just like yours. Of course, there are no more or no less than there were before but at that moment in time red Ford is important to you so you not only see the other cars but your brain registers their presence as important. People who have put their house up for sale have reported that, as if by magic, there suddenly seem to be more for-sale signs in their area – of course, there are no more, they have just begun to notice them.

There are a number of methods of obtaining the attention of a potential customer. One is to do something unexpected. An advertisement printed upside down on a page will present a visual disparity that is likely to catch the attention of the reader, especially if there are other, normally aligned advertisements also in view. Even using bold headlines or outrageous words may have the same effect. More than one supplier has used **SEX** in bold letters followed by: 'now you are reading this . . .', to get the attention of potential customers.

Another ploy that has come into vogue is to run advertisements, especially those on television as a form of soap opera. The UK 'Gold Blend' couple captured imaginations in the late 1990s, using advertisements that featured a growing romantic attachment linked to a particular coffee brand; the times when the advertisements would be shown on television were actually advertised in the media! This was an interesting reversal of the phrase 'soap opera', as the original versions of the genre were so called on their introduction in post-war USA because they were invariably sponsored by washing powder manufacturers.

The pre-advertisement of an advertisement mentioned above serves to sensitise the customer and to build up anticipation. As will be covered in Chapter 12, there is a danger that such sophisticated methods of gaining attention will not just boost the intended product or service but may in fact boost the whole of the sector. It has been suggested that very sophisticated advertisements are remembered more for the generic product than the actual brand and thus boost competitor's sales as well – a result not always to be desired.

Humour and music also form an important method of gaining attention. Evocative music can stop people in their tracks, and jokes are nearly always appreciated.

Icelandair used a slogan of 'Avoid the English' for some of its advertising for Glasgow-based services. Whilst this gained attention, it also caused some offence and it is important that attention does not become negative. Not everybody who lives in Scotland is Scottish by origin; for example, there are many who were actually born in England and to whom such a slogan might imply that the company did not want their business.

Attention on its own is pointless as attention spans can be very short. Attention should lead to the next stage – interest.

Interest

Even a loud noise will attract attention but unless the hearer is in danger etc., the attention will soon diminish. What those responsible for marketing must ensure is that they follow up the initial attention with a sustainable interest.

People tend to be interested in things that meet their needs and wants. The importance of market research, as covered in Chapter 4, and understanding the customer cannot be understated. A knowledge of the behaviour and motivation of the current and potential customer base is what can ensure that marketers sustain interest.

There are three basic types of customer:

1. current customers;
2. potential customers;
3. ex-customers.

Most organisations have data relating to 1 and 3 above. They know who is currently using their products and services, and they should have data on who was but no longer is a customer. They should also have investigated why the latter are ex-customers. It may be because of a quality issue, but it may be price related or even because the organisation has lost their interest. As the customer accumulator covered earlier in this book suggests, one organisation's ex-customer may well be a competitor's current customer.

As regards potential customers, there are two major sub-types:

• already in the market;
• not in the market.

Potential customers already in the market are likely to be the customers of a competitor and can be wooed by better prices, service and quality. Those not already in the market may not know they have a want.

For example, in the late 1990s the commercial facsimile (fax machine) market in the UK was becoming saturated (see Chapter 8). Chapter 8 will use the fax machine as an example of a product that experienced very rapid growth, being almost unknown in the 1980s and an everyday part of business life in the 1990s.

There was, however, a potential market that did not realise that it was in need of the technology – the domestic market. This comprised individuals who used the fax at work and who, by the production of domestic versions (usually combining telephone and fax), were persuaded that a home fax could be a boon. Thus fax machines are now sold in retail outlets that deal mainly with a domestic as opposed to a commercial market. The whole personal computer market is also an example of this unknowing potential market, as the early computer firms did not believe that there would be any domestic applications. It was the minority who saw the huge potential of home computers who reaped the early benefits, mainly by using the game-playing and homework assistance applications of computers to appeal to parents.

Most loyalty schemes, whether plastic-card-based or the membership of an 'exclusive' customer club, work by essentially keeping the customer's interest in the organisation and its products/services by firstly stressing the individual nature of the relationship between the supplier and the customer, and secondly by providing special offers, often exclusive to those in the loyalty club (see Chapter 9).

Interest on its own does not produce business. All customers have competing demands for their income, especially the disposable component. For interest to be translated into acquisition, it is necessary for the product or service to show that it can overcome the opportunity cost.

Opportunity costs relate to those things that a customer must forgo in order to acquire a particular product or service. The vast majority of people have only a finite amount of money or time available at any moment. That money or time will have conflicting demands placed upon it. A person may be interested in purchasing a new washing machine, refrigerator or a holiday, but has only the resources for one. If they choose the washing machine then the opportunity cost of that decision will be a refrigerator and a holiday. Time is also an opportunity cost. One can only use the same money once and one can only use a block of time once so, strange as it may seem, money and time are very similar – they can only be spent once and furthermore it is difficult although not impossible to earn more time. A family may have the choice on a particular day of a trip to the seaside or the shopping mall. If they choose the shopping mall then the opportunity cost is a trip to the seaside. Time can be used to acquire more money. A member of the family in the previous example may decide not to go on the trip and to earn overtime, in which case the seaside and the shopping mall trips are the opportunity costs for the extra income.

For all the products that are interesting a customer there will be opportunity costs, and it is desire that overcomes opportunity costs.

Desire

Psychologically, when we desire something our brain goes into overdrive to obtain it. The object of advertisers is to raise desire in their potential customers. Desires play on the mind. It is almost as though our minds believe that we already have the product or service but just cannot lay our hands on it, leading to a degree of frustration. Frustration is relieved when the desire no longer exists; i.e. one of two things has happened, we either possess what is causing the desire or we no longer want it. An advertiser for most products and services will want the former to occur. Desires are more equated to needs than wants as the fulfilment of a desire becomes a psychological necessity. The purveyors of tobacco and other addictive substances are well aware of this. Nicotine is addictive and the craving for it is not a want but a need that must be fulfilled, otherwise physiological symptoms occur. Hence the increase in sales of nicotine replacement products for those attempting to give up smoking. It has been suggested that the earliest versions of Coca-Cola (first produced in Atlanta, Georgia by Dr Pemberton in 1885) contained traces of cocaine. If this were true, then the drink would have been addictive. It is recorded that Dr Pemberton was a morphine addict. An analysis of Coca-Cola in 1903 showed that by then there was certainly no cocaine present, and it certainly has not contained any since – it is just one of the world's most (if not the) popular soft drinks. The full story of Coca-Cola, including the cocaine rumour, is contained in the highly readable *For God, County and Coca-Cola* by Mark Pendergrast (2000).

Even a pair of training shoes can become a desire if the ownership of the right brand can lead to acceptance in a desired peer group.

The desire for products or services can be a major problem when the resources to acquire them are not available. Such situations can lead to criminal acts to obtain the necessary resources. Fortunately the vast majority of people either forgo another desire or save up to obtain that which they desire. Desire plus the required resources usually lead to action, i.e. a purchasing decision.

Action

As stated above, desire plus the required resource should lead to the action of acquisition. The likelihood of this is also a function of how easy and convenient it is for the potential, or perhaps by this stage proto-customer, to acquire the product. The term 'proto-customer' is introduced here to indicate that this is somebody who has already made the acquisition decision but has not yet physically carried out the final actions. In some cases this may be irrelevant, as it is only the purchasing channel (see Chapter 16) that is at issue. What the customer has not decided is which shop etc. to use, and for retailers there will then be a separate AIDA loop to go through. The customer is going to buy a particular product or service (and thus the supplier of that to the retail sector has more or less done the business) but is undecided how and where to do it.

The importance of distribution channels and payment methods etc. forms the basis for Chapter 13 of this book.

Evaluation

Very few products or services last for ever, and sooner or later the customer may require replacement or enhancements. Even if they do not, they have friends, relations and colleagues that they talk to and these are all potential customers. The importance of repeat business as a key business indicator is widely understood, and depends on the product or service being of the right quality and meeting the needs of the customer.

If, on evaluation, needs are not met or quality is low, the next time attention is called the customer will not listen and will thus not move to the interest etc. stages. Neither will those they have talked to. Indeed, drawing attention to the product, service or even the supplying organisation will have a negative effect, as it will raise memories of negative comments made and thus interest etc. will not follow. There is also the danger that there may still be an interest but that it will be progressed using another supplier. There is nothing more galling for an organisation than to do all the work and expend resources on gaining attention and interest, developing desire and then to see the action benefiting a competitor.

Grudge purchases

It is easy to consider customer relations in terms of the products and services customers actually enjoy – motor cars, clothes, holidays etc. – as these are most definitely wants. Much has been made of repeat business as an indicator of success. Not all organisations however wish to use repeat business as an indicator. Surgeons do not want the patient back, and the police have an actual reduction in repeat business as an indicator. All of society needs hospitals and police stations, but they are not something that individuals actively want to partake in unless as employees. It is, therefore, more problematic to consider those products and services that people actually need but begrudge paying for – products and services known as grudge products and services. Insurance products are classic examples of grudge purchases. They are necessary but the costs are often resented. Indeed, if somebody has to claim on an insurance policy it is because something has gone terribly wrong. Hospital and dental treatment are other examples of grudge purchases, as are home maintenance and essential public services such as prisons and the police force.

It might also be considered that undertakers fall into this category. Despite the fact that everybody will need their services one day, few wish to acknowledge it. Astute marketing by the funeral industry has managed to convince a growing number of people to pre-pay for their own funeral; perhaps this is the ultimate grudge purchase! Such a purchase is 'sold' by referring to its benefits, such as the lack of problems for those relatives having to organise the funeral. By stressing such benefits, the industry has been able to represent pre-payment of funerals as a responsible caring act.

Even where payment is not direct and the services are funded through taxation, there may still be a resentment to pay. The managers and staff of many public sector organisations have a much more difficult task in developing a meaningful relationship with their customers, many of whom may be very reluctant partakers of the product or service. Many doctors' surgeries, dental practices and local/national government offices have become much more customer-friendly, with appointments being made where possible to suit patients and clients rather than the organisation. Even politicians have come to realise that they too may be a grudge purchase but that repeat business, in this case in the form of votes, is very important to them.

It is obvious that the strategies that organisations offering grudge purchases and services need to employ, in many cases to avoid repeat business, will be different from those used by the vast majority of organisations which see repeat business as an important performance indicator. Such organisations have to stress the benefits to the potential customer, and in many cases to his or her family, of such factors as lifestyle changes.

Whilst this book does not intend to be a treatise on selling, those involved with sales make the point that it is important to sell benefits, not products. Even grudge purchases have benefits. Insurance can ease worries, life assurance can allow a person to look after his or her loved ones, and dental care can ensure fewer fillings etc. By concentrating on the benefits, a customer can be convinced of the importance of what is in fact a grudge purchase.

 The passengers on a typical Iceland flight out of Glasgow will have a number of motivations for being on board. Some will have had no choice in the airline they are using, either being booked on that particular flight by their organisation or as part of a vacation package.

The passengers tend to fall into three distinct types:

- business passengers;
- personal passengers;
- tourist passengers.

The passengers also have a series of different objectives. This is illustrated by considering the objectives of passengers interviewed on a particular flight in October 2000. On board the flight were passengers who were:

- British and travelling to Iceland on business;
- British and travelling to the USA and Canada on business;
- Icelandic and travelling back home from the UK;
- British and travelling to Iceland on vacation;
- British and travelling to the USA and Canada on vacation;
- Icelandic and travelling back home from a UK vacation;
- British and travelling to the USA and Canada for personal and family reasons;
- US and Canadian travelling home after business;
- US and Canadian travelling home after a vacation.

The benefits are different for each group. For those on package tours the benefits may be to the organisers through the price discounts offered by the airline. For business travellers it may be a benefit of cost or the avoidance of the transfer at Heathrow. Many Icelanders use the service to access the shops in Glasgow (the second most rated shopping centre in the UK after London).

Those travelling on family business are likely to be attracted by the price. Those vacationing in Iceland will find that the seamless web of the Icelandair service, especially at Keflavik, is a considerable benefit.

For all travelling from Scotland there is a psychological benefit of the journey being in the right direction, i.e. not having to fly south to London in order to fly west to North America.

Icelandair thus have customers with considerably different motivational needs and wants all on the same aircraft. Those wishing for enhanced service can book into business class but the majority will be together in economy. One of the roles of the cabin crew is to meet the needs of the various types by ensuring that their motivation is understood and that the correct assistance is anticipated and offered.

Advertising needs to be such as to appeal to the greatest number of groups at the same time. The main benefit that Icelandair can offer is the convenience of Glasgow, the ease of transfer at Keflavik and the price.

There may well be a number of grudge purchasers on board, either those who do wish to travel (perhaps to a difficult meeting) and those who are afraid of flying. Airlines are very aware of the latter and many now offer special courses to conquer fear of flying and allow nervous passengers to board first and make themselves comfortable with extra special attention from the cabin crew.

Summary

The motivation of customers is a very important facet of marketing management. Needs and wants are not the same and should be treated differently. Motivational concepts, such as those developed by Maslow, Herzberg and Vroom, are important tools in marketing as is the concept of value expectation. The AIDA loop – attention, interest, desire, action – followed by evaluation is an important component of customer behaviour and needs to be considered by those involved in managing the marketing process. Not all products and services are pleasant. Grudge purchases may not be exciting but they are important and need to be marketed.

QUESTIONS

1 Using practical examples, show the difference between needs and wants and why an understanding of this difference can be important to marketing.
2 Using examples of products and services you are familiar with, describe the application of the AIDA loop and its relevance to the marketing process.
3 What do you understand by the term 'grudge' purchases, and how are they different from other products and services offered to customers?
4 How are lifestyle and motivation linked? Why is lifestyle so important a concept to those involved in marketing?

Recommended reading

Useful additional information to support this chapter will be found in *Introduction to Management* by Richard Pettinger (1994), where there is a useful discussion on motivational theories.

Useful website

www.cocacola.com   Coca-Cola website

■ ☑ **7** Understanding the product

Core and supplementary products – Categories of products – Perishable goods –
Merchandising – Service as the prime supplementary – Typologies of service culture
– Pre-sales and after sales service – Consistency of service – Unique Selling Points
(USPs) – Patents and product protection – Branding – Generic branding – Badge
engineering – Product development – Technology and design

Core and supplementary products

Whilst manufacturers and suppliers are interested in the actual product or
service, customers are concerned more with the benefits of the product or service
and how it will meet their needs and wants, as discussed in the previous chapter.
It is benefits that actually sell a product/service, as in the majority of cases a
customer purchases a product/service not for what it is but for what it can do for
them, i.e. the benefit.

In the previous chapter the difference between needs and wants was
considered. Most products consist of two components: a core product that is
designed to meet need requirements, and often supplementary products that
concentrate on the want element. This chapter explores the nature of the core
and supplementary product, goes on to consider the importance of branding
within the marketing function, and finishes with an introduction to product
development. Whilst the phrase product/service is used frequently throughout
this book to aid understanding, it must be restressed that, in the author's opinion,
there is really no difference in marketing terms between a product and a service.
In this and later chapters, service is only considered as a separate concept when
used in the context of the standard of service offered to the customer, an
important use of the word in the context of business.

The life cycle of products, from inception to decline and beyond, forms the
basis of the next chapter.

Most modern private motor vehicles are basically very similar. Any car
purchased in the UK should be of acceptable quality and fit for the purpose for
which it was intended. Indeed, that is an important tenet of the sale and supply
of goods and services legislation enacted by the UK parliament over many years.
Consumer protection throughout most of the world has increased in recent years,
so the basic quality of products has followed suit and in most jurisdictions there
is legislation to ensure that all products provide minimum customer satisfaction
in respect of safety, durability, fitness for purpose etc. Thus what has become

important is going beyond mere satisfaction and actually delighting the customer.

Many of the cars sold look very similar. Where there are differences is in the supplementary products that are attached to the basic core product. For a modern vehicle these include power steering (rapidly becoming part of the core product), extra safety features, air conditioning, the sound system etc., and of increasing importance the after sales service offered. More and more buying decisions are being based on these supplementary components, especially service. It is no use if a customer acquires the car of their dreams if the dealer cannot look after them for what may be a number of years after the original purchase. Indeed, it would not be in the interest of dealers in a competitive marketplace to offer anything less than excellent after sales service, as they will wish the customer to buy another of their vehicles in the future, and the importance of repeat business has already been stressed. It is also in their interest to ensure that the friends, relations and colleagues of the customer only hear positive comments about the new vehicle, as they may well be potential customers.

Some marketing authorities distinguish between tangible products and intangible services. A motor car is obviously a tangible thing, as are washing machines, computers etc. Insurance and health are intangible – we know that they exist but we cannot touch them in the same way as that which is tangible can be touched. However, in the terms of this book, they are both 'goods' in the sense of the word as used by economists. Service, as a separate concept, relates to the ambience that surrounds the acquisition and use of the product, and forms an important component of the concept of a supplementary product.

In general terms, one can distinguish between:

- durable goods that last for a considerable period of time before replacement – examples range from ocean liners through to CD players;
- non-durable goods that have a very short lifespan and need regular replacement, for example food stuffs, washing powders, fuel etc.;
- services which are non-tangible goods.

It is also possible to distinguish between products for the commercial/industrial market and those for the domestic one. The former, which can range from industrial plant to stationery, may have less concern paid to presentation/ packaging etc. than the latter although, as for all products, quality should be high. The modes of purchase and servicing however may well be very different.

Those products in the domestic market are often referred to as consumer goods and can be divided into four main categories (Phipps and Simmons, 1995), as follows:

Convenience goods

These are mainly non-durable goods purchased at regular intervals and include food, toilet paper etc. They can be further divided into: **staple goods**, i.e. bread, butter, day-to-day foods, cleaners etc.; **impulse buys** (to be covered later in this book), for which purchase is not planned but occurs when the customer sees the product on display; and **emergency goods**, such as salt for icy paths etc., which are bought because of a change in the external environment requiring urgent action.

Most products comprise all three components to some degree. Indeed, the concept of planned obsolescence first used in connection with cars made in the Far East showed how a move from durable to less durable could be advantageous. By building in obsolescence after a period of use and by keeping prices low, not only was repeat business generated but also strategic materials were available for recycling. One of the problems with jet aircraft engines that allowed ETOPS (see earlier) to be introduced has been that fewer spares, including spare engines, are sold, because the original product is so durable. Durable products should, in theory, last so long that they remain fashionable. When customers wish to have an up-to-date product, it is a matter of achieving the correct balance between durability and fashion so that they change to another, newer product from the same organisation.

Perishable goods

In marketing terms, 'perishable goods' are not, as one might imagine, foodstuffs that can 'go off' over time, but those products that become worthless if not sold by a certain time. In this respect, certain fresh foods may be termed 'perishable' not only in colloquial but marketing terms. The description also applies, however, for example to a particular performance of a play, to a hotel room over a particular period or to an airline ticket for a specific flight etc. In all these cases, once the play has started or the aircraft has taken off, the product cannot then be sold, i.e. it cannot be put back on the shelf to await another customer. If the aircraft on a Glasgow to Iceland flight leaves with an empty seat, then that seat remains empty and generates no income but incurs the fuel, staff and take-off/landing costs etc. of flying the empty seat.

One feature of perishable goods is that the price charged to the customer often decreases as the last moment to purchase approaches. Students have long realised that supermarkets may well reduce the price of products as they approach their sell-by date. A few days before the sell-by date, the product may be worth £2.00. As the sell-by date approaches, it will be worthwhile for the supplier to drop the price to as low as 50p, because the minute the sell-buy date passes the product will have zero value. The value may actually be negative as to sell it after the sell-by date may result in costs to the organisation in fines and bad publicity. Holidays etc. can often be purchased very cheaply by those who can book late and do not mind the lack of choice.

Products as means and ends

All products are acquired to satisfy a need or want and, as such, facilitate the satisfying of the particular need. Some products however are purely a means of accessing another product. These may be termed **facilitory products**. The products of an Internet Service Provider (ISP) are examples of facilitory products as they exist only to allow the customer to access the Internet. The membership of a book or health club may also be purely to allow the purchaser to access facilities that would otherwise be denied to them. Private health insurance may also fall into this category. As mentioned earlier, all products are facilitory to some degree or other. A motor car allows for personal transport etc. A facilitory product in the context of this book can be defined as a product that exists only to allow access to another product. Credit cards could be considered as an example of facilitory products, as can many forms of education and even the batteries for electronic products. A battery on its own without an appliance to use it in is of little use. People undertake educational courses, in the main, to access new skills, better jobs, career changes etc. There are those, often past retirement age, who access educational programmes (products) purely for the sake of knowledge, but they are a small minority. The providers of facilitory products need to ensure that they understand fully the use to which the product will be put so as to ensure maximum complementation of the end product. Manufacturers of batteries now offer different types of battery for different uses and it is noticeable that more and more products now include a set of batteries within their packaging, so relieving the old Christmas problem of parents buying a toy for their child only to find that a vital facilitory product (the batteries) was not included and it is difficult (but not impossible) to find a shop selling batteries open on Christmas morning. As batteries do not last for ever, even if unused, it may not be possible to include them as an integral part of the packaging, but modern practice is to make sure that the outside of the packaging draws attention to the number and type needed. This is in response to much customer pressure and is a good example of organisations responding to customer needs.

Supplementary products

As alluded to earlier, many buying decisions are based more and more on the supplementary products that surround the core product. To continue with the use of the marketing of motor cars to illustrate and describe marketing activity, it is noticeable that within any particular model there tends to be a range of variants going up in price depending on the extra facilities offered. The core product is the basic model of the vehicle, of which very few may be actually sold or indeed made. In the 1970s, a basic model of a popular vehicle would have had no entertainment system, no wing or door mirrors, little carpeting and possibly no heater. At the start of the 21st century, the basic model of virtually every car sold in the UK had a radio, heater, adjustable door mirrors and full carpeting. In many cases power steering, a luxury in the UK just a few years previously, had become a standard and thus core component. What was extra in the 1970s had become the norm at the end of the 1990s. After sales service had also undergone considerable change to the benefit of the customer. In the 1970s, only the purchasers of very expensive vehicles would have been offered a loan car whilst theirs was being serviced, and coffee machines in garages plus waiting areas with comfortable seats and up-to-date magazines and the day's quality newspapers were almost unknown. Today, this level of service is the expected norm for the vast majority of customers.

Merchandising

The later years of the 20th century saw the growth of a relatively new phenomenon, that of merchandising. As the word has come to be used, merchandising occurs when the supplementary products become at least (if not more important) than the core. In the case of many films, pop records etc., it is the merchandising opportunities for clothing, toys, posters etc. that generate the majority of the income. The core product becomes just the first stage and in effect a means of entry into a particular market segment. In the highly popular ITV series *Popstars* of 2001, in which the formation of the pop group *HearSay* was followed from auditions to first record, it was pointed out that the production of merchandising goods (toys etc.) went on alongside the making of the first records and that the bulk of the income could well come from such activities.

Service as the prime supplementary

As organisations have put the ideas of quality (see Chapter 10) into their cultures, so the products they deliver have moved nearer and nearer to zero defects. There are few consumer items in the Western world that can be differentiated by considerable differences in quality. Defects in new cars are now rare; television sets work first time, computers have very few faults etc. Where companies can differentiate is in the level of service that they deliver. Customers in a free market economy are prepared to pay for good service, and are beginning to see service as moving from a supplementary part of the product to its core.

In discussing the importance of service as an integral part of any product, Clutterbuck *et al.* (1993) describe how organisations can be classified in relation to their actual service standards and their commitment to the delivery of outstanding service. Their organisational typology is as follows:

Naturals

In a 'natural' (as regards customer relations) company, excellent service is embedded into the total philosophy and culture of the company. In many instances this can be traced back to the founder(s) of the organisation who will have set the initial credo and thus standards for the organisation. There is no doubt that the influence of the founder can last for many organisational generations after their demise. Perhaps because they are known for their excellent customer relations, these companies tend to attract, as employees, those who share the customer first philosophy. If service declines, then word will spread rapidly throughout the company and staff will take immediate action, often unofficially in the first instance. Such companies do not need to spend vast sums setting up customer service initiatives, they already form part of the operating procedures, but they do need to ensure that the momentum of continuous improvement is maintained. As such, they are hard to compete against as they are constantly improving the level and standard of service offered.

Aspirants

Aspirant organisations have a keen desire to become naturals and share many of the same characteristics of excellent service and flexibility. Clutterbuck and his colleagues believe that the difference between the two is that aspirants talk more about service but perhaps deliver less, whilst naturals don't talk much about service but are renowned for their delivery. Customers soon discover whether their supplier is just talk or is actually doing something about delivering high levels of service.

Followers

Clutterbuck *et al.* describe followers as organisations that are being forced to adopt a customer-centred approach against the will of the workforce, normally because there has been a lack of communication from higher up the organisation. Top management may well believe in the concepts but these are rarely communicated downward. Clutterbuck *et al.* note that such organisations frequently embark upon costly customer care campaigns because of insistence by their larger customers, and not because of a deeply held belief in a service-oriented philosophy.

It may seem strange that any organisation could undertake customer care unwillingly, but it is unfortunately the case that there are many product-driven organisations still in the marketplace. Anybody who doubts this should consult the consumer advice pages of national newspapers or the television programmes dealing in customer complaints; some of the stories would be farcical if they were not, unfortunately, true. It is often illuminating to see and hear a senior manager defending the indefensible when it comes to poor service. It is perhaps high time that such organisations realised that admitting mistakes is more likely to regain consumer confidence than employing so-called 'spin doctors' to try to twist the facts to put the company in the right. Viewers, listeners and readers are rarely fooled. In many cases the actual complaint is less about the core product but the lack of service when something has gone wrong.

Laggards

The very worst service, according to Clutterbuck *et al.*, comes from laggards. They really do not care. Survival in a competitive environment is naturally very difficult for such organisations and many of them have been in protected, monopolistic situations. They can improve but they have such a bad reputation that they have to work much harder than aspirants or naturals. Even when a laggard improves there may be an uphill struggle to convince the outside world that things really are different. Following the take-over of the much-joked-about Skoda car operation by the German VW giant after the fall of communism in the early 1990s, there was a 2000/2001 campaign by the company to convince buyers that 'it really was a Skoda'. The campaign actually made a joke about Skoda's earlier poor reputation. Students of European history were perhaps among the few who were actually aware of the superb reputation that the Skoda Company had throughout the world prior to World War II, and thus it is perhaps not surprising that once freed of the dead hand of communist economic management the company was able to produce superb products again.

Pre-sales and after sales service

We continue with the motor dealership theme, which provides so many useful examples for a study of marketing and customer relations. Customers purchasing vehicles appear increasingly more interested in the supplementary products that form part of the package. As stated earlier, it can be assumed that the vehicle (if purchased from new) will have very few faults. What distinguishes it from the competition may well be the supplementaries and, of those, service is a vital component.

A customer will be interested not only in the service at the point of sale or delivery but throughout the life of the product. This is why so many people buy extended warranties; they are concerned that the product should receive the proper maintenance it requires over the longest time period possible. More and more organisations are stressing their ability to provide good after sales service, as this is what will lead to repeat business.

Pre-sales service is also important, because the first contact that a person has with an organisation sets the tone for their future dealings; this is when perceptions are developed. Thus the first contact, be it an advertisement, a telephone call or a visit, should be steeped in quality. The importance of first impressions cannot be understated, as it is very difficult to overcome the distrust of an organisation that poor initial contact has caused. The importance of first impressions will be examined in Chapter 12.

Consistency of service

Organisations that operate across multiple sites need to ensure that not only is the quality of the product consistent but also that service is delivered to a consistent level. Local conditions may require differing types of service but the overall standard should be the same. This is one of the reasons why mystery customers are employed, as they can visit a number of sites to check up on service levels. Even within an organisation it is vital that internal service is consistent, as the value chain is only as good as its weakest link. If a company is operating theme parks in different countries, it must ensure that customers receive the same basic standard wherever they are; a chain of shops needs consistency of service, as do the departments of a local authority. Customers will base their overall impression of the organisation on the worst service they receive at one of its sites, and not the best.

The nature of the core and the supplementary product

The core product and the supplementary products can be depicted diagram-matically as shown in Figure 7.1.

The supplementary products surrounds the core. Anything that is essential to the minimum use of the product forms part of the core, all other extras being part of the supplementary. Hence service is not actually essential to the use of a product, desirable as good service is, and thus service does not form part of the core. It is essential to repeat business, hence its position as the prime supplementary discussed earlier.

Other supplementary products can include optional extras and add-ons. In the software industry, the ability to update programs (for instance, those involved in checking for viruses) using the Internet is a valuable supplementary to the core product, as it can assure the customer of the up-to-dateness of the product. A virus checker becomes useless once a virus is developed that it cannot check for, as the user then becomes very vulnerable. However, if the program can be updated, the product remains, in effect, new.

Other supplementary products include products that the core product allows access to (facilitation, as introduced earlier in this chapter). The vast range of telephone services available to subscribers require certain features to be part of the telephone hardware. Basic telephone calls can still be made on the network without these features being part of the customer's telephone, and thus they are supplementary products as far as the basic telephone product is concerned.

Image is also another important supplementary product. Earlier in this book, when lifestyle was discussed, the importance to customers of what the product

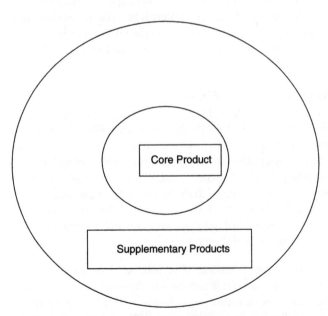

Figure 7.1   Core product and supplementary products.

says about them was introduced. Image is an important part of the buying decision for many core products, and this needs to be kept in mind when considering how to market a diverse range of products from holidays and motor cars through to perfumes for both men and women.

Unique Selling Points (USPs)

With so many similar products to choose from, the contemporary customer in many market sectors can be presented with a bewildering set of choices. Suppliers therefore try to present their product in terms of its Unique Selling Points (USPs). It is the USP that distinguishes one product from another.

Modern consumer legislation, for example the UK Trades Descriptions Act (1968), means that any claims about a product or service must be true. Such legislation is not always followed and false claims about a product have occurred. Similarly any claims about a product based on its relationship with a competitor product also need to be very accurate, otherwise legal action can, and in practice does, follow.

It is important, however, that a manufacturer or supplier is able to highlight the unique aspects of their product or service so that it will have more appeal to a potential customer than that from a competitor. These USPs tend to fall into one of the following categories:

1. *USPs related to function,* whereby the product or service has features that are not present either at all or to the same degree in most competitors' products/services. One of the USPs for Icelandair is the break at Keflavik Airport. As the problem of deep vein thrombosis (DVT) became a matter of growing concern in 2000, Icelandair was able to ensure that customers obtained a degree of exercise because of the change of aircraft in Iceland. What might have been a disadvantage, as non-stop has always been preferable to a change of aircraft, became a useful USP. The method by which the Dyson Dual Cyclone Cleaner performed its task was its major USP, as it worked on a different principle to that of other vacuum cleaners (Dyson, 1998). Dyson protected its patents to a high degree, so important was the USP. When Chrysler introduced its Neon saloon car into the UK, it had the USP that automatic transmission was provided at no extra cost, such a facility usually being a fairly expensive option on medium-value UK vehicles. Unusually for a moderately priced UK vehicle, cruise control was also included on the automatic versions, again at no extra cost. The opportunities for using cruise control are much less in the UK than in North America with its long stretches of Interstate highways, but the possession of such a facility puts the owner into a different category (and therefore image bracket) of UK motorist.

2. *USPs related to performance.* If a vehicle uses much less fuel than its competitors, that is a USP. If a domestic cleaning product will clear up stains that other cleaners cannot touch, that is a USP. Being the quickest between Scotland and Boston is an important USP for Icelandair, and can mitigate

against any concerns that a change of planes in Iceland can cause in the mind of a potential customer.

3. *USPs related to wants* can be very important. As Morden (1991) comments, the first of the electric lawnmowers had the ease-of-use USP over manually operated ones. However they had difficulty in producing the striped effect that the British middle classes deemed appropriate for a suburban lawn. Cut grass is a need, the stripes are a want (see Chapter 6). Modern machines can achieve that effect; it is of no benefit to the lawn but it does meet a need of the customer related to image. As needs change, so new USPs need to be developed. Perhaps one of the most humorous is the development of waterproof radios for use in showers. The use of showers has grown in the UK and thus there appears to be a market to meet the needs of those who cannot be parted from their radio, even for the time it takes to shower. These may, of course, be cases of the birthday or Christmas present for the person who has everything, and it would be an interesting exercise to see how many people actually bought one for their own use compared with those buying them as gifts.

4. *Presentation itself can be a USP.* Ease of opening the packaging and the inclusion of batteries could give a supplier a temporary USP. Recycling of packaging materials provides a psychological USP, as people become more and more concerned about green issues. A product might well be favoured over another purely because its packaging is constructed out of recycled materials. Every advantage, however slight, is important provided that the costs are recoverable.

Unique Selling Points tend to be transitory in nature. No sooner has a product with a new USP been introduced then, unless it is well protected by patents, competitors are likely to jump on the same bandwagon. Patents can provide a degree of protection to allow the introducer of a new product to recoup its development expenses over a period of time, but all patents eventually run out. When patents lapse, reverse engineering can be used to save competitors incurring massive development costs.

Perhaps, and this is a point that will be made under Branding in the next section, the ultimate USP is for the brand name to become synonymous with the product. Many Britons refer to 'hoovering' the floor, but the product they use may be from any one of a number of manufacturers. Hoover, a tradename, has however entered the lexicography as another word for vacuum cleaning. It is given to few products or services to achieve this accolade but when they do the advertising 'comes' free.

Patents and product protection

As mentioned earlier, manufacturers and suppliers who have spent a great deal of time and money in the development of a particular product or service will wish to have their investment protected. The issue of counterfeiting brand names has already been mentioned in this book, and has caused international problems between countries. In the late 1990s, trade relations between the USA and China became fraught because of a perception by the US government that the Chinese government was not doing enough to stop the copying and subsequent resale of US proprietary products, especially those connected with the music and software retail sectors.

As far as the UK is concerned (similar systems operate throughout the developed world), there are three main avenues of protection available to the developer of a new product or service: patents, trademark registration and design registration. As markets become more and more global it is normally necessary to apply for protection under all the jurisdictions that the product or service will be offered in.

Patents

Governments, whilst opposing long-term monopolies, have recognised the need for the developer of a product to enjoy a monopoly for sufficient time for the developmental costs to be recouped and an acceptable profit made. In the UK this can be for up to twenty years. The inventor/developer must make a full disclosure of the product and this is placed on public record. As will be shown below, patents are only applicable to tangible products.

Under the UK Patent Act of 1977, a product (invention) can be patented if:

It is new

The product must never have been disclosed publicly before. Those involved in product development need to search diligently for prior references and patents, as the product may not be new at all.

It involves innovation

The new product must be sufficiently innovative so as not to be a natural progression and evolution from an existing product.

It is commercially applicable

To be eligible for a patent, a product has to have a use. This excludes, say, works of art and books, which are covered separately by copyright law. The invention must be capable of being made or used in some form of industry, including agriculture.

It is more than just a discovery

In many ways this links to the commercial applicability above. Thinking up a new board game would not allow for a patent, but making a special playing surface would. It is the totality that would be patented. Most board games have very similar rules and objectives, and it is the actual format that receives the patent.

Patent law is very complex and if in doubt, the use of the services of specialist patent agents is recommended.

Trademarks

The ® symbol after a name indicates that the trademark is registered and cannot be used without the permission of the owner. Trademarks form an important part of branding (see later) and are valuable assets for the owning organisation as they are a key component in customer identification with the product.

Much thought and design goes into trademark introduction, as they often become the product or organisational logos. Not all logos are registered trademarks – registration is an active step that the organisation must take. Some trademarks are recognised the world over, The Shell Oil symbol is one of the most widely recognised trademarks in the world, together with the McDonald's M. As with patents, infringements of trademark use can lead to hefty damages in the civil courts.

Industrial Design Registration

If the design of a product is completely different from that of competitors then it is possible to have the outward design registered and protected. For some products the shape etc. may be all-important – for example, the well-known mint with a hole, 'Polo' – and this needs protection. 'Polo' is an interesting example, as the USP is in fact empty space, it being the design that is of need of protection as this distinguishes the product from all other mints.

Branding

In presentations Athole Fleming, a Scottish-based graphics designer, has made the point that branding is almost as old as *homo sapiens*. The practice of body painting to distinguish one tribe from another is a very ancient human phenomenon and in fact brands the tribe.

For many similar products it may be only the brand name that distinguishes between competitors and a well-known brand name becomes, in effect, a very valuable USP.

Branding is one of the most important concepts of contemporary marketing. As the Canadian writer, Naomi Klein (2000) has pointed out in her extremely thought provoking book, *No Logo*, for those organisations that have contracted out the vast majority of their manufacturing, their brands are all that they actually have of value.

In the modern world it is actually brands that customers relate to rather than products. Klein shows the importance of the brand by stating that when Philip Morris purchased Kraft for $12.6 billion in 1988, the actual worth of Kraft was about $2.1 billion and the value of the brand $10.5 billion, i.e. six times the paper worth of Kraft was paid to acquire the name. One can only guess what the worth of the name Nike or Coca-Cola would be.

Sir Richard Branson of the Virgin Group makes no apology for the use of Virgin as a brand attachment to his enterprises. Branson is one of the most entrepreneurial people to come out of the UK, and is unique in being a role model for the young and the person that their parents would most like them to emulate. The name Virgin in front of something says a great deal about that product and its quality.

Brands can become very vulnerable to any customer dissatisfaction either with the brand itself or the manner with which it is produced. Nike suffered from picket lines after it was shown that the company was using very-low-paid individuals in the developing world to produce goods at the expense, some in the USA believed, of US workers who could have been employed on similar tasks. A good brand name needs to keep its image.

More and more it is not the product or service that is promoted and advertised but the brand. Brands are what people buy into and are far more than just a mere product.

Counterfeiting

It has become so much a part of image that some people are now prepared to buy something that they know is a fake just for the brand name. That this is dishonest and devalues the brand seems not to bother them. So long as others believe they are promoting a certain image – then this, they say, is OK. Naturally the holders of the brand name take a very different view and are determined to stop others cashing in on their good name with imitations.

In the contemporary world, branding is a very sophisticated tool and poor branding can destroy the commercial opportunities for even an excellent product.

Branding is an important part of the relationship between an organisation and its customers. Brand loyalty (see Chapter 14) can be quite high and the basic concept is to encourage the customer to identify with a particular brand. There are many brands of washing powder on the UK market but most are made by just two or three companies. Chocolate bars of different brands fill the shelves but there are only a few major manufacturers. Certain VW, Skoda and Seat cars look very similar, which should come as no surprise because the brands are all owned by the same group. British Airways are able to franchise their BA brand to regional airlines in the UK and other parts of Europe. BA has a particular position in the marketplace and it is advantageous to the franchisees to be associated with that particular brand. The fashion industry has produced the concept of displaying the brand as part of the customer's image, and the right label can be very important, as discussed in Chapter 6, in terms of peer pressure.

Once a brand gains a reputation for quality then its position is strengthened. Quality is not the only reason for brand success; fashion, as discussed above, may play also a part. It is difficult to tell whether different 'trainers' for children sold in a shoe shop are actually worth the large differentials some brands are able to gain. In this case the name itself is more important than the product, hence the problem of pirate copies mentioned earlier. Branding and the loyalty of a customer to a particular brand are an important weapon in competition and takeover attempts may be purely to acquire a particular brand.

The popularity of particular brands can be culturally and geographically specific. Brands that sell well in Scotland, for example, the soft drink Irn Bru, may be much less popular in England and Wales. Even names can be problematic. The Fiat Ritmo motor car of the 1980s was marketed as the Strada in the UK, as research showed that the name Ritmo would not be acceptable to UK buyers, research at the time suggesting that the name conjured up an image of a lawnmower! The famous VW Golf was for many years the Rabbit in the USA, an acceptable title there but not so in the UK and the rest of Europe. Car manufacturers have begun to use names that are likely to appeal to the global market – Mondeo, Neon etc., even if some like the KA are actually made up. In aviation history, it is reported (Irving, 1993) that the CEO of United Airlines was reluctant to buy the Boeing 707 because of a personal superstition relating to the number, and only bought the aircraft when Boeing retitled a variant as the 720!

Generic branding

A phenomenon of recent years has been the proliferation of so-called 'own brands' appearing on supermarket shelves. These are products that the supermarket has packaged for it by a supplier but branded as though they were the supermarket's own. This is not as new a practice as it may seem. Viewers of BBC's superb *Antiques Roadshow* may note that items occasionally appear with a well-known trade name attached but described as made for them by. . . . In the early days of mail order in the USA, organisations such as Sears would have products made for them and then branded with the Sears name. Contemporary own-brand products are often cheaper than the well-known brands, especially where staple products such as baked beans etc. are concerned. Whether the quality differs or not is a matter for the individual customer to decide. Some own-brand products have a reputation for very high quality, the St Michael trade label used by the UK Marks & Spencer chain being an international byword for quality.

Organisations such as the Goldstar conglomerate from South Korea owed much of their success in the consumer electronics sector to supplying generic products for the retailer to brand as its own.

Where the product is a generic one, the quality standards are dictated by the retailer, as it is the retailer, under UK legislation, who is responsible for the standard of goods sold. If a retailer allows its name to appear on a product, then any deficiencies will be interpreted by the customer as being the fault of the name on the box, i.e. the retailer, and not the actual manufacturer whose name is only likely to appear in very small print, if at all.

Badge engineering

Branding and generic branding are legitimate business activities. What is perhaps less legitimate is the practice of badge engineering, something that the car industry has been accused of in the past. Badge engineering is basically charging different amounts for identical products – identical that is except for the brand name. As certain brand names command more perceived value, customers are more likely to pay a premium for a product badged with that brand even if it does not differ one iota from a similar product badged with a less popular brand.

Product development

New products and services do not appear as if by magic overnight. There may have been years of product development before the particular product or service is offered up into the marketplace. Large sums of money may well have been expended before there is any income to be attached to the product or service, and all product/service development must carry with it a degree of faith that the developmental work will have produced something that is going to be a success. Organisations are not always successful, the Ford Edsel mentioned in a previous chapter being a case in point, as was the Comet airliner. Only 16 examples of Concorde, the Anglo–French supersonic airliner, were sold despite a huge investment by the two governments. The reluctance of the US authorities to allow landings at airports other than New York and Washington, the subsequent refusal of many other countries to allow Concorde overflights for environmental reasons and a tripling of the price of fuel had much to do with the failure of the aircraft to gain orders. Prior to the fatal crash of a Concorde in Paris in 2001, the aircraft had an exemplary safety record since its introduction in commercial service in the middle of the 1970s. British Airways and Air France were able to operate Concorde profitably only because the governments wrote off the development costs leaving only the operating costs (see Chapter 10) to be met.

Not all product development will have the huge development costs of Concorde, but the development costs for even the most modest of projects can be relatively high and monies need to be found that will not be matched by immediate income. The longer the development period, the longer it will be before the product or service can even begin to pay its way. Costs etc. form the subject of Chapter 10 of this book and will be covered in more detail there.

New products and services are usually developed in four major ways:

- totally new developments;
- improvements to previous products;
- spin-offs from previous products;
- near copies of the products of a competitor.

The latter three often incur fewer costs, as there may be less actual new work.

It is not only tangible, manufactured products that can be developed in these ways but also the more intangible services. Many service providers have staff examining and analysing competitor products in order to ensure that the offerings they are developing match and possibly excel those offered by competitors.

Whole books could be written about the travails, successes and failures of product development. The recommended reading at the end of this chapter is

21st Century Jet by Karl Sabbach (1995). This book, which also formed the basis for a UK television documentary, details the development of the Boeing 777 jet airliner in the 1990s. This was a mammoth undertaking and involved the commitment of huge financial and human resources by the Boeing organisation. Students are fortunate that the process was so closely recorded, and the book not only tells the story of the airliner but also of the decisions that led to its inception, first flight, testing and eventual entry into service with United Airlines and British Airways in June and October 1995 respectively. The first design work had started as early as 1988 so that there was approximately a seven-year gap from inception to introduction within the marketplace. *21st Century Jet* is well worth reading by anybody involved in marketing or management and is written in a non-technical but highly informative manner, being more concerned with design, marketing and manufacturing than technical aviation aspects.

Technology

The use of computers has greatly aided product development. Sabbach (the suggested reading to accompany this chapter as mentioned in the previous section) describes how the use of computer aided design (CAD) greatly improved the efficiency of Boeing's design process for the 777. By using linked computers, the problems of interference where two or more components try to occupy the same physical space was greatly reduced. Interference was always a problem prior to CAD, as designers were drawing three-dimensional (3D) objects on two-dimensional paper. As computers can generate a 3D image, such problems can be seen much more easily. CAD also allows for the linking of the systems operated by subcontractors and, as Sabbach points out, every designer can, theoretically, have access to the entire drawings etc.

CAD systems can also be directly linked to manufacturing, again reducing the possibilities of error.

There is no doubt that the ability of computers to produce a virtual 'working' model of a product or the processes involved in a service have greatly aided the efficiency of design.

Totally new developments

This is the most costly method of product development. In many cases the organisation will have had experience of similar products so there will be some organisational knowledge (see the BACK analysis) to draw upon. If the organisation is entering a completely new field it may be necessary to set up design teams, testing facilities and dedicated marketers and sales people from scratch. In competitive forces terms (see Chapter 5) this can present considerably high and costly barriers to entry.

Developing a new product or even an intangible service may not only require the supplier to invest in new equipment and staff training but can also impact upon customers. Will the customer need to retrain staff or acquire additional facilities and if so who will pay for this? Customers may also have to invest development resources before seeing a return, and they will wish to be very sure that the returns will be acceptable within the desired timeframe.

The trend in recent times has been for suppliers to involve their major customers (and subcontractors) in developments as early as possible. Boeing set up a group of eight potential customers to advise on the design of the 777 and was able to bring a customer perception to issues at a very early stage. This does of course mean that secrecy is harder to maintain, and thus a delicate balance between gaining as much information from the marketplace as possible must be weighed against competitors having advanced knowledge of the developments.

The copying of products is not always possible because of the protection given by patents, covered earlier in this chapter. Reverse engineering, the process whereby an existing competitor's product is systematically dismantled and then copied, hopefully with improvements, is a legitimate practice once patents have expired.

In many industries the development and manufacturing of a completely new product may mean committing the majority of the company's assets into that project, and the importance of effective market research cannot be understated. The organisation needs to be sure that it is developing what the market requires. It should not be surprising that the types of analysis covered in Chapter 2 of this book are so important to those involved in product development. It is also important that those who will be involved in marketing and selling the new product are involved in the development process from the very beginning so that they can feed in their market knowledge to the process.

Improvements to previous products

Not all developments are brand new. The concept of product succession introduced in the next chapter is well illustrated by the introduction of a new model of an existing motor vehicle every couple of years or so, until the time comes that the manufacturer believes that the market is ready for a completely new vehicle. The Ford Cortina/Sierra/Mondeo progression is an example, with various marks of each being introduced and with the replacement model (Sierra for Cortina etc.) also taking a loyal customer base from its predecessor. Whilst the transition from Cortina to Sierra fits into the previous category discussed in this chapter, the various marks of Cortina were improvements upon the previous models. This is much less costly, as a foundation for the design work is in existence and it is often a case of improving upon a product or service whilst retaining the original good points. The decision as to when to move to a completely new product can be a difficult one. It may be necessary to convince customers that the old product with which they are comfortable is not so much disappearing as being reborn as something new. However, if it is too similar to what is perceived as old and possibly obsolete, there may be resistance. Careful marketing of the benefits is necessary to retain the loyalty that may have been built up over a considerable period of time.

Spin-offs from previous products

The home computer and domestic facsimile machines have been developed from products originally designed for commercial use, and there have been successful developments of light delivery vehicles from popular small cars. The more commonality of parts there are, the easier it is for the manufacturer, but there is the danger that something that suits one market may not be satisfactory in another, even when modified considerably.

Near copies of the products of a competitor

As has been stated earlier, counterfeiting is both wrong and an actual crime. There is nothing wrong, however, in examining and analysing a competitor's product and reverse engineering it to produce something better so long as patents are not infringed. The balance between a straight copy and a development that is an improvement and a valid input into the market is delicate and sometimes requires a court to rule on whether there has been an infringement.

It is a fact, however, that no lead in a product or service lasts forever. As products enter the marketplace, secrets become harder to keep. Organisations are thus in a continual process of needing to improve their products and services to keep one step ahead of their competitors.

Icelandair's USPs have already been introduced in this book and are a good example of how to change a possible disadvantage into a beneficial USP.

Airlines usually place great emphasis on direct (flights that stop to pick up and land passengers and refuel) or actual non-stop flights, both of which save the passenger the need to transfer aircraft. As mentioned in the text, the concerns about deep vein thrombosis mean that a chance to exercise is a positive benefit. For travellers from Scotland to the USA, the only alternatives to the route via Iceland are either to take longer and go via London or fly on one of the few direct and relatively expensive services.

By ensuring a smooth and quick transfer at Keflavik, Icelandair is able to minimise any inconvenience and still offer a service that is as good if not better than that through London in terms of speed.

An additional USP is the opportunity to stay for a few days in Iceland, a growing short-break destination, at little or no extra cost save for accommodation.

Summary

The vast majority of products and services consist of a basic core product surrounded by supplementaries, of which service may well be the most important. Merchandising, the situation where the supplementary may be more valuable than the core product, has grown over recent years. As the quality of products becomes higher and the similarity of offerings from various competitors makes choices harder, it may well be that levels of service including the all important after sales service become the major deciding factor in customer choices. Organisations vary in their commitment to service and many are led not by conviction but by the higher levels of service offered by their competitors. Organisations operating on different sites etc. must ensure that there is consistency of service wherever the customer goes. Organisations aim to give their products and services Unique Selling Points (USPs) that differentiate them from competitors and will use patent law to protect their position.

Brands and branding form an important facet of customer identification and loyalty, and can command increased prices in situations where the brand is considered desirable.

Product development can be a costly process, and technology can be harnessed to assist designers in developing new and improving old products.

QUESTIONS

 1 Explain the importance of supplementary products in the context of their associated core, and why service levels may be the prime supplementary.
 2 What is *branding*, and why is it an important part of customer identification? Illustrate your answer using well-known brands and products.
 3 Using examples, illustrate the forms that the development of new products can take and show how technology can aid the process.

Recommended reading

As stated in the text, Sabbach's (1995) *21st Century Jet – the Making of the Boeing 777* is recommended as a superb study of design, manufacturing and implementation of a major project. Readers are also recommended to consult Naomi Klein's (2000) *No Logo* to see how important branding has become in the modern world.

Useful websites

www.boeing.com	Boeing website
www.moreover.com	Patent news website
www.napp.org	National Association of Patent Practitioners (US) website

▪ ▾ 8 Portfolios and life cycles

The product life cycle – Families of products – Product succession – Dynamic product life progression – Alternatives to decline – The Manchester Metrolink – Product portfolios – The Boston Matrix – Public sector matrix – Life cycle and portfolio links

The product life cycle

All products and services follow a life cycle that is analogous to that of living things. The life cycle may be extremely short, as for some toys at Christmas time and many fashion items, or it may be very long, as evidenced by the long-term success of many branded products – KitKat bars and Morgan motor cars spring to mind. Interestingly, whilst some toys may be available for just one Christmas, others have achieved long-lasting favour, and teddy bears, Lego®, toy trains etc. have been successful across generations of children in different parts of the world. When thinking about any product or service it is important to consider its life cycle, and this is done using the concept of the product life cycle (PLC), a fairly orthodox marketing idea, and the more sophisticated 'dynamic product life progression', which was developed to represent the more complex situations that can be found in the modern global marketplace. The new model was introduced to alleviate the problems of a self-fulfilling prophecy that had become attached to the conventional PLC model. Decline is not the inevitability that the traditional PLC model suggests, and there are a large number of examples where products have been either reintroduced or whose use has been changed and which then appeal to a new market.

It is important to be aware of the product life cycle in order to understand the behaviour of the market, and the correct times to withdraw and replace products and services. Such an understanding is a key part of the role of those involved in managing the marketing process.

As mentioned at the beginning of this chapter, life cycles can be short, as in the fashion industry or some of the more esoteric products that appear – for example, hula hoops, or those linked to other products, such as Batman accessories, Power Rangers and the vast range of spin-offs from other films and television series (see merchandising in the previous chapter); or they may be very long – P&O's cruise ship, *Canberra* (1961–97), the Boeing 747 (first commercial flight 1969 and still being built) and KitKat chocolate bars being good examples.

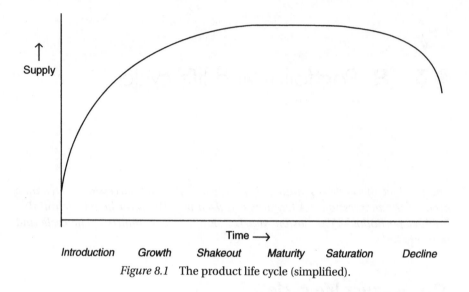

Introduction	Growth	Shakeout	Maturity	Saturation	Decline

Figure 8.1 The product life cycle (simplified).

The classic (and perhaps, too simplistic) view of the product life cycle is shown in Figure 8.1.

Introduction

In order to simplify this study; assume that there is a new product or service that has been developed by an organisation and that there is no competition at the point of introduction. In the case of a completely new product or service this may well be the case, however in real life there will be some competition, however slight, even if it is not competition between similar products or functions but competition for the customer's money. At the moment the product or service has not been introduced to the market, save for testing, but the organisation believes that it will be successful.

At the point of introduction, the organisation may be the only players in the market, although others may be working on a similar product. Airtours, a major UK package holiday and charter airline operator, entered the UK cruise market in 1995 because there was very little provision for lower cost cruising in the UK and it perceived a demand; it was right, because within 5 years it had a fleet of four vessels in service. Icelandair perceived that there was a demand for a more convenient service from Scotland to the Eastern seaboard of North America, and again was proved correct. The importance of market research and market testing, as covered earlier in this book, cannot be overemphasised, as there are examples of seemingly suitable products and services for which there is actually little demand – the electric Sinclair C5 micro-vehicle of the 1980s being a case in point. The C5 may have been technically brilliant but nobody appeared to want to buy it, in part because of safety concerns about so small a vehicle sharing busy roads with cars, lorries and buses.

There are considerable advantages in being the first into the market but there are also some disadvantages. New developments often have 'bugs in the system' and these need to be ironed out. Unfortunately, however much testing is done prior to the launch onto the market it is nearly always the case that it is the early customers who first discover a bug, and they may become dissatisfied. There are certainly many people who wait before upgrading their computer operating system, as they are aware that the first versions may cause problems.

If, at introduction, the organisation can make sufficient impact, a long-lasting set of advantages can occur. If the product is of high quality then customer loyalty (to be considered in Chapter 14) can be enhanced and subsequent purchases will be of the organisation's products. Repeat business is a very important market indicator, and organisations need a range of products to offer both existing and new customers. Existing customers can be encouraged to trade up to new replacements. Of equal importance is making the product synonymous with your name, as covered in the previous chapter with the example of 'hoovering' the floor.

If an organisation is first into a market, competitors will always be playing catch up, but they can benefit from the mistakes and problems of those responsible for the initial introduction of the product or service. Reverse engineering was mentioned in the previous chapter and it may be more profitable to be later into the market and to profit from a competitor's experiences. However what may be difficult to achieve is eroding away the competitor's customer base. Unless the market is expanding, this will mean that there may be insufficient customers to support a number of competing products. An aware organisation will have taken every step possible to 'debug' the product or service, but unfortunately only sustained customer use can reveal the full extent of any problems. The rigorous testing of aircraft in order to obtain an ETOPS rating, covered earlier, occurs because the various safety authorities need to ensure that they have the kind of data that sustained use produces. As Sabbach (1995) pointed out in the Recommended reading for the previous chapter, even the most rigorous testing can fail to discover a problem that only manifests itself in sustained commercial use.

Growth

Provided that the organisation has been successful and the product is in the marketplace and selling well, as success becomes apparent, others will wish to enter the market. The problems of barriers to entry were discussed in Chapter 5, some markets being much easier to enter than others. If a product or service is very successful, it is often the case that demand will be greater than supply and this will make it easier for competitors to enter the market with similar products, e.g. the Airtours cruise operation in the UK being followed by a cruise programme from Thomson (one of Airtours main competitors) offering a very similar product targeted at the same market. Thus as the market grows, the number of supplying organisations increases and those organisations may well increase their capacity. Growth markets are often characterised by a large number of small organisations, as there is sufficient demand to accommodate considerable competition.

Shakeout

As growth begins to peak, weaker organisations leave the market either because they cannot compete or because they are acquired by more successful competitors or larger organisations wishing to enter the particular market (see Chapter 5). Demand tends to reach a plateau and the tendency is for the smaller organisations to merge or to be taken over by one of the bigger existing players, or a large organisation using the shakeout phase to acquire an entry into a new market. P&O acquired Princess Cruises at this point in the Princess product life cycle when P&O was having difficulty establishing its own identity in the West Coast of USA cruise market (Cartwright and Baird, 1999). Smaller organisations are vulnerable at this time to raids by cash-rich predators. Whilst the smaller organisation may be successful, growth usually requires increased resources and cash flow can become a problem, making smaller organisations very vulnerable to those with cash reserves. Unfair it may seem but this is a fact of business life. Growth that is too rapid can produce cash flow problems worse than those produced when growth is too slow. If organisations are unable to satisfy demand without expanding production (and this can carry huge costs), potential and returning customers may become dissatisfied and look elsewhere.

Larger organisations, it is claimed, can produce at lower cost and can benefit from economies of scale; what they have to be careful of is that they don't reduce quality and service along with costs. Service is a very important part of the product, a point made in the previous chapter, and there is growing evidence that customers will pay that little bit more for good service and higher quality (Cartwright and Green, 1997; Cartwright, 2000). The tendency at shakeout is for a position to evolve where there are fewer but larger players competing within the market.

Maturity

As growth slows, the market becomes more mature and possibly dominated by even fewer but increasingly larger suppliers. Entry is difficult, as the existing suppliers will know the market well and will have developed customer loyalty. It requires true entrepreneurship and considerable resources to break into a mature market, Richard Branson and Virgin Atlantic is one of the better known examples. Smaller companies that have tried to break into a mature market have found it very difficult unless they are part of a major group and thus have the financial backing and existing customer base to succeed.

As the marketplace becomes saturated, organisations need to be in a position to bring new products, or adaptations of existing products, to the marketplace.

Families of products

In the automobile market, there are normally a number of versions of each vehicle introduced over time, with a completely new model being introduced

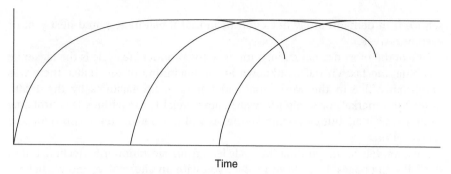

Time

Figure 8.2 Product succession.

every so often. In the cruise industry there are the options of new vessels or new cruising areas. There is also the option of changing the package by moving up-market or by adding a new range of extra services.

Sabbach makes the point that the success of Boeing and Airbus Industrie in the contemporary commercial airliner market stems from their provision of a family of designs covering short-, medium-, long- and very long-haul aircraft. This allows airlines to grow whilst retaining their relationship with one airframe manufacturer. There is a major financial bonus in that training and spare parts provision can be maximised.

Product succession

The previous chapter also raised the importance of product succession with new models and then an eventual new product being introduced over time. The product life cycle for a series of related products looks like that shown in Figure 8.2.

Without a succession of new products, customer loyalty can disappear very quickly, because looking after the customer means anticipating their future needs as well as looking after their current ones.

Saturation and decline

When the market is saturated, supply exceeds demand, possibly because of changing tastes. As demand drops, so profits shrink and competition becomes even fiercer. As decline sets in, players leave the market or are forced out, or old products are removed from the product portfolio. Customers buying an automobile and who don't want the latest model can purchase a bargain at this time, as manufacturers and dealers will often cut prices drastically to clear stocks and free production facilities for new models etc.

For an airliner or cruise liner, the product life cycle is measured in years or even decades; for the latest fashion it may be measured in weeks. But organisations need an idea of how long it is and must be aware that just because a product or service is in demand today does not mean that it will be required next year or even next week.

One of the most dramatic illustrations of the product life cycle is the facsimile machine, the fax. Virtually unknown at the beginning of the 1980s, there was hardly an office in the world that did not have fax facilities by the 1990s. Indeed the market for straightforward commercial fax machines was probably saturated by 1995 but clever marketing, as will be shown later, has produced a rejuvenation.

Most models of the product life cycle lead from saturation into decline, but in the following pages we want to present you with an alternative, and we believe more realistic model, called *the dynamic product life progression*, developed by Cartwright and Green (1997). *Dynamic* because it provides for a series of alternatives, and *progression* because there is life after apparent decline for many products.

Dynamic product life progression

This concept is slightly more complex than the simple product life cycle model and a slightly different graph with two decision points is used (Figure 8.3).

When a product or service first enters the market, there always seem to be some people who must have the latest thing. Thus, whilst initial take-up figures may be very encouraging, they may not point to a continuation of success. Demand may plateau whilst the bulk of the potential customer population makes up its mind. Some of the more esoteric products of the technological age (electric bicycles, the electric mini-mini car etc.) seem never to pass this point,

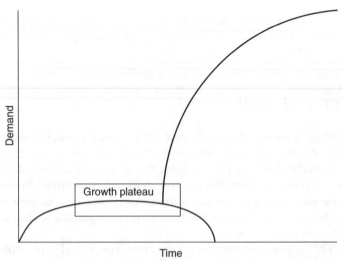

Figure 8.3   Dynamic product life progression – growth phase.

and disappear never to re-enter the market. If the product is acceptable to the mass of potential buyers, the growth phase is resumed; if not, then the product will go into decline. The critical success factor for any new product or service is whether demand picks up after a short time at the growth plateau. The history of marketing is full of products and services that seemed a good idea at the time, had initial success but then disappeared.

The next adaptation to the simple product life cycle model *can* occur at the shakeout phase. It is possible that one supplier or product gains such ascendancy as to *blastout* its competitors. Examples of this have happened in the video cassette market, VHS blasting out Betamax (despite many experts believing that Betamax was actually the better system). The Microsoft Windows® computer operating system has gained the major market share of the global PC operating system market. In the UK satellite television market, the major dominance of BSkyB in the satellite television market was a feature of the 1990s – this system blasted out competing systems and became the norm for users.

The final adaptation by Cartwright and Green (1997) to the classic product life cycle model occurs towards the end of saturation and the beginning of decline (Figure 8.4). As will be shown from the examples, not all decline means the end, it may be the start of something completely new and equally as successful, in effect a new life cycle entirely.

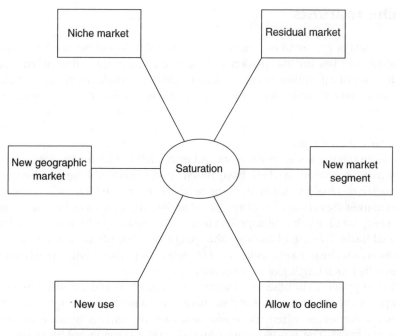

Figure 8.4   Dynamic product life progression – decline and alternatives.
[*Taken from Cartwright and Green, 1997, with permission.*]

There are six possibilities and it is possible that decline *per se* can be avoided and a product or service can be rejuvenated.

Residual markets

In the 1960s, the British Leyland 'Mini' was a revolutionary small car that carried with it considerable customer loyalty. Many UK citizens had a Mini as their first car. The replacement, the Metro (later renamed Rover 100), was intended to serve the whole of the Mini market. There was, however, enough of a residual market for the Mini to justify Rover restarting the production line, albeit with reduced capacity and fewer models. Therefore, in the early 1990s both models were available, catering for similar but slightly different markets. Enough people wanted to buy the Mini to make it profitable for production to continue even after the Rover 100 was discontinued. The last original model Mini as such was produced in 2000 with the replacement already in production, a replacement that kept the Mini name. Residual markets can be very profitable as minor operations for so long as major investment in plant and equipment is not required. In manufacturing especially, the start-up costs can be very high although the running costs may be perfectly acceptable. Thus, provided that the plant is still in working order, it may be possible to make a profit and cater for a much smaller residual market.

Niche markets

Niche markets are small and specialised. They develop either by being set up especially to cater for that market or by a larger company selling off part of its product/service portfolio. Because niche markets are small, they often don't have the economies of scale that larger organisations require and may not fit into corporate plans. Selling an apparent loss-making product to somebody who is prepared to put in the hard work that a niche market requires can be a better alternative than the product leaving the market altogether.

Because the market is small, costs and prices tend to be much higher than in mass markets. Niche markets have much in common with residual markets, although a residual market is often the remnant of a much larger market whilst a niche market may always have been just that. It is often the case that there will be just a very small number of suppliers to a niche market, perhaps organised on a regional basis. The use of Internet shopping has made life somewhat easier for suppliers to niche markets, as it is now far more simple for them to reach out to a potentially much larger global potential customer base.

Many suppliers to hobbies etc. cater for niche markets and, provided that there is support for the more esoteric supplier, the market can be quite buoyant. Problems can occur when niche and mainstream markets operate to similar customer bases. The model railway market (still a thriving hobby in the USA, Canada, the UK, Germany etc.) is supplied by many small retailers and manufacturers. Unfortunately they can be badly affected by a few larger suppliers selling only the more popular items, often by mail order and at a discount. The larger suppliers often do not supply the smaller items that the true enthusiast may require and if these suppliers go out of business because of competition, the whole hobby can suffer.

New geographic markets

As Cartwright and Baird (1999) pointed out, the cruise and holiday companies have become adept at opening up new geographic markets and there is hardly a coast on the face of the earth that doesn't feature in their brochures. As experienced customers search for somewhere new to go, so new markets are opened up and developed, in many cases eventually to become mainstream destinations.

However it is not only holiday providers who access new geographic markets with existing products. The famous Honda 50 motorcycle from Japan was an icon of youth in the USA during the 1960s, later swept through Europe, then India and latterly China. India and China moved from 'bicycle economies' to motor bike economies, with India being slightly in the lead and now becoming a car economy. Honda was able to move the production into these areas. The product was well known and as fast as it became outdated in one area, say Europe, there was India providing a new market. The Morris Oxford car of the 1950s and 1960s was obsolete in the UK but is now manufactured very successfully as the Hindustan Ambassador in India. Fiat sold the production lines of vehicles to Eastern Europe. British Aircraft Corporation sold the jigs etc. of the BAC 1–11 airline to Romania where the final examples were produced. This is a form of the segmentation shift mentioned in Chapter 5 and a phenomenon that will be considered later when considering product portfolios.

New market segments

Earlier, the facsimile machine and the fact that the commercial market was becoming saturated were mentioned. The manufacturers and the telephone companies started marketing the fax machine as a domestic product in the middle of the 1990s. Thus demand has been restimulated. The television market was originally one per household, but now smaller models are available for the bedroom, kitchen and even for boats! Homes used to have one telephone, now many have two or three, all stimulating demand and widening the market into a new segment. The huge growth in mobile telephone sales to young people in the late 1990s and early 2000s in the UK is a very good example of a new market segment being opened up to an established product. By 2001 it was estimated that half of the youngsters in the UK had a mobile telephone!

Keflavik, the base for Icelandair, was originally a military airfield. As the Cold War became less of an issue following the collapse of the communism in Eastern Europe, so a proportion of the military facilities was made available for civilian use, giving Icelandair one of the best equipped airfields in the world at very little cost save for the building of a terminal suitable for commercial customers.

New use

Products that used to be used for baking are now used for cleaning refrigerators! One way of stimulating demand for a declining product is to find a new use for it. Redundant British buses, no longer suitable for the rigours of the rush hour, appear as sightseeing vehicles on the streets of New York. The early generation of cruise ships after World War II were ocean liners displaced by commercial jet transport.

The Manchester Metrolink

In 1849 the Manchester South Junction and Altrincham Railway was opened as a joint venture by the London and North Western Railway (LNWR) and the Manchester, Sheffield and Lincolnshire Railway (later the Great Central) to tap into the growing commuter traffic to the south-west of Manchester. Although the line was electrified as early as 1931, by the late 1980s the line was unprofitable because of competition from buses and the private motor car.

However, important developments in the transport infrastructure were underway in the Manchester area. Central Station, which had closed in 1969 and had been used as a car park ever since, was transformed into the impressive G-MEX exhibition centre, opening in 1986, and the increasing growth of Manchester Airport as a major international airport was such that rail links to the airport from both Manchester and Crewe, and thus the national rail network, were in place by 1995.

As one of the termini of the first commercial passenger railway in the UK, the Liverpool and Manchester of 1830, Manchester has suffered from a lack of a through station in the centre of the city on the north–south axis (Jowett, 1993). There had been many plans to deal with this problem over the years, the eventual solution being the Windsor Link of 1988 and a city centre light railway, the Metrolink. The Windsor Link allowed trains from Manchester Airport to proceed north and is thus of critical importance to the economy not just of the city but of the whole of Northern England.

Manchester abandoned its trams in January 1949 (Yearsley, 1962) but in common with an increasing number of British cities, congestion towards the end of the 20th century led to the examination of tramway practice in continental Europe and plans for light railways/tramways. At the time of writing, tramways have been reintroduced on light railway principles in Sheffield, Tyneside, the West Midlands, Croydon and Manchester, with plans under discussion for other UK cities including the capital of Scotland – Edinburgh. Blackpool, for long the last bastion of tramway operations in the UK, is no longer unique.

The Manchester Metrolink, in its initial form, ran between Altrincham to the south and Bury to the north, passing through the city centre and linking the two surviving railway terminals of Piccadilly and Victoria. Whilst new track was required in the city centre, outwith the centre made use of existing railway tracks, resignalled etc. for light railway operations. To the south, the Altrincham line already mentioned was utilised, whilst from Victoria to Bury the route of the original Manchester to Bury line of the Lancashire and Yorkshire Railway originally opened in 1879 and electrified in 1916 was proposed.

Rebuilding of Victoria Station commenced in late 1992 with the new station being designed to accommodate the Metrolink. The Manchester Metro, as it exists today, was first put forward in 1983, with a suggestion for no fewer than six lines to radiate from the city centre (Hall, 1995). It was proposed that all of the lines would use converted existing rail routes with one exception, that out to Didsbury which was to use the abandoned track bed of the old Midland Railway line from Manchester to Stockport (the South District Railway). In the context of this book, it is the ability to utilise existing infrastructure that makes schemes such as the Manchester Metro so important.

By 1988, Parliamentary consent for the first phase of the scheme, to comprise a line from Altrincham to Bury via the city centre, had been granted and by 1990, a consortium named the Greater Manchester Metro Ltd (GMML) and comprising the Greater Manchester Passenger Transport Executive (GMPTE), GEC, Mowlem and AMEC was in place to construct and operate the Metro. The consortium was awarded a 15-year concession. GMPTE own the infrastructure and vehicles that are then leased to GMML. Originally estimated capital costs were put at £85 million with this sum rising to £130 million in 1990 (Hall, 1995). Government grants covered half of the capital costs but there is no subsidy for the operation, passenger revenues needing to cover all operating costs and overheads (see Chapter 9).

The Altrincham to Bury line opened on 6 April, 1992, and by 2000 an extension line to Eccles had also been fully opened, having run as far as Salford Keys as early as 1997. When Central Station in Manchester was closed in 1969, the approach viaduct was left intact in a far-sighted move, as without this important piece of infrastructure in the centre of the city, the costs of building the Metro might have been prohibitive (Johnson, 1990).

The trams (actually light rail vehicles) were built in Italy and were especially designed to use standard UK railway platforms rather than loading passengers directly from street level, as is the practice on most tramways. Thus the original stations on the Manchester to Altrincham and Manchester to Bury lines could be used with only minimal changes. This new use for what is now old infrastructure greatly reduced the capital costs of building the Metro.

With the exception of a few trams for the route along Pottery Lane and Stanley Grove which passed under a low bridge, all of the original Manchester trams which ran until 1949 were of the traditional British double-deck variety, firstly with open tops and then latterly all enclosed. The new 'supertrams', of which there were 26 by 2000, are single-deck double units built in Italy and carrying 82 seated passengers with a total capacity of 206, i.e. there is plenty of standing room. The original Manchester trams could only accommodate a maximum of 76–80 passengers (Yearsley, 1962), so that the increased capacity of the supertrams means that fewer units are needed.

Whilst there are potential difficulties in designing vehicles that run on their own reserved tracks out of the city centre but need to share the city centre streets with road vehicles, these have been solved to produce a very efficient system. One flick of a switch and mirrors, a street whistle and brake lights become operational, and the transition from railway type operations to street running is accomplished extremely smoothly. Light rail vehicles are able to transport large numbers of passengers without causing the congestion and pollution associated with buses and cars, and this is to be welcomed in urban environments. The opening of a huge shopping complex at Trafford, just off the route of the Metro and to which shuttle buses are operated, has boosted traffic and it is likely that this complex will receive its own direct Metro link at some time in the not too distant future.

The Metrolink operation has also paid considerable attention to passenger safety and security. As Hall (1995) has pointed out, Mancunians have had to relearn how to share their streets with rail vehicles. Continental European countries are used to high-speed trams in the streets, but the inhabitants of UK cities are having to adapt their behaviour to accommodate the new form of transport as, unlike buses, supertrams cannot take avoiding action. Street crime has increased since the late 1940s and the Metro stops are all equipped with closed circuit television (CCTV), recording continuously, and telephone links to the central control. Those working in the field of Organisational Body Language (OBL) have stressed the importance to the customer of feeling safe about the use of a product and service, and the Metrolink has gone to considerable trouble to ensure that security is as tight as possible and that there are facilities for those with disabilities. All stops are announced visually and aurally, and there is wheelchair access to the supertrams.

By using existing facilities wherever possible, Manchester has gained a state-of-the-art light railway system at much less cost than building from scratch, a project that might have been completely cost prohibitive. Older facilities have been given a new lease of life and there has been far less disruption to the general population during the construction phase.

Allow to decline

Some products and services have, of course, outlived their usefulness. New developments and customer expectations have changed the market. In these cases, a swift end is better than a long drawn out one; organisations do not want a declining product affecting their image. If a product or service does not produce a profit (or in the public sector is not required), and if nobody else wants it, then it is possibly time for it to go. It can be reintroduced in a more modern format, as occurred with the famous VW Beetle.

Product portfolios

It is unusual for an organisation to offer just a single product or service. Typically there is a family of related products/services on offer and these form the product portfolio for the organisation. Icelandair offers a family of linked routes, while Boeing and Airbus have a family of products ranging from small airliners to the very large, as described earlier. Motor car manufacturers usually offer the ability for customers to trade up within the same range, thus ensuring that they are able to tap into customer loyalty (see Chapter 14). Within the product portfolio there will be offerings at different stages of the product life cycle/dynamic life progression, covered earlier. The Boston Consulting Group in the USA has developed a very useful method of describing the position of the various items in an organisation's product portfolio.

The Boston Matrix

The Boston Matrix (Figure 8.5) looks at the position of products against the two factors of *market share* and *market growth.*

To illustrate the matrix, let us imagine that an organisation has just introduced a new product or service. To be successful, that product/service will need to capture a certain percentage of market share either by attracting customers from rival companies or brand new customers to the market. Different industries have different levels of market share required to at least break even. In the cruise industry, a vessel for the US market needs to attract 2% of the market share whilst one for the UK market needs a massive 10% share for success. Until customers actually place orders etc., the product or service will have no actual market share at all, just a potential market share. Assuming that the organisation has carried out reliable research and analysis, it will be launching the product or service into a potentially relatively high growth market, there being little point in launching a new product or service into a low growth market unless the aim is to rejuvenate

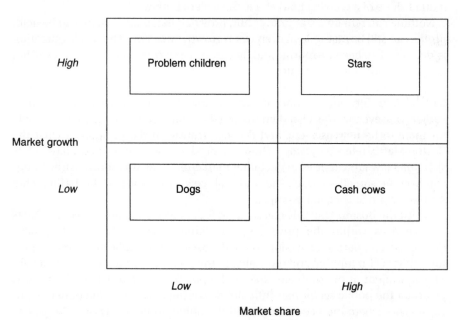

Figure 8.5 The Boston Matrix.

the market. If growth is relatively slow, then the introduction of a new product or service needs to coincide with the removal of an old one.

A product or service, indeed a new company, may be operating in an expanding market, but on introduction the market share will be low unless the product or service is an overnight major success. The combination of a low market share in a high growth regime is known as a *problem child*; a *problem* because there are start-up costs, new customers to attract, perhaps large numbers of staff to train and an infrastructure to build; a *child* because with proper nurturing children grow to become adults earning their way in the world.

Even the best designed operation, however, can have teething problems. Cunard refused delivery of the *Queen Elizabeth 2* in 1968, cancelling an advertised Christmas cruise because the ship was not ready; the company did not take delivery until April 1969. A similar problem occurred in December 1994 when the ship was returned from Blohm and Voss in Hamburg in an unfinished state after a refit. This time passengers were embarked and the ship docked in New York amid much bad press comment and threats of legal action from passengers. The initial problems of the Comet airliner have been well documented, and a number of cars have required high-profile recall action from the manufacturers because of faults that have been found almost immediately the vehicle has entered commercial service.

Some products, service and even companies never make it past the problem child state, disappearing almost as fast as they entered the market, i.e. as they enter the growth plateau stage referred to earlier in this chapter.

However, if the product, service or organisation progresses past the point of low market share and begins to pick up new and repeat business, there is the possibility of becoming a *star*. A star exists when the company etc. has a high market share of a growing market, i.e. the best of both worlds.

Nothing can remain a star forever but, provided that market share can be held, profits can still be maintained even when growth rates slow. The whole operation is 'debugged' to become routine and then becomes a *cash cow*. It is cash cows that generate profits for shareholders and future expansion.

Everything comes to an end, and the vast majority of products and services have a finite life, since sooner or later demand for them declines, as shown earlier. However, as was also demonstrated earlier in this chapter, it is possible for there to be new uses etc. and this can transform the position of what the Boston Matrix refers to as *dogs*. These are products/services etc. that have a low share of a low growth or even declining marketplace. As was shown earlier, dogs can become somebody else's star and cash cows, the Morris Oxford/Hindustan Ambassador being a good example.

Whilst the Boston Matrix is mainly used for analysing the position of products and services within the private sector, Johnson and Scholes (1984) have developed a public sector version where the axes are the public need and support for public sector funding and the ability of the public sector to deliver effectively. The equivalent of the problem child is the *political hot box*, where the need is great but the public sector has difficulty delivering effectively. The public sector *star* occurs where the need is high and the ability to deliver exists. The *golden fleece* has low need but a high ability to deliver, whilst the *back drawer issue* is one

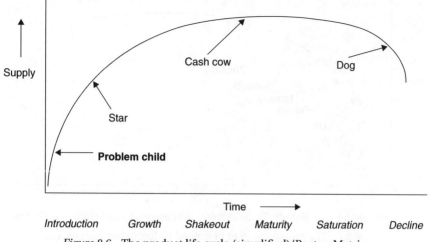

Figure 8.6   The product life cycle (simplified)/Boston Matrix.

where the need is low and the public sector is unable to deliver but that does not matter.

By using this approach, the concept of matrix analysis can be applied to almost all types of operation and provides a useful tool for examining the position of the various products and services for an organisation.

The link between the product life cycle and the Boston Matrix

It is possible to show where each of the components of the Boston Matrix lie on the product life cycle (Figure 8.6).

Whilst for many products and services there is a natural progression from *problem child* to *star* to *cash cow* to *dog*, as was discussed earlier, if a product can be moved to a new market a dog can be transformed into a star etc. What was old hat to one particular market may be the best thing since sliced bread in another. The Manchester Metrolink is an excellent example of a star being created from a dog (the loss-making railway lines).

 In their 1999 Annual Report, Icelandair makes reference to the product life cycle for the tourism market in Iceland by plotting sales regions against the simplified product life cycle curve, as shown in Figure 8.7.

As is pointed out in the report, Germany as a market has reached a definite level of maturity. Icelandair believes that the rapid growth in German visitors in the first half of the 1990s was related to the opportunities for nature study in Iceland. The company is now exploring methods of promoting other aspects of Iceland to this market in order to reach different segments.

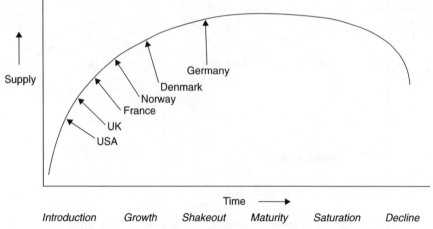

Figure 8.7 The tourism market in Iceland by Icelandair sales region.

The Danish market is likely to be fairly constant as Iceland was a Danish possession until 1944 and thus there are ties of kinship.

The stars (in Boston Matrix terms) are the US and UK markets, as these are showing very rapid growth. Whilst not operated by Icelandair, there has been a growth in day trips to Iceland from the UK operated by one of the major UK package tour companies using its own aircraft. With a return flying time of only 4–5 hours, Iceland is well within reach of UK day-trippers.

The number of US and UK market cruise ships including Iceland as part of their itinerary is also growing.

No longer is Iceland considered an out-of-the-way place at the top of the world but is fast becoming an important itinerary for US, Canadian and UK travellers.

Summary

All products undergo a life cycle from their inception to their decline in the market for which they were intended. Organisations tend to produce families of products to suit different segments of the market and also ensure product succession by bringing out newer versions at suitable intervals. The dynamic product life progression, introduced by Cartwright and Green (1997), provides a more sophisticated explanation of product evolution than the more simple product life cycle. There are alternatives to decline and these may well result in the rejuvenation of the product or service, albeit in a very different market.

The Boston Matrix and the similar version for the public sector provide a useful method of analysing an organisation's portfolio of products/services.

QUESTIONS

1 Using products with which you are familiar, illustrate the *product life cycle* and the *dynamic product life progression*. What alternatives might there be to outright decline for the chosen product?

2 Analyse the portfolio of a company or public sector organisation with reference to the Boston Matrix or its public sector equivalent. Why are cash cows so important even if they may not generate the excitement of new products?

3 'An organisation that does not possess a family of products or that does not plan for product succession may be less successful than it could be'. Discuss this statement with reference to the product life cycle.

Recommended reading

You are recommended to read *In Charge of Customer Satisfaction* by Roger Cartwright and George Green (1997), in which the concept of the dynamic product life progression was first introduced.

Useful websites

www.GMPTE.gov.uk	Greater Manchester Passenger Transport Executive website
www.manchestermetrolink.co.uk	Manchester Metrolink website

■ ⌄ **Part Three**

Price/cost

As Part Two has shown, it is vital that organisations develop the products and services that their customers need, want, value and find of benefit. However for virtually every customer, the resource with which products and services are acquired (usually money) is a finite one. Thus it is important that the right product/service is also offered at a cost that is acceptable to the supplier, who needs to make money to fund future operations, and the customer, who has competing demands on what, for most of us, is a limited resource.

▪ ⊻ 9 Costs

There is little point in having a first-class product unless it is delivered at a cost that is acceptable to both the customer and the supplier.

The Porter *competitive forces model*, introduced in Chapter 5, stressed the balance between the bargaining power of suppliers and that of customers.

Referring to the Porter model, a supplier will want to deliver the minimum acceptable standard at the highest price possible, whilst the customer will want the highest possible standard at the lowest price. As was stressed in Chapter 5, this does mean that suppliers will wish to deliver substandard products, just that they will not want to incur extra expense in delivering a higher standard than the customer actually requires. There is no point in producing something to a higher standard than the customer really needs. Anecdotally it is believed that Henry Ford was not pleased to discover that the kingpins on the famous Model T outlasted every other component by a considerable time. This demonstrated to Ford that the kingpins were over-engineered!

This chapter will examine how the costs of a product or service are built up and how they then relate to the price that can be charged for that product/service.

Costs can be described as a function of the resources needed to deliver a product or service, whilst the price is what the customer has to pay in order to take delivery. In general terms, money is the means by which cost and price are described and measured, and thus it is important that this consideration begins by considering what money actually is.

Money

Money forms an important factor in the success of both organisations and customers (and indeed our daily lives), and yet there is often a misunderstanding as to what exactly the term 'money' means.

Goods are articles produced to be sold or exchanged (and thus the word can include services when used in a strict economic sense). There is a singular of the word goods that is used in business matters, i.e. a good. A good is an article or service produced to be sold or exchanged.

Money is a mutually acceptable, standardised good used as a method of exchange. If organisation A sells an article to customer B, there is no theoretical reason why B should not pay by means of another article that A requires, say fuel supplies, some form of raw material or manufactured goods. The customer could even pay in accountancy or consultancy services. This form of payment, known as *bartering*, is still used in some parts of the world and even within specially set up exchange projects within small communities in the UK. These work on the 'I will bake you a cake if you will mow my lawn' basis. Barter, however, is just not sophisticated enough for anything other than a very small, closed economy or a single, often government-sponsored trade deal or project. Once trade begins to occur with those outwith a barter system, then a common denominator is required for payment, i.e. something that is mutually acceptable to all the parties to a transaction. Humankind has developed the concept of money as that common denominator.

Money is a commodity that has both an agreed and an accepted value to all the parties involved in a transaction and can thus be used in exchange. Technically anything can be used as money but if, say, pebbles off the beach were used there are just too many of them for an individual one to have much worth, although giant stones were used by one South Pacific civilisation for many thousands of years. If you wanted more money, you would just go and collect some more pebbles and so could anybody else. Value comes with rarity and so from ancient times those commodities with rarity value have become accepted as forms of exchange. The precious metals – gold, silver etc. – and precious stones – diamonds, rubies, emeralds etc. – were acceptable because of their rarity value. Although the Chinese invented paper money many centuries ago, a large number of countries and economies retained systems based on rare commodities until quite recent times. Even when notes were introduced, they were backed up by an amount of gold equal to their value held in the central bank. In medieval times, the English Chancellor of the Exchequer used to carry the wealth of the country around with him. Gold has always been a key part of the economic system. Up to the 1930s, exchange rates between currencies were fixed using the gold standard. In theory, this required economies to carry out the promise on their notes. On a UK bank note is the legend: 'I promise to pay the bearer on demand (and then the sum)', and this is signed on behalf of the Governor of the Bank of England or the relevant Scottish bank. A £10 note is really an IOU for £10 of gold, although it is unlikely that the bank would actually give you that amount of gold. In the 1930s, the US government suspended the right of the public to convert notes into actual gold, and now all that remains of the public's link to the gold standard is a line of print on a bank note.

Because gold, silver, diamonds etc. are rare they tend to keep their value, and in times of major crisis people try to convert their assets into these. One of the advantages of gold as an exchange medium is its chemical stability; it is a very non-reactive element and thus it is hard to adulterate or substitute with a fake having the appearance of gold. Up to the early 19th century the UK retained the death penalty for those caught minting their own, forged money, so important is it to retain the integrity of the money supply system. Even today, forging money carries very heavy penalties. The hardness of diamonds makes them, like gold, difficult to fake. The dream of the alchemists of medieval times was to turn base, common metals into rare and pure gold. Gold is the value that it is because people have confidence in its ability to hold this value. Had the alchemists succeeded they would, in fact, have defeated themselves, as the rarity and thus the value of gold would have fallen dramatically. Confidence in the integrity of the monetary system lies at the heart of all economic theory.

If people have confidence in an economic system they are more likely to hold their assets in the intangible symbols of that economy, i.e. bank notes etc., whereas when confidence declines there is a likelihood that those who can will convert their assets into more tangible forms of exchange, such as gold. The use of tangible artefacts such as gold etc. is known as *commodity money*, whereas the money most people use throughout their daily lives, notes and coins, is known as *fiat money.*

Governments through their central banks usually issue money, although in the UK the three major Scottish banks also issue their own notes. By being the currency issuers, central banks are able to regulate the amount of money in the economy and thus aid government fiscal policies.

There are five basic criteria that any good must meet in order to be acceptable as a form of money. The world has developed a series of types of money – coins, notes, cheques, credit cards, bankers' drafts etc. – all of which meet the criteria for a good used as an exchange medium. These are:

- it must be acceptable to all the parties in a transaction;
- it must be standardised, i.e. there should be no difference between two £10 notes issued by the same authority;
- it should last for a reasonable amount of time so that its value does not diminish, i.e. it must be durable;
- it must be transportable;
- it must exist in different denominations.

If the systems of currency in use throughout the world today are examined, they will be seen to exhibit all of the above characteristics. Taking the US dollar as an example, it is acceptable almost universally throughout the world. Tourists, especially in the developing countries, will find that most traders are happy to accept US dollars, often in preference to their own currencies. In Europe and other developed areas, the dollar is less likely to be accepted for individual transactions but changing money in these areas is rarely problematic. Nevertheless, many major international projects will be costed in dollars. The currency is standardised in that there is no difference between any of the dollar bills in a person's wallet and they represent exactly the same purchasing power. The US coins are durable and even the paper money has an acceptable lifespan. Durability is very important, as there would be no point in accepting a $5 bill in payment if it disintegrated before the person accepting it could use it for a transaction of their own. Unlike the huge stones mentioned earlier, notes and coins can be easily carried around and they are divided into easy-to-understand denominations, thus allowing change to be given in an acceptable form.

Fiat money has become the usual means of paying for transactions, however when considering costs a commodity such as time needs to be converted into fiat money so that allowance can be made for it in the costing process.

Supply and demand

One of the most important economic concepts is that of supply and demand.

Assume that an organisation has a product (P) of which 10,000 can be produced per month. The total cost of production, including all overheads etc. for each unit of X, is £10. If the organisation sells all 10,000 at £10, it will break even. At any price that is less than £10 the organisation will make a loss, and at any price that is greater than £10 it will make a profit. The organisation would like to make £3 profit on each unit so needs to sell at £13.

However, once the product is on the market it appears that there is only a monthly demand for 9,000 units at £13, whereas the demand would be 10,000 at £12, 11,000 at £11, 12,000 at £10 and 13,000 at £9. Note, however, that current capacity is only 10,000 units.

In this simplification, remember that the cost of production for each unit is £10, so sales at £9 are unacceptable unless the item is sold as a loss leader in order to stimulate sales of another product, a technique often used by retailers in order to attract customers and one that is covered later in this chapter. It may also be that the marginal cost (i.e. the cost of producing one additional unit) of each item of X over 10,000 units (if production can be extended) is so small as to bring the overall cost of production of 13,000 units down to less than £9.

If the above is it not the case, there are 10,000 customers willing to pay £12 for the 10,000 units produced: demand matches supply at an acceptable cost to the supplier albeit at a profit of only £2 per unit rather than the desired £3.

Supply and demand calculations, as will be shown later, are important in determining prices within the marketplace.

Costs

In order to derive a price for a product or service, the actual cost of delivering that product or service to a customer needs to be calculated and then, for those organisations where profits need to be made, a profit margin needs to be added. There are a variety of costs that need to be considered and these are detailed in the following sections.

Costs can be divided into three distinct elements, namely *material costs, labour costs* and *expenses.*

Material costs

Material costs are for the resources consumed in the course of a work activity. They can include raw materials or components bought in from other suppliers.

Material costs are normally encountered in those sectors of business that produce a tangible product. In service industries, however, the cost of buying in a service from another supplier could be considered as a material cost.

Labour costs

These are the costs associated with the human element in the business activity. In service industries, the bulk of the costs associated with an activity may well be labour costs.

Expenses

All costs that are neither material nor labour related are classed as expenses.

Material, labour and expenses can be further subdivided into direct and indirect costs. *Direct costs* are those that can be attributed directly to a specific product, service or activity, whilst *indirect costs* are those spread over a series of activities and referred to in accounting as *overheads*.

In any business there are staff working almost exclusively on the delivery of a service or product. These are sometimes referred to as *line staff*. There are also those whose role is to support the line staff by ordering supplies and paying wages etc. These can be referred to as *support staff*. Line staff and the materials they use are classed as *direct material and labour costs*, whilst support staff generate *indirect materials and labour costs*.

Costs of energy are direct if they apply to a specific activity. The cost of electricity for a particular machine carrying out a specific task will be a direct expense as it can be costed direct to that product. The lighting for a factory will be an indirect expense as it may illuminate (literally) a number of activities associated with a series of products.

Unit costs and cost units

Unit cost is an important term as it refers to the total costs associated with one unit of production or activity. Another similar sounding term is *cost unit*, which is the minimum quantity that the organisation will normally supply. Screws might be supplied in boxes of 50, in which case the price quoted will be per box of 50 and not per screw.

The unit cost of a product comprises a series of components, namely:

Direct fixed costs associated with the product or service
+
Variable direct costs
+
Overheads
+
Margin added by the supplier

Cost centres

A *cost centre* is a clearly defined section or activity of an organisation to which it is possible to assign specific costs. At the corporate level, each factory or branch may be designated as a separate cost centre. It is also possible to split up a process into different cost centres. In this case, each cost centre in the process becomes a customer of the one preceding it and a supplier to the next along the value chain. Those areas dealing with support services, such as administration, marketing etc., may also be considered as separate cost centres. Even a single person may be a defined cost centre.

One of the major reasons for dividing any organisation or process up into separate cost centres is related to the setting of individual targets. As all the costs for the cost centre are allocated to that centre it becomes easier, so the theory goes, for individual managers to keep a close control on those costs. Individual shop branches, for instance, can then be compared to each other as cost centres to determine efficiency, effectiveness and economy, the so called 3-Es.

Other terms that need to be considered when examining costs are:

- Fixed costs;
- Stepped costs;
- Variable costs;
- Contribution;
- Opportunity costs;
- Storage costs;
- Recovery costs;
- Marginal costing and breakeven;
- Total absorption costing;
- Discounts and promotions;
- Loss leaders.

Fixed costs

Fixed costs are those that are not dependent upon the volume of product or service delivered. Hitching and Stone (1984) state that fixed costs are related to a time base rather than one of activity (Figure 9.1). An Icelandair Boeing 757 flying from Glasgow to Reykjavik incurs the same staffing costs, landing costs and more or less the same fuel costs whether it carries 50 or 100 passengers. A shop's rental, rates, staffing etc. are the same regardless of the number of customers. Owners of motor cars pay fixed costs of insurance and road tax regardless of the number of miles they travel. Servicing is also often a fixed cost, as most warranties require servicing either every so often (time-based, e.g. 6 or 12 months) or after so many miles. Car hire prices often contain a fixed and a variable component, i.e. so much per day (fixed cost) and so much per mile (a variable cost – see later).

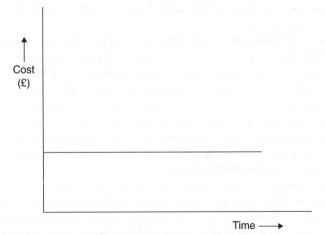

Figure 9.1 Fixed costs.

Fixed costs are very important because unless they are covered, the organisation cannot be successful. It is impossible to go into profit until all of the fixed costs are covered, as will be shown in the consideration of marginal and total absorption costing later in this chapter.

The fuel for the Boeing 757 mentioned earlier is considered a fixed cost because, whilst slightly more fuel will be required for each additional passenger, this is a marginal amount and makes little difference to the total cost of the operation.

Overheads

Car owners are only too well aware that there are costs attached to a vehicle even if it never actually leaves their garage. It will still need to be insured, it will need the engine turned over occasionally to prevent seizure, it may need to be taxed so that it can be used if necessary, and time will have to be found to clean it etc.

As the section on fixed costs has demonstrated, organisations like car owners also have costs even if they undertake no business. Some of these fixed costs can be associated with a particular product whilst others, known as overheads, are concerned with activities across whole areas of the organisation.

One of the reasons for the development of cost centres is to control overheads. By associating them with a particular cost centre it is believed that there will be a greater incentive to control them. As the term 'overheads' actually encompasses many organisational activities, there is always a danger that nobody is taking responsibility for the overhead costs and that they may get out of control.

Overheads generally include all those items that cannot be ascribed to an individual product, process or activity; for example, administration, personnel, salaries, finance, logistics/distribution and of course marketing. In this respect they are indirect fixed costs.

There are two basic methods of allocating overheads to the cost of a product. The organisation can calculate the total overheads for an accounting period and then allocate them on an equal basis to each product, so if there are three products each will carry one-third of the total overheads. Whilst being simple, this method does not carry any recognition that different products or services may 'consume' more overheads than others may. For example, if the machinery for a particular product takes up three-quarters of the floor space and the other two products share the remaining quarter, should not the first product have three-quarters of the overheads allocated to it?

It has become more common to allocate overheads proportionately using a measure such as direct labour hours, direct machine hours or floor space as the input factor. Thus if product A required 10 direct labour hours and product B 5, then 2/3 of the overheads would be allocated to product A and 1/3 to product B.

Marketing costs

Marketing as a function will also have costs associated with it. In the case of an advertising campaign for a particular product it may be possible to allocate these costs directly to that product, but for those areas of marketing that are concerned with promoting the organisational image or gaining knowledge about customers the marketing costs are likely to be regarded as overheads.

One of the problems that organisations may face is to judge the effectiveness of their marketing in terms of value for money. It may be relatively simple to sample the effectiveness of an advertisement to see how many new customers were gained. It is likely to be less simple to discover how normal operations help to retain customers or how good practice promotes word-of-mouth re-commendations. Marketing managers need to ensure that they know what their customers are saying about their effectiveness, as they may have to account for the sometimes large overheads that marketing can generate.

Stepped costs

Imagine that a piece of equipment can produce a maximum of 1,000 items in a given time period and that the fixed cost per hour of using it is £100. If an order came in that required 1,100 items to be produced each hour, then a second piece of equipment would be needed and the fixed costs would immediately double to £200. This is known as a *stepped cost* and occurs when the capacity of equipment etc. reaches its limit, at which time the fixed costs go up considerably (Figure 9.2).

Organisations need to be very careful when expanding their operations, as activity that takes them beyond current capacity, although not by much, may incur considerable additional extra fixed costs.

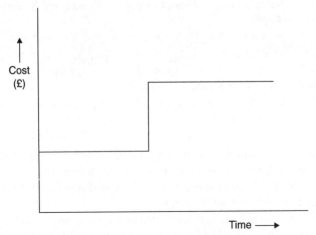

Figure 9.2   Stepped costs.

	Week 1	Week 2
Number of items produced (*A*)	8,000	10,000
Fixed costs	£3,000	£3,000
Variable costs @ £2 per item	£16,000	£20,000
Total costs (*B*)	£19,000	£23,000
Cost per item, *B*/*A*	£2.38	£2.30

(Figures for cost per item are rounded up to the nearest 1 p)

Figure 9.3   Faversham plc costings.

Variable costs

Variable costs are those costs that increase according to the level of activity. In manufacturing, if one item requires 100 g of steel, two items will require 200 g and three items 300 g etc. Thus the costs vary in proportion to the activity.

Fixed costs, as covered earlier, tend not to vary much with the levels of activity under normal circumstances. As was shown in the previous section, a sharp rise in activity over a short timescale can give rise to stepped costs where the fixed costs go up dramatically.

Overhead costs, spread as they are over many activities, are usually regarded by accountants as fixed costs.

As is often the case with the study of numbers and money, a simple example may be worth many words.

Faversham plc, a fictional company, produces a component for the electronics industry. The fixed costs associated with the particular product are £3,000 per week and the variable cost per item produced is £2. The total capacity per week is 10,000 units.

Figure 9.3 shows the costs per item for a week when 8,000 items were produced and for the next week when full capacity was reached:

As the figure shows, the increased production reduces the cost per item by 80 p because the fixed costs of £3,000 are spread out over more units. Assuming that a

	Week 1	Week 2	New order
Number of items produced (A)	8,000	10,000	15,000
Fixed costs	£3,000	£3,000	£6,000
Variable costs @ £2 per item	£16,000	£20,000	£30,000
Total costs, (B)	£19,000	£23,000	£36,000
Cost per item, B/A	£2.38	£2.30	£2.40

(Figures for cost per item are rounded up to the nearest 1 p)

Figure 9.4   Faversham plc costings showing stepped costs.

new machine etc. would double the fixed costs, the effect of stepped costs can be seen in Figure 9.4. Assume now that Faversham plc has received an order for 15,000 units per week. To satisfy the customer they will need another machine, as current capacity is only 10,000 per week.

Unless Faversham can sell more than 15,000 units per week, it has a problem, as the unit cost (see earlier) for 15,000 units where the machinery has a capacity for 10,000 is actually slightly higher than it is for 8,000 units. Perhaps the order is not such good news after all!

Contribution

Referring to the Faversham plc, week 2 example, quoted earlier, the unit cost was calculated at £2.30. Of that £2.30, £2.00 went towards the cost of materials etc., i.e. the variable costs associated with each unit (V) The remaining 30p was a proportion of the fixed costs carried by the product. Suppose for argument's sake that the unit selling price (S) is £3.00. Then contribution (C) = $S - V$. Here C is a contribution towards the fixed costs and when they have all been met, it becomes a contribution towards profit. In the example, C = £3.00 − £2.00, i.e. £1.00.

Other types of costs

Having considered fixed costs and variable costs, there are other types of cost that need to be considered when determining the true cost of delivering any product or service. The first of these involves the concept of an opportunity cost.

Opportunity costs

Any resource is usually finite. In general terms, an individual or organisation with a sum of money to spend will find that having spent it, it is no longer available to them. It is true that purchasing an appreciating asset may lead to even more resource being made available later. Where time is concerned, however, the time resource is fixed. Once time has been used it is never available again.

An opportunity cost relates to what could have been done with the resource had a different decision been made. An organisation with £10,000 to spend and a requirement for both a new computer system and a new brochure, both costing

£10,000, can have one or the other but not both. If the computer is chosen then the brochure becomes the opportunity cost, and vice versa. In personal terms, most of us make such opportunity cost decisions every day when spending our disposable income. It may well be either a holiday or a washing machine but not both.

Those responsible for the management of marketing have a duty to ensure that their colleagues in the organisation make the choices that the market will support and that such choices are customer centred. Losing the customers' goodwill is always an opportunity cost that it is never worth paying.

Storage costs

Of especial relevance when considering tangible products are the costs of storage. In the case of goods that require special environmental conditions, e.g. low or high temperatures, these can be very high indeed. However, even more mundane goods may take up valuable floor space and will need insuring. It is important to suppliers to minimise these costs. In recent years the concept of JIT (Just In Time) has become very important in manufacturing. In a Just In Time operation, the manufacturer keeps no stock of raw materials or assembly parts. Instead of maintaining stocks, materials are delivered as near to the point in time of need as possible. This means that suppliers need to work to the laid down schedule that has been agreed with the customer, and supply the material exactly to schedule. This may mean that a delivery will be made sometimes as frequently as every day or half-day. In some cases it may mean deliveries timed to the hour, as without further materials the operation will quickly be brought to a standstill. Because each of the separate parts of the customer's operation will also be working on a Just In Time basis, the next process which is supplied from this production line will also stop until in a very short space of time the whole production system is at a standstill.

Not only must the delivery schedule be met but also the agreed quality must be achieved, for any faulty material will also cause the line to stop until it is rectified.

The entire Just In Time operation is built upon the need to reduce the holding of stock and have it drip fed as necessary. Whilst this may cause problems if supplies are delayed, there are considerable savings in storage and its associated costs.

Recovery costs

The next chapter of this book considers quality and value. Even in the best run organisation, things will go wrong. It is probably impossible to guarantee that every product or service will always be 100% defect free. Machines break down and people make mistakes. Customer service experts have realised that what is important to the supplier–customer relationship is less that there is never a mistake but how errors are rectified. As will be shown in the next chapter, it often costs much more to correct an error than to try to ensure that it will never happen. The techniques of cost–benefit analysis are useful here. If an error occurs only very infrequently then it may be concluded that the systems etc. are adequate, but even so the customer who suffers from the error will need a replacement and possibly compensation.

Modern statistical techniques can indicate the error rate, and the costs of rectification can be built into the price paid by all customers.

Organisations can be much more generous with their guarantees if they are confident about the robustness of their processes. In the 1990s, UK motor car manufacturers, beginning with Rover, started to offer unconditional money-back guarantees within one month on new vehicles if the customer was dissatisfied with their purchase, even if there were no actual faults. Rover would not have taken this step (which is a powerful marketing tool) if it had not been confident in the quality of the products in the first place. In fact, very few vehicles are returned under such schemes, but they do provide the customer with a safety net when making what is a major purchasing decision involving considerable sums of money for the individual.

Sunk costs

One of the reasons put forward for continuing with projects that appear unsuccessful is that of 'we have spent so much, we must try to recoup our costs'. This is actually a fallacious argument. If a project is not going to be successful, the resources put in may well be lost and are known as *sunk costs*. It is perhaps better to be honest, admit this and cut further losses than to continue.

Development costs

The costs of developing a new product may be huge. These costs have to be covered through sales. It is permissible to treat costs as an asset on the balance sheet for each item sold, although this is not always wise. Instead each item sold up to breakeven should carry a part of its price as a repayment of development costs. Obviously, adding development costs to the price will push the breakeven figure out even further.

One of the reasons for co-operation in major projects is the fact that development costs can be spread over the partners, the opportunity cost being secrecy!

Marginal costing and breakeven

The concepts of fixed and variable costs and contribution allow a point known as the *breakeven point* to be calculated.

Davies (1990) points out that marginal costing is not a complete costing system but a means by which managers can focus their attention on costs that can be controlled in the short-term. By concentrating on the cost of producing one more

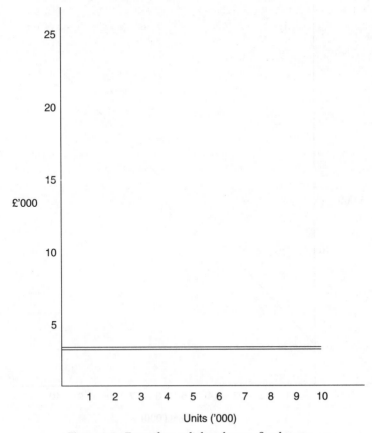

Figure 9.5 Faversham plc breakeven, fixed costs.

unit of product or service, the concept of marginal costing allows for the unit cost to be divided into its two main components – the variable cost element, i.e. the cost of the materials etc. used, and the contribution discussed earlier.

Considering Faversham plc, week two, again (assuming a selling price of £3.00), Figure 9.5 can be constructed.

The horizontal line represents the fixed costs of £3,000 that will have to be paid regardless of the number of units produced or sold.

The variable costs are added in Figure 9.6.

Note that the variable costs line starts not at zero but at £3,000 to take account of the fixed costs that must be met. The final stage is to add on the line representing sales (Figure 9.7).

Breakeven

The sales line does begin at zero because it represents income, and no sales equals zero income. Where the sales line crosses the variable costs line, when

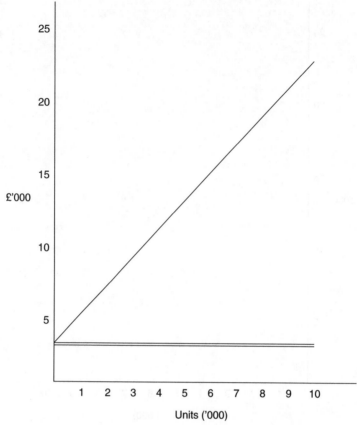

25

20

15

£'000

10

5

1   2   3   4   5   6   7   8   9   10

Units ('000)

Figure 9.6   Faversham plc breakeven, fixed costs + variable costs.

set over the fixed cost line this represents the breakeven point. In this case it is 3,000 units. If Faversham plc sell fewer than 3,000 units at £3.00 each, it will make a loss. Sell 3,000 and it breaks even; sell more than 3,000 and it will make a profit.

Similar charts can be drawn up for different prices and costs. For example, if the selling price were reduced to £2.50, then the breakeven point would move out to 6,000 units, as shown in Figure 9.8.

There is a very simple set of formulae for calculating breakeven figures:

F = fixed costs
V = variable costs per unit of product/service
P = selling price per unit of product/service
n = number of units of product/service
C = total cost, i.e. $F + (n \times V)$
R = revenue, i.e. $(n \times P)$

As breakeven is the point at which revenue is exactly the same as costs, $R = C$, then at breakeven:

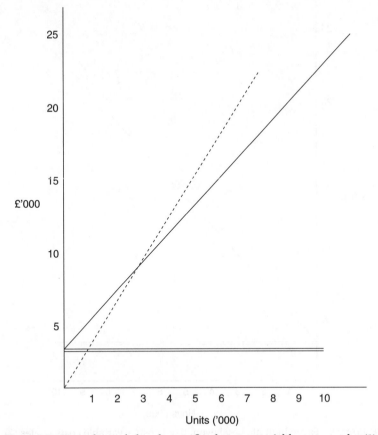

Figure 9.7 Faversham plc breakeven, fixed costs + variable costs + sales (1).

$$(n \times P) = F + (n \times V)$$

Using simple algebra, the price required to break even for a given volume is:

$$P = F/n + V$$

and the volume required to be sold at a given price is:

$$n = F/(P - V)$$

Pricing is considered in the next chapter.

Unless the fixed costs are met, then there will never be any chance of profit. This is one of the most important points about marginal costing, as it also means that once the contribution has met the fixed costs then everything else is profit. The organisation can take on extra work at a lower price once the fixed costs are met without risking a loss, provided that the lower price covers the variable costs

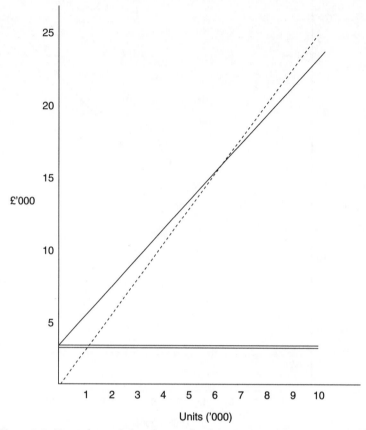

Figure 9.8 Faversham plc breakeven, fixed costs + variable costs + sales (2).

of the extra work. For organisations operating in the perishable goods market, covered earlier in this book, this is very important as it means that an airline can sell the seats that remain after breakeven has been reached quite cheaply. This is where the bargains can often be found.

One of the objections often made to marginal costing is that it concentrates too much on the variable and not enough on the fixed costs.

Breakeven is of considerable importance to those involved in the marketing function as it represents one of the first major goals for any project. Recalling the dynamic life cycle progression model introduced in Chapter 8, it should be apparent that breakeven is likely to occur somewhere between sustained growth and saturation, i.e. it is stars and cash cows that break even, not problem children! It is unlikely that the breakeven point will be reached in the early stages of a project, however positive the initial uptake or rapid the early growth.

Where a project costs many millions of pounds or dollars, breakeven may be some way in the future and a great deal of faith is needed. To finance such projects requires both faith and understanding banks, whose money is likely to be exposed for some time.

For an airline such as Icelandair it is important to calculate the breakeven load factor for each flight. If there are not sufficient passengers to make the breakeven point, then the flight will make a loss. Not only are airline seats 'perishable', as described earlier in this book, but the nature of the operation makes cancelling a flight difficult as the aircraft will have passengers waiting at the other end, hence the discounting often undertaken as flight times approach.

Marketers need to be involved in price setting etc. to ensure that the product/service is priced attractively enough to allow breakeven to be reached before cash flow problems occur.

Cash flow

Many organisations become financially embarrassed despite the success of their products and services because they run out of money. Cash flow is a very important financial concept. The materials etc. needed to meet the variable costs of a product/service are acquired before the customer pays. Organisations are happiest when the customer pays a deposit that covers the variable cost. As a project gains momentum, current sales can pay for future orders but this is not true at the beginning. It is no use having huge order books (in accounting, an order can count as an asset) unless there is sufficient cash to pay one's bills. Banks and other financial institutions will want to study the cash flow forecasts showing monies in and out and the potential market very carefully before committing funds to a new project.

Cash cows (see the Boston Matrix introduced in Chapter 8) are very important for providing cash flow for newer projects. Much of their development costs are in the past and they are generating profits, some of which may be paid as dividends but some of which prudent companies use to fund current developments.

Learning curve

As time goes by, for any product or service the organisation should be able to deliver it cheaper and better. Early prototypes will have bugs that need to be ironed out and workers need training. Irving (1993) reports that the first fifty Boeing 747s to be built required a workforce of 27,500. By the time the breakeven four-hundredth was produced, the workforce was only 7,500. This is the learning curve. As time goes by, mistakes become less and the time taken, especially in manufacturing, drops thus aiding cashflows and recovery costs.

Total absorption costing

The other main means of costing is known as *total absorption costing* because it spreads the fixed costs out over a range of products/services. This method allocates the fixed costs across the products and then adds the variable, thus absorbing all of the costs.

The following example is for a product with a variable cost of £50.00 per unit, the relevant fixed costs being £1,000. It is interesting to see the relationship between unit cost and quantity as the latter increases (Figure 9.9).

Shown graphically, these figures produce the result shown in Figure 9.10.

Every quantity above the line represents profit and every one below it a loss. Sell 50 units at less than £70 each and there will be a loss. Equally, selling

Quantity (Q)	Fixed costs (£)	Variable costs (50 × Q) (£)	Total costs (£)	Unit cost (T/Q) (£)
1	1,000	50	1,050	1,050
2	1,000	100	1,100	550
5	1,000	250	1,250	250
10	1,000	500	1,500	150
50	1,000	2,500	3,500	70
100	1,000	5,000	6,000	60

Figure 9.9   Total absorption costing (1).

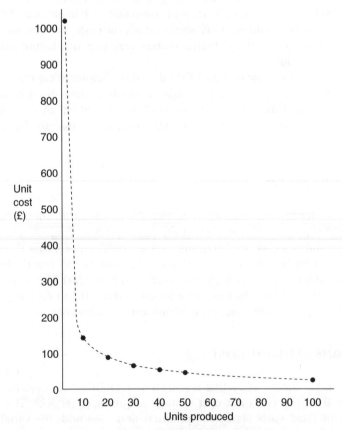

Figure 9.10   Total absorption costing (2).

fewer than 50 units at £70 will also lead to a loss, as some of the costs will be unabsorbed.

Value chain

In a simple transaction, an individual may deal directly with the customer with no intermediaries. In modern business, however, there may be a number of organisations and individuals along the value chain. Each of these entities adds value and thus will require to make a percentage of the margin that in turn will need to be added to the cost (Figure 9.11).

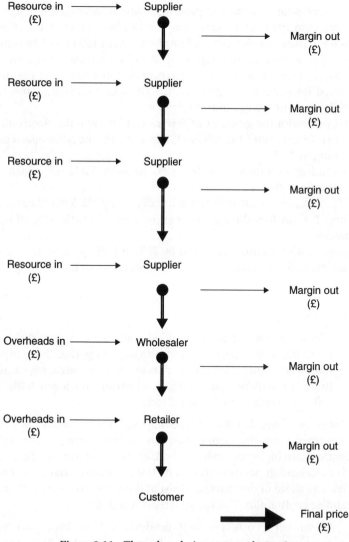

Figure 9.11 The value chain, costs and margin.

Each organisation or person in the chain has costs and if all goes well, each takes out their costs plus the margin. The sum of the margins over the cost of all the resources and overheads is the value added that the customer pays.

As will be shown in the next chapter, a bargain is a product/service where the added value is perceived by the customer to be greater than the margin added.

 The sums involved in the airline industry are huge. A Boeing 737–700 jet, the smallest of the Boeing family, costs about £30 million, a considerable investment.

The following figures taken from the Icelandair 1999 accounts show the scale of the sums involved and the importance of maximising reources (Icelandair, 2000).

The Icelandair Boeing 757 passenger aircraft averaged a daily usage of 14.6 hours in 1999, an increase from the 13.7 hours recorded in 1990.

As a measure of efficiency and productivity, in 1999 the 2,490 employees in the group produced a figure of 236,874 revenue ton-kilometres per employee, well up on the 137,024 revenue ton-kilometres per employee recorded for the 1,428 employees in 1990, although slightly down on the 1998 figure as noted in the annual report.

Net profits for the group in 1999 were 1,515 million ISK (Icelandic Krona, £1 = 131 ISK), up from 151 million ISK in 1998 despite passenger-kilometres dropping by 1.5%.

Operating expenses rose by 9.2% to 30,023 ISK, of which staffing accounted for 26.8%.

Of key concern to an airline, fuel prices rose by 4%. Icelandair spent 2,247 million ISK on fuel during the year, this being nearly 10% of operating expenses.

Cargo traffic revenue increased by 25%, a large growth, the majority of which came from imports into Iceland, reflective of the growing stature of the country in the European economy.

In his introduction to the 1999 report, Sigurdur Helgason, the President and CEO writes:

> 'The decade which has just ended marked a very remarkable turning point in Icelandair's operation. During this period the company has managed to turn a very difficult position to its advantage and rapidly build up activities and services which are on a par with the best offered anywhere in the world today.'

Whilst stating later that the 1999 results were not as good as they could be, he comments on the strong position of the company overall. Airline operations are highly competitive and, as shown above, costly. A company such as Icelandair needs to market its USPs to ensure that these bring it an increasing share of the market, whilst at the same time controlling costs to maximise profitability. The report later states that:

> 'Icelandair's costs per unit production have kept pace with the revenue trend. Unit costs have fallen by more than 30% in real terms

over 10 years. Icelandair has achieved its reduction in costs through three main channels:

1. Expanded activities which spread overheads to more units of production. Primarily the company has increased its activity by building up and expanding its hub connection network which creates the opportunity for utilising equipment and manpower jointly to serve more markets than would otherwise be the case.

2. The introduction of new technology has enabled unit cost to be reduced. Above all this has involved a new generation of aircraft, while the company will increasingly seek ways to cut costs with the introduction of new information technology in all areas of operation.

3. Dedicated cost analysis of operations has twice produced very good results and at the same time contributed to introducing better control and management of costs and operations in the company as a whole.'

In 1999 the seat load factor was 71.4%, i.e. flights were on average 71.4% full. This is above the necessary breakeven figure.

Summary

Money is the accepted means of carrying out most business transactions. The supply and demand calculations determine how much can be charged. Costs are built up of a variety of components, including variable and fixed costs. Fixed costs must always be covered before there can be any possibility of profit.

Organisations need to take into account opportunity, storage, and recovery and development costs when deciding prices.

The two major costing techniques are marginal costing and total absorption costing.

Breakeven is the point at which profit can be made. Cash flow and the learning curve feed into breakeven calculations. The more an organisation does something, the cheaper and more efficient it should be.

QUESTIONS

1 What is meant by the terms 'contribution' and 'breakeven'? A product has fixed costs of £1,000 and a variable cost of £4.00. Market research suggests that the maximum a customer will pay is £8.00 per unit. At £8.00 per unit, calculate the breakeven point.

2 What do you understand by the term 'opportunity costs'? Give examples from your own experience of opportunity costs either faced by yourself or your organisation.

3   What is 'money'? Describe the major characteristics of a monetary system.
    [Answer to question 1 = 250 units]

Recommended reading

Useful information on the financial aspects of management can be found in *Management and Cost Accounting* by Colin Drury (1985).

Useful website

www.moneyweb.co.uk   Information and history about money

■ ⊻ **10** Quality, value and price

Value and cost – What's it worth? – Excellence equilibrium – Value expectation – Bowman's strategic compass – Excellence and quality – Total Quality Management (TQM) – Legal aspects – Sale and Supply of Goods Act – Product liability – Legal remedies – Codes of practice and arbitration – Quality standards – Price – Price elasticity – Discounting, promotions and loss leaders

Value and cost

The previous chapter was concerned with costs, this chapter centres on value and pricing. Costs are tangible, value is less so. Whilst the value of a product may be related to the costs of assembly, delivery etc., as discussed in the previous chapter, it does not follow that there will be a straight-line relationship. The cost of a human being in terms of the chemicals in our body is just a few pence. The value of a human life is such that it is beyond price. In the case of a person, the added value is massive compared with the basic cost.

What's it worth?

'The Great House Selling Conundrum' has been used by a number of authorities to illustrate the nature of perceived and actual value.

A couple wish to sell their house but unfortunately it is in an area where prices have been at best fairly static, a scenario that became all too real for many householders in the 1990s. Those who had bought when prices were high and had taken out huge mortgages found that the anticipated further rises in prices did not occur and in many cases prices dropped, leaving them owing more than the property could fetch in the marketplace, i.e. with negative, not positive equity.

If, three years ago, they had paid £70,000 for a house and then £6,000 for a new kitchen and a conservatory for £10,000, the total cost to them would have been £86,000. Unfortunately, the estate agent values their house at £75,000 since new kitchens etc. do not often add the full cost of purchase and installation to the value of the property for a potential buyer. Their insurance agent, however, advises that the insurance value for rebuilding should be £95,000.

Plenty of potential customers (and not a few time wasters) come to see the house, and eventually they are offered £72,000.

Is the house worth the £86,000 spent on it, the £75,000 the estate agent has valued it at, the £95,000 it would cost to rebuild or the £72,000 being offered?

In reality, anything, including property, is only worth what somebody else is willing to pay for it. This is a key concept when considering value for money. It is only the customer who decides whether something is value for money. An organisation can make as many statements as it likes regarding its beliefs that its products/services represent the best value for money in the marketplace, but those statements can only be proved to be correct if customers are prepared to pay the price that the organisation asks.

Value for money, or VFM as it will be referred to in this chapter, is a very individual matter, as it comprises a series of factors, which may be very personal to the customer:

- desire for the product/service;
- amount of finance available;
- cost of competing products/services.

A product/service can only be deemed VFM if the targeted customer can actually afford it. A top-of-the-range sports car or a world cruise may well be considered good value but very few will be able to partake of such an offering.

A Rolls Royce is possibly the best car in the world and in pure engineering terms there is no doubt that the product is truly excellent. Prior to the fatal crash of 2000, Concorde was the fastest and most exciting method of flying across the North Atlantic. Rolex watches are undeniably among the best in the world (and the most expensive!). Rolls Royce and Rolex products are undoubtedly excellent but for most people, excellence is connected with things that they can do or experience, and not the experiences and possessions of others.

Tesco in the UK and Macy's in the USA may not be in the same league as the more expensive stores such as Harrods but they offer an excellent service to a large number of customers. VW, Ford and General Motors may not be perceived as in the same class as Rolls Royce but they provide good, reliable transportation for millions of people across the world. Icelandair operates a reliable, fast and economical service across the North Atlantic. Its product does not have the glamour of Concorde but it is available to a larger number of travellers.

Excellence, as presented in this book, is a balance between the best service or product for the price, with the highest quality, delivered to a consistently high level. All this is done through people. Excellence is the equilibrium between the various components. If a conscious decision has been made to go for a small 'niche' market, then one cannot compare the products or services so developed with those that are aimed at a wider market. When considering excellence, it is important that like is compared with like.

The excellence equilibrium (Figure 10.1) illustrates this balance.

Value expectation

Value expectation as a concept was introduced in Chapter 6 when considering needs and wants. The point was made about the link between perception and value. When value, quality and excellence are considered, they are not what may

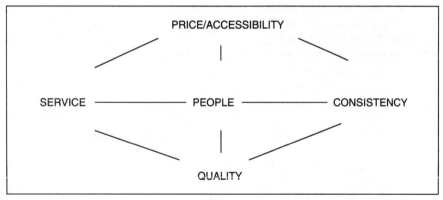

Figure 10.1 The excellence equilibrium. [*From Cartwright* et al., *1998b, with permission.*]

be described as absolute absolutes. An absolute is something that can have an agreed fixed value attributed to it. A non-absolute absolute has a value that can fluctuate according to the perceptions of the individual valuer. One person's idea of high quality may be very different from another's and thus quality is a non-absolute absolute. It shows components of absolution, i.e. very clearly defined limits, especially at the lower end where a situation can occur whereby the product/service is rejected because the quality does not reach the minimum standard. There is also a degree of absolution in the quality standards that governments and trade organisations may set for a product/service. These are independent of the value that an individual may ascribe to the product but will be based on average perceptions.

As was covered in Chapter 6, one of the major theories of motivation is that proposed by Vroom (1964) and commonly known as **expectancy theory**. Vroom's concept was that the perceptions that effort will lead to effective performance, that effective performance will lead to rewards, and that such awards are available, produce a motivational effort on the part of an individual, this effort leads to performance and the performance to some form of reward. Achieving the award starts a feedback loop in that it reinforces the original perceptions. From Vroom's ideas it is possible to develop the concept of **value expectation**.

Based on these ideas, the value expectation model (from Chapter 6) can be used to explain the perception–value links (Figure 10.2).

As was further explained in Chapter 6, the model is based upon four basic perceptions held by the person ascribing value to the product/service:

1. perception of a direct relationship between price and quality;
2. perception based around the strength of the need (or want) for the particular product or service;
3. perceptions gained from previous experiences;
4. perception in regard to the market.

These four perceptions together produce an overall perception of value, albeit an individual one based as it is on an individual's perceptions. If the valuer has a

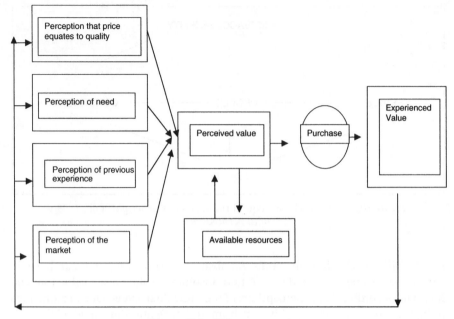

Figure 10.2   Value expectation.

good idea of the true relationship between price and value, i.e. they understand that prices are based on costs (see previous chapter), and if they have a high level of need, good previous experiences and know the market and what is on offer, then there will be the likelihood of a high perceived value provided that the standards of the product/service are high. The model shows the value to be expected to be ascribed. The actual value will be highly dependent on the standards of quality of the product/service.

After experience of the product or service, the valuer will be able to make an objective judgement of its actual value to them. It is possible that this will bear no true resemblance to the actual costs of production/delivery. This can then feed back to inform revised perceptions of price v. quality, and there are new experiences, a measure of need fulfilment and enhanced knowledge of the marketplace.

Bowman's strategic compass

Clutterbuck *et al.* (1993) use Bowman's strategic compass as a tool to inform organisational decision-making as to the direction that an organisation should take in respect of costs and added value.

The model uses two axes, one relating to price and the other to perceived added value (Figure 10.3).

Examining each of the strategies in turn provides examples of a variety of approaches within the marketplace.

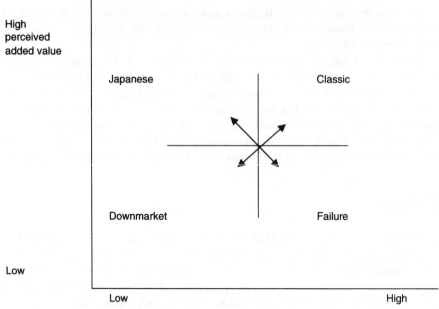

High
perceived
added value

Japanese   Classic

Downmarket   Failure

Low

Low   High

Figure 10.3 Bowman's strategic compass.

Classic

The traditional strategy that has been in vogue for centuries is based on the concept that an increase in perceived value leads to the ability of the supplier to charge more. The key issue is, based on the previous section of this chapter, who ascribes value?

For much of commercial history, value was set by the suppliers who told customers what was and was not value for money. Not surprisingly, the organisation's products and services always were VFM, at least in the organisation's eyes. Such an approach may seem incredible in our communications-oriented society but demand value, like demand economies, can be imposed. If the culture of questioning is not present then people will accept what they are told.

Downmarket

This is the opposite of the classic strategy. Just as price can be increased if the perceived value increases, so lower value allows for price to be cut. Discounting often follows this strategy. Organisations sometimes appear to behave as if their customers will not notice that little bits of the experience are being removed to cut costs. Unfortunately, soon the customer can notice that it is not just costs that are being cut but value as well. Once value is cut then the customer will expect to pay less and a vicious downward spiral can develop.

Many organisations have adopted what might be termed an 'incremental decrease' in costs/quality, hoping that a succession of small cuts in service will be less noticeable than a few larger ones. They are probably wrong. Sooner or later the customer will notice.

There is nothing intrinsically wrong in adopting a downmarket strategy provided that the organisation does not try to portray its products and services as being anything other than downmarket. There will always be room at the lower end of almost any market for suppliers who offer VFM to that segment. Downmarket does not mean less VFM. VFM is a balance between what is offered and what is expected. A cheap, downmarket product or service that exceeds expectations is actually better VFM than a more expensive one that fails to satisfy.

Failure

It perhaps stands to reason that an attempt to charge a high price for low perceived value is a doomed strategy. It can only work in a monopoly situation (as often found in demand economies) with a very highly desired or staple product. It is certainly not a medium- to long-term strategy for success in a free market economy, where competitors will be able to offer much better VFM.

Japanese

This is an interesting strategy as it links high value with low price. This is a classic method of gaining market share. Pascale and Athos (1981) have pointed out the many differences between the Japanese and the Western style of management after World War II. The Japanese and other Pacific Rim economies (South Korea, Taiwan etc.) have traditionally regarded market share as a prime success criterion, whereas the West tends to look for Return On Investment (ROI) – up to 15% pa in many cases. Japanese electrical goods and cars made massive inroads, initially in the USA and then in Europe after World War II, by offering quality products at low prices. The Japanese were, at times, accused of dumping goods onto the market and making no profit at all. True or not, Japanese companies employing these strategies were able to gain a massive market share through this approach whilst raising overall quality standards considerably. UK motorists, who had been used to returning a new car to the dealer time and again to have faults rectified, prefered (and then demanded) zero defect products that required little or no post-purchase rectification. Interestingly, in the late 1990s, Japanese goods were no longer the cheapest, Taiwan and South Korea having also learnt how to play the strategic compass game!

Excellence and quality

Excellence and quality are key factors associated with VFM. The *Concise Oxford Dictionary* (1990) defines excellence as:

'. . . surpassing merit or quality'

Quality comes first, excellence goes beyond it. It follows that a consideration of quality is key to any study of customer relations. It could be said that VFM is achieved whenever quality exceeds expectation.

A number of authorities have considered precisely what is meant by excellence, collectively they may be termed the 'quality gurus'. The work of these people – Deming, Juran, Crosby, Peters and Waterman, Clutterbuck *et al.* – is important not because they have provided a detailed prescription of how to achieve quality (which some have tried to do) but because of the debate they have stimulated.

Peters and Waterman's *In Search of Excellence* made a major impact in the UK when it was published in 1982. Its themes were taken up with great gusto, especially by the public sector, which was perhaps unusual at that time as it might have been expected that the lead in considering and debating excellence would have been taken by the private sector.

Total Quality Management (TQM)

The concept of Total Quality Management (TQM) gained a high profile from the early 1990s onwards. In effect, the ideas of the various quality gurus mentioned earlier were combined into a concept that saw quality as the responsibility of everybody in the organisation and placed quality, like customers, at the centre of the organisation's activities.

Quality and the need for a balance between value and quality, with minimum standards for the latter, are not new concepts. Going back to ancient times, there is a quotation from King Hammurabi of Babylon in 1700 BC:

> 'If a building falls into pieces and the owner is killed then the builder shall be put to death. If the owner's children are killed then the builder's children shall also be put to death.'

Whilst this is rather harsh by Western 21st century standards, it does show a concern about quality and the concept of the provider being responsible to the customer for the standard of workmanship. The craft guilds of medieval times were formed both to control the market and to impose quality standards, so that a customer who purchased products or services from a guild member would have a guarantee of quality and would know that shoddy work would be rectified and that culprits could be punished by fines or expulsion from the guild. Organisations such as ABTA (Association of British Travel Agents) and the BMA (British Medical Association) are the modern-day successors to the medieval guilds.

Modern thinking, as promoted by the quality gurus, centres around the concept of continuous improvement, often referred to as *kaizen*, this being the term for continuous improvement in Japanese. Continuous improvement leads to a belief in the totality of quality. Total quality is not just a control system based on constant inspection (QC – Quality Control), nor is it purely an assurance mechanism reliant on self-checking (QA – Quality Assurance), but an holistic approach that requires an organisational attitude and culture that runs through every operation (TQM – Total Quality Management).

TQM is very much a people-oriented as opposed to a control-centred approach. TQM considers that all employees actually have two work roles, one being their actual job and the second being to find ways of improving the work that they do. Given that the second role involves personal initiative, it is obvious that the TQM approach has implications for the senior management of an organisation. Senior management must subscribe and support the TQM approach, as it is their commitment that will lead to the TQM culture pervading the whole organisation.

Legal aspects

Sale and Supply of Goods Act 1994

The original Sale of Goods Act was enacted in 1893 in an attempt to codify certain parts of common law. The main aim of the Act was to clarify the rights and responsibilities of the parties involved in the sale and purchase of goods in respect of those areas not explicitly covered by the terms of the contract. The Act was amended in 1979 and again in 1994 when it was retitled the Sale and Supply of Goods Act. In contract law there are explicit and implicit terms to a contract. The Act does not forbid any explicit terms. For instance, if a non-working motor car were to be sold, perhaps as a static display, then the fact that it was not working causes no problem provided that this is stated clearly in the contract. This is of especial importance when dealing with items that are regarded as 'seconds', i.e. usable but with blemishes. If this is not stated then a breach of the Act has occurred.

The 1994 Act provides considerable protection for the consumer by stating that: **goods should be of satisfactory quality**. Prior to 1994, the concept of reasonableness had to be applied to the term 'merchantable quality', as it had also to be applied to the vendor's description of the goods. If they were described as seconds, then it would be unreasonable to expect them to be perfect. If there is a defect, then, provided that the vendor makes the defect clear to the purchaser, no breach of the Act occurs as the purchaser is deemed to have accepted a contract. The Act specifies five aspects of satisfactory quality:

- fitness for all the purposes for which goods of that kind are commonly supplied;
- appearance and finish;
- freedom from minor defects;
- safety;
- durability.

Durability is a key aspect that again raises the question of reasonableness. If goods break down after normal use but within an unreasonable time scale, then the Sale and Supply of Goods Act can be invoked. The definition of a 'reasonable amount of time' will vary from product to product. In the white and brown goods markets (see Chapter 3) there has been much selling of extended warranties over recent years. Manufacturers' guarantees are normally for 12 months. Many extended warranties are sold on the grounds that the purchaser will not be covered for repairs or replacement after 12 months unless they purchase an extended warranty. A washing machine that broke down after 18 months of normal use might well not be covered by the manufacturer's guarantee, but the aggrieved purchaser would most certainly have a case under the Sale and Supply of Goods Act.

The Act makes it clear that the purchaser is entitled to a product that is as near to perfect as possible. Obviously, 100% quality, whilst desirable, cannot be achieved every time and thus there are remedies available to the purchaser should the goods be imperfect in any way.

A key point relating to contract law is that **the contract is between the vendor and the purchaser and thus the onus for providing redress lies with the vendor and not the manufacturer.** Thus a vendor who claimed that it had to send a faulty item to the manufacturer, or, worse, insisted that the purchaser returned the item to the manufacturer, is committing a breach of the Act.

It is not permissible for a vendor to insist that it will provide *no refunds, no exchanges* or *credit notes only,* indeed signs stating such may constitute an offence under the Act. It is for the purchaser to decide the remedy that they require. Provided that the time since purchase is reasonable and that the item has not been altered or had abnormal use, then if the purchaser wishes the item to be repaired this should be done free of charge, if he or she wishes for a refund this should be provided, or the item exchanged if that is the purchaser's wish.

The addition of the word 'supply' to the title of the Act reflects the fact that it applies not only to the sale of goods but also to hire and barter arrangements. The law is very clearly on the side of the purchaser. As Wotherspoon (1995) has pointed out in an article that all those involved in selling or supplying goods should read, '. . . the buyer should receive goods that are of a satisfactory quality'. If buyer do not then they can, and increasingly do, sue the vendor.

Many vendors seem unaware of the fact that it is they and they alone who have a contract with the purchaser. If the item is faulty then the vendor may have a case against their supplier who in turn may have a case against the manufacturer. However the legal relationship is between adjacent links in the customer value chain (see earlier). Combining the legal and the economic imperatives for excellent customer relations, it is the vendor that has the relationship with the customer, it is the vendor that they may take to court and it is the vendor that will be criticised for any breach in the relationship.

Should a person receive an item as a present then, according to law, they are not the purchaser and thus any claim has to be made by the person who actually made the purchase. Notwithstanding the above, many retailers will exchange presents, but they are under no obligation to deal with anybody except the original purchaser.

It should also be noted that the cost of the return of faulty goods lies with the vendor and not the purchaser.

Services, as opposed to goods, have been covered in law by the Supply of Goods and Service Act 1982. In receiving a service, a customer is entitled to:

- reasonable care and skill in carrying out the service;
- to have the service performed within a reasonable time;
- a reasonable charge if a price was not fixed in advance.

Any materials used in carrying out a service are covered by the same statutory rights as if the customer purchased them personally.

Product liability

Product liability is a term imported from the USA where there have been a number of high-profile financial settlements to customers injured as a result of defective products. In July 1995, General Motors was ordered by a Californian court to pay the sum of $3.2 billion to a family of six, badly burned when a fuel tank on one of its vehicles exploded. The contention was that the company knew that there was a fault and did not issue a recall notice. General Motors immediately appealed and gained a reduction of damages to £750 million, but the case shows how careful companies need to be.

Safety is a key aspect of the Sale and Supply of Goods Act and since 1988, a European Union Product Liability Directive has been in force which allows for action by anybody injured by a defective product *regardless of whether they were the actual purchaser*. A causal link showing that it was a defective product that brought about the injury will need to be shown, but the Directive shows the importance that is now placed on consumer safety.

Remedies

Recourse to law has always been expensive, and cost has often been a deterrent to the ordinary consumer taking action. The introduction in 1973 of the first Small Claims courts in the UK made it much easier for actions relating to relatively small amounts to be brought. In the 1990s these courts became part of the new Civil Court in England and the Sheriff Court in Scotland. The amounts that can be claimed are different in England and Scotland and have been increased upwards a number of times since the original £500 English limit in 1973. Without the formality of a normal court and requiring little or no outlay on legal costs by the plaintiff, these Courts have made it much easier to gain redress. In 1999, the total cost to a claimant in England was £150 for a claim of up to £1,000 and £180 if the claim was between £1,000 and £5,000 (the maximum that could be claimed). Where the plaintiff wins the case, these fees are paid by the defendant.

Larger amounts need to be claimed through the County Court system but with an ever increasing number of solicitors willing to undertake 'no win – no fee' cases, derived from the contingent approach allowable for some time in the USA but actually illegal in the UK until recently, it seems likely that more and more dissatisfied customers may bring legal actions.

It behoves organisations to ensure that they comply fully with the legislation to meet the rights of their customers and to build up relationships such that disputes can be settled amicably without the cost of legal action and the subsequent bad publicity that it can bring.

In 1999, the UK government announced its intention of increasing the powers of Trading Standards Officers in a white paper entitled *Modern Markets, Confident Consumers*. Among the proposals made were:

- a clampdown on rogue traders, using powers to force them out of business;
- additional codes of practice;
- legislation on Internet shopping;
- increased consumer protection.

Codes of practice and industry arbitration

Many industries have now set up arbitration schemes to resolve disputes without recourse to the courts. The decisions of such arbitration services may be legally binding but customers cannot be forced to use them if they would rather go to court. The arbitration scheme of the Association of British Travel Agents (ABTA) is typical. The arbitration fee in 1999 was £65 for claims up to £1,500 and £112 for claims up to the maximum claim under the scheme of £7,500. In 1998, ABTA handled 18,000 claims of which 10% went to actual arbitration with the customer winning 85% of these (*Daily Mail*, 14 July 1999). There is a Chartered Institute of Arbitrators which sets the professional standards for those involved in this work. There are normally time limits on applying for arbitration. As the arbitration service is often linked to a trade association, it is in the supplier's interest to ensure that it has met its obligations, as it may face the wrath of its industry colleagues if it brings bad publicity on the entire industry. Whole sectors have adopted the ombudsman principle, first applied in Scandinavia to the public sector and later adopted by many governments and latterly commercial organisations. Banking, insurance and financial services are examples of sectors that have appointed an independent ombudsman to rule on disputes.

Following the privatisation of many UK public sector industries in the 1980s and 1990s, regulators were appointed to ensure that consumers received a fair deal. OFTEL (telecommunications), OFWAT (water) and OFGAS (gas) are examples, as are the regulators for the National Lottery, electricity and the rail industry. Appointed through the government, the regulators have the power to penalise unfair practices and monitor standards to see that these are in accordance with the franchise agreements. If they are not, then penalties can be applied and ultimately a franchise could be removed.

Quality standards

Many organisations boast about the quality standards they have achieved. ISO 9000 and BS 5750 are two of the better-known quality standards (ISO standing for International Standards Organisation and BS being a British Standard). Clutterbuck *et al.* (1993) make the very valid point that gaining a standard only represents part of a service quality approach. Many organisations are required to gain standards in order to be suppliers to large concerns and especially governmental bodies. Being able to undertake this paperwork may be no indication that the customer will actually receive a better standard of care than that given by an organisation that has not gained the standard. Standards may be of more practical use when they can be removed as well as awarded. In the summer of 1999 the UK Passport Agency lost the 'Charter Mark' it had been awarded by the government, following huge delays experienced by its customers. The award of a recognised standard to a hotel is only meaningful if customers can be assured that, if standards slip, the number of crowns, roses etc. can and will be reduced. Standards need to be reviewed regularly; it is no use achieving the standard and then allowing things to slip back – customers will soon notice.

Price

In the previous chapter, costs were considered and it should be apparent that no product or service should be delivered for less than its variable cost (the only exception being a loss leader, as covered later in this chapter).

The variable cost V and the required contribution to fixed costs $F(c)$ represent the minimum price that an organisation can charge for a product, i.e. $V + F(c)$. As even not-for-profit organisations (see Chapter 2) may need to show some form of return, there is likely to be a requirement for some margin to be built in, making the minimum price to be charged, $OP(min)$, where the O stands for the organisation:

$$V + F(c) + M(min)$$

where $M(min)$ is the minimum margin. As will be shown later, the organisation may choose to forfeit much of the margin and build up market share as an alternative.

The maximum price that the customer will be prepared to pay, $CP(max)$, where the C stands for customer, will be a function of the value expectation as described earlier and thus based on need, perceptions of quality, price of competitors etc.

Remembering that < stands for 'is less than' and > for 'is greater than': if $CP(max) < OP(min)$ there will be no purchase as the customer perceives that the product/service is too expensive, as shown in Figure 10.4.

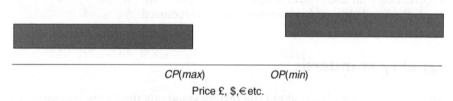

CP(max)   OP(min)
Price £, $,€ etc.

Figure 10.4   Pricing – no sale.

At the point where $CP(max) = OP(min)$, a sale is possible but with little flexibility either way (Figure 10.5).

If, however, $CP(max) > OP(min)$, as shown in Figure 10.6, there will be flexibility for the supplier to offer a discount and for customers to pay more if they really want the product or service.

A major part of the marketing task is discovering the position of the zone of flexibility, as it allows the customer to think that they have achieved a bargain.

Texts on negotiation make great play on allowing for flexibility and achieving a win/win situation. These are four outcome possibilities of any interaction between parties, as shown in Figure 10.7.

When the supplier wins, the customer pays a sum equal to or greater than $OP(min)$. When the customer wins, he or she pays a price equal to or less than $CP(max)$, i.e. exactly what or less than they expected to pay.

When they both lose, there is either no sale at all or the customer feels cheated, perceiving that he or she has paid too much.

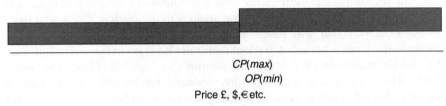

CP(max)
OP(min)
Price £, $,€ etc.

Figure 10.5 Pricing – sale but no flexibility.

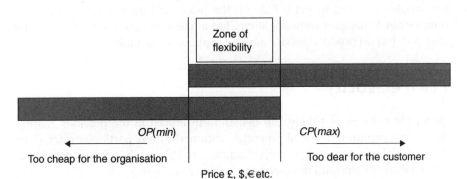

Zone of flexibility

OP(min)

CP(max)

Too cheap for the organisation

Too dear for the customer

Price £, $,€ etc.

Figure 10.6 Pricing – sale with flexibility.

Result for supplier	Result for customer
Win	Win
Win	Lose
Lose	Win
Lose	Lose

Figure 10.7 Outcome options.

The ideal state is obviously win/win where both sides are satisfied, i.e. the customer pays less than $CP(max)$ and the supplier gains more than $OP(min)$, something that can happen in the zone of flexibility.

A situation where the organisation wins but the customer loses is to be avoided because, as discussed above, this will lead to a dissatisfied customer and little chance of repeat business, making for a very short-lived victory especially if other current and potential customers are lost because of what the 'loser' says about the organisation. There may be some short-term satisfaction to be gained from 'getting one over' on a customer, which may be one of those destructive 'games that people' play as described by Berne (1964), but in the end customers will nearly always win as they will end up patronising another supplier!

A situation where the customer wins but the organisation loses may not be as disastrous for the organisation but, having gained a low price once, the danger is that the customer will continue to expect bargains, and a customer that generates no margin is probably one that the organisation does not want to keep.

For many, lose/lose is perhaps the next best option to win/win, paradoxical as that might seem. Davies (2000) uses the analogy of the nuclear defence strategy in the Cold War that was based on a concept of MAD – Mutually Assured Destruction. If the other side launched their missiles at us, in the few minutes we had left we would launch ours at them. We might be dead but at least they would be dead too – a classic (and sad) lose/lose scenario! Davies calls this *The Samson Option*. This reference to Samson bringing down the temple and destroying his enemies and himself in the process can be described as 'if I am going to suffer, so will you'. Lose/lose has the customer refusing to pay a little bit more and the supplier refusing to cut a little off the price, and both being at the same time satisfied that they were not 'done', but at the same time dissatisfied as the customer has no product/service and the supplier no income!

Price elasticity

Under the concept of supply and demand introduced in the previous chapter there are a certain number of potential customers at any particular price level. The aim of the vast majority of organisations is to balance the greatest number of potential customers with the highest price possible.

Those involved in marketing management are also interested in the phenomenon of price elasticity, i.e. the effect of price changes upon product/service uptake.

The standard supply and demand curve suggests that uptake should decrease as the price increases, Foster and Davis (1984) use the example of instant coffee. If the world price of coffee beans rises, it is likely that the cost of the product will rise for all suppliers of instant coffee and that they will all be forced to put up their prices. Coffee is not an essential item for most of us (it is a want rather than a need), so it is likely that some purchasers will switch to other forms of refreshment (perhaps tea) for which the price has not risen.

If the percentage rise in the price charged to the customer is, say, 3% and demand falls by more than 3% then the demand is deemed to be elastic. If the demand is elastic then it falls at a greater rate than the price rises. If the fall in demand was only 1% then it is deemed to be inelastic. When the rise in price is exactly equal to the fall in demand, the elasticity is 1 (one).

Price elasticity is calculated as the percentage change in sales (%S) divided by the percentage change in price (%P), that is:

Price elasticity = %S/%P

It will be seen that, as the revenue generated by a product or service is the price multiplied by volume, even small price increases can (over a large volume) lead to large increases in revenue if the product displays inelasticity. Staple products are inelastic, petrol being a very good example. In the late 1990s and early 2000s the UK government stated that it intended to curb vehicle use (and hence pollution) by raising the price of petrol at the pumps. The number of vehicles on the road and the number of vehicle journeys were relatively unaffected. Motorists just had to pay more, although commercial drivers in 2000 blockaded petrol supply sites causing a nation-wide fuel shortage. Petrol is inelastic – if the price rises, demand is not greatly affected.

Life experience also suggests that there are cross-elasticities. As mentioned above, a rise in the price of instant coffee may lead to a rise in the consumption of tea without there being any change in the price of tea. Relative prices may be as important as absolute ones.

Brand image and elasticity

The importance of a strong brand image has already been stressed in this book, and it is one way in which suppliers can mitigate the effects of elasticity. If a particular brand becomes more desirable than a competitor's, it is possible that customers will absorb greater price increases. There will come a point, however, when even the most loyal and satisfied customer will pay not a penny more and will then consider switching to a competitor or a substitute.

Deciding the price

Prices are decided all along the value chain, with each decision having a knock-on effect on subsequent ones.

To come back to the coffee example used earlier in this chapter. If one year there is a poor world crop of coffee following adverse climatic conditions, then there will be a shortage of coffee. As coffee is a product popular throughout the world there is thus likely to be a shortage and, under the concept of supply and demand, demand will exceed supply and the price of coffee beans to the manufacturers will rise.

In the interests of maintaining the customer base, the manufacturers may decide that this is a short-term problem and that they will absorb some of the price increase. There is likely, however, to be a price increase to retailers. The retailers may, like the manufacturers, decide to absorb some of the increase, thus passing on a smaller increase to customers.

Given that all manufacturers are likely to be affected by the increase in price of coffee beans, all prices are likely to rise by similar amounts without there being any illegal price fixing. Coffee will now be sold at a higher price range. If the world price falls, the price to the customer should drop. Whether it will in practice depends on whether the suppliers believe they can get away with charging the higher price. It only requires one major supplier to reduce prices and the rest are likely to follow suit in a domino effect.

Prices are basically determined by the variable costs, the contribution, the required margin, the actions of competitors and what the market can stand. The latter will, in turn, be affected by the available cash of the target group and factors such as seasonal demand. The turkey market is seasonal in the UK (Christmas) and North America (Thanksgiving). At these times, prices will be at their highest as demand is high. In order to ensure a reasonable price (and thus decent demand all year round), suppliers make strenuous efforts to encourage the customer base that turkeys are not just a seasonal treat but a suitable food for everyday use.

New products/services

As Foster and Davis (1984) point out, these are the hardest to price as there is little history to go on. It is likely that much market research will have to be undertaken to determine the price range that is acceptable to the potential customer base. The price will have to cover all of the costs mentioned in the previous chapter, including development costs.

Very few products or services are genuinely completely new and thus there may well be a body of knowledge that managers can access to give a fair idea of a reasonable price. This price needs to be set carefully as if it is too low the demand will be too high and may outstrip supply, as happened to Sinclair computers in the 1980s. If this happens, customers whose appetite has been whetted may well seek a substitute if they cannot obtain their first choice. Setting the price too high will mean that it will have to be reduced, and this may produce a perception in the customer base that the product/service is not of the quality first supposed.

There are two main strategies that can be used in setting prices:

- skimming;
- penetration.

Skimming

Skimming, as defined by Foster and Davies (1994), involves setting the initial price as high as possible and reaping the benefits until competition forces a reduction. The earliest digital watches are a good example. They were very expensive and there was little competition as the earliest models had patent protection, and yet today they cost just a few pounds.

The fact that setting a skimming price (skimming the profits off) can produce high initial returns that help pay off development costs will also encourage competitors to enter the market, as they see the returns that can be made. It is almost inevitable, therefore, that prices will fall as the market matures.

Those involved in planning need to be aware that the huge potential returns will probably be short lived.

Penetration

Where there are existing competitor products/services it is possible to set prices so as to penetrate the market by fairly aggressive pricing. Unless a new product/service has a large USP (Unique Selling Point), its initial impact may be purely on price. In many ways this is the opposite of skimming. In penetration, the initial price is low and then rises as market share is gained. The danger is that existing suppliers, well-established in the market, may be able to cut their prices to undercut the newcomer and forcing sales at a loss.

Airlines often use this method to enter markets, offering initial fares that are very low in comparison with competitors in order to build market share. The ultimate in penetration is that used, initially by the Japanese and then by other Far Eastern economies, of buying market share by entering markets with prices that are very low and quality that is high (see Bowman's strategic compass, earlier in this chapter).

In the motor industry, this technique was used in the UK market by manufacturers such as Proton, Skoda and latterly Chrysler, whose products were initially much cheaper than those of the competitors. Over the years, prices have risen although at the time of writing these products are still at the cheaper end of the market.

Governments (and especially the EU) have reacted against these practices by restricting imports that are being dumped at a low cost to the customer in order to build up market share.

Discounting, promotions and loss leaders

'How can they sell it for so little? – there must be a catch' is a not infrequent refrain of incredulous customers.

The discussion on marginal and absorption costing above has shown that there is indeed a level of price below which the organisation will be making a loss, and no organisation wishes to make a loss – or does it?

Once all the fixed costs have been covered, it is perfectly possible to reduce the price charged to that of the marginal cost plus a small markup. This is what happens with last-minute booking deals. The organisation will not lose and neither will the customer. There is the danger, however, that other customers will resent having paid nearer to the full cost. Such deals are often for the least popular products.

Icelandair, in common with many airlines, has offered promotions linked to newspapers. Such promotions (Icelandair promoted their Glasgow–Reykjavik–North America service in the *Scotsman* newspaper – a sensible plan given the similarities between the *Scotsman*'s customer base and the customer base that Icelandair wished to tap) often involve the collection of tokens, thus increasing newspaper sales and providing additional customers for the airline.

At one time in the UK it was common retailing practice to buy in goods to offer on special sale, usually in January. Such practices are less common today, given the increased level of consumer legislation. If a retailer wishes to offer goods on special sale, they have to state when and where the goods have been sold at the normal price.

Nevertheless, 'sales' are still very popular. They provide a useful method of clearing out old stock that is costing money by taking up storage space. Customers believe that they are receiving a bargain and whilst the margins may be reduced, provided that fixed costs have been covered, then as was shown earlier a profit can still be made.

The discounting problem

When everybody in a sector discounts everything, there can be a problem because the customers do not discount their perceptions. If a customer books a holiday that was quoted at £1,000 but has been discounted down to £750, that customer will still expect the quality and value to equate to £1,000 and with margins cut this may be impossible for the supplier. In this case the customer will perceive that they have not received VFM and this can lead to resentment, complaints and a loss of repeat business. Perception is usually based on the original price, not the discounted one, a point taken up in the next chapter.

Loss leaders

It is acceptable to sell at a loss on just two occasions. The first is to clear inventory, as stock that is not moving is incurring costs, as described earlier. This is thus a case of cutting losses and it is hard, as described earlier in this chapter, to recover sunk costs.

The other occasion is that of a loss leader – a product or service that is offered at a loss to entice further business. Such operations need careful planning and costing. The idea is usually to build up customer loyalty by apparently offering an exceptionally good bargain in the hope that a more expensive product/service will also be purchased and long-term customer loyalty built up. If the package says 'buy one, get one free', the customer should be aware that the organisation is not making a loss but less profit. It is a mathematical fact that to sell 50 items at a profit of £1.00 is better than selling 20 items at a profit of £2.00. Again, once the fixed costs have been met, additional items can be sold on a marginal costing basis.

Summary

It is organisations that decide the price to be charged dependent upon costs and market conditions, but it is the customer who ascribes value to a product or service depending upon their value expectation etc. The worth of a product or service may differ depending upon the circumstances of the customer. There are various strategies that can be adopted for setting the price of a product or service depending upon the degree of market share required and the elasticity associated with that product or service. Discounting, promotions and loss leaders may all be used to achieve an increase in sales and the customer base.

Quality is often enshrined in legislation, and consumers have increasing rights to redress where quality standards are not up to the required level.

QUESTIONS

1 Using examples, demonstrate what you understand by the term 'elasticity'. Ensure that you provide examples of both elastic and inelastic demand for products/services.
2 What is meant by the terms 'quality' and 'value for money'? Who determines the value of a product and what criteria do they use?
3 What legal implications are there in the UK for suppliers of products and services and how might these impact on their relationships with their customers?

Recommended reading

Useful information on quality is provided in Wille (1992) in *Quality – Achieving Excellence* and Heller (1997) in *In Search of European Excellence.*

Useful websites

www.asqc.org   American Society for Quality Control website
www.iso.ch   Internation Standards Organization website

■ Ⅳ Part Four

Promotion/communications

If despite having the right product/service being offered at a cost that is acceptable to both the supplier and the customer, the latter never actually heard about it then the organisation would be facing a bleak future.

Humankind in the contemporary world is bombarded by information, some news related, some concerned with entertainment, and much about products and services that are available.

Effective communication is vital to the building of the relationship between supplier and customer and thus to marketing management. A great deal of the information is through advertising and the first chapter of this Part is concerned with the marketing role of advertising followed by a chapter that looks at the importance of image and public relations in marketing management.

Communications

One of the distinguishing factors between human beings and the rest of the animal kingdom is the complexity of our communications compared with even our closest relatives. Human beings, in common with most other higher animal species, have five senses:

- vision;
- hearing;
- touch;
- smell;
- taste.

Of these five, the one humans, as members of the primate family, use most often to communicate is vision. Primates are very visual animals, possessing colour vision (important for animals that began as fruit eaters) and stereoscopic vision that is vital for gauging distance. As many primates swing from branch to branch through trees, the ability to judge distance extremely accurately is of critical importance. After vision in order of importance comes hearing. In fact, vision and hearing account for over 90% of primate communication. Other animals communicate using different senses, for instance dogs have a much more highly developed sense of smell than humans. Indeed when it comes to smell, humans are very low down on the list for the effective use of this sense. Many animals take advantage of chemicals known as pheromones, which are produced by the body, and use the sense of smell to communicate (Zdarek, 1988). The best we can usually manage is to apply perfumes and aftershave, although there are such expressions in the English language as 'to smell the fear'. It is quite probable that we produce pheromones but that our noses are not sensitive enough to detect them.

Whilst sight is the predominant human sense, accounting for perhaps as much as 80% of communication using writing, signs and body language, it is apparent that the body is able to compensate for deficiencies in a sense. Visually impaired people often have a more highly developed sense of touch, thus they can learn to read using Braille, which requires considerably more sensitivity in the fingers than humans usually display.

It remains a fact that the vast majority of communication between people is firstly visual and secondly through sound. (Note that our colour vision is restricted to the visible spectrum, so called because it is defined as the range of colours that humans can see, and does not include infra-red or ultra-violet radiation; and that our hearing covers a much more restrictive wavelength of sound compared with that of a dog or a whale – animals that can hear sounds that we cannot.)

The importance of feedback

By definition, communication involves a minimum of two parties. To be effective, communication should also be two way. Even if the process is one whereby the first party purely provides information to the second, the first party should always elicit feedback to ensure that the message has been understood.

To illustrate the importance of feedback, consider a situation where *A* has asked *B* to pass on an important message. Such communications are best carried out in writing but all too often, as in this case, it has been carried out verbally. Imagine that the message is 'send out the Robinson file today, OK?' Such messages are unfortunately all too often shouted at people in corridors. The usual response to 'OK?' is 'yes', whether or not the person really understands.

There might be more than one Robinson file and the person may be unaware of who to send it to. This is why feedback is so important. Messages should be passed on in calm surroundings, not when people are rushing about, and at the end there should always be a summary with feedback – 'what are we going to do?' – to check that the message has been understood. It is a matter of historical record that the British Light Brigade at the battle of Balaclava in the Crimean War was never told to charge the Russian guns. A message was misinterpreted and no clarification or feedback sought. The result was a military blunder of the highest order and a tragic loss of life.

The importance of two-way communication

Part of our programming as animals involves the receiving of feedback in communications – we actually expect it. How many people, watching a quiz show on television, actually *yell* out the answers to the contestant? In some way our brains must expect that we will be heard and that there will be a response, i.e. some form of feedback to our shouts. It is quite clear that this is not an isolated phenomenon, as quiz show hosts comment on it in the vein of: 'hundreds of people at home will be shouting the answer at their television sets!' Despite the fact that logic dictates that the contestant cannot hear people at home, the behaviour continues. In many ways this illustrates the problem of television (and associated technologies) as a medium of communication, because two-way communication is virtually impossible and therefore feedback is at best delayed. Feedback works best when it is instantaneous. There is currently considerable expenditure on technologies to assist television in becoming more interactive. As homes become equipped with more and more digital communications systems, this concept becomes closer to reality.

Body language

Whatever anybody, be it supplier, customer, colleague or employee, may say in words, there is one easy method of telling what they are really feeling in a face-to-face situation – through an observation of their body language. Whilst it is obvious that somebody with a red face and who is gesticulating wildly is obviously annoyed, there are more subtle clues that a knowledge of body language allows those dealing with customers to ascertain the true feelings that are being expressed. It is also obvious that if a member of staff can work out the mood of a customer using body language, then the customer can work out whether the member of staff dealing with them is interested or bored with the conversation etc. Body language is one of the most infallible means of discerning true feelings and is thus a very important part of the communications process. It should be noted that body language is not confined to humans, as those dealing with animals (including pet owners) know well. The true feelings and thus intentions of an animal can often be gauged from the body language clues given out. In many species, body language forms the major part of the communications process considering the lack of a verbal language. Given the importance of vision as a sense in many animal species, this is hardly surprising.

Konrad Lorenz (1963) was one of the first to study the posture and mannerisms of animals and link these to behaviour. In his work on aggression he was able to show how dogs signalled their aggressive intent through the facial gestures they made, and since then many others have studied this area.

Human beings are unusual for primates in that we are 100% bipeds, i.e. we always walk in an upright position. This confers major advantages on us as a species as we can use our very complex arm, hand and finger joints to manipulate tools whilst still being able to move about. The major disadvantage is that the soft, vulnerable parts of our bodies are exposed to attack. The human skeleton is designed to protect the back and deep in evolutionary history suggests that we moved on all fours with our fronts close to the ground. Thus, when threatened, humans tend to use their arms as a defensive shield across the front of the body and this can be very noticeable in body language terms. All of those involved with dealing with customers, whether face to face or through the medium of advertising, need to consider the aspects of body language in the message they are sending out.

If a person is being frank, honest and open, they will not adopt any defensive postures, and such an approach is important in the visual component of any advertising copy. Honesty, integrity and lack of fear are often the most important messages that advertisers wish to put across.

Observation makes it easier to recognise the clues and thus act accordingly. A knowledge of body language is innate. Bullies become more aggressive on seeing a defensive posture, while those who value relationships act in the opposite way and try to build up confidence.

Objects can sometimes form part of body language. At least one ex-Prime Minister of the UK was believed to use lighting a pipe to gain time when asked a difficult question. Keys, pens and almost anything that people hold can be played with and, if this happens, the person is displaying nervousness. Removal of such mannerisms is an important part of presentation skills training, as they can be very distracting to an audience.

Hands can be useful tools for illustrating points, but it is considered rude and even threatening in most cultures to point directly at a person. It is important to remember when preparing advertisements (and even in meetings etc.) that innocuous gestures in one culture, an example being the thumbs up sign used in Britain to mean 'OK', can be deeply offensive to some cultures.

One of the reasons for using members of the acting and entertainment professions in advertising, apart from the fact that they are well-known faces, is that they have usually been trained in the nuances and subtleties of body language.

■ Ⅳ ▮▮ Advertising

What is advertising? – The role of advertising – Binding suppliers and customers – Sales promotions – Free gifts – Free and semi-free advertising – Different markets – Advertising design – AIDA – DAGMAR – ATR – Product v. advertisements – Types of advertising – Limitations of advertising – Advertising budgets – Advertising agencies – Advertising campaigns – Media – Sponsorship – Advertising and the product life cycle – Advertising effectiveness – Direct marketing – Ethics, law and control

What is advertising?

Giles (1990) defines advertising as non-personal communication directed at target audiences through various media in order to present products, services and ideas. Morden (1991) also defines advertising in similar non-personal terms, although in view of the advances in target direct advertising, to be discussed later in this chapter, advertising can now be much more personal. By understanding the individual potential customer and his or her precise needs and wants, very personal advertising copy can be sent to specific individuals.

The inclusion of products, services and ideas in the Giles' definition is also of considerable importance. Whilst the advertisements that people most remember are those for tangible products, services are also advertised as are ideas such as those connected with health and political activities.

There are, in fact, four communication activities carried out by organisations, and these are sometimes confused. Advertising, as discussed above, is different from sales promotion (a concept considered later in this chapter). Personal and direct selling is another separate concept covered in this chapter, whilst publicity forms a major part of the next chapter.

In 2000, the UK Channel 4 television company in association with Sunday Times Newspapers asked viewers to vote for their favourite '100 Greatest TV Ads', the results of which were televised and also released in book form by Robinson (2000). Of the 100 advertisements featured, 93 were tangible products and only 7 could be described as services (travel, newspapers and utilities). Seemingly the advertisements that are most memorable were those associated with tangible products.

The role of advertising

The role and complexity of advertising increased considerably in the 20th century. Whilst early advertisements served purely to alert potential customers to the product, the modern form seeks to exert considerable influence. A scan of early 20th century newspaper advertisements will demonstrate the apparent lack of sophistication in the copy, although statements could and were made then that would be legally unacceptable today. Certainly the claims for many of the patent medicines that filled the pages of newspapers would come under considerable scrutiny at the present time.

Whilst advertising is a term used in general parlance to describe the promotion of products, services and ideas, as covered above, the role of advertising can be broken down into a series of linked tasks, all of which have promotion as their prime objective. Advertisements are produced to:

Create awareness of products, services or ideas

New customers are usually constantly being sought by organisations. The exceptions are areas such as law enforcement where the aim is to reduce the numbers of 'users' of a service, and these are a special case. Nevertheless, police forces etc. advertise crime prevention measures in the hope that their take up by the general public will reduce the activities of criminal elements or the numbers drinking and driving etc.

In order to become a customer or user, there has to be an awareness of the product, service or idea on offer. Even the best product in the world will fail if its potential customer base is unaware of its existence. The raising of awareness in the run in to the launch of a new or changed product etc. is an important part of modern advertising. It is important, as discussed earlier in this book, to ensure that once anticipation has been induced there are sufficient stocks to meet demand. The Attention and Interest components of the AIDA acronym introduced in Chapter 6 are concerned with this anticipation. Advertisements such as 'tell Sid', used to promote the privatisation of the UK gas industry in the 1980s, deliberately sought to build up the anticipation in the public, such privatisations being an important part of the ruling Conservative Party's philosophy. It was important for political as well as economic reasons that the campaign was successful, so a long lead-in time was required.

Products such as airliners have a long development period and yet need firm orders before the manufacturer will commit to cutting metal. Boeing began discussions with Pan Am (the launch customer for the 747 Jumbo Jet) in 1965, and yet the design was not finally agreed until late in 1966. Despite this, early on in the discussions Boeing had already made promises to Pan Am on payload, speed etc. The first aircraft was not delivered until December 1969, by which time Pan Am had 33 Boeing 747s on order in addition to orders from other major air carriers (Irving, 1993). In the case of major projects such as this, advertising may need to commence years in advance of first delivery.

When Icelandair decide on a new route, it needs to advertise well in advance of the first service as many of the buying decisions will have been made weeks or even months before customers actual make the flight. Market research can, of course, indicate the average time lag between decision and delivery and thus ensure that market opportunities are not missed by commencing advertising either too late or even too early.

In January/February of 2001, Independent Television in the UK put out the programme *Popstars*, in which the whole process of forming a band from nation-wide auditions to the release of the first record was recorded for posterity. The programme grabbed the attention of the viewing public and built up the anticipation covered above, more or less ensuring early successes for the band – 'hear'say'. It must be stated that the band members were actually very good musically, despite claims that they had been manufactured. What the manufacturing actually consisted of was a very public set of auditions followed by equally public voice training etc. The group eventually adopted the name 'HearSay' and went on to break a number of records as their first single CD and albums raced to the top of the UK pop charts. The length of the anticipatory period is quite crucial as if it is too long interest may begin to wane. Human attention spans are not all that long!

The term 'soap opera' given to a genre of popular television drama is derived from the fact that the original productions in the USA were sponsored by washing powder (soap) manufacturers. In some cases the wheel has come full circle. The highly popular Gold Blend coffee advertisements that were first screened in 1987 became the subject of advertisements of their own. The format, according to Robinson (2000), was based on a US television series called *Moonlighting*, in which one of the sub-plots involved a 'will they, won't they?' romantic situation. This was used for the advertisements, which featured the build up etc. to a romance. So popular did these advertisements become that the next 'instalment' would be advertised with the screening time in newspapers for a couple of days before it was first shown. It may have been one of the few cases of people watching a television show with the intention of viewing an advertisement and not vice versa.

To attract enquiries for the products etc. of an organisation or group of organisations

A second role of advertising is to encourage the Action part of AIDA. Sufficient Interest and Desire should be generated so as to prompt some form of action by the potential customer. In many cases this will be an enquiry for more information.

It is important, therefore, that follow-up material is sent out promptly and is to the same standard as the original advertisement.

To reinforce the behaviour of existing customers and users

Whilst new customers are nearly always to be welcomed (too rapid growth can lead to as many problems as too slow growth), existing customers must never be

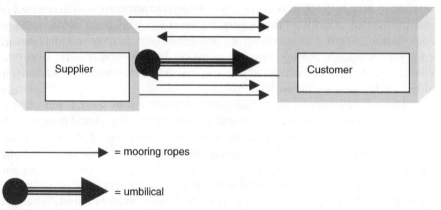

Figure 11.1   The binding of supplier and customer. [*From Cartwright (2000),* Mastering Customer Relations, *with permission.*]

forgotten. Existing customers may need reminding about the product/service and they should be among the first to receive details of any changes or developments. There is an important role for the loyalty schemes covered in Chapter 14 in this respect. As will also be covered below, the more a customer feels that there is a strong bond between themselves and the organisation, the closer they become bound to that organisation. Cartwright (2000) described this as a system of mooring ropes and umbilical, as shown in Figure 11.1.

The umbilical represents the core need of the customer and the channels through which it is delivered.

Each time there is a successful transaction between the supplier and the customer, then a mooring rope is set up between them. As any sailor knows, the greater the number of mooring lines between a ship and the shore there are, the more tightly the ship is held fast and the harder it is to cast off. Advertising also forms part of the mooring rope. Each time a customer feels that a message is somehow addressed to them personally, this too can form a mooring rope. Research for this book suggests that owners of a new car feel (provided they are pleased with their purchase) a slight thrill when they see it advertised.

When the supplier does something to the customer's satisfaction, the rope goes from the supplier to the customer. When the customer praises the supplier or recommends them to somebody else, he or she in fact binds themselves closer to the supplier. The mooring ropes of customer relations go both ways and thus bind the supplier and the customer into an ever-closer relationship and, as mentioned above, advertising can form part of this process.

To create/reinforce organisational and brand image

It may be that an advertisement is less targeted on a particular product or service and more on the image of the organisation and its associated brands. Department stores will perhaps wish to advertise convenience rather than individual products. Skoda, the car manufacturer, ran a series of advertisements in 2001 in the UK that were designed to show how the company had improved its image following its acquisition by the German VW Group. Cruise operators tend to advertise on a company-wide rather than an individual-ship basis, as they are promoting a type of vacation rather than just one of their particular products. The importance of image has already been stressed within this book. The feelings of pride and loyalty referred to in the previous section are connected to perceptions about corporate and brand image. Advertisements that centre on image tend to promote the idea of the organisation being caring, honest and concerned with quality – the things that customers tend to value most in the organisations with which they interact. They are also often concerned with promoting an image similar to what the customer would like to believe reflects themselves as one of being rich, sexy, intelligent, shrewd etc. Perhaps the ultimate in this role for advertising comes at election time when the whole focus tends to be on image rather than specifics.

To influence the behaviour of others in the supply chain

Whilst a great deal, possibly the majority, of advertising is directed at the end user, a proportion is targeted at others in the supply chain. Wholesalers and retailers may need the persuasion of advertising to stock certain products or to offer particular services. In many cases such advertising is now as sophisticated as that aimed at the more general market. In addition there are often special events aimed at such members of the supply chain, trade fairs being a good example. The advertising at these events will be sophisticated and of a high standard because if products are not stocked, customer demand will remain unsatisfied thus emphasising the important role every member of the supply chain plays.

To facilitate changes

Not only do products and services change as they develop but, as discussed in Chapters 3 and 8, so do markets. Organisations wishing to enter new markets with their products and services need to alert the customers in that market to their offerings, and this may mean a change in the manner of advertising. In the 1960s, as television advertising began in earnest in the UK, a number of US manufacturers believed that they could just repeat their successful American advertising copy on British screens. This was not the case, because advertisements need to be produced with cultural sensitivity. The successful Gold Blend advertisements mentioned above needed changing when introduced in the USA, as the UK characters and language did not appeal to the US viewers. It is often forgotten that whilst the UK and the USA (and Australia, New Zealand, Canada etc.) all speak English, each culture speaks it with their own idioms etc. and these do not always translate well. There have been some very successful global advertisements: the British Airways' Face (voted as 62/100 in the Channel 4/Sunday Times survey quoted earlier) and the 'I'd Like to Teach the World to Sing' (sung as: 'I'd like to buy the world a Coke') advertisement for Coca-Cola (16/100) are two advertisements that were designed for and succeeded with global audiences. One wonders, however, how even other English-speaking countries would have responded to uniquely UK culturally based advertisements – Hovis, John Smith's Bitter, the Carlsberg spoof on the Dambuster's theme and the famous 'Luton Airport' of Campari spring to mind.

Sales promotions and their role

In distinguishing between advertising and sales promotion, Wilmshurst (1984) considers that the former is usually carried in media outwith the advertisers direct control, whereas the latter is within the control of the advertising organisation.

Sales promotions are usually short campaigns, often run in association with the media. Many involve the collection of tokens either from other products produced by the advertiser or carried in newspapers. The Icelandair/ *The Scotsman* sales' promotion from Scotland to the USA via Reykjavik at a much reduced price was of this form.

Wilmhurst also makes the very valid point that whilst advertising is often strategic and forms part of an overall, global plan for the organisation, sales promotions may well be tactical and concentrated on the point of sale. Advertising is often concerned with market share, whereas sales promotion is centred more on the immediacy of an individual sale.

The major roles associated with sales promotions include:

Encouraging dealers to stock products

There may be separate promotions for dealers as opposed to the general customer base. Stocking a product can be costly for dealers. They often have to pay for stocks up front, and the costs of space, insurance etc. (see Chapter 10) will fall on them. Thus they may need considerable incentive to lay out money to stock a new product.

The encouragement of sampling by customers

If a new product is being launched or an existing one changed, the less risk a customer feels under, the more likely they are to buy. Provided that the product/service is of the correct quality, letting the customer sample without financial risk is one of the best ways of firstly letting them experience the benefits of the product so that they will, hopefully not want to be without it in the future, and secondly demonstrating the organisation's faith in its products/services.

Sampling has developed a long way since the inclusion of small sachets of hair conditioner in magazines.

Motor car manufacturers have developed 'return it undamaged within 30 days if you are dissatisfied and pay nothing' schemes. Apparently very few customers ever do return the vehicle. One of the first of these schemes in the UK was that operated by Rover in the 1990s.

In the holiday industry, during 2000 both Carnival Cruises and Renaissance Cruises offered a 'vacation guarantee' that stated the customer could leave the cruise ship at the first port of call and have all their money refunded. Organisations need to be very sure of their product and service levels when making that kind of offer. According to Ward (2000), only one-tenth of one per cent of customers took up such an offer. The remainder might have been that tiny bit more likely to book with those companies offering the money-back guarantee. As it is an unconditional guarantee, it is not necessary to prove that there was anything the organisation failed to do in order to invoke its terms. Legal action can gain redress when something is faulty but not when the customer just does not like it.

Competitive action

In cases where the competition runs a promotion it may be necessary for others to follow suit. If brand X offers a two-for-one promotion, then brand Y (a competitor) has to offer either the same or perhaps more effectively something different but to the same value. Such offers may well be costly. Free insurance for a new car is only free to the customer. The manufacturer will be charged by the insurance companies in more or less the normal way.

Revitalising a product or service

Familiarity breeds contempt. However well known a product is, it needs 'perking' up every now and then in order to maintain market share. This is often accomplished by means of competitions. It is problematic as to whether much extra is generated in sales value but loyalty is reinforced, which is often the major objective.

Free gifts

One of the most frequently used methods of sales promotion involves the provision of free gifts. Depending upon the value of the product or service in question, the value of gifts can range from worthless to quite valuable. What they often have in common is the inclusion of the name of the brand or the organisation, to act as a reminder of whose largesse was responsible for the gift. Where gifts become expensive, a careful line has to be drawn between a promotional gift and a bribe. Many organisations, especially in the public sector, have strict limits on the value of gifts that can be accepted by staff in order to avoid any accusations of impropriety. In many parts of the world, however, the giving of such expensive gifts is the norm and a perfectly acceptable (in that culture) method of doing business.

Free and semi-free advertising

Occasionally the opportunity arises for an organisation to receive free and semi-free advertising through making facilities available to others – usually the media, or by featuring in a related story. When a ship owned by a major cruise company takes part in a rescue at sea and if that rescue is then reported in the media, good free publicity (see the next chapter) and thus advertising is generated. In the context of this section, such publicity is not deliberately generated but comes as the result of normal business activities.

Many of the newspapers and television companies feature programmes that test household appliances, drive new cars or send their reporters to try out different holidays. Organisations that have their products reviewed in this way are able to gain good free advertising (they can, of course, gain bad advertising as well if the product or service does not come up to scratch).

The third type of free or semi-free advertising comes from the product or service being involved in a book, play, film, article or television programme. If the hero drives a Ford, then Ford will benefit. This is different from sponsorship (see later), where the organisation puts up money to be associated with a programme. Here the name of the organisation or recognition of the product is incidental, but nevertheless an association may be made by the viewer.

Different markets

In the early chapters of the book, concepts such as market segmentation were introduced. Different markets respond to different types of advertising, in major part because of the different nature of the customer and potential customer base.

FMCG (Fast Moving Consumer Goods) market customers are likely to behave very differently from customers of an industrial market.

According to Morden (1991), FMCG companies may well commit up to 80% of their advertising budgets to the type of media advertising and promotional activities that pervade much of our daily lives. This strategy is referred to as *demand pull*, as the advertising etc. lead to increased demand that then serves to pull the product through the channel of distribution. (Channels of distribution form the content of Chapter 13.)

Organisations in industrial markets are more likely to allocate monies to brochure production, publicity and a very specialised salesforce (technical expertise being very important as markets become more specialised). Sales staff in these industries may also be involved in more complex price and contract negotiations than their colleagues in FMCG markets. One of the complaints about the FMCG market has been the lack of expertise displayed by many younger sales staff in retail outlets. This can lose custom, and product knowledge and technical training for sales staff has received considerable attention by many retailers.

Advertising design

AIDA (Attention, Interest, Desire and Action) has already been introduced in this book and forms part of what may be termed the persuasion process – a key role of advertising. Another example of this process is DAGMAR, standing for Defined

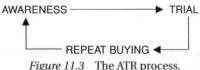

AWARENESS ⟶ COMPREHENSION ⟶ CONVICTION ⟶ ACTION

Figure 11.2 The DAGMAR process.

Figure 11.3 The ATR process.

Advertising Goals for Measured Advertising Results. Foster and Davies (1984) describe DAGMAR as working through the process shown in Figure 11.2.

A third process is that of ATR, standing for Awareness, Trial and Repeat buying, proposed by Ehrenberg in 1974 and quoted by Foster and Davies. This is a useful model in that, like the concept of value perception introduced earlier in this book, it provides a feedback loop as repeat buying (which, of course, will only occur if there is satisfaction and delight with the product/service) leads to enhanced awareness (Figure 11.3).

There is a similarity in all three processes in that *awareness* leads to a wish to acquire or partake, and this in turn leads to action to acquire or partake. It is the step between the wish and the action that usually requires the customer to expend some of their precious resources (money, time etc.), and it is at this point that the stressing of benefits by advertisements becomes of considerable importance.

Advertisements therefore need to be designed with these processes in mind. You are advised to analyse current advertisements from a variety of sources and consider how their copy raises awareness, generates interest and desire, and promotes action. Advertising designers have come up with many methods of appealing to the customer base, including:

- convenience;
- well-being;
- envy;
- sex appeal;
- humour;
- emotion.

None of the above are self-contained and a successful advertisement will often include more than one of them. In the section on Humour below, the Top 20 of the Channel 4/Sunday Times 100 'Greatest TV Ads' research is analysed (Figure 11.4) for the combination of the above factors.

Convenience

By stressing the convenience benefits of a product or service, the advertiser is using 'opportunity' cost as a major selling point – 'buy this appliance and you will have time for this or that activity'.

Time has become a very precious commodity in the modern world and thus needs to be 'spent' wisely. The freeing up of time has become an important selling point for many products/services, as evidenced by the number of times it appears in the analysis shown in Figure 11.4 later in this chapter.

Well-being

Physical and emotional well-being are sought-after commodities in modern society. Products that promote our 'feeling better about ourselves' can be best sellers. Foods, drinks etc. are sold not only for their nutritional benefits but for their effect on well-being. A certain beer that 'refreshes the parts that others cannot' is a classic example.

In addition to this type of well-being, many advertisements use emotion to produce an inner sense of well-being (see later).

Envy

Envy is perhaps a subliminal factor. It is not often used directly by advertisers for fear of giving offence and belittling the potential customer. Nevertheless, the message that he or she has this and you have not is often quite strong in advertisements. The use of respected celebrities to promote products/services may have some root in considerations of envy, as many people wish to be like those they admire and one way of doing this is to acquire the things those celebrities promote. Whether, of course, they ever use them or even like them is a mute point.

Sex appeal

Sex it appears nearly always sells, provided that the images are not too blatant or raunchy. Many of the complaints to the UK Advertising Standards Authority (ASA), see later, concern overt sexuality in advertisements and the belittling of a particular gender.

In contemporary society, advertisers probably do best when they stick to romance as opposed to sex appeal, because romance has emotional connotations and, as will be shown later, emotion is a very powerful persuader indeed. Packard (1957), in *The Hidden Persuaders*, a superb text from the early days of studies in the subject (and recommended reading at the end of this chapter), relates some of the barriers and taboos that advertisers began to break after World War II, many of which were unacceptable before that time and might well be unacceptable today. The use of human beings of either gender as sexual objects to help sell anything is becoming, quite rightly, unacceptable.

Humour

As Figure 11.4 shows, humour forms a very important and powerful persuasive element. Nearly all of the advertisements that capture public imagination appear to have a large humorous element.

No.	Advert/factor	Convenience	Well-being	Envy	Sex appeal	Humour	Emotion
1	Guinness		*			*	
2	Smash	*				*	
3	Tango					*	
4	Heat Electric	*				*	
5	Boddingtons		*		*		
6	Levi's				*	*	
7	R. White's Lemonade					*	
8	Hamlet cigars		*			*	
9	Walker's Crisps	*				*	
10	Impulse		*	*	*	*	
11	Cinzano					*	
12	Renault Clio	*		*	*	*	*
13	Yellow Pages	*				*	*
14	BT	*				*	
15	Nike					*	*
16	Coca-Cola						*
17	Carling Black Label					*	*
18	Shake'n'Vac	*				*	
19	Andrex	*				*	*
20	Real Fires	*				*	

Figure 11.4 Analysis of the Top 20 'Greatest TV Ads' from the Channel 4/Sunday Times survey.

One of the problems, however, with humour relates to cultural barriers. What one culture finds funny, another may deem offensive. Even where the language is the same, humorous nuances might be lost. It was Oscar Wilde who remarked that the only difference between the UK and the USA was language, reflecting the divergence between American and British English. Whist many US comedy shows and films work in the UK and vice versa, many others do not. In cases where the language is different, humour relying as it does on nuances and subtlety may well not travel well. At number 17 in the Channel 4/Sunday Times list of 'Greatest TV Ads' is the famous Carling Black Label 'Dambusters' advertisement, a spoof based on the *Dambusters* film that commemorated the raid on German Dams by 617 Squadron RAF in 1942 using the famous 'bouncing bomb' designed by Barnes Wallis. That piece of history has become part of British folklore and thus the implications of the advert were well understood by the target audience – how it would have been received in Germany or Austria is open to question. It is worth considering whether it would be understood in the USA.

Humour forms a very important part of advertising copy but must be used carefully to ensure that offence is not given and that the humour is not too subtle so that the point of the advertisement is missed.

Emotion

The advent of television advertising led to a re-popularising of classical music. Music is a very emotive means of gaining attention. *The Planets* suite by Holst, Elgar's *Enigma Variations*, especially Nimrod, and the largo from Dvořák's *Symphony Number 9 in E minor*, Op 95, 'From the New World' are just three of the classics that reached a huge audience through advertisements. Part of their appeal was the well-being (see earlier) that they seemed to induce in the listener, and this was then carried over into the perception of the product/service. Anything that links a product/service with positive customer emotions is to be welcomed by advertisers. Not only music but also children and anthro-pomorphical representations of animals seem to do this. Anthropomorphism is the attribution of human characteristics to animals and has been used very successfully by advertisers. The UK Electric Association advertisements of the early 1990s, using characters designed by Nick Park, the creator of the characters of Wallace and Gromit and the film *Chicken Run*, had plasticine figures successfully selling electrical appliances and systems to large numbers of people – and it worked. It made people laugh and, more than that, they could empathise with the characters. Animals feature in many successful advertisements. People find them appealing and humorous (and in many cases non-threatening), and these are important virtues that can assist the promotion of a product or service. As an experiment you are advised to analyse just a few nights' television advertising to see how many times animal images are featured.

It will be noted that much modern advertising is connected with image rather than the product/service *per se*. In fact, image and glamour are often seen as benefits by customers in the same way as convenience.

Jingles

The use of music in advertising has been mentioned earlier. The short musical phrase, often accompanied by words that becomes closely identified with a product/service through advertising, is known as a jingle.

Many of the jingles and catchphrases have become well known enough to be almost part of a society's folklore. In the UK these include:

'I'm going well, I'm going Shell'
'Murraymints, Murraymints – the too good to hurry mints'
'Beans means Heinz'

Because these jingles and catchphrases stick in the mind, they act as reinforcement to the advertisements.

Product v. advert

There have been times when the advertisement has become more memorable than the product. There is little point in spending large sums on advertising a product or service only for the recipients to remember the advertisement but not precisely what was being advertised. Even worse is the situation where the majority of recipients believe that the advertisement was for a competitor! In this case money really has been wasted.

One of the problems associated with successful advertising campaigns is that they often have a generic effect in that they promote not only the product but also its competitors. A successful campaign for a particular coffee brand will boost sales of that brand but is also likely to boost overall coffee sales, including those of competitors.

Types of advertising

There are, of course, many physical means of bringing a product to the notice of potential customers. They tend to range from the simple, i.e. leaflets, at the cheaper end of the market to the very sophisticated and expensive types of advertising seen on television. The media aspect of advertising is covered later in this chapter. Advertisements tend to fall into three main types, namely:

- persuasive;
- informative;
- corporate.

Persuasive

Persuasive advertising tends to be the most common. Basically these advertisements, often very carefully planned according to message, are designed to persuade the recipient to do something. It may be to purchase a product or service, or to perform or not perform an action. Negative advertising always carries a risk. 'Don't drink and drive' or 'Don't smoke' are messages that need to be presented with care as they bring drinking and smoking into the consciousness.

An example of how advertising can misfire is illustrated by the famous (or infamous) advertisements for Strand Cigarettes in the 1960s. The advertisements, shown on television, cinemas (before such advertising was banned in the UK) and on advertising hoardings showed a man, late at night, alone on a bridge lighting a Strand Cigarette and carried the caption 'You're never alone with a Strand'. Unfortunately the message that the buying public received was not one that said people would never be lonely if they smoked a Strand but rather that people who smoked Strand had no friends, and who wants to go into a tobacconist and say, in effect, 'Twenty Strand please because I'm a lonely person nobody wants to know?'

As mentioned earlier, it is vital that the product/service brand name is given prominence as the advertiser will wish to avoid boosting the sales of competitors. They will want to boost the market for their brand, not other brands of the similar products/services produced by their competitors.

Informative

This type of advertising is often combined with persuasive advertisement on the grounds that as customers become more sophisticated they will require more information about products. In 2000/2001 Chrysler provided a small number of their retro-styled PT Cruise car to a sample of the public who then ran the car for some months, Chrysler producing an advertisement with their comments and including negative items – i.e. the things the sample did not like.

Advertisements for the public sector may be completely informative although the trend has been for these to be more sophisticated, including humour. The campaign by the UK Inland Revenue to ensure that tax returns were submitted in time following the introduction of self-assessment in the late 1990s used humour and cartoons to get its message across. In this respect it was an example of the informative and the persuasive.

As Foster and Davies (1984) have pointed out, the British Code of Advertising Practice has rules to ensure that customers know that informative advertising is still advertising, especially when it is written in the style of an editorial. This type of advertisement often appears in magazines and appears at first glance to be an endorsement of the product/service by the magazine, and there is a requirement in the Code to draw readers' attention to the fact that it is in fact an advertisement.

Corporate

The raising of awareness etc. may not be for a single product/service but for the offerings of a whole organisation. Airlines will advertise certain routes but will often produce corporate advertisements showing their strength within the marketplace, depth of experience and routes, and comfort on board. British Airways produced an award winning advertisement in 1989 featuring large numbers of people who eventually made up a face that turned into the globe. Filmed in the USA, the core message was that British Airways brings people together – and in fact an aircraft did not feature in the advertisement.

Limitations of advertising

At the end of the day, unless a product/service satisfies the needs and wants of the customer after acquisition, advertising can only really produce an initial sale. It cannot compensate for a lack of quality or value. As will be shown later when considering effectiveness, advertising, being costly, must produce more than it costs. Unless it does it wastes precious organisational resources. The Strand advertisement mentioned earlier in this chapter was well produced but was probably responsible for a diminution in sales – which is not an effective use of resources.

Advertising budgets

Advertising and sales promotion, like all organisational (and indeed personal) activities, need to budgeted for. A budget can be defined as **a plan in financial and numerical terms which forecasts the results of a specified future trading period**. A budget is a plan, and plans change. Two of the most important aspects of any form of budgeting are the initial setting of the budget and the monitoring of it to deal with any variance.

The money to place in the advertising budget will come from activities undertaken in advance of the advertising or promotion. The money needs to be generated by the current and not future activities of the organisation. Money from cash cows (see Chapter 8) is often used to generate the advertising/promotion budget for stars and problem children.

Those setting budgets need to have a very clear indication of the anticipated level of activity, as the money will need to be in effect 'repaid' to the organisation. Part of the revenue will go towards meeting the advertising/promotion costs, whether they are considered as a fixed or variable cost as described in Chapter 10. Very often the budget will be set on a percentage basis of the anticipated turnover. This method ensures that those responsible for the budget have a clear indication of the amount they can spend and can plan accordingly. It does mean, however, that sales targets need to be met.

Another method, perhaps less accurate, is to base the budget on that of the competition. At some stage, however, one of the organisations concerned will have had to set an original budget without competitor data.

Yet a third method involves calculating the spend required to achieve a specified objective – a certain level of sales being an obvious example. Advertising as an art/science is sufficiently sophisticated for these to be adequate data to state that a certain level of spend in a particular market is likely to produce a particular level of customer activity. Provided that the revenue is sufficient to pay all the costs, including promotion, then all should be well.

According to Morden (1991), by the start of the 1990s, of the £3,096 million spent on advertising annually in the UK at the time, approximately 23% or nearly £700 million was by the food and drink industry with the financial sector, i.e. banks, building societies, insurance companies and investment concerns, coming next with 17% (approximately £515 million). Third in the advertising spend league was the motor industry, accounting for approximately £450 million, i.e. about 14%.

Hardly surprising is the fact that it is the consumer market that receives the greatest concentration of advertising spending. Advertisements for the consumer market have to reach millions of individuals rather than a smaller group of organisations and this is always likely to be more costly.

Advertising agencies

Almost the only people preparing their own advertisements in the 21st century are individuals compiling small, classified advertisements for newspapers. Even the smallest companies and organisations tend to employ the services of specialist advertising agencies. As advertising has become more sophisticated – a movement in part driven by the ability of television companies to transmit advertising copy on a sub-regional level and thus allowing for localised TV advertising – so the need for specialist assistance and advice has risen.

Advertising agencies are specialists not just in the design of advertising but also in campaign planning and the placement of advertising copy. They perform a vital linking role between the organisation that wishes to advertise and the media in which the advertisements will be placed. The relationships between an organisation and its agency, and the agency and the media, are necessarily close as the agency needs to understand both the organisation and the media to ensure a careful match of needs and wants.

Agencies range in size from the huge multi-national household names (Saatchi & Saatchi being an example) to small operations using only one or two people. However, the 50% of agencies who are members of the Institute of Practitioners in Advertising (IPA), the professional organisation setting the standards and ethics for agencies, account for over 90% of the total UK business.

There are two major means by which agencies receive remuneration. The traditional method is the taking of a commission of the advertising spend from the media. The organisation that wishes to advertise employs the agency and pays it the full amount. The media's fee less commission is made to the media by the agency, which then retains the commission, the amount being based on time or space booked. Commission traditionally ranges from 10 to 15%. As it is the agency that pays the media, any contract issues are between the media and the agency, so that in case of default etc. the claim would be by the media against the agency and not the organisation. Naturally the agency will have a separate contract with the organisation. It is not difficult, however, to imagine the following scenario. An organisation contracts with an agency for an advertising campaign. The agency creates the advertisements and places them with the media, but the organisation is unhappy with them, perhaps claiming that the finished product does not correspond with what was agreed. Under UK law, if the media have done what the agency asked, they have a right to be paid by the agency; but if the organisation can prove that its wishes were not followed by the agency, it does not have to pay the full amount. In this case the agency may well be out of pocket, hence the need for a professional approach.

More and more agencies are changing to a straight fee basis. In part this move has been driven by the growth of specialist operations dealing with just a small part of the advertising process on a sub-contractual basis. Commission calculations can become very complex in such cases and a fee basis works better when allocating costs and revenue.

Advertising campaigns

For the purposes of this section let us assume that an organisation is embarking upon an advertising campaign and has employed a middle or large advertising agency to handle the campaign.

The marketing department (or individual(s) in a small organisation), working with those in product/service development, will have at least some idea of the benefits etc. that they wish to promote.

The advertising agency will appoint an **account executive** to manage the client–agency interface. If the relationship has a history then this person will probably have worked with the organisation before, will understand the culture, structure, products etc., and will have built up a working relationship with the relevant members of staff. The account executive, normally quite senior in the case of large accounts, has overall responsibility for agency–organisation links and thus is a very important role indeed.

The agency will then task a **creative team** to plan the campaign. The role of this team is to translate the benefits etc. of the product or service into advertising copy, i.e. to get the message across in a manner that is both effective in terms of the market and acceptable to the client organisation. Organisations may hold certain values that they will wish to be promoted. They will not want advertisements that conflict with those values. For example if the client puts great stress on family values, the use of sex appeal in the campaign might be deemed unacceptable.

Creativity requires a special type of person. In the 1990s the author was senior tutor and later development manager for the Certificate in Management programme provided by the Oxford Consortium for British Airways on a world-wide basis (the programme was originally branded as 'Fundamentals of Supervision'). Part of the marketing module for the programme involved the analysis of the award winning British Airways 'Global' advertisement mentioned earlier in this chapter. British Airways had produced a video showing how the advertisement had been conceived, planned and made (British Airways, 1989). Of particular note was a senior member of the creative team explaining how the idea of the face made up of people had been conceived – coming, it was stated, from the deepest recesses of the mind.

The third vital team in the process is that of the **media team**. Its role is to decide how and where to place the advertisements. Obviously it needs to liaise closely with the creative team, as some types of advertising work better in certain media than others. Music is irrelevant to print media but of considerable importance to television and radio, whilst vision, important on the screen and page, has no impact on radio. The media team will have a good knowledge of the various formats and excellent contacts within each of them.

The production of advertising uses talent from all other fields, as necessary. The Global advertisement covered above was directed by Hugh Hudson, whose credits also include the very successful feature film Chariots of Fire. The use of celebrities to present advertisements and thus endorse products has already been mentioned earlier in this chapter. Whilst a household name may cost more, the benefits in linking respected personalities to a product or service may be large enough to make the cost worthwhile.

Media

Advertising appears in a wide variety of media. It may also be local, regional, national or even international. Classified advertisements in newspapers tend to be local in character, although for specialised items they may be national. Indeed, magazines such as the UK *Exchange and Mart* provide a national platform for classified advertisements, often from individuals on a national basis. Many local newspapers now offer free classified sales advertising for non-commercial subscribers, provided that the item(s) advertised are of low value.

As is mentioned in the next chapter, newspapers and magazines often have clearly defined readerships and thus the media team in an agency will be careful to place newspaper and magazine advertisements in the paper etc. that tends to be read by the target customer base.

As radio and television becomes at the same time more and more international and yet broadcast on a more regionalised basis, so it becomes possible to offer advertising using broadcast media on a regional and even sub-regional basis. This can allow smaller organisations to access broadcast advertising at a level of cost that is acceptable to them.

Billboards are still an important form of advertising and whilst, in the UK, roadside advertising is not as conspicuous as in North America, this form of promotion is still used to good effect. It is especially popular with political parties at election time as it allows a message to be got across to large numbers without any problems of technology.

In the section on direct marketing later in this chapter, the importance of targeting the customer will be stressed. Media teams are able to assist this process in a more general way by ensuring that advertisements are seen by the potential customer base. For instance, a railway company could use billboards of a congested stretch of road to put their benefits across to motorists and encourage a switch in transport modes. A university in Scotland bought up advertising space on billboards near a College of Further Education, encouraging potential students to consider their degree programmes. As the College also offered degrees, some staff considered this an unfair tactic but perhaps 'all is fair . . . etc'. In fact, provided that the law or codes of practice are not broken, then the advertising market is a very open one.

Modes of transport often form a very suitable medium for advertising. The holiday resort advertisements that adorned railway carriages in the age of steam (up to the late 1960s) are now, as originals, highly collectable. Buses have become useful mobile advertising hordings, sometimes with the whole vehicle covered in images promoting a single product. Buses are especially useful for local advertising. The Icelandair campaign promoting the Scotland–North America service made much use of buses, especially in Glasgow, as an advertising medium. By covering a whole bus with a single advertisement, a very high-profile moving billboard can be produced. The advertising trams covered in lightbulbs that appear each year during the Blackpool Illuminations (a longstanding attraction at this Lancashire holiday resort) are perhaps the ultimate in high-profile billboards, as are the advertising 'blimps' pioneered by Goodyear.

Sponsorship

Once tobacco advertising became very severely restricted in the UK, it became necessary for the tobacco companies to find alternative methods of ensuring that their brand names were kept in the public eye. A very successful means of achieving this is through the sponsorship of the arts, sport and entertainment. It is not just tobacco companies that are involved in sponsorship. A wide range of organisations sponsor football teams, concerts, horse races and individual athletes – in fact, if it is in the public eye it is open to sponsorship.

Sponsoring an event ensures that the name of the organisation or brand will be mentioned and provides the possibility of logos being displayed prominently. It is sometimes difficult to see a Formula One racing car these days, or even the driver, as both are likely to be covered in the logos of their sponsors. There are few football teams whose players do not carry the name of the sponsor on their chest.

Not only is the name displayed but also the organisation can bask in the glamour of the sport or entertainment. Where charitable works are concerned, the organisation can be seen to be putting something back into society. The UK Do-It-Yourself chain, B&Q, ran a series of advertisements in February and March of 2001 stressing the community work that was being sponsored by themselves and their employees. Such advertising is usually very positive and aids the corporate image, in addition to promoting a brand.

If, of course, the football team etc. ceases to perform well, the organisation might withdraw sponsorship. There is no benefit in being associated with failure.

Advertising and the product life cycle

The product life cycle and the dynamic product life progression were introduced in Chapter 8. The means of advertising differ depending upon where the product or service is in its life cycle. At introduction and growth, the emphasis will be on creating awareness. Similar tactics may be necessary during decline where there may also be considerable promotional activity, if only to clear stocks and production lines to make way for new products.

In the middle of the life cycle, the promotional activities are likely to be those designed to encourage customer loyalty and also to attract new customer groups.

One advantage that can be used at this stage is that there is likely to be plenty of data from current customers, and they may be able to provide endorsements based on experience.

Advertising effectiveness

It is often difficult to measure the quantitative effectiveness of advertising, i.e. how would the product or service have sold if there had been no promotional activities?

Experience suggests the patterns that ought to be linked to the AIDA model to show the effectiveness of different types of promotional activity at different stages, and these are shown in Figure 11.5.

What is of especial interest is the manner in which effectiveness tends to rise over time with sales promotions and personal selling, but to drop with advertising and publicity.

Personal selling is in fact better at engendering action than it is as a means of raising awareness, an area in which advertising scores. Thus the linking of advertising and a personable sales person is likely to produce good results. The former raises awareness and generates interest, and the human factor completes the sale.

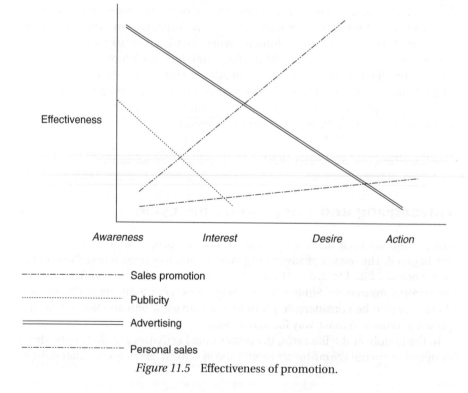

Figure 11.5 Effectiveness of promotion.

Direct marketing

It is logical that the more a potential customer perceives that an advertisement or promotion is designed with him or her directly in mind, the more he or she is likely to partake of the product/service.

Whilst it may appear non-cost-effective for the organisation to make a direct appeal to individual customers, it is becoming easier to target specific groups and in many cases individuals directly.

There are, of course, major advantages in the organisation removing the middle sections of the value chain and having a direct relationship with the customer. Not the least of these is the keeping of a greater percentage of margin by the organisation. There will, however, be no buffer between the organisation and the customer if things go wrong.

Mail order, a form of direct sales that became very popular as the USA grew and more and more customers began to live tens if not hundreds of miles away from retail outlets, is still a popular method of purchase today. Modern Internet shopping can trace its ancestry back to the great mail order companies of the USA, for example Sears.

Modern technology has also allowed far greater analysis of customer needs and wants, and it is now possible to send out direct marketing material only to those whom the organisation knows are interested in the product or service. This knowledge comes from either the organisation's databases, built up from previous business or enquiries, or from bought-in databases. People fill in many questionnaires and these often contain (as covered in Chapter 4) information on lifestyle. It may well be that there are data of interest to a range of organisations, data that will allow an organisation to offer model railways books only to those it knows are interested in model railways – say subscribers to the various model railway magazines in the USA, the UK and other parts of Europe. That way, much wasted marketing can be avoided as the Awareness and the Interest are already firmly in place.

Ethics, law and control

A situation where there is no control over advertising and promotion would, in the medium- to long-term, benefit nobody. Customers and potential customers would become so distrusting that they could never believe a single word of advertising copy.

There is a balance to be struck between glamorising and putting forward all the best features of a product or service, and going beyond the truth. Governments legislate for this in order to ensure that advertisements are factually accurate or are so fanciful as to ensure that no reasonable person could actually believe that.

Thus Heineken has no particular metabolic properties that would enable it to affect parts of the anatomy that similar products had no effect on. However, it is perfectly possible for Heineken to advertise that it is the 'lager that refreshes the parts that other beers cannot reach'.

In the UK, the major piece of legislation regulating advertising copy and promotion is the Trades Descriptions Act, first passed in 1968. Certain products such as tobacco have major restrictions on their being advertised (tobacco advertising is not allowed on the television screens of many jurisdictions), as have banned substances, weapons other than in specialised magazines etc. The controls on these are absolute in that the government controls the whole process and not just the honesty element.

Trades Descriptions Act 1968

Often considered a landmark piece of legislation because it attempted to stop growing practices relating to false or inaccurate descriptions of products, the Act regulates the way in which goods can be described to potential customers.

The Act deals with three basic aspects of description – claims about the goods themselves, false statements relating to services, and incorrect pricing. Section 2 of the Act sets out areas that constitute a trade description, namely:

- physical characteristics;
- history;
- quantity;
- size;
- method of manufacture;
- fitness for purpose;
- testing;
- manufacturer;
- use;
- previous ownership.

The Act requires the person selling the product or service (the vendor) to be truthful about these areas. If a box of matches has an approximate number of contents labelled at 100, then provided that on average there are 100 matches to a box the Act will have been satisfied. If tests showed that the average was 95, then an offence would have been committed. It would be interesting to postulate on what would happen, or indeed if a case would be brought, if the average were 105!

Interestingly, availability is not covered by the Act and thus items advertised in order to 'lure' customers in but which are not available are not covered, and nor are the contents of books or CDs where there is clearly a subjective view as to their quality etc. However, if a CD were advertised as being by a band and that band only appeared on one out of twenty tracks, there could well be a case under the Act. It should also be borne in mind that the offence needs to be committed in the course of business, and thus purely private transactions are excluded.

The Trades Descriptions Act carries strict liability in that an offence can be committed even if it is not intended to do so. There is a defence for organisations, however, if a member of staff who should know better carries out an act that renders the organisation liable under the Act. In Tesco v. Nattrass (1972), a supermarket manager made a false description of a product unbeknown to his employer. He had received proper training etc. and the Court ruled that Tesco was not liable. This case has been used as a precedent to say that there needs to be some proof before a company can be held liable for false advertising claims if an employee makes a false description.

The Trade Descriptions Act not only applies to goods but also to services. It is an offence (although strict liability does not apply) to make false statements about specified aspects of service. As strict liability does not apply, it is necessary to prove that the statement was known to be false or was reckless, i.e. not sufficient attention being paid to the truth or falseness of the statement.

The Trade Descriptions Act also covers pricing of products and services, and again is related to the truthfulness of statements. Prior to the Act it was not unknown for companies to make blatantly untrue statements about prices: 'was £50, now £20', when in fact the item had never ever been sold at £50.

Under the Act, where a recommended price is quoted and then undercut, that price must have been in operation. Where a sale price is quoted, then the original price should be shown together with details of where it applied. There must be evidence that the non-sale price had been applied somewhere within the organisation for at least 28 days over the previous 6 months. If you look carefully at the sale prices in many large retail outlets you will see statements like: '. . . as offered in our Manchester store for 28 days between January and June'. It is permissible to make a disclaimer for specially acquired products, and this does limit the applicability of this part of the Act.

Pricing, as regards the Trade Descriptions Act, only applies to goods and not to services. Thus an untrue statement claiming that the outlet is closing and this is the last chance to buy would not commit an offence.

Many actions under the Trade Descriptions Act are brought by the Trading Standards Department of local authorities. They have been especially vigilant in the area of counterfeit goods. As designer labels have become more and more popular, so there has been a flood of fakes, often sold in markets. Offering such an item for sale is clearly a breach of the Act, as it is clearly not what it purports to be.

It stems from the above that lying is an offence not only against the customer but also against the society that has passed the laws regulating trades descriptions. Unfortunately, organisations still do lie to their customers and it is thus necessary that there are laws to protect customers from the small but significant number of organisations that either do not deliver on their promises or that may have had no intention of delivering all that they promised.

Many other pieces of legislation on a wide variety of issues have implications for advertising. It used to be illegal for UK solicitors to advertise their services; the law changed and advertisements for legal services are now found in all the media, including television. A change in the law on solicitors has brought about a change in advertising practice and a new client group to the industry.

Control of Misleading Advertisements Regulations (1988)

These UK regulations define a misleading advertisement as one that in its presentation deceives or is likely to deceive anybody it reaches (whether they are an intended recipient or not), or by reason of the deception damages a competitor. Those who believe that they have been deceived or damaged can seek an interdict or interim interdict (injunction or interlocutory injunction in Scotland).

The regulations lay a duty on the Director General of Fair Trading to investigate any complaint made under them, and the Director can then approach the Courts for action. The regulations also place a duty on the BBC, the Independent Broadcasting Authority (IBA) and the authorities responsible for cable broadcasting under the Cable and Broadcasting Act (1984) to investigate complaints regarding deception.

ASA

Many advertisements do not breach legislation in that they do not tell a lie, yet are considered by some to breach some form of moral code.

In the UK, the Advertising Standards Authority (ASA), established in 1962 as a company independent of the advertising industry, is tasked with investigating complaints of a moral as opposed to a legal nature. As such, the ASA considers breaches of decency, public taste and areas where offence might be caused. The more innovative campaigns may often run into opposition from minority groups who have taken offence, whilst the rest of society cannot see where the problem is. Nevertheless it is better to offend nobody – they might be potential customers. The ASA advertises its existence to the public in magazines and newspapers, and publishes the results of its inquiries.

The British Code of Advertising Practice

Adopted by the major players in the UK advertising industry, the Code covers the areas of:

- exploitation;
- threats;
- public decency;
- advertising to children;
- privacy for individuals;
- testimonials;
- guarantees;
- product/service comparisons.

First published in 1962, the Code represents the wish of the industry to maintain high standards and to achieve effective self-regulation.

Any industry that wishes to self-regulate needs effective codes of practice in place if governments are not going to intervene. Thus the advertising industry is keen to ensure that it is seen as honest and having integrity.

Children

Governments, industry watchdogs and not least parents have become very concerned at the impact of advertising on children. Whilst adults may be able to sift fact from fantasy fairly easily, children have often not acquired the life experience necessary to do this.

Great care needs to be taken to ensure that advertising directed at children does not raise unobtainable expectations about the product or service. This can be difficult because the purpose of items such as toys is to stimulate imagination, and imagination is hard to limit.

There is also the moral dilemma of children wanting products that their parents can ill afford. Research suggests that at Christmas, many parents will move heaven and earth to satisfy their children's wants (not necessarily needs), and advertising at these times needs careful control if social problems are not to be exacerbated.

 In the main, airline advertising has tended to stress glamour, comfort and convenience. As Eddy *et al.* (1976) have pointed out, airlines never advertise their safety record. Even if they have an excellent safety record (as Icelandair), there is still the possibility that something will go wrong.

Except in rare circumstances it is unusual for one airline to disparage another in its advertising, although Virgin did so in respect of British Airways during its long running battles in the 1990s. When a merger between British Airways and American Airlines was proposed, Virgin had the slogan 'No way, BA–AA' placed on its aircraft.

easyJet, the UK low-cost airline, uses on-plane advertising, as do similar airlines in the USA. Whereas British Airways called themselves 'The world's favourite airline', easyJet has the slogan 'The Web's favourite airline' on its aircraft, thus emphasising the Internet-based nature of its booking system.

In the early days of the jet age there was considerable emphasis placed on the glamour attached to the flight crew. Both British Caledonian and Singapore Airlines had long-running advertisements extolling the beauty of their flight attendants. By the 1990s this form of advertising was much more socially unacceptable. The more sophisticated market of today responds to advertisements that stress comfort and convenience. Quite rightly, the modern traveller is more concerned about the competence of the cabin crew rather than their physical appearance. The job of cabin crew is actually to look after passenger safety; the serving of meals, drinks and duty free goods is an incidental task.

The Icelandair 'avoid the English' advertisement used in Scotland was not designed to be disparaging towards the English but to reflect the convenience of flying to North America from Scotland. During the month of February 2001, Icelandair undertook a new advertising campaign in Scotland. Icelandair UK & Ireland and Icelandair Holidays introduced a special deal for customers, with an 'Icelandic Cocktail' theme supported by a major advertisement campaign in the Scottish region. The advertisements were placed in prominent outdoor locations in both Glasgow (60) and Edinburgh (30), using billboards measuring 6 metres by 3 metres in order to create a major impact on the Scottish leisure market. The posters included bright, eye-catching colours to inject some colour and atmosphere into the outdoor poster market. The billboards were designed to be informative while grabbing the attention of commuters, and feature scenes from Iceland incorporated into a cocktail theme.

The 'Icelandic Cocktail' concept had proven a tremendous success in the past, with the previous campaign generating huge interest and increased sales. This prompted Icelandair UK & Ireland to expand the campaign for 2001. Icelandair said of the campaign:

> 'The Scottish public demand a quality service to the US from Glasgow and Icelandair meets this requirement. This campaign will alert the travelling public to the excellent service available to them from Icelandair, and the level of our investment demonstrates how seriously we take the Scottish market.'

The idea was devised by the agency BDP Creative in conjunction with Icelandair UK & Ireland.

This campaign was the most comprehensive ever undertaken by an airline in Scotland and it served to reconfirm the commitment of Icelandair to the Scottish market. The Scottish public endorsed this commitment, when they recently voted Icelandair 'Passengers Choice – Scottish Airports'.

The key areas that major airlines tend to stress in their advertising are:

- the route network;
- comfort of the aircraft;
- special facilities at airports;
- the reputation and integrity of the airline;
- the bringing of people together.

To do this they produce very sophisticated advertisements that reflect the technological and social aspects of air travel. The British Airways 'Global' advertisement of 1989 was remarkable in that it did not feature an aircraft, just images of people from across the world coming together.

Summary

Advertising and promotions are a regular feature of daily life for the majority of the inhabitants of Planet Earth. Advertising is a powerful tool in the AIDA process.

Advertising and promotions take many forms, often put together by specialist agencies.

Depending on the product or service, humour, emotion, sex appeal etc. may all be used to advertise products and services, and to assist the customer in achieving identification with both the product/service and the supplier organisation.

Given the impact of advertising on daily life, governments and the industry are keen to ensure the highest standards of truth and honesty.

QUESTIONS

1 Using current newspaper, magazine and television advertising, analyse a sample of advertisements (at least 10) to show how they use convenience, well-being, envy, sex appeal, humour and emotion to promote the product/service.

2 Show the correlation between effectiveness and type of advertising/ promotion, and explain how this can link to the Product Life Cycle.

3 What is the significance of AIDA, DAGMAR and ATR? Using examples, show how they form part of the advertising process.

4 'Advertising is immoral'. Discuss this statement with reference to current advertisements.

Recommended reading

For a background to the success and making of advertisements you are recommended to read: Robinson (2000), *100 Greatest TV Ads*, and Packard (1957), *The Hidden Persuaders*, both texts being referred to in this chapter.

Useful websites

www.asa.org.uk	Advertising Standards Authority website
www.crossculture.com	Richard Lewis website, contains useful details on cross-cultural communication
www.sage.uk	Sage UK website
www.sage.com	Sage main website (Sage publish a number of journals in the promotion/communication field)

■ ⊻ 12 Image and public relations

Public relations – Publicity and advertising – Definition of public relations – Needs of the various publics – Product recalls – Pressure groups – The media – Gaining stories – Marketing and corporate public relations – LICAL – Public relations' techniques – Organisational Body Language (OBL) – Feng Shui

Three terms that are often confused are *public relations*, *publicity* and *advertising*. Having dealt with advertising in the previous chapter, this chapter considers public relations in some details. One of the major differences between advertising and public relations is that the former is directed towards the promotion and take-up of a product or service, whilst the latter concerns itself with the image of the organisation to the whole of society – a society that will, of course, include the target market. Public relations is concerned with the corporate message that the organisation wishes to promote. Thus public relations cannot but help advertise the organisation and its products/services, and is thus a legitimate area of study when considering marketing management.

Publicity is the result of actions by or to the organisation and is managed through the public relations process. Publicity can be active, where there is a deliberate attempt to put over a message or image about products, services or the organisation, or passive, where something happens that is outwith the control of the organisation but an organisational response is required.

The Institute of Public Relations, quoted in Brassington and Pettitt (1997), defines public relations as:

'The deliberate, planned and sustained effort to institute and maintain mutual understanding between an organisation and its publics.'

▬▬▬

The use of the plural form for 'publics' is important. Marston (1979) states that: 'a public is any group, with some common characteristic, with which an organisation needs to communicate.' There are, therefore, a number of publics with whom any organisation needs to communicate, as listed below:

- customers;
- suppliers;
- shareholders in the private sector;

- the electorate for the public sector;
- local and national government;
- competitors (where there are matters of mutual concern);
- the media;
- its own employees;
- pressure groups;
- professional and trade bodies.

Some of the above, such as customers, are also the target for advertising as discussed in the previous chapter, and a distinction needs to be made within the organisation between public relations and advertising activities. Customers may well expect a degree of hype for the latter but will expect pure facts for the former.

Each of these groups will require different information to be used for different purposes. The Institute of Public Relations' definition is rather wide and could almost be deemed to include both advertising and related activities. It is proposed therefore to use the following definition to distinguish between advertising and public relations:

Whereas advertising is related to the raising of interest in products or services, public relations is concerned with presenting a positive image of the organisation to its various publics in response to events and with regard to the needs of those publics.

As Jefkins (1980) has pointed out, public relations embraces everyone and everything, whereas advertising is limited to special buying and selling tasks. Public relations may use advertising to achieve its aim but is itself neither a form of nor a part of advertising.

As Jefkins also points out, public relations is not publicity. Publicity is the result of something that has happened, public relations is the response to that publicity which may in turn generate more publicity. We shall now consider a practical example.

A tour company has a number of clients on a holiday package. Unfortunately their hotel is badly damaged by fire. This will generate *publicity*, which may be negative, and the company will be asked by the media to comment. Good *public relations* (perhaps showing how the company has relocated their customers) will generate positive *publicity* and this may be used in future *advertising* ('We will look after you whatever happens etc.'). Poor *public relations* ('Customers should note that their contract with us excludes problems relating to Acts of God etc.') will produce further negative *publicity*.

Complaints can be used positively, and negative publicity can be transformed into positive publicity by good public relations. Recently there has been much comment about so-called 'spin doctors', normally referring to those in the political arena. 'Spinning' is the putting forward of a positive message about something that may be viewed in a negative manner in the first instance. Unfortunately it has become almost the norm in political circles to use spin doctors to 'prove' that the particular politician or party was not and apparently never could be wrong. Time after time this appears to have backfired, as the public is only too well aware that all people have human frailties and that mistakes happen. Always spinning so that there is never any bad news does not fool the voting public.

The needs of the various publics

Each group that has a relationship with the organisation is part of the public for that organisation and will have different needs, as discussed below. A key component of an effective public relations strategy is to cover as many of the groups as possible and to avoid providing conflicting messages to different publics.

Customers

The individual nature of the relationship with customers is very important, but there will be times, for example when there is the recall of a faulty product or the introduction of a new product/service, when the organisation needs to 'speak' to its whole customer base. This can be achieved through a number of means.

Product recall

It is especially important to make urgent contact with customers when a fault that requires immediate rectification has been found in a product. Whilst the organisation may not wish to let it be known that there are faulty products out in the marketplace, silence may lead to very negative publicity indeed. If the organisation has a list of purchasers then they can be contacted directly, but it must be remembered that the purchaser is not always the end user of a product so that additional steps need to be taken. Notices can be placed in the various outlets that stock the product and also in the appropriate media, e.g. newspapers, magazines and trade journals. This will, of course, bring the problem out into a much more public domain. Such notices need to do two things. They must provide clear and concise details of how the fault is to be rectified and they must give information of the nature of the fault. If the item must not be used, then this must be clearly stated. It is also possible to use such a notice to reassure the customer. Statements such as 'in a small number of instances' etc. may help achieve reassurance but it is important that there is no complacency. As product liability has become very important, organisations are tending to veer on the side of caution in issuing recalls. Obviously any recall is likely to generate bad publicity but, as discussed earlier, dealing with the problem quickly and effectively can generate good publicity. It is important that the need for a recall should, ideally, come from the organisation proactively and not from the media as a result of complaints or incidents. There have been a number of cases where faults in products have been highlighted by consumer organisations and television programmes, forcing the manufacturer to issue a recall. Good public relations should be proactive rather than, in this case, reactive.

Customer newsletter

The computer systems that have enabled the introduction of sophisticated loyalty schemes (see Chapter 14) provide organisations with an easy-to-access database that can be used to send regular mailings to customers. Dot.com organisations, Amazon is a good example, use the Internet and e-mail to keep customers informed about new promotions, special offers etc. Such newsletters need not be purely for advertising as they provide a useful vehicle for promoting the image of the organisation and for strengthening the customer–organisational bonds.

By developing this form of communication, all sectors of business including the public sector can show customers that they care enough to want to keep in touch.

Customer events

The launch of a new product or service can be an ideal method of gaining extra personal contact with customers. This is a technique that has been used successfully by a number of vehicle dealerships. Examples of a new model are put on show, and past (and any identified potential) customers are invited for a drink and a buffet snack. Sales staff can then circulate and talk to customers on a more informal basis than normal. Even if there are no immediate sales, the exercise generates good public relations and shows that the organisation is trying to get close to its customers.

The airframe manufacturers make a great show of the roll-out of a new model, with customers (and potential customers) being invited to meet staff and view the product. It is rare for the media not to be invited to such events, and their reports generate not only good publicity but may also provide a degree of free advertising.

Customer comments

Comments from customers, especially those that are unsolicited, can provide a useful public relations opportunity. Such comments, which often appear in brochures etc., generate a useful link with advertising. The comments of a delighted existing customer are likely to carry more weight with potential customers than comments by the organisation or from a celebrity who will have been paid to take part in the advertising.

Suppliers

The importance of the value chain has already been discussed earlier in this book. The relationship between suppliers and an organisation is both delicate and dynamic. Suppliers will operate to their own values and culture but if the organisation they are supplying is a large one, then that organisation may be able to insist on its values being applied within the supplier. There may well be issues, especially those of product liability, that concern a number of members of the value chain. Eddy *et al.* (1976) have shown how, in the case of the 1972 Paris DC10 air disaster, the public relations exercise involved not only Douglas as the main builder of the aircraft but also Convair, who built the fuselage and the defectively designed rear door (to the specification, it must be said, insisted upon by Douglas), and Turkish Airlines, the operator of the aircraft. Indeed had the engines been considered to be contributory to the crash, then General Electric would also have been involved. In this case the public relations exercise was not conducted well, with members of the value chain actually suing other members. The case serves to illustrate the dependency on mutually supporting public relations for the various members of the value chain.

Shareholders in the private sector/ the electorate for the public sector

The UK Labour government, elected in 1997, brought the word 'stakeholders' into common use. Stakeholders are those who have an interest in the function and performance of an organisation. As such, the term encompasses customers, suppliers, employees and crucially those who have a financial stake in the organisation. In the private sector these are the shareholders, in the public sector the whole of the electorate (at least those members of it who pay tax, a group which tends to include everybody, because although direct taxation may not encompass the whole of society, indirect taxation most certainly does) has a financial interest in the organisation.

In the 1980s and 1990s the UK Conservative government began a series of privatisation exercises, taking a large number of publicly owned enterprises into the private sector, as discussed in Chapter 2. The aim was to produce a shareholding democracy with those sections of the public who had never previously owned shares buying into these enterprises. British Airways, British Gas, the electricity generators and British Telecom were among the larger enterprises privatised.

These new private sector organisations had very large numbers of shareholders indeed, ranging from financial institutions down to individuals, many of whom were entering the stock market for the first time and held just a hundred or so shares.

Private sector organisations have a legal obligation to communicate to their shareholders. They are compelled to produce an annual balance sheet showing the financial position of the enterprise, and it has proved a good public relations exercise to provide easy-to-read summaries of the yearly accounts for those who have never previously had to read a balance sheet. The early annual general meetings of some of the newly privatised organisations occasionally descended in uproar as small shareholders attempted to make points. As time has gone on, the senior managements of these companies have demonstrated a growing awareness that small shareholders have different needs from those who have traditionally held large numbers of shares. In the case of many of the privatised enterprises, shareholders are also customers and this can provide an interesting view of the Porter model in Chapter 5 with regard to bargaining power. As a customer, one wants the lowest price possible; as a shareholder, higher prices may well mean higher dividends!

Many local councils and even the UK government have begun to issue a form of annual report to their electorate. Under education legislation in England and Wales, state schools have been compelled to issue an annual report to parents, the report being issued in the name of the school's governing body.

Demands for council tax now come with an explanation of how the money is allocated, and many councils hold public meetings on planning and budgetary issues to ensure that the electorate can gain information if they so wish. As regards the payment of council tax, the electorate is in a hostage (see Chapter 14) situation but whilst it cannot legally withhold money, it can 'spend' votes.

The UK Labour government elected in 1997 decided to issue a public booklet on how well it was fulfilling its promises, although it came in for considerable criticism for the employment of so-called 'spin doctors' who were employed to put a positive spin on policies and actions.

In addition to the annual report and general meeting, there are two other methods used by private sector companies to communicate with their shareholders.

Firstly, large companies make considerable use of the media and often employ their own public relations consultants. Any stories about the company are likely to be seen by their shareholders and they will always want to present the company in the best light. The stock market can be very volatile and any story that diminishes confidence in a company may lead to shareholders selling stock, normally the largest shareholders doing so first. It is interesting to note that the share price of a company has little to do with its performance and more to do with how the stock market values it. When one reads that a vast sum has been wiped off the share price of a company it does not mean that the company is any worse off than it was the day before. Stock markets can collapse for reasons that have nothing to do with the performance of an individual company. The share price is an indication of how investors value the company. Shareholders, of course, wish the share price to remain high, as they will want to obtain maximum income if they sell.

Secondly, many companies also offer discounts on products and services to shareholders. This is a deliberate bid to make the shareholder into a customer. This approach has a certain degree of commonality with the loyalty schemes covered in Chapter 14.

A phenomenon that has been seen regularly since World War II has been the public relations aspect to armed conflicts. In 1939 the British Prime Minister, Neville Chamberlain, actually wanted to close down BBC Radio for the duration of the conflict. Today news is broadcast directly from the front line, and governments employ spokespersons to brief the press and through them the general public. Even as late as 1992 the UK government was criticised for the handling of the Falkland's conflict with Argentina in respect of the way it handled the public relations aspects of the conflict, especially when dealing with operational matters and the tragic loss of personnel, ships and aircraft, the manner in which the sinking of the destroyer *HMS Sheffield* was reported being considered particularly inept (Hastings and Jenkins, 1983).

As more and more democracies enact Freedom of Information legislation, the role of the public relations staff in governmental organisations is becoming increasingly important and challenging. It might, of course, be argued that every election campaign is in fact a major exercise in public relations, although given the low turnout in some recent UK elections especially those involving the European Union, it may well be that the parties have not really succeeded in putting their message across.

Local and national government

The previous section considered the need for local and national government to undertake public relations for themselves. However, for a whole range of organisations, some of their most important publics (as defined earlier) are local, regional, national and even supra-national (e.g. the European Union) governments. Individual organisations, trade bodies and professional associations who lobby politicians often employ specialist public relations consultants (known as lobbyists) to put forward their views to politicians and their advisors. Many organisations provide overt and covert sponsorship of individual politicians and political parties. Increasingly, as in the UK, it is a requirement for politicians to register any such interests to allay accusations of corruption. Nevertheless, such accusations are made and every so often a major political figure receives very negative publicity when accused of allowing individuals or organisations undue influence in return for favours.

Smaller organisations that cannot afford to employ lobbyists may be able to lobby through their trade organisations, and such bodies are often invited to provide the trade or sector viewpoint to legislative procedures.

Competitors

Whilst it might sound strange at first that a competitor can be regarded as a stakeholder, within any sector of business there will be matters of mutual concern. For instance, if the government is bringing forward legislation on a matter that has implications for all the players in a particular market, there may be an advantage in putting aside competitive instincts and adopting a common approach. In these cases a trade body may handle the public relations' aspects in order that there is a co-ordinated response. Whilst many organisations may be fiercely competitive, they may also work collaboratively on matters of safety. This is only common sense as a lack of confidence in one player in a market, or even a single product, may cause a lack of confidence in that sector of the marketplace in general, to the detriment of all of the players.

Employees

All employees have a vital, if often informal role in public relations. It is often forgotten that for many retail and public utility companies, employees are also customers, often receiving discounts. The image and the message that an employee sends about his or her company can be very important. Nothing is more likely to dent confidence in a product, service or organisation than an employee talking about it in a derogatory manner. One of the Golden Rules of Customer Care is 'if you don't believe, how can you expect others to?', i.e. if the employee has lost confidence in the organisation and its products then it will not be surprising if customers also lose confidence. It is vital, therefore, that the organisation makes sure that employees know what is happening and to that extent they become the recipients of internal public relations. Brassington and Pettitt (1997) stress the importance of such internal PR. Rumours can be incredibly damaging to organisations and the more information employees have about the organisation and its strategy, the less likely they are to make up or twist stories that may then enter the public domain.

Pressure groups

The final half of the 20th century saw a growth in the number of what became known as *single-issue pressure groups*. This was not a new phenomenon, the anti-slavery movement of the 19th century and the suffragettes of the first two decades of the 20th century being good examples of earlier single-issue pressure groups. Many contemporary groups are often highly organised, well financed and have access to excellent information and communications technology (ICT). Such pressure groups can be very focussed and may be local, national or even international. They normally campaign on a single issue that allows them to put over a very simple message, perhaps on an issue as local as stopping a local road programme or as international as protecting a particular part of the environment. There are also groups that are formed to seek redress or justice for a particular individual. In effect this is their product and they have become as adept at marketing as those dealing with commercial products and services.

Such groups are often very effective in their own public relations but are sometimes reluctant to listen to the message put out by other organisations. Any issue always has at least two sides and there is very often a public relations 'war' going on alongside the real issue as each party attempts to rally public support to its point of view. Whilst organisations should never lie, one can be sure that a single-issue pressure group will uncover any untruths from their opponents and then use the fact against the offending organisation. Pressure groups usually have opponents, i.e. those, often in authority, who are doing something the pressure group disapproves of, and competitors, these being other such groups who are competing for the publics' time and money. Single-issue and indeed other pressure groups are usually very tenacious and highly committed, and will probe any and all messages put out by their opponents.

Klein (2000), in her best selling book *No Logo*, has shown how a major US organisation such as Nike was forced to respond to consumer concerns about work conditions at its plants in Indonesia by a campaign designed to turn its core, youth customer base against the product and the company.

Professional and trade bodies

In terms of public relations, professional and trade bodies often act as a clearing house and co-ordinating centre for their members. By their very nature they are able to speak with a greater degree of authority than individuals or small organisations (strength in numbers, economies of scale etc.). They are also able to co-ordinate a response to any issue across a range of organisations. To do this, they rely of course on receiving accurate, up-to-date information from their members. Membership of such a body brings many benefits to an organisation, but if the organisation is consistently at fault there is the possibility of it being expelled and it is likely that the professional/trade body will be able to use public relations more effectively than the organisation can. The organisation will have to explain its expulsion whilst the professional/trade body can use it to show how concerned it is about maintaining standards, and protecting customers and the reputation of the profession/trade and those who remain within the trade grouping. Organisations as prominent as those dealing with the standards of medical professionals were forced into undertaking considerable public relations in the UK in the opening years of the 21st century, as public confidence was undermined by a series of issues relating to doctor–patient relations, including the case of the mass murderer Dr Harold Shipman.

The media

The media has been left until last, not because it is unimportant but because it encompasses much of what has gone before, as the method of communication with regard to public relations between the organisation and the outside world is often through the media. The power of the press (the Fourth Estate), television and radio companies, and increasingly the Internet, to reach and influence huge numbers of people on a global basis cannot be overestimated.

Much of the information that people receive comes via the media and however pure that information was initially, it is in some way transformed by the time they receive it. The media have their own agendas (and often political ideologies) and deal with stories accordingly.

Public relations and the media may be either proactive or reactive. It is proactive if the organisation initiates the story, it is reactive when the media carry out the initiation and then approach the organisation.

The various sectors of the media operate in slightly different ways, a review of which follows.

Newspapers and journals

In the same way as there are typologies of organisations, there are also typologies of newspapers and journals. The vast majority of newspapers fall into the following categories:

- broadsheet nationals – daily, e.g. *The Times, Herald Tribune*, and *The Scotsman*;
- tabloid nationals – daily, e.g. *Daily Mirror, USA Today*;
- Sunday broadsheets, e.g. *The Observer, The Sunday Times* (these are often linked to daily broadsheets);
- Sunday tabloids, e.g. *The News of the World, People* (again often linked to a daily newspaper);
- regional dailies, e.g. *Manchester Evening News*;
- regional weekly or bi-weekly, e.g. *Perth Advertiser*;
- local weeklies, e.g. *Strathearn Herald* and *Stockport Express*;
- specialist dailies, e.g. *Financial Times* and *Racing Post*;
- specialist weeklies, e.g. *New Musical Express*.

Each type of newspaper has a particular type of reader, as a humorous comment in the book '*Yes Minister*' by Lynn and Jay (1989) and also a successful television sitcom remarks;

'*The Times* is read by the people who run the country, the *Daily Mirror* is read by the people who think they run the country, *The Guardian* is read by people who think they ought to run the country . . .'

This is a very true if humorous method of looking at newspaper coverage. Suppliers of goods and services are normally fairly adept at knowing which newspapers are likely to be read by a particular target audience. Many of the questionnaires on lifestyles or even at the end of package holidays ask which newspapers the respondent reads. This is so that advertising, which is very expensive, can be properly targeted. It is unlikely that an expensive car or holiday will be advertised in the *Daily Mirror*, but it may well feature in *The Times*, and the reverse is true for the less expensive products.

Whilst all of the daily newspapers may carry the same story, the manner with which it will be treated varies according to the readership and the views of the newspaper editor or owner. Newspapers often espouse a particular political viewpoint or may take up a campaigning stance on an issue, especially if that is likely to increase sales. The newspaper industry is an example of where the customer accumulator introduced earlier in this book is especially relevant; a reader gained is normally a reader lost to the main competitor, and the newspaper industry is fiercely competitive as advertising revenue is inevitably linked to circulation.

Regional and local newspapers tend to concentrate on a narrower front but, like the nationals, they may well take up particular issues, especially where there is a more local interest. There are also specialist newspapers covering a range of subjects from finance to music, the *Financial Times* being a very well-known example. The essential difference between newspapers and magazines lies in the word 'news'. Newspapers deal with the more ephemeral issues of the moment; a story that is page one today may be on page three tomorrow and forgotten by the end of the week. The articles in magazines usually have a longer shelf life. All newspapers employ a considerable number of journalists and researchers. If they believe that there is a story then they will approach the organisation concerned, normally through the press officer or the public relations department. Dealing with the press is a specialised skill and best left to the experts. A throwaway line by a member of staff could end up as a damaging banner headline in a national paper.

Magazines tend to fall into three groups:

- special interest;
- professional interest;
- general interest.

Special interest magazines, for example *Homes and Gardens* and *Model Railroader*, are targeted at particular interest groups, whilst the general interest publications, e.g. *Woman, Esquire* etc., are designed to appeal to a wide range of readership, often gender specific. A number of trades and professions publish their own magazines, some of which may be on general sale, whilst others are issued to members of trade organisations or are available on special subscription.

Television and radio

Despite ownership by virtually all of the population of the developed world by the start of the 21st century, mass ownership of televisions did not commence until some years after the end of World War II. There are now few homes in developed countries that are without at least one television set and many have additional sets. Radio was developed earlier, in the 1920s, and by 1939 there was a mass market for radio sets. Television and radio have not taken over the whole world as yet. Hutchings (2001) reports that at the start of the 21st Century only 12% of China's 1.3 billion population owned a television set and that the figure for radio was a mere 18%. However those figures are growing very quickly indeed.

Television and radio have an advantage over newspapers in that they are able to react much more quickly to news items, as newspapers have to await the printing of the next edition whereas television and radio can break into a programme. Where newspapers have an advantage is in the depth of analysis they can provide and, as with all written material, there is the ability to scan pages and return to items of interest. However, many television systems can now accommodate teletext, and there are large numbers of text pages available to the viewer bringing increased competition against newspapers and magazines.

Radio does not have this advantage but is able to produce analytical programmes related to the news in interviews with relevant personalities. Up to the 1970s, an advantage that radio had over television was the ease of outside broadcasting, with radio just needing a car as against the outside broadcast van required for television. The development of video cameras of increasing sophistication has led to the introduction of Electronic News Gathering (ENG) using lightweight cameras, allowing television crews to gather news in more remote areas and to broadcast it back to base. Jefkins (1980) considers that radio has four special characteristics that should guarantee its survival alongside television:

- the attractiveness of the human voice regardless of the appearance of the presenter who is, of course, not seen;
- the speed with which material can be produced and the immediacy of interactive programmes such as 'phone ins';
- the low cost of personal radios;
- the ability to broadcast in many different languages, thus allowing ethnic groups access to news etc. in their own languages.

To the four above can be added a fifth:

- the ability to listen to the radio whilst driving.

It should be noted that whilst it should never be possible for a driver to watch television whilst at the wheel, more and more visual entertainment systems for passengers are being developed as optional extras for cars.

Television has become an important, some might argue essential, part of people's lives. There has been a growth in consumer-related programmes where organisations have had their products and services put under the public spotlight, often unfavourably. In the late 1990s, organisations began to fight back. The holiday industry has complained that such programmes are actively seeking complainants and are thus a magnet for attention seekers who may have no real complaint but just wish to appear on television. It cannot be doubted, however, that programmes such as *That's Life*, *Watchdog* etc. have put companies on their mettle as regards the treatment of their customers.

Starting in the USA, recent years have seen a growth in regional and local television and radio stations that provide a more focussed localised mode of news dissemination. These also aid smaller organisations in obtaining coverage (and advertising) for their public relations' stories.

How the media obtain their stories

Given the power of the press, it is useful to consider how they obtain their stories. The ten major methods used by newspapers, as well as journals, television and radio are:

Reporters

Reporters, perhaps the most well-known method of news gathering, are employed directly by the newspaper and may be specialists, e.g. sports, crime, science etc., or general reporters which is how most specialists start their careers, often on small more local newspapers, radio and television stations. The role of reporters is to seek out information and, as such, they are required to have good inter-personal skills as they are required to probe into stories and may have to interview people on sensitive or distressing issues.

Special correspondents

Special correspondents are employed by the media to provide in-depth coverage of their specialist subject, the special correspondent often having a world-wide brief. War correspondents are often attached to military forces. Of particular relevance to this book are those special correspondents who cover particular commercial sectors. A reporter may not have the in-depth knowledge of the special correspondent and if contacted by the latter, it is as well to be aware that the correspondent has probably gained a considerable depth of knowledge about the subject.

Foreign correspondents

The larger media organisations station foreign correspondents in strategic locations abroad. An alternative to employing one's own staff is to make an arrangement with a local media organisation for the use of one of their staff (see Stringers, below).

Stringers

Smaller newspapers cannot afford to have reporters all over a country and abroad, and will use the services of a local journalist who will usually be employed by a newspaper based in the area. One of the roles of a stringer is to feed local stories to the national and international press. Stringers often possess local knowledge and contacts far in advance of those held by visiting journalists.

Feature writers

Newspapers employ feature writers to produce articles rather then news stories. Like special correspondents, they have a considerable depth of knowledge about their specialist field. They are often used to provide background material for news stories.

Contributors

Outside writers who are experts in their field may be commissioned to produce articles for the press. The newspaper or magazine usually approaches them as an expert and asks for so many words on a given topic, the contribution then being edited in house, sometimes under the byline of one of the in-house journalists.

Syndication and picture libraries

If a newspaper or magazine gains a 'scoop', it may sell the material, especially pictures, to other newspapers and magazines. Picture libraries collect photographs from a huge range of sources and then make them available to newspapers and magazines. Such libraries are often used to obtain pictures to accompany articles.

Wire and news services

Reuters, Associated Press etc. are well-known companies which collect news items from whatever sources they can and then put these out to newspapers and magazines who subscribe to the service. The growth in Internet usage has also led to Internet news channels that provide up-to-the-minute news coverage, which is available to the public. The Internet has proved to be an ideal channel for getting breaking news to a large audience very swiftly.

PR departments

Large organisations, trade bodies and governments usually have their own public relations department who will respond to press enquiries, set up interviews and press conferences, supply background material and issue press releases. The PR officer needs to maintain active communications with the press whilst at the same time protecting the organisation when necessary.

The public

The general public themselves can be a valuable source of news items. Local groups can and do issue press statements, and individuals often contact the press to inform them of a news event. Not all such events are actually newsworthy but occasionally a member of the public with a camera takes a picture that is of interest to the press, sometimes world-wide. The video and stills footage of an Air France Concorde with flames gushing from it prior to the fatal crash in 2000 is such an example of the public providing the photographic coverage of a very dramatic event. Widespread ownership of video cameras has meant that it is not only the print media that can benefit from public contributions but television as well. Dissatisfied customers may use the media as a means to gain redress, and many newspapers, magazines, television and radio stations have consumer affairs columns or programmes where the public is encouraged to come forward with 'horror' stories.

Complaints against the media

As is human nature, organisations (and individuals) seldom complain about stories that show them in a positive light, but often complain bitterly when there is an equally correct but negative piece of reporting. The media are not however infallible. Complaints against the media tend to fall into three categories:

- complaints about accuracy;
- complaints about intrusion;
- complaints about bias.

Accuracy

The vast majority of reporters are very concerned about the accuracy of their stories for good reason. In UK civil law, the strongest and most reliable defence against a libel charge is the truth! In 1999 Jonathan Aitken, who had been a government minister in the 1992–97 Conservative government, sued a UK newspaper for making a libellous statement about him. Not only was the statement proved to be true but the case bankrupted Mr Aitken and led to him being given a prison sentence for perjury. Had the statement been false then he could well have received a considerable sum in damages.

Inaccuracies should always be pointed out to the publisher of the story as soon as possible in order for a correction to be printed. Court action is rare as even if the publisher has printed in error, few organisations wish for the publicity of a court case that will keep what may be a sensitive issue in the public domain for some considerable time. Minor inaccuracies are normally corrected by a statement in the newspaper, magazine or by the television/radio company. However it is often the case that the corrections appear in smaller print than the original story.

Intrusion

There is a delicate balance between the privacy of the individual and the right of the public to have access to information. There have been a number of high-profile instances of personalities complaining of undue intrusion into their lives, not least of which have been the complaints by the British Royal Family. The usual defence given by the media is 'public interest'. Journalists, whilst having a great deal of influence are, of course, covered by laws of trespass etc. and may not commit offences in order to gain information.

Bias

Organisations and groups often complain about media bias. In many cases this is just because the media have not presented the organisation's view in the manner that the organisation would prefer, i.e. the media have undertaken a journalistic role rather than acting as unpaid PR consultants for the organisation! In recent years the BBC has been accused of bias against nearly every political party in the UK. If all the parties are complaining then perhaps the Corporation's claim that it is neutral is perfectly logical and factually correct.

In a democracy there is theoretical freedom of the press. In practice, all governments reserve the right to suppress stories on the grounds of national interest and security. Such powers are normally used sparingly by democratic regimes. Non-democratic regimes control the media to a much higher degree, often being the actual owners of the major national newspapers and radio/ television stations. Even in 2001 there were complaints in one African country that the government had ordered the bombing of the premises of a newspaper that had vociferously opposed certain government policies.

In the UK, the Press Complaints and the Broadcasting Standards Councils are able to adjudicate on complaints made against the media and act as a valuable safeguard against charges of inaccuracy, intrusion and bias.

Marketing and corporate PR

It is possible to make a distinction between marketing public relations and more general corporate public relations, although it must be stressed that every PR opportunity is also a marketing one. Even a negative story can promote the organisation if there is seen to be a customer-centred response dedicated to solving a problem rather than priority being given to protecting the organisation at all costs. Marketing public relations normally forms part of the wider promotion of the organisation and its products/services. As such, it is a form of active public relations in that it will be generated internally. Corporate public relations is more concerned with the image of the organisation as a whole and may well be a defensive reaction to an externally generated issue.

Marketing public relations is capable of being planned well in advance and may well form part of an advertising campaign. Sponsorship (see later) can be considered a form of marketing PR as it is often linked to a specific individual or range of products/services. Whilst corporate PR can be planned, as in the case of a major development, it also needs to contain contingency plans to cope with the unexpected. 'Be prepared' is not only a suitable motto for the Scout/Guide movement, it applies as much to PR. There is nothing more damaging to an organisation than a spokesperson who has been poorly briefed. It is perhaps better to say nothing rather than to make a statement that is neither accurate nor considered.

LICAL

Cartwright and Green (1997) introduced the acronym LICAL – Lying, Ignorance, Complacency, Arrogance and Lethargy – to customer relations, and it is just as applicable to public relations and marketing management. This acronym was considered in the previous chapter with respect to advertising. LICAL comprises the five worst things that any organisation can do in its advertising. They are certainly the things that should never, ever happen in public relations.

In the developed world with its enhanced communications and media systems, it is very difficult to keep anything secret. A free press is particularly adept at finding out the truth, especially if it believes that a cover-up is going on. The *Washington Post* journalists, Bernstein and Woodward (1994), uncovered the Watergate conspiracy in the USA and caused the resignation of President Nixon – a classic example of the power of the media. As the story unfolded, it could be seen that the White House staff committed every one of the LICAL sins, but to no avail as the full story was eventually revealed despite the efforts of the holder of the most powerful position in the world and his closest advisors.

Techniques for public relations

Public relations does not just happen. Regardless of whether the issue requires reactive or proactive PR, there are a number of methods open to an organisation to put its message across, as detailed below.

Press releases

Speed may well be of the essence in ensuring that an organisation is able to forward the message that it wishes to. Whether it is a response to an externally driven event or an internal one that the organisation wishes the public and the media to know about, a press release can be a very useful tool. A typical press release will be succinct, covering the main part of the issue only and not cluttered up by detail, and will state clearly who to approach for any additional information. The PR departments of larger organisations will have a list of media outlets that press releases should be sent to, and modern facsimile machines and e-mail can ensure that this is carried out in an effective and speedy manner directly to the relevant newsroom. It is, of course, important that the contact name on a press release is thoroughly briefed, as a lack of knowledge when contacted could lead to a public relations' disaster.

If an organisation knows that there is likely to be public and media interest in one of its activities, products or services, it is best to be proactive and issue a press release prior to the media contacting the organisation.

Press conferences

Major issues often result in the need for the organisation to call the media together for a press conference. The advantage is that the organisation can make a statement once, rather than dealing with individuals from the media, and there is the option of allowing questions. The disadvantage is that the person or persons delivering the press conference cannot predict the nature, tone and direction of the questions. Again, thorough briefing is required.

Publicity stunts

Most people are well aware of 'stunts' that are arranged to promote a particular product or service. In many ways this is a form of advertising, but not being as controlled as commercial advertising there is always the danger that the stunt can go wrong and thus produce the wrong image. If a publicity stunt is successful, it carries with it more credibility than advertising because the customers are well aware that advertising is both paid for and controlled.

Sponsorship

Sponsorship has become a major part of commercial operations. It is based on the concept of association. An organisation that is linked to a successful football team comes to be associated with that success. Whilst there is a degree of altruism in sponsorship, the main aim of a sponsor is to ensure that its name is put before the public and thus reaches potential customers. As with publicity stunts, as mentioned above, there is always a danger of being associated with failure, and sponsors do remove their sponsorship if they feel that they are receiving neither enough exposure or the wrong form of exposure. Sponsorship can be used as a subtle means of targeting customers, in that the sponsor can choose events and activities that are likely to be enjoyed by its own particular customer base. There are huge ranges of sponsored activities, from football to classical music. There is even sponsorship in academia, with organisations sponsoring professorships and research positions within colleges and universities. The important requisite of successful sponsorship is that the organisation's name is always spoken or written in association with the event or activity. For a long time in the USA, and more recently in the UK, the sponsorship of popular television programmes has been taken up by commercial organisations. Whether viewers actually link *Coronation Street* (probably the most successful UK television soap opera), *Emmerdale* or *Friends* with their respective sponsors is a moot point, but the sponsors obviously feel that it is money well spent. The term 'soap opera' derives from the fact that it was US soap manufacturers who first sponsored that particular form of serialised drama.

Trade shows etc.

Trade shows, county shows, military tattoos etc. all present an opportunity for organisations to meet their publics. Retailers and others in the value chain are an important public, and trade shows provide an opportunity for organisations to meet them and to provide corporate hospitality. For many years, banks have provided a mobile unit at major events. This provides a good public relations' opportunity, even if it is actually a loss-making activity for the bank.

Charities

Many commercial organisations support named charities. Whilst there may well be a purely altruistic element to charitable donations, it is also true that such donations can offer tax advantages and help to show the caring nature of the organisation.

Corporate image and Organisational Body Language

The importance of product branding has already been discussed. Branding is concerned not only with the function of a product/service but also with its image. Corporate image is also a form of brand. A corporate image that is perceived by the customer to be customer centred and focussed will aid customer relations. The opposite is also of course true.

Much public relations' activity is directed at showing the corporate body in a good light. There may well be problems with an individual product, but it is important to the organisation that such problems are perceived as isolated to that product and not related to the organisation in general.

Organisational Body Language

As part of the work for their book *In Charge of Customer Satisfaction*, Cartwright and Green (1997) introduced the term Organisational Body Language (OBL), a concept expanded by Cartwright (2000) in *Mastering Customer Relations*. They had discovered that it was not only individuals who signalled their true feelings through body language and the resulting dissonance that can occur with the spoken or written message. Organisations also exhibited a form of body language that revealed true image, regardless of what they might say about the corporate culture etc.

OBL relates to the whole atmosphere that an organisation creates. There are organisations that clearly welcome the customer with open arms and there are those that may claim to, although the message the customer actually receives is one that seems to state the customer is actually rather a nuisance who has to be tolerated! There are organisations that state that staff are respected but the experience of their employees is exactly the opposite.

It might seem strange that there would be any organisation that does not positively welcome its customers or does not value its employees, but unfortunately they abound. A typical example from OBL research was of the organisation that arranged its car park in such a manner that customers were forced to park at the end furthest from reception. The parking spaces next to the reception area were 'reserved for company vehicles'. A company mission statement that claimed that customers came first was of little consequence to customers who had just walked from their cars to reception in the pouring rain and passed the company parking spaces right next to the reception area.

An organisation that has thought about OBL will have first and foremost put its customers first. In the example above, customer parking arrangements should have been for the convenience of customers and not the organisation.

Reception, as the first point of contact and therefore key to corporate image, should be easy to find and provide somewhere for the customer to sit with newspapers and magazines – there may even be a pot of coffee available!

When the researchers were developing the OBL concept, they found many examples of messages that send out negative OBL signals to the customer and give the impression that the organisation thinks about itself first and the customer second. Examples from their work include the following:

- there is no car parking space reserved for a customer who is expected;
- the customer arrives to find a locked door and no explanation – a door may need to be locked for security reasons, but the means of entry should always be made clear to the customer;

- there is nobody in reception;
- there are people there but they have their backs to the customer;
- there is somebody there but he or she walks off as the customer approaches;
- there are people there but they are interested in each other, not the customer;
- there is a large queue and only one person is serving, while others are walking about doing other things;
- there is loud music blaring;
- there is someone at reception but nowhere to sit and wait;
- reception have never heard of the customer, even though he or she has an appointment;
- no-one answers the telephone;
- the customer leaves a message on an answering machine but no-one calls back;
- no-one answers the customer's letters;
- the customer arrives in reception and no-one has ever heard of the person that the customer has arranged to see!

The last point may seem far-fetched but often happens when a new member of staff joins the company and nobody remembers to tell reception and the switchboard. OBL proactive organisations ensure that staff changes are notified to reception and the switchboard in advance, with a note of the date and time they take effect.

Outstanding organisations usually pay close attention to Organisational Body Language and ensure that those who interface with the organisation are not only told that they are important but that their experience will bear this out. It is a known fact that a good initial feeling leads to a 'halo' effect, whereby subsequent events are judged from a positive point of view. A bad start to a customer–supplier relationship can lead to a 'horns' dilemma. For example, if the first few transactions between an organisation and a customer are good and there is then a less than satisfactory transaction, the customer is most likely to put the bad experience down to a temporary aberration – they have put a 'halo' around the organisation. If the first couple of transactions are less than satisfactory then, provided that the customer has not gone elsewhere, a subsequent good transaction may be thought of in terms of 'well they managed to get it right that time but will it last?' The customer is on the horns of the dilemma as to which transactions really represent the organisation and should they defect anyway in case subsequent transactions follow the initial pattern. Organisations have a perennial problem that one bad event can wipe out many good ones in an instant!

With OBL, as with all interactions between an organisation and its stake-holders, the halo/horns effect will apply. If the organisation is open and welcoming, customers and others will assume that this reflects the rest of the organisation (halo). If it is the opposite (horns), then they will assume the worst.

Organisations need to be aware that there is an aural version of the halo/horns effect. If customers, potential customers or other stakeholders overhear someone talking about an organisation, this is likely to influence them. Staff need to be aware that if they are wearing company identification, any comments that they make about their organisation may have a halo/horns effect on any listeners.

Another very important aspect of Organisational Body Language is communicating very negatively. This is often manifested in the extremely negative notices that organisations display, for example:

- don't lean on the counter;
- no credit; no cheques; no refunds;
- broken counts as sold;
- do not touch;
- no push chairs;
- no food to be consumed on these premises;
- no children;
- no dogs;
- no cameras;
- keep off;
- no change telephones;
- no bags beyond this point.

There may be very valid reasons for the above strictures, but it is the manner in which they are communicated that sets the tone for those who read them, including customers, suppliers etc. Every one of the above would send a more positive message if the word 'please' was included. The message would appear much more positive if some form of explanation was given, for example:

- for security reasons, please leave your bags with the attendant;
- newly sown grass, please keep off;
- dangerous area, please keep children away.

Customers who meet a barrage of prohibition notices are likely to interpret this as 'go away, you're too much trouble', and this is a very foolish message for any organisation to send to customers and potential customers.

Organisational Body Language can even include the sense of smell. It is possible to purchase essences to place in air conditioning systems so that the smell of roasting coffee or baking bread can waft through a supermarket and trigger an autonomic reaction in the customers. Having a pot of coffee sending its aroma through a property is a well-known ploy of those trying to sell their house!

Organisational Body Language determines what an organisation actually thinks about its stakeholders, especially customers, as opposed to what it says its policy is. There is no point in an organisation claiming to be family friendly if there are no facilities to change or feed babies and if the seats and counters are too high for children. The British Airports Authority (BAA) is among a growing number of organisations that provide baby facilities in the male as well as the female toilets. Many organisations that claim to be family friendly do not provide lowered urinals and toilets for children, a small point perhaps but one that goes a long way to showing how much the organisation has thought about its customer base.

The major aspects of Organisational Body Language

In considering the impact of OBL on customers, organisations need to consider a series of factors, namely:

- location/buildings;
- security;
- convenience;
- communications;
- ambience.

Each of these aspects has its own OBL implications which the organisation needs to consider not just in respect of the external customer but also of its own internal customers, suppliers and other stakeholders who form part of the value chain.

Feng Shui

Towards the end of the 20th century, many in the West were made increasingly aware of the oriental (especially Chinese) concepts embodied in Feng Shui. Feng Shui involves the harmonious placing of objects, and there are few Chinese organisations that would not include a Feng Shui consultant and take his or her advice on the design of new buildings etc.

Whilst this text is not the place to debate the applicability of Feng Shui to Western methods of business and as to whether the placing of objects can affect prosperity, it is probably self-evident that an organisation that takes such an interest in its physical and mental environment is one that is also likely to think deeply about quality and customers etc. Whether one considers that Feng Shui is effective because of its stated attributes or because it reflects a thinking organisation does not detract from the success that many oriental organisations attribute to it. OBL also involves the organisation thinking about its place in the scheme of things, and thus there are definite linkages between OBL and Feng Shui on both the practical and philosophical levels.

Whilst perhaps not using the term Organisational Body Language, airlines and airframe manufacturers are cognisant of the effect of image. Liveries are chosen to provide a contemporary look. In November 1999, Icelandair introduced a striking new livery. The previous livery was reminiscent of that of Aeroflot, the carrier of the USSR and latterly Russia, and Icelandair wished to move away from any possibility of customers linking the airlines. American Airlines use a steel effect finish that is quintessentially American and reminiscent of US steel railroad cars.

In the 1990s, British Airways experimented with a multi-cultural tail-fin livery to stress the global nature of its operations. In fact this livery appeared to put off many UK customers, and the airline later began to repaint aircraft with the traditional logo.

Inside the aircraft, designers have put much effort into colours etc. that fool the eye into thinking that the passenger is in something other than a long, narrow tube. This is easier in a wide-bodied jet such as the Airbus A300, 310, 330 and 30, or the Boeing 747, 767 and 777. However, by careful design even narrow-bodied jets, such as Icelandair's Boeing 757, can benefit from the work that Boeing carried out on its earlier 727 models in making the fuselage seem higher and wider. As Green *et al.* (1987) point out, careful use of fabrics can be designed to break up the appearance of the long thin tube that is the fuselage of the Boeing 757, despite the fact that passenger accommodation is only 148 inches wide with a headroom of 84 inches.

Airlines are among the large number of organisations that also use the Internet to make information available to the public through their web pages, many of which include the press releases issued by the airline. Icelandair are just one of the air carriers that place their press releases on the Web in the form of an on-line press office. In this way, interested members of the public, in addition to the media, can have access to company information. A recent trend has been to place the annual reports and financial information onto the web pages, furthering public access and disclosure.

Summary

This chapter has examined the relationship of an organisation with its various publics and the need to ensure effective communication with them. The nature and role of the media were discussed, as was the difference between publicity and advertising. The importance of understanding the LICAL model was raised, together with the need to ensure a good corporate identity. Many oriental organisations use the concepts of Feng Shui in designing buildings and setting out workspaces etc. The thinking that Feng Shui requires is very similar to that for Organisational Body Language.

QUESTIONS

1 How would you define the difference between *public relations* and *advertising*? How do the differences manifest themselves through organisational behaviour?

2 Explain the importance of LICAL to the public relations' function of an organisation. What effects can a failure to avoid the LICAL terms have on potential and existing customers?

3 What do you understand by the term 'publics'? Using an organisation you are familiar with, explain its relationships with each of its publics.

4 Use the concept of Organisational Body Language (OBL) to show how the message that an organisation sends out may actually be different from the one it believes it has communicated to its customers.

Recommended reading

For more information on public relations, you are advised to consult

Haywood (1990), *All About Public Relations*, and Cutlip *et al.* (1999), *Effective Public Relations*.

Useful website

www.pri.ie   Public Relations Institute of Ireland website

■ ⫶ **Part Five**

Place/convenience

This is the shortest Part within this study of the 4Cs but that is not indicative of any lack of importance. Although this Part consists of only two chapters, the first concerned with the distribution and delivery of products/services and the second with customer behaviour, it should be self-evident that even if the product or service is tailored to the needs of the customer, is delivered at a cost acceptable both to the supplier and the customer, competitive enough to generate business and promoted in an effective manner, unless the customer can actually take delivery etc. all the previous effort will have been wasted.

As the customer has acquired more and more bargaining power (see Chapter 5), so convenience and ease of delivery have become more and more important.

Chapter 13 considers how convenience forms a vital part of the marketing mix, particularly as technology has enabled more and more organisations to compete in making it easier for potential customers to access their products and services across previously difficult-to-penetrate boundaries, especially those of a geographic nature. Chapter 14 looks at the importance of understanding the customer and his or her behaviour patterns.

■ ⊻ **13** Distribution channels

Channels of distribution – Channel length – Short channel – Typologies of retailer – Long channel – Direct channel – Title of goods – Channel objectives – Selection, purchase and delivery – Credit – Stock control issues – Direct marketing – The Internet

Channels of distribution

Distribution channels are the means by which goods and services are transferred from the manufacturer or originator to the end user (the final customer). In many cases the product itself has to move along the distribution channel. However, in the case of services there may be no physical movement of a tangible good but rather a flow of ideas and information. With the advent of firstly paper-based and then electronic methods for moving money, no longer does actual cash have to travel along the distribution channel (for obvious reasons, money will travel in the opposite direction from the product, see Figure 13.1). In medieval times the Kings of England carried the nation's wealth around the country, as this was the only means of keeping it safe and facilitating payment.

If one considers the case of a customer purchasing a piece of software over the Internet and using a credit card for payment, there is no actual movement of product or money in a physical sense. All the movement is that of electrons through circuits and down a wire.

How different is this from the situation that has existed for much of human history where a customer has needed to travel, perhaps to a market, as has the supplier. They then exchange payment for goods, and each then returns to their original place.

Channel length

In Chapter 5 the balance between the bargaining power of the supplier and that of the customer was discussed. A similar situation exists in respect of distribution channels. It is to the advantage of the supplier to have the customer come as near as possible to the supplier's premises, just as it is to the advantage of the customer to have the product delivered as near as possible to the point of use.

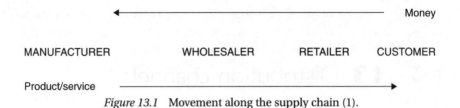

Figure 13.1 Movement along the supply chain (1).

Whilst it may be more cost-effective in terms of logistics to have the customer come to the supplier, it may well give a marketing advantage for the supplier to make it as convenient as possible for the customer to take delivery of the product/service. Distribution channels have been traditionally divided into two major types – the short channel and the long channel – to which should now be added a third – the direct channel. Originally the direct channel was a specialised example of the short channel but the growth in information and communications technology, especially since World War II, has meant that direct marketing and sales should be considered as a separate entity. Paradoxically, as will be shown below, it is the long channel that can provide the most convenient service both to the initial supplier or manufacturer and the customer.

Services are often delivered in a more direct manner than are physical products. As there is nothing physical to transport it may be easier to maintain a direct face-to-face relationship with the customer. Many services, such as accountancy, legal etc., have traditionally been delivered locally in a direct manner with no intermediaries. In recent times, however, there has been a trend towards the development of larger organisations in many of the service fields – organisations that still deal directly with the customer but over the telephone or Internet rather than face to face.

Short channel

The short distribution channel consists of either:

SUPPLIER–CUSTOMER

in which case one must go to the other (this is a form of the direct channel and will be covered in more detail later), or:

SUPPLIER–RETAILER–CUSTOMER

where the retailer is situated, either in marketing terms or physical terms or both, between the customer and the supplier. There is thus little or no actual relationship between the supplier and the customer. In the UK, consumer law is quite clear on this point. Sale of Goods legislation (1982/94) puts the contractual obligation for the quality etc. of products and services firmly on the vendor. It is no use a retailer demanding that the customer return a faulty product to the manufacturer. The contract that the customer has is with the vendor and the vendor alone. The vendor will have a contract with its wholesaler or the manufacturer if it was supplied directly, but the vendor is responsible to the customer.

In many cases the retailer will be situated in closer proximity to the customer than to the manufacturer, retailers acting as nodal points that link products and customers. This indeed was the original function of medieval markets – they brought suppliers and customers together. Gradually retailers began to act as facilitators in the process.

There are many good reasons for a supplier to use retailers as intermediaries; the most important of which also serve to make the acquisition process more convenient for the customer. The main reasons for this are as follows:

Physical location

By supplying retailers in different physical locations or branches of the same retailer, the supplier is able to concentrate its operations on a small number of locations. The distance that the majority of customers need to travel to obtain the product is lessened.

Stockholding

Using retail outlets may lessen the stockholding costs that the supplier might incur by transferring them to the retailer.

Sales techniques

The retailer will be responsible for the relationship with the customer and thus the supplier can concentrate the sales effort on commercial promotions to retailers. It is the retailer who will be responsible for ensuring that staff possess the necessary direct selling and retail customer service techniques.

Assistance

Provided that there has been adequate training in respect of product knowledge, the staff employed by a retailer will be a source of local, face-to-face assistance and information to the customer.

The short channel (Figure 13.2) minimises the loss of contact between the manufacturer/supplier and the customer, and also allows for the building of a close relationship between the manufacturer/supplier and the retailer. As the supply chain is usually relatively short, the retailer and the manufacturer, a supplier may be able to co-operate on promotions, training and the methods by which the product is displayed etc. The disadvantages of the short channel include the fact that the manufacturer/supplier may be dealing with a large number of retailers on a separate basis, and this will require the setting-up of separate invoice systems etc. Where the manufacturer/supplier deals with only a small number of wholesaler outlets, as in the long channel (see later), then economies of scale would come in to play.

A large number of retailers to be supplied is likely to need a large fleet of vehicles, especially if the retailers are situated over a wide geographic area. Even

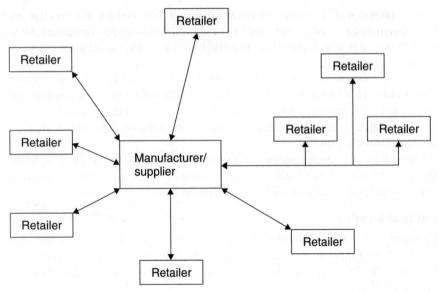

Figure 13.2 Short channel operations for a single manufacturer/supplier.

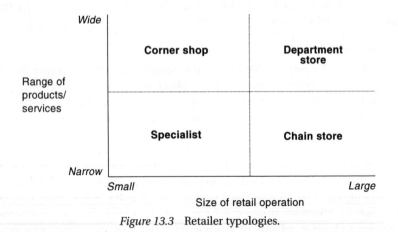

Figure 13.3 Retailer typologies.

if logistics is outsourced, the costs of supplying a large number of small outlets is likely to be far in excess of that incurred in dealing with a few larger wholesaler outlets.

Types of retailer

Before considering the long channel, it is appropriate to examine the wide range of retailer typologies. They can be divided into four distinct types, as shown in Figure 13.3.

As with all typologies, there are no absolutes and the positions within the grid for any particular retailer are likely to reflect a combination of typologies. There is, however, normally a dominant typology, as explained below with examples from the UK and the USA.

Specialist

Typically a specialist retailer is small and deals with a particular type of product or service. Very often this may be a niche product as described in Chapter 8. Examples include local bakers, butchers, and small electrical and household goods outlets. This type of retailer has been hit in recent years by the economies of scale available to larger organisations and the increasing ease and willingness of customers to travel in order to obtain both increased choices and lower prices. One of the responses, following strategies employed by corner shops (see the next section), has been to band together to form a buying consortium and thus take advantage of bulk buying. A number of local household electrical retailers in the UK undertook this strategy in the early 21st century with some success, although it is too early to say whether they will be able to slow down decline and compete with the major chains.

Another popular form of specialist in the developed world is the garden centre. As leisure time and disposable income increase for many people, so hobbies such as gardening also grow in popularity and there is a market whose needs are there to satisfy.

Corner shop

Corner shop is the term that can be given to small, local retailers selling a variety of products, often foodstuffs, newspapers, cigarettes etc. As they stock a fairly wide range (but not as wide as a supermarket) and provide a local service, they have survived but with reductions in numbers due to the growth of large supermarkets. Unable to offer the same discounts as larger organisations because of lack of economies of scale, they have been able to open for longer hours (although supermarkets have responded with longer hours, including even 24-hour shopping) and do not involve a lengthy journey for most of their customers. For the customer it is a trade-off between the convenience of a local outlet set against higher prices and less choice.

In order to compete, at least to a degree on price, many corner shops have banded together to form buying consortia, Spar and Mace being UK examples.

In the past, many corner shops offered a delivery service – a feature of the offering by many supermarkets today.

In many rural communities local petrol outlets have also taken on a corner shop role, thus maximising use of space and ensuring the continuance of a retail outlet for an area that might be unable to support either a pure petrol outlet or a pure corner shop.

Department store

The department store, a concept that developed from the 1860s onwards, is the large-scale equivalent of the corner shop. Many are household names: Harrods, Debenhams, Macy's etc. The House of Fraser in the UK has a number of brands for its department stores, and they tend to sell a huge range from food to clothing to household items. Many of the supermarkets, a genre that began as chain stores (see the next section), are rapidly moving into a more department store mode as they add clothing etc. to their core food products.

Franchises are covered later but many of the department stores have franchised out space to various other suppliers. In the latter part of the 19th century, Isador Strauss and his brother sought permission to sell glass and chinaware in a corner of a successful department store – R. H. Macy. In return they paid the Macy operation 10% of their takings. In ten years they owned Macy's, still on its site in Herald Square, New York, and one of the best known department stores in the world. Isador Strauss and his wife were in Europe in 1912 and on the night of 15/16 April of that year were returning home to New York on the maiden voyage of the White Star liner, *Titanic*. After the liner struck an iceberg and began to sink, Mr Strauss, despite being over eighty years old, refused a place in a lifeboat, as he did not consider it proper that a man should accept. Mrs Strauss gave up her place to remain with her husband and they were last seen sitting together on deck (Davie, 1986), a sad end to a very successful business and marketing career.

Chain store

Chain stores are large and thus similar to department stores, but tend to offer a more restricted range of goods. They are likely to concentrate on particular markets such as white and brown goods (kitchen and entertainment items) and other domestic electronics. Examples are Currys and Dixons which are both part of the same group. They may centre their operations on food and clothing, which would include Marks & Spencer and the major supermarket chains. B&Q and Homebase are UK examples of DIY (Do It Yourself) chain stores. Both belong to groups with wider commercial interests.

Chain stores buy in huge quantities and can often offer the best prices to customers. They have also taken the lead in providing parking, petrol facilities, late night and even twenty-four hour shopping. Because of the high cost and often low availability of city and town centre building land, many of the supermarkets are situated on the edges of urban areas and thus the provision of parking for customer vehicles is paramount. Many of the chains also operate buses to these sites for those who do not own their own transport.

Just as the corner shop was, in former days, known for delivering products, usually using a boy on a bicycle, so many of the supermarket chains have developed home delivery packages, a number of these being based on placing an order over the Internet. Aldrich (1999) calculates that physical grocery shopping, including unpacking, took the average American 1 hour and 40 minutes in the late 1990s, whilst the same operation using the Internet took only 40 minutes. The time for delivery is excluded because when the customer actually goes to the supermarket, the time spent travelling and walking up and down aisles is actually an opportunity cost. Whilst the supermarket van is in transit, the customer can be doing something else. The one thing that is difficult, nay impossible, to accomplish using the Internet is physical browsing – something that many customers enjoy as it forms part of the social side of shopping.

Franchises

Setting up a retail operation can be a time-consuming and costly business. One of the key things that an organisation needs to be a success is a good reputation, and that can take years to build up.

There is a short-cut available in some sectors – the franchise. In a franchise operation the franchisee buys a name and possibly training, equipment etc., and then operates under that name **to the quality standards laid down in the contract between franchiser and franchisee.** It is the franchiser who sets the standards, as it is its name that is at stake. There is likely to be a management fee and a share of profits to be paid to the franchiser, thus the profits for the franchisee may be less than if they were the outright owner, but they have the support of the franchiser behind them.

Whilst there are franchise scams, many franchises are backed by large, global organisations. McDonald's is probably the best known franchise in the world, with few cities not having a branch. The franchiser, in effect, puts in much of the initial effort of developing the product but does not have the retail staff costs as these are borne by the franchisee. In a good partnership there will be training and support. For many, franchising has been a useful first step in running their own business, many franchises being bought using redundancy and early retirement lump sums. One of two things seems to come out of all the stories about franchising – either success and failure. Hard work is required by the franchisee. Franchising is not a 'get rich quick' option.

Long channel

The long channel has an expanded supply chain that includes:

MANUFACTURER–WHOLESALER–RETAILER–CUSTOMER

A wholesaler operates so as to supply retailers and not the public. In effect they act as an intermediary between the manufacturer/supplier and the retailer.

The advantages of including a wholesale operation relate to economies of scale. Therefore it is more economic (see Figure 13.4).

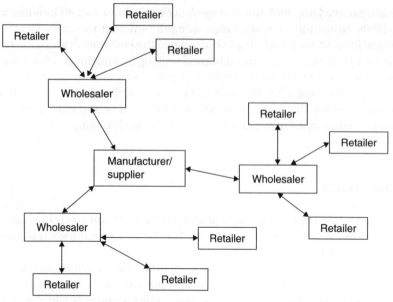

Figure 13.4 Long channel operations for a single manufacturer/supplier.

The model is in fact very similar to the hub and spokes concept introduced when discussing the Icelandair operation in Chapter 1. In fact, both concepts are derived from the same basic idea, that of simplifying logistics.

The advantages of the long channel centre on the cost-effectiveness of the operation, as each retailer does not have to be supplied directly but via the wholesaler. It is quite likely that wholesalers will order in greater bulk than will retailers (as they will need to service a number of retailers), and the economies of scale associated with bulk orders aid planning and production. Perhaps the biggest disadvantage is that by adding an extra link to the supply chain, the manufacturer/supplier needs to accept less money as the wholesaler will want to take a cut and is likely to be able to negotiate larger discounts than retailers can on account of the size of orders.

Direct channel

The direct channel involves the manufacturer/supplier dealing directly with the customer. Direct marketing is considered later in this chapter, and this section will be concerned solely with the physical delivery of the product.

The direct channel was once the preserve of the very large and the very small organisation, the latter often in the local service and individualised product markets. Thus Boeing and Airbus will normally deal directly with airlines. Indeed, the larger airlines often have staff stationed at the builders to act as their representatives during the construction process. Similarly a local blacksmith or plumber will deal directly with the customer. There are organisations that order aircraft for resale but this is not the norm in the airline industry.

The advantage of the direct channel is in its ability to build up a very close relationship with the customer and to respond to individual need. The disadvantages lie in logistics and economies of scale. During the expansion of the American West in the second half of the 19th century there was a growing demand for products from settlers who lived a considerable distance from the major retailer outlets, indeed from any retail outlets at all. Some of the distances involved were huge, with families living tens and in extreme cases hundreds of miles from their neighbours. To satisfy their need for even basic items, a system of mail order was developed. Companies such as Sears produced catalogues and then supplied the goods through mail order. This was a time of the growth of efficient transportation systems based on railways, and with this came the development of a postal service that could increasingly serve remote areas. Almost anything could be obtained using mail order (including in some cases brides!). Mail order and latterly modern computer technology have been able to overcome both physical and political barriers.

Whilst there have been some notable failures of the Internet (the so-called dot com) companies, the use of the Internet for trade is increasing.

Cash and carry

Cash and carry operations are a mixture of the short and long channel designed to benefit small retailers, especially those dealing in domestic products that have a short shelf live, e.g. foodstuffs.

The cash and carry wholesaler deals with the manufacturer/supplier in the long channel manner, but the retailers come to the cash and carry warehouse to collect the goods they need as and when required. The retailer, in effect, trades the costs of storage for the logistic costs of collection. Provided that the cash and carry operator is reasonably close to the retailer, the latter can just stock what they need for immediate use and resale. The major function of the cash and carry operator is to act as a huge warehouse and distribution point. They do not deliver and therefore save on the maintenance of a vehicle fleet.

Title of goods

In commercial contracts it is often of considerable importance to determine who owns goods. The parties to a contract must have the **legal right to make the agreement**. If a person entered into an agreement to sell some goods known to be stolen, then the contract would be invalid as *nemo dat quod non habet*, i.e. no one can give that which he does not have, and possession is not nine-tenths of UK law. Despite the well-known saying, only the owner of goods can transfer the ownership of them to somebody else. Young people under the age of 18 are limited in the contracts they can make, organisations may limit which staff may

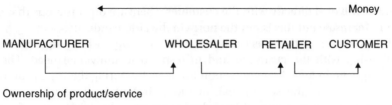

Figure 13.5   Movement along the supply chain (2).

enter into contractual obligations on behalf of the organisation, and those certified as insane are forbidden from entering into contracts. Signing a contract whilst under the influence of alcohol or drugs may also affect the validity of the contract. It can be seen that the right to make a contract and the actual ownership of the goods may be of considerable interest to the various parties if there is any form of dispute.

Provided that all is legal and above board, movement along the supply chain as shown in Figure 13.1 can be amended to that shown in Figure 13.5.

It is possible to own a service. If you look back to page iv at the front of this book, you will see the phrase:

> © then the author's name and date of the edition, followed by the restrictions on copying

and later:

> 'The author has asserted his right to be identified as the author of this work in accordance with the Copyright, Designs and Patents Act 1988'.

Note that the author does not own the book. Either yourself or the library from which it is borrowed are the owners of the book, but the author does hold the copyright. In buying a book, the purchaser does not acquire copyright.

As shown in Figure 13.5, each time money changes hands along the supply chain, title of the goods passes to the person or organisation that has paid for them. This is why it is the vendor who is responsible to the external customer under Sale of Goods legislation in the UK and not the manufacturer, as it is the vendor who has acquired title.

The exception to the acquisition of title occurs when an agent is used as part of the supply chain. If an agent is used to facilitate a purchase, he or she does not acquire title. Their payment is for their services and not for the goods. This can provide employment for lawyers specialising in commercial contracts. It is possible for customers to believe that they are actually purchasing from somebody who is just acting as an agent. The onus is on the agents to make their role very clear.

Many people deal with estate agents (realtors in the USA) and travel agents. The person in a high street store who sells a ticket on an Icelandair flight is acting as a facilitator between the customer and Icelandair, and never has title to the ticket. There are strict rules in place to stop estate agents acting as agents but then buying a property using their inside knowledge and making a personal profit.

Channel objectives

The choice of a channel is one that is shared between the members of the value chain and the customer. The customer has the ultimate word in that it is the customer who ultimately decides the means by which they make a purchase and the channel they use. That choice can only be made from the choices that are available however. If, for instance, the customer wishes to have something delivered to their home but there is no manufacturer, supplier or retailer willing to deliver, then that choice cannot be made. If a number of customers begin to express the convenience of home delivery, then of course it is likely that an enterprising organisation will offer this as a service, to be followed later by their competitors.

Marketing managers and those involved with logistics and distribution are likely to have the following objectives when considering channels of distribution:

An effective (in terms of both logistics and cost) distribution mechanism

An effective distribution mechanism is one that ensures that the right product is in the right place at the right time. The advent of Just In Time (JIT) manufacturing and stock systems has highlighted the need for effective distribution methodologies.

In Just In Time operations, the manufacturer or supplier keeps little or no stock of raw materials or assembly parts. Instead, they will have the materials delivered just as they need them in their manufacturing or service process. (A local plumber can operate such a system, acquiring parts only as and when needed. Specialist suppliers exist to serve the small operator end of the building/plumbing market, although some stocks will need to be held to cope with emergencies.) This means that suppliers need to work to the laid-down schedule that has been agreed with the customer and supply the material exactly on schedule. This can involve deliveries being made every day or even every half-day. In some cases it can mean deliveries timed to the hour, or else the assembly line will be halted and production and revenue lost.

In the extreme case above, because the customer only has enough material to last until the agreed delivery time, if the supplier fails to deliver then the production line will stop. Because each of the separate parts of the customer's operation will also be working on a Just In Time basis, the next process which is supplied from this production line will also stop until, in a very short space of time, the whole production system is at a standstill.

Not only must the delivery schedule be met but also the agreed quality must be achieved, for any faulty material will also cause the line to stop until it is rectified.

Tight delivery schedules and high quality can be seen as vital success criteria for the customer. The supplier who can provide these is likely to enjoy a good and profitable relationship with the customer.

Clearly, the longer the supply/value chain is, the more opportunity there is for something to go wrong. Therefore, the closer the working relationship between the various suppliers and customers, the more effective they are likely to be in meeting each others' needs. The importance of the distribution system cannot be overstated. If part A has to be in place B by a certain time, then a mechanism to ensure that this can be accomplished must be in place.

The means of distribution also need to be cost-effective and use the appropriate delivery mechanisms. The latter can be different depending upon the organisation and the product/service. The type of question that marketing managers should be considering includes the following. Should the organisation invest in its own distribution and delivery system? If the answer to this is 'yes', then should vehicles etc. be owned outright or leased? Leasing is often a more effective option as it involves another organisation having responsibility for maintenance etc. What is the best delivery mode for the product/service? Is it road, rail (useful for bulk items), air (costly but fast) or sea/river? The UK government has been encouraging the use of rail transport in order to decrease heavy traffic on the roads, especially for bulk items. Up to the 1970s, the railway companies and latterly British Rail operated a version of the hub and spokes system (see earlier), using rail transport between centres with initial collection and final delivery being by road, often using their own vehicles. The decline in rail operations and the increase in motorways led to the demise of this system as it became less economic for small items. For the larger bulk loads there has been financial encouragement for organisations that are near to main line railways to lay sidings and arrange for the operation of dedicated block trains. Anybody enjoying a glass of wine in a bar on the banks of the Rhine will see an endless procession of heavy freight trains on the rail tracks that border both sides of the river, trains that remove a large number of lorries from the roads. The huge trains in the USA are legendary, with wagons apparently as far as the eye can see pulled by a large number of locomotives. Whilst river and canal transport has declined in the UK, many of the major rivers of the world still accommodate huge barges moving bulk goods. The seas too are the main conduit for the movement of heavy machinery, ores and oil between continents, although the tramp steamer plying its trade with smallish quantities of mixed goods has given way to the container ship usually following a fixed route.

If an organisation has its own delivery system, this provides an extra advertising mechanism as the sides of lorries etc. can be used to promote products and services. If disaster strikes or the vehicle is dirty or badly driven, negative images may be given out of course. There is an apocryphal story in the USA that after a non-fatal plane crash, the first thing that the airline did was to paint out its name off the aircraft to avoid negative images appearing on news programmes.

Access to target markets

The planning of a logistics and distribution system must take place against a background of the needs and location of the current and potential customer base. Although it may sound pure common sense, it is important that the logistics are in place prior to any serious attempt to penetrate the market. If an organisation is offering free trials etc. it may be acceptable to have only minimum logistics in place, but once customers are being asked to purchase a product or service as part of normal operations, there needs to be a mechanism in place to:

1. ensure that the product/service is delivered on time to the customer;
2. distribute any spare parts or ancillary items that may be required;
3. operate a returns/repair service as required.

It is no use waiting until problems have built up to an unacceptable level, the above must be in place before commercial operations begin.

Whilst it may be the case that the organisation is building up a distribution network from scratch, in many cases there will be such a network in place for other products and it will just be a case of adding to this.

Assisting others in the supply chain

The provision of an effective distribution system and the supply of display materials can aid the others in the supply chain, especially at the far end, i.e. the customer interface. Many organisations supply retailers with display stands and even freezers if the retailer deals in frozen goods such as ice creams. The organisation may wish to place restrictions on using competitor's products in its displays, and in the case of ice cream this has been the subject of official investigation. The easiest way around charges of unfair practice is to make the display stand suitable for only the organisation's products.

Value added

Just In Time, home delivery etc. add value to the product and are thus more than only a means of ensuring that the product/service reaches the end user. They are in fact an integral part of the product/service.

After sales service

After sales service plays an important role in today's customer-centred commercial environment. Part of offering an effective after sales service is the ability to ensure ease of access to spare parts. The aim should be the minimum loss of use to the customer. An effective logistics system is vital to securing this aim. There is little use in delivering a product or service if it becomes difficult for the customer to obtain spares or to access repair facilities in a manner and at a time convenient to the customer.

Selection, purchase and delivery

In any supplier–intermediary (wholesaler, retailer etc.) link, there are likely to be variances between the locations, selection and purchase.

In the simplest scenario where, for instance, a customer visits a tailor for a suit that the tailor will cut and make up, all of the process may occur on the tailor's premises with the tailor very much in control of the whole operation.

In the case of a domestic electrical or car purchase, the customer will probably never have contact with the manufacturer, the ordering and collecting being done via the dealer.

For the customer, it is possibly most convenient to have selection, purchase and delivery as near to the place where the product/service is to be used, with the proviso that the selection may be interesting and fun if carried out elsewhere – shopping can be a therapeutic and social activity.

Organisations need to consider not only the physical places where selection, purchase and delivery take place, but also the means by which they can be made more convenient to the customer – hence the changing of *Place* to *Convenience* in the marketing mix. The time span between each activity is important. The longer the time between selection and purchase and purchase and delivery, the more likely a form of 'buyer's regret' (as it is termed in the USA) will occur. Buyer's regret is the phenomenon, well known in sales activities, whereby a keen and interested customer becomes less and less interested in completing the purchase by taking delivery as time goes by. The longer the time before delivery, the more likely it is that the customer will cancel. Stringent penalty clauses can force delivery, but the customer will then have a negative image of the organisation and is unlikely to provide repeat business.

More and more organisations are prepared to deliver domestic products at the customer's convenience or at a time that suits the customer. Those who sell double glazing become creatures of the evening. Most customers will be out at work during the day so if a sale is to be made, it needs to be made in the evening. Experience shows that few potential customers actually visit the salesrooms of double gazing companies and thus most activity for domestic sales occurs in the customer's home. This has the advantage that this is where the product will be fitted and therefore measurements can immediately be taken and checked.

Unsolicited sales

Selling to people in their home or office is nothing new. Door-to-door sales staff have been employed since at least the Victorian age to offer unsolicited goods, i.e. they visit homes on a speculative basis. This is different from the sales staff who visit commercial premises on a regular basis, and with whom the organisation often has a long relationship with mutual knowledge and respect being built up over time.

In the UK there is legislation in place through the Unsolicited Goods Act to protect consumers from unscrupulous sales techniques. Organisations that send out goods that have not actually been ordered, but in the hope that the recipient will buy, do so at their peril. The title to such unsolicited goods can pass to the recipient if the organisation does not reclaim them (it should be noted that the organisation must take all the steps involved in reclamation, including costs). All the recipient needs to do is to sit tight and wait for title to pass to them or for the organisation to collect. Unsolicited goods used to be a fairly common hazard – not any more, as the legal changes make it financially risky for any organisation to be involved in giving away complete products.

Payment

Some payment methods are more convenient to particular customers than to others. Some will of course be more acceptable to the supplier than will others. The main methods of payments are:

- barter;
- cash;
- cheque;
- banker's draft;
- credit card.

The role of money was discussed in Chapter 9. Barter is only advantageous if all the organisations involved possess products/services required by the others. In recent years, barter has formed part of international trade at governmental level with weapons-for-oil etc. deals. Barter removes the need to convert goods into money but also removes the flexibility that money can provide.

Provided that it can be transmitted safely, the type of payment may be less relevant than the amount of credit given. Methods of payment such as banker's draft have been developed to aid security.

The lapse between delivery and receipt of payment can often be considerable – 30 days is usually considered perfectly acceptable. An organisation requesting payment will be aware of the need for the payee to process invoices and issue cheques or whatever type of payment is being used. The problems tend to occur when the payee holds up payment. If the payee is not satisfied with the goods/services received, this may be legitimate. In the late 1960s, Pan Am held up payment on the first batch of the Boeing 747 because it was unhappy with the performance that the early examples delivered (Irving, 1993). What is not acceptable is the holding-up of payment to ease the payee's cashflow. Whilst large organisations may be able to wait for 90 or 120 days for payment, this length of wait may cause serious cashflow problems to small organisations. Thus many organisations offer discounts for prompt payment of accounts.

Credit

Many organisations offer credit to their customers, some actually lending money to customers to make purchases. On a global scale, governments and their associated financial operations may be involved in the guaranteeing of payment.

Lynn (1995) has detailed the complex financial arrangements used to assist airlines to buy aircraft. In the 1960s the Douglas Company in the USA was involved in deals that led to the bankruptcy of the company as it was lending money to its customers at a lower rate of interest than it was paying to its bankers from whom the money had been borrowed by Douglas in the first place. Such a policy may seem completely irrational but sometimes the need to achieve market penetration and clear stocks may override short-term financial considerations.

DFS, the UK furniture retailer, has long offered up to four years free credit, often with no payments in the first year. Car manufacturers also offer zero per cent interest deals to customers. This ensures a customer but means that the financial institution underwriting the deal needs plenty of free cash, as there will be a long wait for payment.

Credit, debit and store cards

Credit cards are issued by banks, building societies and similar financial institutions. Many charge an annual fee but interest is only charged if the account is not paid off in full each month. There are useful legal reasons for possessing a credit card in the UK, not least is the card issuer's liability if the supplier of goods and services purchased using the card fails to deliver or goes into liquidation. Many of the issuing banks etc. also provide accidental damage insurance for a limited period in respect of items purchased using a credit card.

Corporate credit cards may be issued to staff to allow business-related expenses to be processed without causing the employee to use his or her personal funds. It goes without saying that there need to be organisational rules and safeguards to prevent misuse.

The vast majority of hotels and cruise ships provide facilities for customers to register their credit card details at the start of their holiday; the customer then signs for any purchases, with the account being settled automatically. This is obviously of considerable benefit to the organisation as it makes non-payment for services much less likely, and the customer benefits from not having to carry large amounts of cash around.

Credit cards can be very useful when undertaking foreign travel as they obviate the need to change currencies with the losses that always occur during currency conversions.

As with the debit cards covered in the next section, suppliers are able to seek authorisation from the issuer for any amounts over the suppliers own 'floor limit', i.e. the amount over which a member of staff must seek authority before accepting payment other than in cash. Thus if a customer is over their credit limit or the card has been reported stolen, action can be taken.

Credit cards can also be used in many cash dispensers (ATMs) all over the world.

Whilst credit cards may be rare in inter-organisation trading, they are becoming one of the major methods for domestic end users to pay for their purchases, especially as Internet trading grows and a reliable method of payment is required.

Organisations pay the card issuer a percentage on transactions and this has led some organisations to place lower as well as upper floor limits on the amounts they will accept. It does not pay to accept small amounts on credit cards in the same way as UK cheques, for amounts below £10–£15 are not cost-effective given the time required to process them and the bank charges incurred.

Similar in appearance to credit cards are debit cards, again issued by banks etc. Whereas only a proportion of the balance on a credit card needs to be paid off, a debit card acts like a cheque with the amount of money being debited from the customer and transferred to the supplier. Such cards are nearly always a dual-purpose combined debit and cheque guarantee card.

Debit cards avoid the customer getting into debt as they are, in effect, paperless cheques with strict limits as to the amounts they can be used for.

Store cards are specific credit cards that can only be used in a particular store or grouping of outlets. They are part of the marketing effort to encourage repeat business, often using revolving credit facilities whereby once, say, £1,000 has been paid off then £100 is available for the customer to spend.

Stock control issues

There is little point in having carried out a successful marketing exercise if there is no product or service available for the customer. Once the customer wishes to take action, it is possible that he or she will be unwilling to wait. The skill is in the building-up of an inventory that is large enough to meet initial demand but not so large as to incur excessive storage, handling and insurance costs. Storage alone can eat into profits as the costs of heating, lighting, staff and the purchase of materials can account for up to 25% or more of the net value of an organisation. Lynn (1995) suggests that a failure by Pratt and Whitney to deliver JT-9-D engines for the 747 airframe to Boeing in mid 1969 led to airframes whose worth was rapidly approaching that of the company being stranded outside the construction facility, with concrete blocks replacing the engines to avoid the airframes tipping over.

Inventory and Pareto Analysis

Inventory is potential cash but inventory does not generate revenue. Inventory control is an important part of the role of those managers concerned with production, but they need input from marketing managers on levels of demand. We are all aware that demand cycles often vary depending upon the season. When to stock up and by how much is ultimately a function of potential demand, and thus links to the market research processes discussed in Chapter 4.

Whilst customers may benefit from the holding of high buffer stocks, the costs of such stocks tend to drive up the price that has to be charged and therefore suppliers are very interested in what is known as the **economic order quantity (EOQ)**.

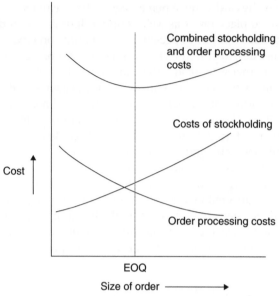

Figure 13.6 Economic order quantity.

The EOQ is a function of the cost of stockholding and the cost of processing orders. The more stock that is held, the more costly it is, but larger orders provide for a reduction in the order processing costs, as shown in Figure 13.6.

In order to calculate the desired level of the buffer stock, the cost of not having stock needs to be considered.

Stockout

There is nothing worse, whether it be in a business or even a domestic situation, than running out of something that is needed. Consider a domestic example. It is 7.00 p.m. on Christmas Eve and a vital ingredient for Christmas dinner has been forgotten. The item's retail cost is £2.50.

If you live in a city or large town there may be somewhere nearby still open but those in the country may have to drive to the nearest late-opening store. To the £2.50 will need to be added the cost of petrol and the opportunity time cost at one of the busiest times of the year. How much worse is it for a manufacturer who has run out of a vital component? As was quoted above, Boeing 747 s without engines are useless and thus are tying up capital for no revenue.

The desired level of buffer stockholding occurs when the cost of holding that stock is equal to the cost of not holding it, i.e. the price that the organisation will have to pay if it runs out of stock. This is shown in Figure 13.7.

The costs of a stockout include not only loss of revenue but also the opportunity costs of disappointing the customer. It is important that the optimum level of buffer stock, Z, is maintained. If it drops too low a stockout may

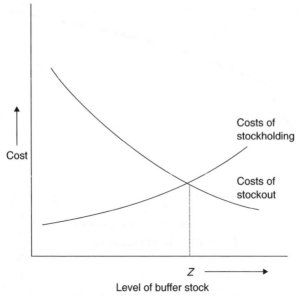

Cost

Costs of
stockholding

Costs of
stockout

Z

Level of buffer stock

Figure 13.7 Desired buffer stock levels.

result, and if it is too high additional storage, insurance and handling costs may occur. Perishable goods may deteriorate to the point where they are useless and thus have no intrinsic value.

However it is nearly always possible to obtain emergency supplies but the usual rules of supply and demand as introduced earlier in this book apply. The more urgent the demand, the more can be charged for the goods. Delivery next week costs X, delivery today costs X plus a premium.

Some organisations have a market niche in offering a Just In Time service to their customers as a matter of course in order to alleviate the need for the customer to hold high stock levels. Viking Direct, the UK stationery and office supplies company, will normally deliver to any part of mainland UK within 25 hours. Customers of such organisations should not, however, let stocks run down to such a low level that weather and other problems affecting transport mean that they run out of essentials. A little caution should always be employed.

Texts concerned with operations management will normally provide all of the equations and charts required to calculate both re-order periods and re-order quantities.

Pareto Analysis

In an organisation with, for example, three products or services, *A, B* and *C*, it is likely that each will have different levels of turnover and indeed different values.

Item *A* may be only 10% of the stock in terms of numbers but 60% of turnover, i.e. a low-volume–high-margin product, whereas item *B* may account for 50%

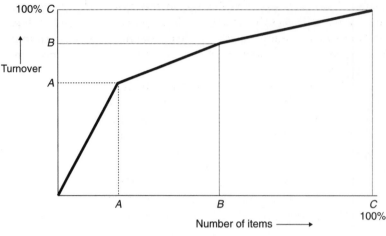

Figure 13.8 Pareto Analysis.

of numbers but only 20% of turnover, with the figures for item *C* being 40% and 20%. If these figures are plotted as a Pareto Analysis, as shown in Figure 13.8, it becomes apparent that an inventory management should be prioritised on item *A* as a stockout on it will be the most disadvantageous of the three. The steeper the line, the more important it is to avoid a stockout.

Much of management is about setting priorities and it is important that marketers ensure that those involved in production are aware of the priorities that each product/service has. When time or resources are limited, the correct priority can be applied to the range to ensure that if a stockout occurs, it will have the least possible detrimental effect.

In the late 1990s, following the release of the movie *Toy Story* in the UK, the demand for Buzz Lighter action toys became so great that the manufacturers could not supply UK retailers fast enough. Some parents, desperate not to disappoint their children, actually flew to the USA to purchase the toys, thus adding the costs of the airfare and accommodation to that of the product – a very expensive Christmas present.

Direct marketing

Modern information and communications technology (ICT) has enabled not only a greater degree of accurate information about the customer to be collected and analysed (see Chapter 4) but has also made it possible for the supplier to have a closer, more individualised relationship with the customer.

Prior to the introduction of computers as a regular part of business and then domestic life from the mid 1980s onwards, variation in marketing materials was a costly option. ICT allows organisations to tailor their marketing materials at particular customer groups and in many cases at individual customers.

By knowing what customers have bought in the past and then using the information in word processed materials, it is possible to send a highly personalised piece of marketing material that can not only remind a customer of what they may need but also show the interest that the organisation takes in its customers.

There is also what might be termed **pseudo direct marketing** where ICT is used to make contact with the customer but all customers receive a similar message. An example of this is the telephoning of large numbers of people to see if they require a new kitchen, roof, windows etc. Many of the companies undertaking the telephoning do so purely on the basis of having acquired a telephone number and have no actual knowledge of the customer. Much money is wasted telephoning the owners of brand new properties offering replacement kitchens etc., when a little research would have shown that the owners of a house that is just a few months old are unlikely to be in the market for such replacements.

To be successful, direct marketing requires the organisation to analyse current and potential customers, and to show them that they appear special by personalising what is offered to the highest degree possible commensurate with the costs.

The major methods of direct marketing will now be described.

Mail

Mail order has already been mentioned and much business is still conducted using postal services either as a marketing tool (i.e. from the organisation to the customer), as a marketing/supply tool (i.e. organisation–customer–organisation–customer) or as the supply methodology for one of the other forms of direct marketing.

There are few parts of the world that have not developed an effective and relatively cheap mail service. Transit times have been slashed with the development of airmail services. As Irving (1993) has pointed out, the growth in the US aircraft industry was linked to the awarding of mail contracts, whereas in Europe it was the railways that gained much early business carrying the mails.

From a marketing manager's point of view, the beauty of using the mail is the simplicity and speed of the operation coupled to the fact that mail deliveries are (in most cases) made direct to the customer's premises. The distribution and logistics network is provided by the mail carrier, often a government agency. There is also the security that mail is protected by reciprocal international agreements.

There is also still a romance about receiving mail. Auden's famous poem *The Night Mail* has an evocative feel about it, even to those who have never even seen a steam train let alone travelled on one.

Postal services often enter into commercial agreements with organisations for the collection, prepayment etc. of mail, and so using the mail as a complete service can remove the need to set up a distribution service. However this will extend the time taken for deliveries and may reduce flexibility.

Telephone

Any review of the implications of technology on marketing must include a consideration of the telephone, invented by Alexander Graham Bell at the end of the 19th century and today a standard feature in nearly every home in the developed world and every business world-wide. It is a piece of equipment often taken for granted and yet at the heart of the communications and computer revolution.

Even in the 1950s, most telephone calls in the UK were made either from business premises or from a public call box. The domestic telephone, although gaining in popularity, was not installed in the majority of homes. By 2001 the telephone had become a fixture in nearly every house in the developed world, with many people owning two or three landline telephones plus a mobile telephone. The telephone is possibly one of the great icons of the later 20th century and when, from the 1980s onwards, it became possible to link computers using telephone lines, whole new possibilities of communication and business were opened up.

The basic workings of a telephone system are relatively simple. A number of instruments that can both transmit and receive the human voice are connected either by wires or radio to a central switching point where the message is routed to the other desired receiver transmitter. Originally the switching of calls was a manual task, with switchboard operators plugging wires into the relevant sockets.

Writing in a companion text to this, Cartwright (2000) recalled that in the 1950s until the introduction in the UK of STD (Subscriber Trunk Dialling), any calls other than local ones (which could be handled at a semi-automatic telephone exchange) required the intervention of the operator who would connect the call. International calls needed to be booked in advance. As electronics improved, so it became possible to dial anywhere directly from home. In the UK, until the 1980s, telephony was a government monopoly, subscribers not buying but having to rent a telephone (like Henry Ford's famous Model T, you could have your telephone in any colour you liked as long as it was black!).

An average UK domestic telephone set (or sets, as there are likely to be at least two in most homes) enables the customer to:

- choose a telephone provider of his or her choice, not necessarily British Telecom;
- have separate lines – most new properties are constructed with at least two telephone line connections;
- place extension sets throughout the house;
- see who is calling;
- receive answerphone messages;
- redial the last number automatically;
- see who was the last person to call;

- set up call waiting;
- divert calls;
- set up three-way calls;
- send and receive faxes;
- access the Internet and e-mail using a modem.

The first telegraphic connection between Europe and North America was laid by the giant (for the time) steamship *Great Eastern* in the late 1860s, and the development of telephone services was limited by wires until well after World War II when space-based technology was developed. The 'space race', which led to the first moon landing in 1969, produced as a by-product the telecommunications satellite and freed the telephone from a total dependency on wires and thus made it possible to use many more channels.

The introduction of ISDN (Integrated Services Digital Network) in the 1990s led to an explosion of telephone-related services. Digital messages, unlike those sent by analogue means, allow the signal to be broken up into discrete packages. Thus a single wire can carry more than one 'conversation'. This allows computers (which use digital codes) to communicate very quickly as well as permitting much more complicated signals. Digital communications have made video-conferencing much more accessible as well as improving the quality of the vision and sound. ISDN is rapidly gaining ground not only for business communications where vast amounts of data need to be transmitted, but also in the home where a modem linked to an ISDN line can handle data much more quickly than a traditional analogue telephone system can.

As the number of home computers has grown, so has the requirement to access the Internet and e-mail from home as well as at work, leading to the development of faster and faster modems and ISDN, as covered above.

The telephone allows a marketer to speak to the customer, and the technology has also been taken up by those involved in direct selling. The boundaries between direct marketing and direct selling can be rather blurred. Many of the calls received by potential domestic customers that claim to be marketing related are actually a form of cold call selling, designed not to acquire information but to make a sale.

Facsimile machines

The facsimile machine, developed during and after World War II, matches telephone and photocopier technologies to allow documents to be sent over telephone lines. Whilst it may well be superseded by a scanner + PC + e-mail combination, many business rely on 'fax' to send messages quickly and conveniently. It is especially useful when complex instructions or diagrams need to be seen by somebody many miles away and a reply or amendments sent back. It may be mundane technology in the 21st century, having had a very rapid life cycle from introduction to maturity (see Chapter 8), but the 'fax' can still help build useful relationships with customers.

Call centres

It makes economic sense, as customers become more and more distant geographically, to provide a central point of telephone contact. Given the benefits of the technology, this does not have to be in the same country, although the cost of telephone calls needs to be kept in mind as more remote customers should not be disadvantaged. Fortunately it is possible to set up either freephone telephone calls or local rate calls to ease the burden on customers.

Airlines, especially British Airways, have used their telecommunications network to obviate time differences. A call for information on the London to Glasgow shuttle made at 2000 (GMT) may well be answered in New York where it is the middle of the day and thus the maximum number of staff are on duty.

Many of the financial and large retail institutions have set up centralised call centres where customer enquiries can be dealt with, often on a 24-hour basis. The computer systems have access to the customer's details and routine matters can normally be dealt with efficiently and effectively, with supervisors on hand to deal with the more difficult queries.

In the UK, a fair number of such centres are located in the central belt of Scotland, as it is believed that the Scottish accent is particularly appreciated over the telephone. Banks which only operate in England and Wales have been known to set up their call centres in the Glasgow area, despite having no (or only a few) branches in Scotland.

Ticketing for flights etc. can be performed in India just as easily as in London as data travels at the speed of light and so distance is no problem.

Call centres provide a point of contact with a human being, and that is still of vital importance to the majority of customers no matter how good the technology is.

It does appear that customers, whilst appreciating a 24-hour customer service arrangement, prefer to deal with people who understand their area and any local issues. Call centre staff can only respond to the computer data that they have to work with, whereas a local shop may be able to take other factors into consideration. By 2001 there were also issues about the way staff in call centres were treated by the organisations, some staff referring to the call centres in terms more reminiscent of high-technology production lines, or even sweat shops with a considerable degree of 'spying' on staff. Such employer activities do not aid motivation.

The Internet

e-mail

Electronic mail (usually shortened to e-mail) is one of the major manifestations of the synergy gained by linking computer and telephone technology. Virtually unknown in the UK before the 1980s, e-mail has become a normal method of business communication and has spread rapidly into the domestic market. With its ability to send document files, pictures, greetings cards etc. to anybody in the world equipped with an Internet connection, e-mail has meant that time and distance have been truly overcome. A message typed in London can be in the inbox of somebody in New York in seconds, and at the cost of a local telephone call.

Colleagues, family and friends who are on-line can be readily contacted and as there is no telephone bell to ring and disturb people, the problem of time zones is eliminated. Despite its protocols, e-mail lacks the personal touch but for instant messages and indeed communications it is hard to beat. Organisations can send the latest information on products and services directly to a large number of customers and suppliers at very little cost.

The more information that is sent increases the risk of virus infection, and this can make recipients wary about opening electronic mail. There is also the danger that the supplier–customer relationship could suffer serious damage if either party inadvertently infects the system of the other.

Just examining an e-mail address can provide a number of clues about the sender. For example, **.ac** near the end of an address indicates that the address is at an academic institution, **.gov** indicates a government body, **.co** is used for companies etc. and **.com** is used by communication providers with others organisations using **.org**. US addresses have nothing at the end, but **.uk** represents Britain (the United Kingdom), **.ca** Canada etc.

The Internet itself

Whole books have been written about the development and use of the Internet. The combination of telephone and computer technology through a gateway provided by one of the many ISPs (Internet Service Providers) allows people owning a computer with a modem to gain access to millions of Web pages covering every possible subject.

There are three major implications of the Internet for marketing, namely:

- information for customers;
- information about customers;
- e-commerce.

Information for and about customers

Nearly every major organisation from retailers to governments and charities, and an increasing number of smaller concerns, have set up easily accessible web pages where customers and potential customers can find information about the organisation. Whether the customer is searching for a new motor car, wishes to know about a piece of legislation, ferry times between France and the UK or wants details of a book, video, CD or DVD, the chances are it can be accessed through a simple Internet search. Some searches require the use of passwords but most commercial and public service are open to anybody wherever they are in the world. All that is required is either the URL (Unique Reference Location) of the organisation in question or the use of the search engines provided by the *Internet Service Providers*. Most addresses begin as http:///www etc. Like e-mail addresses, to which they are related, they may appear complex but follow a logical pattern.

The growth in the use of the WWW (World Wide Web) has been nothing short of explosive, and many individuals as well as organisations now have their own personal web pages where they provide details about themselves.

As more and more people have become 'connected', there has been a massive growth in an area of business known as electronic commerce, or e-commerce for short.

Every time a customer or potential customer accesses a web page, they leave an electronic calling card and the page can send a cookie to the customer making it easier for them to access the page in future. In this way the organisation can discover information about the customer's interests and preferences covertly. Properly regulated, this information can be used to ensure that customers are sent marketing information related to their needs and interests.

e-commerce

In September 1999, UK television news services reported that the UK Prime Minister, Tony Blair, was to appoint an 'e-envoy' to promote the effective use of commercial activities carried out using the Internet. The reports quoted the fact that in 1999 there were 500,000 companies actually conducting business on the Internet, a figure that was expected to grow to a staggering 8 million by 2002 with revenue exceeding £5 billion by 2003. In the UK alone it was predicted that by the end of 2000 no fewer than 9 million Britons would have access to an Internet connection (*source*: ITV Teletext service, 12 September 1999).

Companies using the Internet for business in 1999 ranged from the major holiday companies, airlines, travel agents, book suppliers and antique houses down to a small bakery in Whitby in the north-east of England.

Internet home shopping

As was covered earlier, there is nothing new about the concept of home shopping. As the settlers poured across Middle America in the 19th century, companies such as Sears realised that the massive distances involved in reaching the nearest department store created a market for mail order shopping. Such companies produced mammoth catalogues containing items as diverse as clothes and farm implements. Even today, many people still use a home-shopping catalogue for mail order as discussed above, and this is a thriving sector of the retail industry. No longer do orders have to be placed by mail and an agent used to collect payment. Modern mail order uses the telephone and facsimile technology coupled to credit card payments for those who wish a quicker and more convenient service.

US television stations pioneered the introduction of shopping channels devoted entirely to promoting products and taking orders over the telephone, a development that is now gaining ground in the UK with the introduction of cable, satellite and digital television which allow more channels to be accessed from home.

Electronic commerce is a natural extension of home shopping, recent developments allowing those without a computer but with a digital television to become part of the marketplace.

Given such diversity it would be impossible to mention every type of business operating on the Internet, as new companies and sectors are being added continually. In 1999, one of the latest applications of e-commerce was the conducting of antique auctions by the major antique houses. No longer did a buyer need to fly from New York to London to bid for a piece or employ an agent. They could see the piece on their personal computer at home, examine its provenance, bid electronically and, if successful, pay using a credit card.

The UK budget airline easyJet commenced operations by only accepting telephone bookings paid for by credit card. However, in the late 1990s it began an Internet booking service, one in three bookings being made over the Internet by May 1999. Internet bookings even receive a discount. In May 1999 there were over 1 million visits to the company's website which provides flight details etc. as well as a booking facility.

Not only are flight details readily available on the Internet but so are virtual tours of cruise ship facilities and railway timetables for many parts of the world.

The Internet has made the acquisition of travel information far more convenient for potential customers, who can make their plans in the comfort of their own home or office.

There is a downside in that facilitating such tasks by computer can lead to job losses among high street travel retailers; in effect, the Internet brings the same facilities into the home as have been enjoyed by the travel trade for some time. It is too early to see how this will affect traditional trade and how that trade will adapt to accommodate the new technology.

This section will concentrate on the means by which obtaining and accessing the airline product has been made much more convenient for the customer. It is also a fact that on-board convenience has been much enhanced in recent years, with electronic developments allowing for the provision of telephones, facsimile machines, armchair shopping etc. for passengers.

Buying a scheduled airline ticket has never been easier. All of the major airlines have their own website that nearly always includes a booking facility in addition to information about routes and timetables. The operation of these pages is designed for the convenience of the customer.

Web pages also carry information about the airline and its fleet, many including a section on press releases. You are advised to visit Icelandair's website in the UK on:

in order to see an example of an airline web page.

Whilst the traditional travel agent still books airline tickets for customers, bargains can also be had from the booking agencies that advertise in the newspapers (especially the UK Sunday newspapers) and the specialist web booking agencies. By pre-purchasing seats in bulk, these suppliers can often supply tickets at a considerable discount.

As a rule of thumb, the more inflexible a ticket is and the earlier it is booked, the cheaper it will be, albeit the less convenient to the customer. The cheapest tickets nearly always have an in-built inflexibility that does not allow for a change of flight without an additional (often large) payment. Full fare tickets usually allow the passenger to change flights without penalty, but they can cost two to three times more than the cheapest ticket.

The earlier a ticket is booked, the cheaper it is likely to be. Many of the newer low-cost airlines have blocks of seats at discount prices. Once a price block has been sold, the next highest price seats are offered. Thus the earlier one books, the more likely it is that a low-price seat will be available.

On 5 April 2001, a UK carrier quoted a price of £137 for a single ticket from Glasgow to London for travel on that afternoon. The cost of travel on the next day was between £32 and £77 and that for 5 May 2001 a mere £18.

Not only is it now easier and more convenient to book a ticket but the situation regarding convenience at airports is changing rapidly in favour of the passenger. In many ways airports place considerable limitations on airlines. Firstly, it is rare for an airline actually to control the airport and thus its operations need to fit into the objectives of the organisation operating the airport. In the UK, airport operators are either the BAA (British Airport's Authority) or in cases like Manchester Airport a consortium of local authorities.

The nature of airport operations means that they need considerable land, and for this and obvious safety reasons are situated on the edges of urban areas. The one UK exception is London City Airport, which is situated on a converted dock in the East End of London and can only operate short take-off and landing aircraft.

When British Rail electrified the West Coast main line between Manchester and London in the early 1960s, a race was organised from Manchester to London (city centre to city centre) between a car, a train and an aircraft. As was expected, it was the train that proved the quickest, with the aircraft second and the car a poor third. Whilst the aircraft only took 30 minutes from Manchester Airport to Heathrow, the passengers had to travel out to Manchester Airport using a car as there was no rail link at that time, check in, pass through security and wait to board before taking off, i.e. 1 to 2 hours of time from leaving the city to taking off. On arrival at London it could take at least an hour from leaving the aircraft to finding a taxi and driving into London. The train was able to run from Manchester Piccadilly (virtually in the city centre) to London Euston in just over 2 hours 30 minutes, beating the aircraft passenger over the total journey. A similar situation occurs between London and Paris and Brussels now that the *Eurostar* trains can use the Channel Tunnel. These trains have gained a great deal of traffic from the airlines because they can take a passenger from city centre to city centre in less time than it takes by flying and with less disruption.

Airlines and airport authorities have been well aware of the time delays that can occur at either end of the journey, delays that can wipe out time savings gained by flying.

To improve the situation, all of London's airports (plus Manchester and Birmingham) have rail connections. The connections to Heathrow and Luton are relatively recent, whilst those to Gatwick and Stanstead have been in place for some time. This brings the major UK airports into line with many in Europe such as Brussels or Schipol (Amsterdam), where there has long been a rail/air interchange. The rail links mean that travel to the airport is no longer hindered by congested roads, especially during the rush hour.

Once the passenger has arrived at the airport, check-in facilities have been streamlined, especially for those carrying only hand baggage. Icelandair passengers staying at the hotel linked to the airline can even check in there the night before their flight and receive their boarding pass, thus saving time at the airport. The waiting areas are much smarter than they used to be. Airport management has realised that waiting passengers form a captive retail market and many airports now resemble a shopping mall.

Where passengers need to change aircraft and they remain in transit within a secure customs and immigration area, there have been many improvements in the facilities for refreshments, shopping and information available. The Icelandair passengers transiting through Keflavik will find that the small airport caters for all their needs in very pleasant surroundings. Part of Icelandair's convenience is the short wait between flights, and the airport is well geared to handle the waiting passengers.

Summary

The changing of Place in the marketing mix to Convenience reflects the changes that have taken place in the supplier–customer relationship in the 19th, 20th and now the 21st centuries. There are many methods of bringing customers and suppliers together in a manner that is cost-effective to both. The modern customer expects the minimum inconvenience in selecting, purchasing, paying for and delivery of products and services.

The chosen channel of distribution is a function of the value/supply chain with each member, be they manufacturer, wholesaler or retailer, adding convenience value to the product or service.

Modern technology allows those involved in marketing management to target customers directly. This is a two-way process with the organisation using the information it acquires from customers to make its offerings to them as personal as possible.

QUESTIONS

1 Describe what you understand as a *channel of distribution*. Using examples of both short and long channels, explain the role of wholesalers, retailers, agents etc. and show how value is added to the product/service.

2 What can be the effects of poor stock control? Describe the issues surrounding too much and too little stock being available. How might the price charged to the customer be affected?

3 'The Internet is revolutionising convenience'. Discuss this statement with reference to products/services that you are familiar with.

Recommended reading

You are recommended to read *Managing Channels of Distribution* by Kenneth Rolnicki (1997) and *Mastering the Digital Marketplace* by Douglas F. Aldrich (1999).

Useful website

www.dmg.co.uk Distribution Magazine website

▪ ⋈ 14 Understanding the customer

Importance of good customer relations – Comfort zones – Loyalty – Customer behaviour and loyalty – Loyalty schemes

Customers can be the marketing manager's best friends or worst enemies. Satisfied customers can be among the most effective channels of marketing, whilst dissatisfied customers can undo expensive advertising campaigns using just a few well-placed comments.

In Chapter 5 the *customer accumulator* was introduced and the point made that the loss of a customer by one organisation usually means that a competitor gains that customer, thus strengthening the position of the latter in terms of relative market share. It is therefore very important that organisations not only attract new customers but also actually retain them after the initial experience of the product or service. Ward (2000) makes the point in *The Complete Guide to Cruising and Cruise Ships, 2001* that Carnival, the largest cruise company in the world at the time, offers a product that he believes (page 297 of the Guide) many will only want to use once and then move on to a more upscale one. As has been shown earlier, Carnival owns a number of brands, which is possible within the same company. It would be a problem if the company hooked its customers on cruising, only for them to continue but on the products of its competitors.

The lifetime value of the customer, i.e. their purchase of products and services, over a prolonged period of time is very important. If one considers it carefully, the single shopping basket presented at a supermarket till translates into many thousands of pounds' worth of business over the period that the customer has a relationship with the organisation. It is estimated that each customer could spend upward of £100,000 with a supermarket over time, and thus should be considered in these terms and not in respect of the single £30 to £40 of shopping on each visit. With the exception of those few organisations normally in the criminal justice or medical sectors, whose aim is to never see the customer again, successful organisations view the initial transaction with a new customer as just the first of many. It actually costs far more to gain a new customer than to retain an existing one. The actual cost difference has been placed as high as a factor of 5. This cost reflects the amount of advertising (see Chapter 12) and the time it will take to build up a working relationship with a new customer. There is also a hard-to-define but very real benefit in having loyal customers, as they often act as a marketing organ for the organisation. Unfortunately, satisfied customers seem to have fewer friends than dissatisfied ones, and the latter appear to have louder voices. Put simply, people are far more likely to be vocal about things that go wrong as opposed to those that go right. Whilst there have been a number of television and radio programmes in the UK dealing with consumer problems, there has not been much mention made of the things that have been done well. Bad news sells better than good news, as a casual glance at any newspaper will show.

It is clearly to the advantage of the vast majority of organisations to have a loyal customer base. It is perhaps also advantageous, psychologically, for customers to be loyal to a particular product or organisation. The motivational theory ascribed to Abraham Maslow (1970), introduced earlier in this book, stresses the importance of belonging as a motivational factor. Belonging, according to Maslow, is quite a high-level need for humans. As a species we gain comfort from a feeling of belonging and being with others who share similar ideas and values to ourselves. Organisations that can provide this sense of belonging to their customers are tapping a very important psychological vein within humans.

Much of the fashion industry works on the sense of belonging. It is important to members of fashion-conscious consumer groups to be identified with others of a like mind. As a whole generation of parents have been made aware, it matters what name is written on the side of a pair of trainers that their children wear. Peer pressure, as covered earlier, is an important aspect of marketing.

Comfort zones

Change of any type, even if for the better, can be very uncomfortable. Kurt Lewin (1951) suggested that people become frozen into a particular situation and whilst it may not be the best situation available, the effort and uncertainty of changing can inhibit even a change for the better.

Tice (1989) has developed the concept of a comfort zone in which people operate. Any movement away from the zone of comfort, be it for better or worse, is resisted. This can explain why people who upgrade into first class on airline flights can feel uncomfortable, and why a huge lottery win may well bring discomfort as the winner is moved completely out of his or her economic and possibly social comfort zone into unfamiliar surroundings and experiences.

In terms of the relationship between customers and loyalty, the concept of comfort zones can be used to explain why customers stay loyal to an organisation or product even if another is just as convenient thus making the change relatively easy. Even if the new product or service is of marginally higher quality, customers may still decide to stay with the product or service with which they are familiar. Customers tend to stick to what they know, or as the saying goes 'better the devil you know . . .'. Cartwright (2000) has coined the phrase **comfort loyalty** for this form of behaviour.

Linked to the effect of comfort zones is the cost to the customer of switching to another supplier or product. In the case of everyday household goods (Fast Moving Consumer Goods, FMCG) there may be no cost. However switching, say, computer operating systems may require the purchase of new software, while changing to another make of car may require building up a relationship with a new supplier and dealer, and these costs can be perceived as too high. They may not be monetary at all, often they are time and effort, but they are costs to the customer nevertheless.

Product and brand loyalty

Loyal customers are an important facet of marketing management. Firstly, they cost less to market to and secondly, they can act as marketers themselves by telling family, friends and colleagues about the product or service. Word-of-mouth and personal recommendation will, all things being equal, be more effective than even the most glossy advertisement.

Wind (1982) has examined customer loyalty and has postulated that there are six classifications of customers in respect of loyalty:

- current loyal customers who will continue to use the product or service;
- current customers who may switch to another brand;
- occasional customers who would increase consumption of the brand if the incentive were right;
- occasional customers who would decrease consumption of the brand if a competitor offered the right incentive;
- non-users who could become customers;
- non-users who will never become customers.

It is important to distinguish between loyalty to the generic product, the brand and a particular supplier. Examining customer loyalty, one can define a number of discrete forms of such loyalty.

Many people are loyal to coffee as a beverage. There are also those who are only occasional coffee drinkers and those who never drink coffee, often for medical or religious reasons. Those who drink considerable amounts of coffee can be described as having a product loyalty. Within that group there will be some that buy just the cheapest coffee or drink whatever is available. For them another term is **aloyal**. They are product loyal but brand **aloyal**. They are not disloyal, as that implies that there has been a loyalty, but they have no loyalty at all to a particular brand, Later in this chapter, these brand aloyal customers will be equated to a type of customer known as a mercenary (Jones and Strasser, 1995). Within the group of those who are product loyal there will be those who have a particular **brand loyalty**. They always buy a particular brand or at least a brand from the same producer.

According to Alsop (1989), who studied brand loyalty in the USA, cigarettes, mayonnaise and toothpaste carried a 60% brand loyalty, with plastic bags and tinned vegetables having very little brand loyalty, i.e. the name on the packaging appeared to matter little to customers who equated all products as being of equal quality etc. The situation has become more complicated as suppliers have begun to introduce their own brands, a point already covered in this book.

Supplier loyalty

As was mentioned earlier, many customers are creatures of habit. Not only are they loyal to particular brands but there is also a loyalty to particular suppliers. The work on customer behaviour to be covered later in this chapter introduces a type of customer known as a hostage, i.e. somebody who has no choice but to be a customer of a particular brand or supplier. Such a situation could occur in a small village community where there is only one shop selling perhaps just one brand of breakfast cereal. A customer who is without transport could be forced, although they do not really want that particular type of cereal, to be loyal to that one brand and that one supplier. The term introduced for this is **pseudo-loyalty**. A statistical analysis of that customer would show considerable loyalty but it is pseudo-loyalty because, given the opportunity, the customer might well choose another brand from another supplier. The introduction of large edge-of-town supermarkets in the UK provided a dramatic illustration of pseudo-loyalty as smaller shops saw customers they had previously thought of as extremely loyal defecting to the supermarkets in large numbers, lured by lower prices and increased choice. Whenever loyalty is considered, organisations need to make sure that the customers they believe are loyal are behaving as they do for reasons other than a lack of choice.

In cases such as the above there may well be product and brand loyalty but no supplier loyalty, i.e. the customer might well buy the same brands etc. in a recently opened supermarket as in the village shop, but will use the supermarket because of the increased choice (even if no choice is exercised) and improved facilities etc.

Supra-loyalty

Supra-loyalty is a term used to describe those who are extremely loyal to an organisation, product or service. In the case of loyalty to an organisation they have normally built up a personal relationship with the organisation over a period of time, or in the case of a product/service they identify themselves with it. It is as if they have internalised the relationship and consider themselves almost part of the organisation instead of being a customer. They may well be knowledgeable about the history and operations of their preferred company. Such supra-loyalty can be very beneficial to an organisation as its customers actually perform a marketing function for it by telling their friends, relations and colleagues, but if they become disillusioned then they can wreak havoc, as will be shown later, and then they can undo much of the organisation's marketing effort.

De-loyalty

A customer who makes a deliberate decision to move to another organisation because he or she has been let down by an organisation that they were previously loyal to can be described as being **de-loyal**. This is not the same as disloyalty, which suggests that it is the customer who is doing something wrong. In the case of de-loyalty, it is the organisation that has let the customer down. There is evidence that people are willing to forgive one mistake or one case of poor service – that this forgiveness is actually inherent has been suggested by Dawkins (1976), and Cartwright and Green (1997) have pointed out that customer loyalty can be retained even after a mistake provided that rectification (and an apology) is speedily forthcoming. However if supra-loyal customers become disenchanted they may take their business elsewhere, in effect becoming de-loyal. If they are very disappointed they may become **anti-loyal** and seek retribution against the organisation, becoming what are known as terrorists, a phenomenon that will be covered later in this chapter. Customers who reach this stage of dissatisfaction after previously being delighted often feel betrayed, and this is especially dangerous as they are likely to voice their feelings to other potential customers. The growth of consumer articles in magazines and newspapers and the popularity of consumer programmes on radio and television give these dissatisfied customers relatively easy access to a wide audience for their stories, a type of marketing that no organisation requires or relishes.

Disloyalty

It is a moot point as to whether a customer can actually be disloyal. Customers owe nothing, in terms of loyalty, to suppliers. Many customers may feel that they are being disloyal if they go elsewhere, but feeling disloyal is not the same as being disloyal. The only obligation actually placed on a customer is to render payment for the product or service provided either in monetary or other terms.

Organisations, however, carrying as they do a responsibility to their customers, can be disloyal. Disloyalty is not providing a product or service deliberately to a previously loyal customer. An example of this would be an organisation that treated a new customer better, deliberately or not, than an existing customer, a scenario that is all too common. Organisations often forget that it costs far less to market to existing customers than to new customers, and often go out of their way to promote new business at the expense of retaining existing customers. A retained customer is often worth more and costs less than a new one. Of course, new customers are needed but not at the expense of existing ones. In cases like these, the organisation is being disloyal to the relationship that had been built up. If the existing customer decided to go elsewhere then they would be making a perfectly valid and proper decision. Disloyalty implies an act that is somehow immoral, and one can argue that only the organisation and not the customer is capable of such an act. The customer may be aloyal, deloyal or even anti-loyal, as discussed earlier, but never disloyal.

Customer behaviour

This chapter has introduced a number of terms that can be used to describe the degree of loyalty a customer has to a particular generic product, brand or supplier: *aloyal, supra-loyal, de-loyal, pseudo-loyal* and *anti-loyal*. In effect, these terms describe a variety of customer behaviours. Work by Jones and Sasser (1995) in the USA has also considered customer loyalty and in particular why satisfied customers defect. This is a very important question for organisations. It is easy to see why dissatisfied customers go elsewhere but why might those who are apparently satisfied behave in this manner? In short, the question can be answered by stating that mere satisfaction is no longer enough. The aim of any supplier of goods or services should be to delight the customer. Unless they are aloyal, delighted customers do not defect unless they cease to become delighted or are even more delighted by the offering of a competitor. The concept of comfort zones, discussed earlier in this chapter, indicates that a competitor will need to provide considerably more delight in order to woo a customer, and that may well not be a cost-effective method of gaining new customers.

Jones and Strasser have made the point that many organisations believe that if their customer feedback mechanisms indicate satisfaction then the organisation is in a good position. Their research however showed a weak link between satisfaction and loyalty, the strong link being between delight and loyalty! As products and services improve then satisfaction becomes, in effect, the minimum acceptable standard. As this book has used the terms supra-loyalty and pseudo-loyalty, Jones and Strasser have referred to long-term loyalty and false loyalty. Many commercial operations have competition curtailed either by government restrictions or by (sometimes illegal) arrangements between the various players. Whilst monopolies are becoming rarer in free market economies, as discussed earlier in this book, situations such as duopolies where there are only two main players in a particular segment of the market, or oligopolies where the supply is restricted to a limited number of suppliers, are more common. High cost barriers to entry, as discussed in the previous chapter, may restrict membership, as may the illegal setting-up of cartels. The oil and airline industries have been accused of restricting membership to the favoured few, situations that benefit the suppliers but not the customer (Sampson, 1984; Gregory, 1994). Jones and Strasser have concluded that in the case of monopolies or oligopolies, as soon as there is increased competition then the level of satisfaction required to retain previously 'loyal customers' increases. They point out that whilst in monopoly/oligopoly situations it is the customer who has restricted choice, as soon as competition opens out it is the suppliers who have only one real choice. They must provide their existing customers with higher and higher levels of satisfaction. The easier it becomes to switch, the more likely it is to happen.

UK banks have made a point of targeting students to open accounts with them, despite the fact that students have little if any disposable income and may incur considerable debts whilst studying. The fact is that graduates are likely to earn more over their working lives and thus provide more business and revenue for the bank. There has also been a considerable lack of switching of bank accounts. Part of this may be due to loyalty but it has also been relatively complicated to do so. Banks are now making it much easier for customers to change to them by easing the complexities that the customer could experience. This is, of course, a two-edged sword. If an organisation makes it easier for somebody to switch from a competitor, their competitors will make it easier for customers to defect to them.

When the UK government deregulated telephones, gas and electricity in the 1990s, the various suppliers made it relatively simple for customers to switch provision. British Telecom, as the UK market leader for telephone services, also made it easy and cheap for defectors to return.

The importance of total satisfaction (or delight) against mere satisfaction was demonstrated by the example of the reprographics giant Xerox, as profiled by Jones and Strasser (1995). They found that delighted Xerox customers were a staggering six times more likely to give repeat business to Xerox than merely satisfied customers. As it is unlikely to cost six times more to delight a customer than to merely satisfy him or her, the financial advantages of delighting the customer seem self-evident.

Jones and Strasser have developed terminology for six types of customer behaviour that can be linked closely to the typologies of loyalty discussed earlier.

Apostles

Apostles demonstrate supra-loyalty. The apostle is a customer who is extremely delighted with the service or product and, as stated earlier when considering supra-loyalty, may actually identify with the organisation or the product. This is, of course, good news for any organisation. Apostles, in effect, carry out a marketing function for the organisation. They are highly loyal and delighted, and they tell their friends, colleagues and relations. As they have, apparently, no stake in the organisation, they are as near to an unbiased marketer as it is possible for the organisation to obtain. Potential customers who may be suspicious regarding the claims made in an advertisement are more likely to believe somebody they know. The use of celebrities etc. in advertising is linked to this form of trust and belief, as potential customers are more likely to believe the endorsement of somebody they revere in another field – irrational but true.

There are downsides to having too many apostles in the customer base. Their identification with the organisation may be so close that they can come to believe that they are actually part of the organisation. When this happens, the distance that should rightly be present in the customer–supplier relationship is destroyed. Apostles can become a nuisance by demanding special treatment and interfering in matters that are really not their concern, such as internal arrangements that have no effect on the customer. There is a delicate balance to be struck by organisations that want the benefits of apostles but must militate against the disadvantages.

The biggest danger associated with the apostle is the tendency to become highly disruptive if dissatisfied. Apostles are paradoxically the most fertile source of the organisation's worst enemy – the terrorist (see later). It is said that 'Hell hath no fury like a woman scorned' but to an organisation, Hell hath no fury to compare with a highly dissatisfied apostle. The dissatisfied apostle does not just feel let down but because of their perceived close link to the organisation, they can also feel betrayed and with betrayal may come a wish for revenge and retribution. Many of the complaints that make the headlines originate from ex-apostles who some time earlier would have been singing the praises of the organisation, product or service that they are now decrying.

Apostles are unlikely to switch organisations unless they become very dissatisfied, but when they do it will be in such a manner as not to go unnoticed and they are very unlikely to return unless recovery of the situation by the organisation is swift and effective.

Loyalists

Loyalists form the most important component of the customer base. They are akin to the 'cash cows' described by the Boston Consulting Group (see Chapter 8) to describe those products that form the basis for organisational success. Loyalists require much less effort on their behalf than apostles do and are very loyal customers, coming back time and again. They tend to be less volatile than apostles are and thus more tolerant of mistakes. They are less voluble in their complaints but that does not mean that the organisation can afford to ignore them. An organisation that loses the support of its loyalists is on the downward spiral to major problems. Loyalists are the source of the all-important repeat business that is a major performance indicator for the vast majority of organisations.

Whilst there might be a certain glamour attached to apostles and their effusive praise of an organisation, loyalists are the true firm foundation for any customer base. Loyalists provide the stability and objectivity required for sustained growth. Loyalists also form useful members of focus groups as they will not be afraid to tell the truth as they see it, but they will be objective in doing so and that will provide useful data for the organisation.

Jones and Strasser make the point that loyalists are the easiest customers to deal with. That is true but customers only become loyalists as a result of high-quality products and services delivered over a period of time, and the experience that when there have been complaints, these have been rectified expeditiously.

Mercenaries

Mercenaries are the hardest customers to deal with, as they are basically aloyal. Mercenaries will tend to go for the cheapest or the most convenient option. They are difficult to deal with because they may well be satisfied but they are not loyal. Mercenaries may demonstrate product loyalty but brand aloyalty; they may be brand loyal but supplier aloyal. They may well move from brand to brand or supplier to supplier. If asked why they moved, the answer may be in terms of cost or convenience but it may well be just a desire for a change. This makes developing a marketing strategy aimed at mercenaries based on anything other than cost or convenience very difficult.

The problem for an organisation is whether to expend energy or indeed money on trying to turn a mercenary into a loyalist. The organisation will need to satisfy the mercenary, as even they will tell people about bad products and services, but unless they are incredibly pleased it may well be that they will continue to shop around. From the organisation's point of view it is important not to pander too much to the mercenary. Too big a discount on the first transaction may well mean that they will always want such levels if they return, but they are just as likely to go down the road and quote your discount to a competitor in the hope that it will be bettered. Certain modern marketing strategies based on always undercutting the quoted price of a competitor play into the hands of mercenaries completely. However, even the most mercenary customer should be aware that there is a price below which no organisation can or should drop in order to gain or retain their business.

Hostages

Hostages appear to be very loyal but that is only because they have no choice. If a town only has one toyshop then that shop will receive the vast majority of the toy trade. An organisation will not know whether its customers are loyalists or hostages until a competitor or a substitute appears on the scene, and by then it may be too late.

Hostages have no choice; there is only one convenient shop, one local supplier, one hospital to go to etc. They have no choice but to demonstrate attributes of loyalty even when dissatisfied, hence the use of the term pseudo-loyalty.

The time for an organisation to assess the loyalty and the satisfaction of its customers is not when a competitor opens up but before then. Hostages will leave as soon as they have an opportunity if they are dissatisfied. Even satisfied ex-hostages may leave for a while in order to assess a new competitor. The original supplier will have to hope that the original product/service was of sufficient quality to tempt them back. It is too late to offer discounts and or enhancements after competition starts. Hostages will ask, and rightly, 'why are you offering this to me now and not before?' Customers are not, in the main, stupid and may well resent levels of service being enhanced to retain them after the opening-up of choice.

Defectors

Dissatisfy even the most dedicated loyalist often enough (or once in a major way) and they may well defect from the organisation. Once a customer has defected and given custom to another organisation it may well be difficult to recover the situation, as their comfort zone (see earlier in the chapter) will have changed. In effect, the new organisation will have become their comfort zone. This can occur very rapidly indeed once the decision to defect is made.

To ensure minimum defection, organisations need to have effective procedures in place to deal with complaints in an expeditious manner so that any temporary dissatisfaction does not become permanent and thus lead to defection. One organisation's lost customer is a gain for a competitor, with the financial penalties as shown in the customer accumulator introduced earlier.

The defector displays characteristics of de-loyalty, as discussed earlier.

Terrorists

The terrorist in customer relations' terms is the worst nightmare that an organisation can have. Just as the political terrorist acknowledges no rules, neither, it appears, does the customer relations' terrorist.

Terrorists were often apostles displaying supra-loyalty until they were let down and the situation was not recovered. They are not so much dissatisfied with the organisation, product or service as at war with it. They have a desire for revenge and retribution. Many of those who appear on consumer affairs television programmes have been previous apostles. On being let down, they have no problem in letting the world know about it.

The longer a situation remains unresolved, the angrier the terrorist becomes and sometimes their actions may be extreme, irrational and even criminal. The threat of a court appearance for harassment or breach of the peace in respect of their relationship with an organisation may well have an unexpected and negative effect. Court appearances mean publicity and by the time a customer becomes a terrorist, putting the problem right is no longer enough. They want to see the organisation humiliated and even if they are punished for a breach of the peace, they will have generated massive negative publicity. The larger the organisation, the more media interest there is likely to be and, human nature being what it is, the more sympathy the underdog (the customer) is likely to receive from the public.

The best method of dealing with this type of terrorist is to do what should never be done to a political terrorist – give them what they want, and more if necessary, and hope that they go away. The organisation will not want them as customers in the future, however much business they generate, as by the time they have reached the terrorist stage the disadvantages far outweigh the benefits of their custom. The organisation should concentrate on cutting its losses rather than trying to win back the custom. Terrorists are not de-loyal or even disloyal, they are anti-loyal; to use a metaphor, love has turned to hate!

Jones and Strasser's work is useful in that it provides an easy-to-understand explanation of why mere satisfaction is no longer enough to generate loyalty. Loyalty must be earned and should never be taken for granted. A summary of loyalty and satisfaction is shown in the *loyalty matrix* of Figure 14.1.

	Low		High
High	HOSTAGE (PSEUDO-LOYAL)		APOSTLE (SUPRA-LOYAL)
			LOYALIST (LOYAL)
LOYALTY			
	DEFECTOR (DE-LOYAL)		MERCENARY (ALOYAL)
Low	TERRORIST (ANTI-LOYAL)		

	Low	SATISFACTION	High

Figure 14.1 The loyalty matrix. [*Taken from Cartwright (2000), with permission.*]

Can loyalty be measured?

This is a question that can only be answered in a situation where there is considerable choice available to the customer. Customers will be truly loyal and not displaying pseudo-loyalty when the quality and value for money that they receive are sufficient for them to ignore the competition, even when the competitor can offer either a slight cost-saving, or enhanced convenience, or both.

Even changing one's regular supermarket can affect the comfort zone and it appears that there is a threshold that needs to be reached before many customers will defect. The easier the procedures to change supplier are made, the lower the defection threshold. It must be remembered however that even in a monopoly situation, there may well be one actual choice to the customer – that of going without.

Loyalty schemes

The latter part of the 20th century saw a proliferation of loyalty schemes, in part due to the opportunities presented by the introduction of new information technology systems and increasing competition in a global marketplace.

Loyalty schemes have, however, been around for some considerable time. Since the earliest days of commercial activity, discounts have been offered to repeat customers, thus encouraging them to come back to the same supplier. What new technology has allowed is for loyalty schemes to become highly sophisticated.

However, as Brassington and Pettitt (1997) have pointed out, when every supermarket, every airline and every department store have their own loyalty scheme, much of the competitive advantage may be lost. Cobb (1995) has reported that once the market for loyalty schemes becomes saturated they generate very little extra revenue. Mitchell (1995) has shown that over 25% of scheme members are happy to switch to a scheme offering marginally better benefits and as such display aloyalty, as discussed earlier. Once saturation is reached it may be that lower prices may well become, once more, the determinant in customer choice. Nevertheless, loyalty schemes grew considerably in the 1990s and seem set to be a feature of retail operations for the foreseeable future. Customers seemed to require larger wallets and purses not for increased cash but for the growing number of dedicated charge and loyalty cards that were being issued. The UK Supermarket chain of Safeway actually decided to terminate its loyalty card scheme in 1999 as it was apparent that customers were not being loyal to the supermarket because of its loyalty scheme *per se* – in fact, many customers were members of a number of such schemes.

Brassington and Pettitt (1997) provide a useful case study on supermarket loyalty schemes in their book *Principles of Marketing* (pp. 694–5), where they examine the highly successful Tesco scheme in the UK (to be discussed later).

A number of the schemes that will be discussed in the following sections involve the awarding of points, stamps or vouchers to the loyal customer. Such rewards are known as alternative currencies, as they can be traded in for goods and services at an agreed exchange rate in the same way that actual cash is used to purchase goods and services (Brassington and Pettitt, 1997)

Dividend and stamp schemes

The various Co-operative Societies that sprang up in the UK during the Industrial Revolution, the first being opened in Rochdale in 1844 under the title of 'The Rochdale Pioneers', were based on the concept that they were owned by their members. In effect, they were an early example of the share-holding democracy that became a touchstone of the Thatcher government after 1979. The major benefit of membership was the dividend that was paid out either as cash or goods at the end of the year. As such, the societies also had a banking function and this became formalised in later years with a separate banking operation. Each transaction that a member made attracted a certain discount, which was recorded on a slip and placed in their dividend book. 'Divi' was an important source of extra income and helped with the purchase of luxury items at Christmas and special occasions. It was the concept of customers sharing ownership that set the Co-operative movement apart from other retail operations, and it is only in recent years that other retailers have begun to operate similar loyalty schemes. The Co-operative movement was also different in that, at least at its beginning, it had social and political aspects to the operation. The movement was closely associated with the working class of the time and the Labour Party. It should also be noted that in its earliest years there was no provision for the transfer of benefits from one Co-operative to another, the operations being very much based on local geographical location. Not surprisingly, as the movement grew, it became necessary to operate in a more UK-based manner. Even up to the end of the World War II there was much less mobility of labour than there is today, and thus the need to transfer benefits did not affect the vast majority of the members of a particular local Co-operative.

Trading stamps

After the merger of the locally based Co-operative stores, the organisation replaced the dividend with a stamp scheme. Stamps were given by each store based on the value of the customer's spend, and could then be used to pay for subsequent items exactly as cash and which were redeemable at any participating store. The Co-operative scheme was, naturally enough, confined to Co-operative outlets, but a much larger, nation-wide multi-organisation scheme was developed that offered Green Shield Stamps.

Large numbers of outlets across the whole of the retail sector offered these stamps (there were also some smaller, less successful competitors to Green Shield Stamps), which were collected by customers who then redeemed them for items out of the Green Shield catalogue. One of the problems with this type of scheme was the tendency to drive prices up as retailers had to pay to take part, just as they have to pay to accept credit cards. Nevertheless, up to the 1970s, large numbers of consumers collected the stamps and there was pressure on retailers to offer them in order to match their competitors. The introduction of cards that could be read by computer helped hasten the demise of stamp schemes, as the cards could be read quickly and easily at the point of sale whereas stamps had to be placed somewhere safe and then stuck into a book, which then had to be redeemed against catalogue goods. The Somerfield supermarket chain was using an electronic variant of the scheme into the 21st century. Their loyalty card is processed at the till but then needs to be placed into a special machine, usually near the exit, for the new points to be accumulated. The points can then be redeemed from the catalogue issued by the Argos chain of stores.

Vouchers

The idea of a voucher included with each purchase of a particular product was used by the cigarette companies in the years after World War II with considerable success. The best known UK scheme was that run in conjunction with the Embassy brand of cigarettes. Given the increasing campaigns against smoking, such a scheme that encouraged increased purchases of cigarettes would be much less acceptable today. However, in the 1950s and 1960s large numbers of smokers collected Embassy and other vouchers that were, like trading stamps, redeemable against goods in a catalogue. As with trading stamps, the vouchers had to be stored, counted, collated and then sent through the post. Unlike trading stamps, the vouchers were product specific and designed to reward product loyalty rather than supplier loyalty.

Air Miles

One of the most successful UK loyalty schemes has been that of *Air Miles*. According to Churchill (1999), the scheme was conceived almost informally by

Keith Mills, an advertising executive, and Alan Deller an ex-British Caledonian Airlines marketing director in the late 1980s. Instead of the more mundane goods offered by the trading stamp and voucher companies, *Air Miles* was designed to offer the glamour of air travel. All airlines have a proportion of empty seats on many flights, and the concept was that *Air Miles Promotions* would purchase seats from British Airways that it could then sell on to retailers in the form of vouchers in a series of air mile denominations. British Airways took a 51% stake in the company but eventually in 1994 decided to acquire the operation in its entirety. Various large organisations had begun to offer *Air Miles* to both loyal customers and as a staff incentive, and with the arrival of electronic registering of *Air Miles* both the Sainsbury supermarket operation and Vodaphone began to offer the scheme. It was also a sensible strategic move to offer other rewards in addition to flights and these now include admission to theme parks and holidays. Only about a third of *Air Miles* are actually used for flights. As Churchill (1999) points out, it is also possible for a customer to increase their reward by using a credit card from a bank that offers *Air Miles* to pay for goods at a retail outlet also offering *Air Miles*. By switching to electronic registering, *Air Miles* has been able to bridge the gap between the earlier voucher and trading stamp schemes and the current loyalty cards as offered by more and more organisations.

Icelandair operates a similar scheme in conjunction with Hertz and Radisson (a number of the airline schemes have links to hotel and car rental operations) and their airline partners. Accumulated points can be used for purchases and upgrades.

Loyalty cards

The ability of the magnetic strip and its later derivatives on the back of a credit-card-sized piece of plastic to record and store information has in many ways revolutionised the relationship between customers and suppliers.

The importance of marketing as the process of finding out as much as possible about the customer has already been stressed. The loyalty card can greatly increase the research possibilities for organisations. By recording use at the point of sale, the organisation is able to determine buying patterns etc. This allows demographic correlations to be made and can provide a very comprehensive picture of individual customers to be drawn up. There are some who have raised ethical objections to the degree of information that can be gleaned about an individual's lifestyle although, in the UK, such information is controlled under data protection legislation. By 2000 there were, as discussed earlier in this chapter, a large number of loyalty cards in circulation. The benefits of the loyalty card as opposed to stamps etc. is the ability of the card to provide detailed information about the customer. Whilst the customer may receive loyalty rewards for using the card, they pay for these rewards not only through their purchases but also through the information that they provide to the supplier. A supermarket can glean vast amounts of information about lifestyle just by analysing what (and when) a customer purchases.

Pseudo-loyalty schemes

The major car manufacturers operating in the UK began to offer payment options that had many of the hallmarks of loyalty schemes from the early to middle 1990s. By guaranteeing a residual value for a new vehicle after so many years (normally 2 or 3) and with an allowable annual mileage, a customer would need to pay only the difference between the purchase price and the residual value. There was also a guarantee that there would be enough money left over in the deal for the deposit on a new vehicle at the end of the scheme period. Thus the customer received lower repayments and the manufacturer, in effect, locked the customer into buying a new vehicle on a regular basis. The scheme works well provided the customer is happy with the products of the chosen manufacturer but, as with all such arrangements, there are financial penalties if the customer wishes to leave the scheme early.

Forms of credit arrangement as offered by certain retail outlets also lock customers into deals which may sound an attractive method of making an initial purchase, but can considerably increase the customer's financial indebtedness to the supplier. Such options are not really loyalty schemes as such but a financial arrangement between customer and supplier.

Features of a successful loyalty scheme

The Co-operative dividend scheme discussed earlier was successful in attracting customer loyalty in that it displayed most but not all of the attributes of a successful loyalty scheme. The most important attribute of a successful scheme is that customers perceive added value. If they do not, then the scheme is doomed. To add value, it must offer benefits that customers want as opposed to those that the organisation may wish to give. As has been discovered in recent years, when all suppliers in a given sector offer a similar loyalty scheme then customers may find it difficult to distinguish between them, and whilst they hold and use a loyalty card for one supplier they may also do the same with other suppliers thus removing any competitive advantage.

The major attributes of a successful loyalty scheme are that it should:

Be mutually beneficial

The original Co-operative schemes need to be viewed from the sociological perspective at the time. By owning the organisation, the members were able to control prices and quality to some degree. The degree to which individual members had control is open to question but like all shareholders, they were able to question managers at periodic intervals, usually at the annual general meeting. In a similar manner, members of those UK building societies that have remained mutual are theoretically in control of the society but in practice the individual has very little say, just as individual holders of small shareholdings have little real influence. The Co-operatives benefited from a customer base that was locked into it via ownership culture and the reward of a dividend.

Today the benefits to the organisation of an effective loyalty scheme can be viewed not only in terms of customer loyalty but also in the information they can provide to the organisation about the customer, as discussed earlier. As was covered earlier, Electronic Point Of Sale (EPOS) equipment linked to the information held on the cards issued to members of a loyalty scheme can allow an organisation to build up a profile of the customer.

This new technology may be able to bind the customer and the organisation even closer together. By identifying buying patterns it may be possible for organisations to be even more proactive. It should be possible for the cashout operator to be able to ask customers if they have forgotten an item; it only requires the EPOS computer to compare the current spend with previous ones to produce a very personalised service. Whilst this may be pleasant when it happens occasionally, too frequent a display of just how much the organisation knows about the customer may become threatening.

Reward increased spending

A successful loyalty scheme will reward spending differentially. Whether it is a points system, such as that operated by many supermarkets, or a percentage scheme, such as the 'POSH' Club operated by P&O Cruises for repeat cruisers who care to join (who are then offered in addition to a newsletter and extra shipboard activities, percentage discounts on items purchased on board), the scheme should provide higher rewards as spending increases. The British Airways' 'Executive' Club for frequent travellers, in addition to awarding *Air Miles*, has three levels of entry available to most customers depending on the number of flights they undertake in a year. The Blue, Silver and Gold cards offer an increasing range of privileges both in airports and in the air. Thus the more a customer spends on air tickets, the more privileges they receive. It is interesting that one of the Unique Selling Points (USPs) of the easyJet airline operation based at London's Luton airport is that it does not offer any such loyalty bonus, concentrating instead on cheaper seats. easyJet make the point to staff that more expensive seats may be booked with airlines offering a loyalty programme in order to benefit personally, but if a booking is made on an easyJet flight then there will be cost savings to the company.

Provide communication

One of the most important functions of a loyalty scheme is that it provides the organisation with the name and address of the customer. This then allows the organisation to send mail to the customer. Mailings cost money and anything that can allow those monies to be targeted is welcome. General details about the organisation can be sent to the customer, as can special offers both of a general or a targeted nature. Receiving a personalised mailing can also strengthen the customer's sense of belonging, thus binding the customer closer to the organisation.

Have no cost to customers

In the main, the costs of a loyalty scheme should be borne by the organisation and not the customer. It may well be that there is a barrier requiring a certain level of initial purchase to enter the scheme. Many of the loyalty schemes operated by companies in the travel industry allow entry automatically after the customer's first purchase with the company. The POSH Club operated by P&O Cruises is unusual in the industry in that there is an annual subscription required in order to continue membership, but the scheme does provide for discounts on shipboard purchases. The Captain's Circle loyalty scheme operated by Princess Cruises, P&O's US-based operation, is free but does not provide for discounts onboard. Both provide special offers etc. for members. All of the major operators in the sector operate similar schemes.

Be multi-site

The original Co-operative dividend schemes were very restricted in that there were no transfers between Co-operatives in different parts of the country, as discussed earlier. It was only when the Co-operatives merged to form a nation-wide organisation in the 1960s that a national stamp-based loyalty scheme was introduced (see earlier).

The development of card reading computer systems has allowed organisations to offer multi-site loyalty schemes. Thus a Tesco Clubcard can be used in a Tesco branch anywhere and, as will be shown later, at branches of certain other organisations. Modern customers are much more mobile than their predecessors were. Prior to the introduction of cheque guarantee cards by the UK banks, special arrangements to draw out cash had to be made by customers going on holiday; today they can withdraw cash either at the counter or at a cash dispenser at any branch of their own bank, or indeed at competitor banks. As customers have become more mobile so the need for organisations to operate loyalty schemes across a wider geographic area has become more apparent.

Be multi-organisational

Not only have successful loyalty schemes developed a multi-site function but many are increasingly offered as a multi-organisational scheme. Hence the Tesco Clubcard could at one time also be used at branches of the Do-It-Yourself (DIY) retailer B&Q. The loyalty scheme operated by the British Airports Authority (BAA) allows the customer to collect points based on purchases at a wide range of retail and food outlets in the airports controlled by the BAA. As airlines have formed strategic alliances, so their loyalty schemes have expanded to cover the partners in the alliance, as discussed earlier in respect of Icelandair, Air Canada etc.

Whilst the logistics of operating a multi-organisational scheme may be more complex, they are eased by the ability of computers to communicate very effectively and thus there is no real problem in operating such a scheme provided that the partners have the equipment in place to read each others' cards. The scheme operated by the Somerfield supermarket chain involves premier points that are redeemed at the Argos stores group. These points can also be collected at certain petrol stations. Points are added to the card, which has magnetic storage facilities and is thus able to keep a record of the accumulated points. The total can be checked on a simple machine that is located in each Summerfield store.

The Tesco Clubcard has been a very successful loyalty and promotional scheme since its introduction in 1995. At that time, UK supermarkets were undergoing a major expansion especially in the form of 'edge of town' sites offering increased facilities. Whilst Sunday trading had been the norm in Scotland for many years, changes in the law in England in the 1990s allowed the supermarkets to offer a seven day per week service. The provision of ample parking spaces, café facilities, cash dispensers, florists and an increasing product range allowed a successful supermarket operation to become a 'one stop shop' for customers. The competition for suitable sites that provided both the space needed for customer vehicles and proximity to major roads and motorways was intense, and the supermarkets were keen not only to acquire new customers but to retain those customers in order to boost their market share. The Tesco Clubcard scheme recorded the monetary value of a customer's purchases at the cashout point and then sent the customer a series of money-off vouchers according to the spend made. The scheme was very successful and by June 1996 there were over eight million members (Brassington and Pettitt, 1997). The expansion of the scheme for a short period to allow customers to collect points not only at the B&Q Do-It-Yourself stores but also at branches of Lunn Poly travel agents provided not only an increased bonus for customers but further added to Tesco's database of its customers and their spending habits and preferences.

Brassington and Pettitt (1997) claim that the Clubcard scheme assisted Tesco in boosting its turnover by 25% and profits by 15% in 1995 alone, despite the fact that over £40 million had to be given back to customers as a result of Clubcard discounts.

Whilst the Clubcard scheme in its original form provided for discounts on spending at Tesco, by 1999 members could receive discounts at theme parks and on holidays, air tickets, entertainments, rail travel, ferry crossings and a host of other products and services. To this extent Clubcard has moved nearer to the *Air Miles* concept.

To celebrate the fourth anniversary of the Clubcard scheme in 1999, Tesco introduced an enhancement known as Clubcard Deals. For every £25 spent, Clubcard holders received a 'Clubcard key', each key being valid for one year. Holders of 50 keys could receive a series of half-price offers, including holidays, travel etc., from a special brochure, whilst holding 100 keys gave a 75% discount.

It is not surprising that Tesco's competitors have followed suit. Loyalty schemes in the UK have flourished, mirroring the US experience, and nearly every purse and wallet contains a series of such cards issued by a variety of organisations.

Provide ease of redemption

One of the problems with earlier types of loyalty schemes was the effort required by customers to redeem their reward for goods. Modern technology makes it very easy to store the accumulated rewards on a magnetic strip on the customer's loyalty card, and to use this information to ease redemption. The easier it is to redeem a reward, the more likely the customer is to use that particular scheme.

These characteristics of rewarding increased levels of spending, personalised communication, ease of redemption and wide inter- and intra-organisational use typify the vast majority of contemporary successful loyalty schemes.

Whereas most current loyalty schemes are based around a card that can be read by a computer, there are two earlier types of scheme which have been largely superseded by modern technology but were very popular and built on the Co-operative dividend schemes.

Summary

In considering the relationship with customers and ensuring their loyalty, this chapter looked at the types of loyalty that can be displayed, namely product loyalty, brand loyalty, supplier loyalty, supra-loyalty, aloyalty, de-loyalty, anti-loyalty and disloyalty. These were linked to the work of Jones and Strasser and their concept of apostles, loyalists, mercenaries, hostages, defectors and terrorists, leading to the construction of the loyalty matrix. A variety of loyalty schemes using cards, stamps etc. was then introduced, and the benefits and disadvantages discussed.

QUESTIONS

1   Using the descriptions of various types of loyalty given in this chapter and the work of Jones and Strasser, explain why the link between satisfaction and loyalty is not straightforward. In what circumstances may loyal customers actually be dissatisfied and why might satisfied customers defect?
2   Why might a supra-loyal customer (apostle) present such problems to an organisation that it would rather the customer defected to a competitor?
3   Describe, using examples, the attributes of a successful loyalty scheme and explain the mutual benefits to the organisation and to the customer. How can marketing effectiveness be increased through the use of loyalty schemes?

Recommended reading

You may wish to read Cartwright (2000), *Mastering Customer Relations*, a companion volume to this text, for further information about customer relationships.

■ ⊻ Part Six
Conclusion

■ Ⅴ 15 The marketing plan

At the beginning of Chapter 1 of this book, marketing was defined (Wilmhurst, 1984, quoting from the Institute of Marketing) as:

> '. . . the management process responsible for identifying, anticipating and satisfying customer requirements profitably'.

As such, marketing forms part of the management function of any organisation for without customer or clients, however they may be defined, there is little reason for the existence of the organisation.

This final chapter seeks to bring together the components of the organisational analyses and the 4Cs of marketing, as covered throughout the book, into a set of questions that can be used to plan and implement the marketing of an organisation's products and services.

The aim of this book has been to show that marketing is an activity that forms part of the general management role of any organisation. All managers, whatever their specialism, need to know as much as possible about the needs and wants of their customers and potential customers, and to have a knowledge of the benefits and specification of the organisation's products and services.

At the centre of marketing is the need to balance the customer and the product/service and to ensure that the product/service is delivered to the customer in a manner that is cost-effective and convenient to both sides of the transaction.

The planning of marketing lies in the careful analysis and answers to the following questions.

What factors feature in the PESTLE/SPECTACLES analysis?

The external environment needs to be considered throughout the derivation as a marketing plan, as it is within that external environment that the products and services of the organisation will be offered. The only exception would be in the case of the development of a product or service for use wholly within the organisation, and even then the objective is likely to be one that supports a product/service designed for an external customer.

The key external factors that must be considered in a SPECTACLES analysis are:

Social

What is happening in the society containing current and potential markets that may present opportunities and threats to the organisation's products/services?

Political

Are there political implications that need to be taken into account when planning marketing? It is rare for such implications to come as a surprise, as most governments and political parties make their views known well in advance of any action. So, is the organisation monitoring the political scene?

Economic

What is happening in the economies of the markets served by the organisation? In planning the management of the marketing function, organisations should be considering factors such as exchange rates, interest rates, employment levels, levels of disposable income etc.

Cultural

Of particular importance when moving into new markets, the cultural analysis requires the organisation to consider the values and norms of the target customer groups and to ensure that both what is offered and the manner of offering correspond to the cultural norms.

Technological

Of particular importance to the management of marketing is a consideration of how new technologies can aid the promotion and delivery of products/services. In recent times the impact of ICT (Information and Communications Technology), including the Internet, has been particularly relevant in this regard.

Aesthetic

The aesthetic analysis is concerned with the image that the organisation displays both through its infrastructure (buildings, staff etc.) and through the products/services and their packaging etc. How have these been considered in respect of current and future customer groups?

Customers

Customers form a major part of this section (see later). As part of the SPECTACLES analysis, the organisation will be looking at general trends, e.g. are customers becoming more demanding? Specific customer-centred planning will occur later.

Legal

Is there any legislative action proposed in any of the organisation's markets that will have an impact? Legislation may be concerned with customer rights, safety, finance etc. The managers from the respective parts of the organisation should be able to inform those in marketing at an early stage of any proposed legislative changes.

Environmental

Organisations have to be much more responsive to environmental concerns and this can have a positive benefit on the image that the organisation presents. What opportunities are there for the organisation in this area?

Sectoral

The results of the analysis are likely to vary between organisations although many will be common within the same sector or regional economy.

The analysis provides the external framework within which the marketing plans may be formulated. In all probability the external analysis in respect of competitors will be very similar but there may be regional or sectoral differences that need to be taken into account.

SWOT

Once an analysis of the external environment has been completed, consideration needs to be given to the strengths and weaknesses of the organisation and then this should be added to the external threats and opportunities derived from the SPECTACLES analysis.

The strengths and weaknesses are internal to the organisation, whilst threats and opportunities are external. A similar analysis should be carried out for competitors to see how strengths can be maximised against competition and weakness minimised.

C-SMART

The next stage is to consider and list the major objectives of the organisation, putting them into C-SMART criteria:

- Customer centred;
- Specific;
- Measurable;
- Agreed;
- Realistic;
- Timely.

Product portfolio

What products/services are offered?

Unless the organisation is starting from scratch, there will be an existing product/service portfolio. The questions that need to be asked are:

How balanced is the portfolio?

Is the organisation dependent upon a range of products/services or perhaps there is just one main source of income, making the organisation vulnerable to changes in taste etc.?

Where is each product/service in its life cycle?

It is important that all products are not at the same stage of the life cycle and that product succession has been considered, with new models etc. replacing those coming to the decline stage of the life cycle.

How can products/services be developed?

What scope is there to develop existing products or services into new areas or segments, or does the organisation need to be developing related or completely new ranges?

What are the USPs (Unique Selling Points) for the range?

List what makes the organisation's products/services unique and therefore different from those of the opposition.

Who are the current customers?

List the current customers of the organisation. What similarities are there between them? What market segments are they in?

Who are the internal customers and are they aware of their role in the value chain?

Who are the internal customers within the delivery process? How can service to them be improved and how will this benefit the external customer?

What benefits are external customers gaining?

List the products/services and alongside them the current benefits they provide for customers. This is important for promotion and advertising as it is benefits that sell, not products.

What new products might they benefit from?

Are there potential benefits and synergies that can be developed?

Who are potential customers?

Who could be a customer but isn't yet? Why are they not customers, i.e. what barriers are they encountering?

What new markets can be tapped?

Are there new segments, uses or geographic regions that can be tapped by the organisation? What will be needed to do this?

Who are ex-customers and why?

Most organisations are able to identify recent ex-customers. It is illuminating to find out precisely why they no longer have a relationship with the organisation. Has something gone wrong, or has a competitor offered a better deal?

Whilst it might be difficult to ascertain why a customer has defected, the exercise can prove valuable. Customers leave for reasons other than complaints, and a study might point out demographic factors such as population shifts that the organisation may be able to make a positive response to.

Who are the competitors?

It is rare that there is only one supplier to a particular market segment. It is as important to find out (fairly) what the competition is offering and their prices and delivery methods. The organisation will also want to know about the quality of products/services offered.

Other competitor aspects that need to be addressed are:

New entrants

Are there any new entrants that need to be investigated and in particular are they backed by a large organisation that may have considerable resources available to support a new venture?

Substitutes

Is substitution a possibility (see Chapter 5)? Substitution can often catch existing competitors by surprise.

Competitor SWOT/PEST

It is not enough just to analyse the external environment and the SWOT factors for the organisation. As much information as possible should be gathered about competitors in order to perform comparative analyses. This will assist the organisation is assessing its position within the market when compared with the position of competitors.

Costs

The organisation needs to consider how its costs are derived and where savings can be made that do not impact on quality of product, service and delivery. Whatever information can be obtained regarding competitor costs should also be gathered and compared with the costs that the organisation incurs.

Price

There are three major questions to be asked:

- What is the maximum price that the market can bear?
- What price are competitors charging for similar quality?
- What is the minimum price that the organisation can charge in order to break even and make the required profit?

These are three out of the four key questions to be resolved before setting a price for the organisation's products and services. The fourth, relating to supply and demand, is considered next.

Supply and demand

The fourth key question in pricing relates to the levels of supply and demand. Much will depend on the capacity of the organisation, as it is important to ensure that demand can be met or else the customer may seek an alternative supplier.

Advertising

The organisation needs to consider the means of advertising that will allow it to access the greatest number of customers with the maximum impact. For all but the smallest organisations this is likely to involve the use of an advertising agency that will advise on format and location. Advertising costs can be very high and need to be considered in relation to the total costs of the product/service. As with all market planning, the advertising undertaken by competitors also needs to be taken into account.

Promotion

The organisation also needs to consider what promotional activities can and should be undertaken in conjunction with advertising. These normally need to be planned well in advance. Organisations have received bad publicity for making offers that they cannot fulfil – this tends to lead to very dissatisfied and lost customers.

Channels of distribution

It is not enough to have the right products and services at the right price. They need to be delivered in a convenient manner to the customer along the channels of distribution.

The organisation must analyse the various channel options and pick those that are most convenient predominantly for the customer but also for the organisation. If the cost of delivery becomes too high, then the price charged might have to rise and this may lose custom for the organisation.

Law

Naturally the organisation must ensure that all of its marketing activities fall within the law, be it legislation relating to contracts, customer rights, finance or safety. Large organisations will normally have their own legal team and many smaller operations retain the services of solicitors etc. Keeping up with legislation may well be time-consuming but it is worth while.

How trained are staff?

The final part of the planning relates to the competence of the staff all along the value chain. How well do they know the product or service, the customer and the role of others along the chain? The better informed the staff is, the more the organisation can do. Training needs should always form part of the marketing process.

The nature of the questions is such that they require an holistic approach, i.e. one that includes managers drawn from across the organisation. Production, sales, finance and personnel management staff input is as important as that from those concerned purely with marketing. The role of the latter is to take the answers and draw up a plan for the interface between the organisation and the customer, and then to communicate that plan to colleagues so that each function within the organisation is aware of its role and of the part it plays in the value chain.

This book has attempted to show how marketing is part of the management process for an organisation. All organisations have customers in one form or another, and the basic aim of the vast majority of them is to deliver a product or service to their customers at a cost or a price that is mutually acceptable. Marketing is the name we give to this relationship between an organisation and its customers.

Useful websites

www.instcustserv.co.uk   Institute of Customer Service webpage
www.tesco.com   Tesco webpage

■ ⱽ   Bibliography

Aaker D (1984) *Strategic Market Management*, Wiley

Adler E (1969) *Lectures in Market Research*, Crosby Lockwood

Aldrich D F (1999) *Mastering the Digital Marketplace*, Wiley

Alsop R (1989) 'Brand Loyalty is Rarely Blind Loyalty', *Wall Street Journal*, 19 October, p. 1

Anderson D, Sweeney D and Williams T (1990) *Statistics for Business and Economics*, West

Argyris C (1960) *Understanding Organisational Behaviour*, Tavistock Institute

Berne E (1964) *Games People Play*, André Deutsch

Bernstein C and Woodward B (1994) *All the Presidents Men*, Touchstone

Bower T (2000) *Branson*, Fourth Estate

Bradbury A (2000) *Successful Presentation Skills*, 2nd edn, Kogan Page

Brassington F and Pettitt S (1997) *Principles of Marketing*, Financial Times/ Pitman

Brech E F L (1957) *Organisation – The Framework of Management*, Longman

British Airways (1989) *The Making of Global*, British Airways Video Production

Cartwright R (2000) *Mastering Customer Relations*, Macmillan (now Palgrave)

Cartwright R (2001) *Mastering the Business Environment*, Palgrave

Cartwright R and Baird C (1999) *The Development and Growth of the Cruise Industry*, Butterworth Heinemann

Cartwright R and Green G (1997) *In Charge of Customer Satisfaction*, Blackwell

Cartwright R, Collins M, Green G and Candy A (1997) *In Charge – Managing Yourself*, 2nd edn, Blackwell

Cartwright R, Collins M, Green G and Candy A (1998a) *In Charge – Managing People*, 2nd edn, Blackwell

Cartwright R, Collins M, Green G and Candy A (1998b) *In Charge – Managing Resources*, 2nd edn, Blackwell

Churchill D (1999) 'Can I have my change in Air Miles please?', *British Airways Business Life*, July/August, pp. 83–6

Civil Aviation Authority (1994) *ATOL Business*, December, CAA, London

Clancy T (1987) *Red Storm Rising*, Collins

Clutterbuck D and Goldsmith W (1983) *The Winning Streak*, Orion

Clutterbuck D and Goldsmith W (1997) *The Winning Streak Mark II*, Orion

Clutterbuck D, Clark G and Armistead C (1993) *Inspired Customer Service*, Kogan Page

Cobb R (1995) 'Testing the Ties', *Marketing*, 6 April, p. 18

Cole G A (1993) *Management – Theory and Practice*, DP Publications

Crimp M (1990) *The Marketing Research Process*, Prentice Hall

Crosby P B (1979) *Quality is Free*, New American Library

Cutlip S, Center A, Brum G *et al.* (1999) *Effective Public Relations*, Prentice Hall

Davie M (1986) *Titanic – The Full Story of a Tragedy*, Bodley Head

Davies D (1990) *Finance and Accounting for Managers*, IPM

Davies M (2000) *The Samson Option*, Harper Collins

Dawkins R (1976) *The Selfish Gene*, Oxford University Press

Deming W E (1988) *Out of Crisis*, Cambridge University Press

Donald D (general ed.) (1999) *The Encyclopaedia of Civil Aircraft*, Orbis Publishing/Aerospace Publishing

Drury C (1985) *Management and Cost Accounting*, Van Nostrand Reinhold International

Dyson J (1998) *Against the Odds*, Orion

Eddy P, Potter E and Page B (1976) *Destination Disaster*, Hart-Davis

Fayol H (1916) *General and Industrial Administration*, translated from the French by C Storrs (1949), Pitman

Fenton J (1984) *How to Sell Against Competition*, Heinemann

Foster D and Davies J (1984) *Mastering Marketing*, Macmillan (now Palgrave)

Giles G B (1990) *Marketing*, 5th edn, M&E

Green W, Swanborough G and Mowinski J (1987) *Modern Commercial Aircraft*, Salamander

Gregory M (1994) Dirty Tricks – *British Airways' Secret War against Virgin Atlantic*, Little, Brown & Co

Hall S (1995) *Rail Centres: Manchester*, Ian Allan

Handy C (1976) *Understanding Organisations*, Penguin

Handy C (1978) *Gods of Management*, Souvenir Press

Handy C (1989) *The Age of Unreason*, Business Books Ltd

Hanlon P (1996) *Global Airlines*, Butterworth Heinemann

Harrison D (1992) Tourism and Less Developed Countries, Bellhaven

Hastings M and Jenkins S (1983) The Battle for the Falklands, Michael Joseph

Haywood R (1990) *All About Public Relations*, McGraw-Hill

Heinecke W E (2000) *The Entrepreneur*, Wiley

Heller R (1997) *In Search of European Excellence*, Harper Collins

Herzberg F (1962) *Work and the Nature of Man*, World Publishing

Hitching C and Stone D (1984) *Understanding Accounting*, Pitman

HM Government (1984) *The Cable and Broadcasting Act 1984*, HMSO

HM Government (1994) *The Control of Misleading Advertisement Regulations 1988*, HMSO

HM Government (1994) *The Sale and Supply of Goods Act 1994*, HMSO

HM Government (1982) *The Supply of Goods and Services Act 1982*, HMSO

HM Government (1968) *The Trades Descriptions Act 1968*, HMSO

Hutchings G (2001) *Modern China – A Companion to a Rising Power*, Penguin

Icelandair (2000) *Annual Report, 1999*, Icelandair

Irving C (1993) *Wide Body, the Making of the Boeing 747*, Hodder & Stoughton

Jefkins F (1980) *Public Relations*, Macdonald & Evans

Johnson E (1990) *The Midland Route from Manchester, Part 1*, Foxline

Johnson G and Scholes K (1984) *Exploring Corporate Strategy*, Prentice Hall

Jones T O and Strasser W E Jnr (1995) 'Why Satisfied Customers Defect', *Harvard Business Review*, Nov–Dec, pp. 88–99

Jowett A (1993) *Railway Centres, Vol. 1*, Patrick Stephens

Juran J (1964) *Managerial Breakthrough*, McGraw-Hill

Juran J (1989) *Juran on Leadership*, Macmillan (now Palgrave)

Klein N (2000) *No Logo*, Flamingo

Kotler P (1980) *Marketing Management*, Prentice Hall

Lavery P and Van Doren C (1990) *Travel and Tourism – A North American–European Perspective*, Elm Publications, Huntingdon

Laws E (1997) Managing Packaged Tourism, International Thomson Business Press, London

Lewin K (1951) *Field Theory in Social Science*, Harper

Lewis R D (2000) *When Cultures Collide*, Nicholas Brealey

Lorange P and Roos J (1992) *Strategic Alliances*, Blackwell

Lorenz K (1963) *On Aggression*, Methuen

Lynn M (1995) *Birds of Prey*, Heinemann

Lynn J and Jay A (1989) *The Complete Yes Prime Minister*, BBC

MacDonald J and Piggott J (1990) *Global Quality – The New Management Culture*, Mercury

McGuirk M (1999) *The New Haven Railroad Along the Shoreline: The Thoroughfare from New York City to Boston*, Kalmbach

Manes S and Andrews P (1994) *Gates*, Simon & Schuster

Marston J E (1979) *Modern Public Relations*, McGraw-Hill

Maslow A (1970) *Motivation and Personality*, Harper & Row

Mitchell A (1995) 'Preaching the Loyalty Message', *Marketing Week*, 1 December, pp. 26–7

Morden A R (1991) *Elements of Marketing*, 2nd edn, DP Publications

Neave H (1990) *The Deming Dimension*, SPC Press

Packard V (1957) *The Hidden Persuaders*, David McKay

Pascale R T and Athos A G (1981) *The Art of Japanese Management*, Simon & Schuster

Peters T (1987) *Thriving on Chaos*, Alfred A Knopf

Peters T and Waterman R (1982) *In Search of Excellence*, Harper & Row

Pettinger R (1994) *Introduction to Management*, Macmillan (now Palgrave)

Pettinger R (2000) *Mastering Organisational Behaviour*, Palgrave

Phipps R and Simmons G (1995) *Understanding Customers*, Butterworth Heinemann

Porter M (1980) *Competitive Advantage*, Free Press

Porter M (1985) *Competitive Strategy*, Free Press

Porter M (1996) *On Competition*, Harvard Business School Press

Prendergrast M (2000) *For God, Country and Coca-Cola*, Orion

Price C (2000) *The Internet Entrepreneurs*, Pearson

Pugh D (ed.) (1971) *Organisational Theory, Selected Readings*, Penguin

Robinson M (2000) *100 Greatest TV Ads*, Harper Collins and Channel 4/Sunday Times

Rolnicki K (1997) *Managing Channels of Distribution*, American Management Association

Rolt L T C (1955) *Red for Danger*, Bodley Head

Sabbach K (1995) *21st Century Jet – The Making of the Boeing 777*, Macmillan (now Palgrave)

Sampson A (1984) *Empires of the Skies*, Hodder & Stoughton

Sampson A (1993) *The Seven Sisters – The Great Oil Companies and the World They Made*, Coronet

Stewart S (1986) *Air Disasters*, Ian Allan

Swarbrooke J and Horner S (1999) *Consumer Behaviour in Tourism*, Butterworth Heinemann

Taylor F W (1911) *Principles of Scientific Management*, Harper

Tice L (1989) *Investing in Excellence* (Multimedia), Pacific Institute

Trompenaars F (1993) *Riding the Waves of Culture*, Economist Books

Vroom V H (1964) *Work and Motivation*, Wiley

Ward D (1994) *The Complete Guide to Cruising and Cruise Ships, 1994*, Berlitz

Ward D (1999) *The Complete Guide to Cruising and Cruise Ships, 2000*, Berlitz

Ward D (2000) *The Complete Guide to Cruising and Cruise Ships, 2001*, Berlitz

Warner O (1975) *The British Navy, A Concise History*, Thames & Hudson

Watts A (1976) *The U Boat Hunters*, Purnell

Wille E (1992) *Quality – Achieving Excellence*, Century Business

Wilmhurst J (1984) *The Fundamentals and Practice of Marketing*, Heinemann

Wind J (1982) *Product, Policy and Concept, Methods and Strategy*, Addison-Wesley

Wotherspoon K R (1995) 'The Sale and Supply of Goods Act 1994', *Journal of the Law Society of Scotland*, March, pp. 88–91, Law Society of Scotland

Yearsley I (1962) *The Manchester Tram*, Advertiser Press

Zdarek I (1988) *How Animals Communicate*, Hamlyn

■ ⌄ Index of subjects

◼◼ ✹ Index of names